THE CONSUMERS UNION REPORT ON
LIFE
INSURANCE

The Consumers Union Report on ★ Life ★ Insurance

A GUIDE TO PLANNING AND BUYING THE PROTECTION YOU NEED

Fourth Edition

The Editors of Consumer Reports Books

HOLT, RINEHART AND WINSTON / NEW YORK

Library of Congress Cataloging in Publication Data
Main entry under title:
The Consumers Union report on life insurance.
1. Insurance, Life—United States—Handbooks,
manuals, etc. I. Consumers Union of United States.
HG8951.C62   368.3'2'00973   80-25733
ISBN Hardbound: 0-03-059109-0
ISBN Paperback: 0-03-059108-2

The Consumers Union Report on Life Insurance is a Consumer Reports Book
published by Consumers Union, the nonprofit organization that publishes CON-
SUMER REPORTS, the monthly magazine of test reports, product Ratings, and
buying guidance. Established in 1936, Consumers Union is chartered under the
Not-For-Profit Corporation Law of the State of New York.

The purposes of Consumers Union, as stated in its charter, are to provide
consumers with information and counsel on consumer goods and services, to
give information and assistance on all matters relating to the expenditure of the
family income, and to initiate and to cooperate with individual and group efforts
seeking to create and maintain decent living standards.

Consumers Union derives its income solely from the sale of CONSUMER
REPORTS and other publications. Consumers Union accepts no advertising or
product samples and is not beholden in any way to any commercial interest. Its
Ratings and reports are solely for the information and use of the readers of its
publications.

Neither the Ratings nor the reports nor any other Consumers Union publications, including this book, may be used in advertising or for any commercial
purpose of any nature. Consumers Union will take all steps open to it to prevent
or to prosecute any such uses of its material or of its name or the name of
CONSUMER REPORTS.

Printed in the United States of America
1 3 5 7 9 10 8 6 4 2

Preface

Consumers Union has been keenly interested in life insurance for more than four decades. Our first report on the subject was published in CONSUMER REPORTS in 1937, one year after CU was founded, and additional major reports appeared in 1938, 1945–46, 1967, 1974, and 1980. CU has also published a number of shorter life insurance articles in the magazine, testified before governmental bodies, and prepared surveys of life insurance costs in 1973 and 1979. In 1967, we published our first book on life insurance—an expansion of the magazine's three-part series that year. Revised editions appeared in 1972 and 1977. Now we present the fourth edition of this book.

The impetus for this new edition was the publication in CONSUMER REPORTS in early 1980 of CU's Ratings of more than four hundred life insurance policies issued by more than one hundred major insurance companies. The Ratings published in the magazine were limited to as many of the lowest-cost policies as space permitted as well as the five highest-cost policies of each type rated. The complete results of

Consumers Union's survey comprise Part II of this book.

Inevitably, the cost information in the Ratings will become dated to some extent with the passage of time. Yet, while life insurance premiums and dividend scales will change, it is not commonplace for them to change dramatically. As we note in Chapter 8, individual policies may move up or down the price ladder, but the ladder itself (that is, the range of costs from highest to lowest) moves much more slowly.

Consumers need some guidance in deciding which of the hundreds of life insurance companies to consider, and the comprehensive Ratings by company and policy name should be helpful in that regard. As a starting point in the shopping process, readers will be able to use CU's Ratings as a yardstick against which to measure an offered policy.

Also new to this edition are chapters on life insurance dividends, how to read a life insurance policy, whether you should replace a policy you already own, and how the life insurance marketplace can be demystified for consumers. Other chapters have been extensively revised and updated.

This book is the cumulative product of years of effort on the part of Consumers Union staff members. As with the third edition, John Dorfman, a freelance writer, assistant editor of *The Insurance Forum,* and a former CONSUMER REPORTS assistant editor, was the coordinator and writer of this edition. CU has also benefited extensively from the help of consultants, including a team of actuaries, university professors specializing in insurance, and several individuals active in governmental regulation of insurance on both the state and federal levels. Criticisms of past reports and suggestions for future reports made by members of the life insurance industry—from company presidents to agents—also have been useful. The final recommendations, judgments, and opinions, however, must be considered those of Consumers Union alone.

Contents

Introduction   9

Part I. What You Should Know About Life Insurance

1. Who Really Needs Life Insurance?   15

2. Social Security   23

3. How Much Life Insurance Do You Need?   41

4. The Basic Policy Types   61

5. Term Versus Cash Value   72

6. Par Versus Nonpar   87

7. Deciphering the Price   97

8. Shopping for a Policy   108

Contents

9. Other Types of Policies, from A to V   122

10. Riders   140

11. How to Read a Life Insurance Policy   147

12. Should You Switch Policies?   177

13. Demystifying the Life Insurance Marketplace   190

Part II. Consumers Union's Ratings of Life Insurance Policies

14. Introduction to CU's Ratings   201

15. CU's Ratings of Term Policies   206

16. Alphabetical Summary of Term Policies   252

17. CU's Ratings of Cash Value Policies   263

18. Alphabetical Summary of Cash Value Policies   333

Appendixes

I. A Note to Beneficiaries   347

II. Term Versus Whole Life: Investment Values   349

III. Addresses of Insurance Departments   354

IV. Estate Taxes   361

Glossary   366

Index   375

8

Introduction

Many people don't buy life insurance—they're sold it. Rather than try to figure out how much life insurance they really need and of what type, they let an agent or a company decide for them. In fact, a recent study suggests that one-third of all life insurance buyers still don't know what kind of life insurance they've bought even *after* they've purchased it. As for costs, more than 20 percent of those surveyed in that study thought that life insurance rates were set by state officials. Indeed, many consumers tend to assume that policies are all pretty much alike and that they all cost around the same amount. Of course that's not true. Policies can differ widely and shopping for a policy can pay off.

This book is designed to help you become knowledgeable about life insurance and about how to plan and, if necessary, to purchase the protection you need. To accomplish this, Consumers Union believes you have to start with a decision about how much life insurance you need, then settle on the type you want, and finally shop for the best price. This book will help you make those decisions.

The first question to ask is whether you really need any life insurance coverage at all. If you have dependent children, the answer is almost certainly yes. If you don't, it might well be no, but not necessarily. Chapter 1 will help you make this initial determination.

You can't very well figure out how much life insurance you need until you have an idea of what Social Security benefits your family would get when you die. So, Chapter 2 discusses Social Security (with special emphasis on survivors benefits) and reviews the various steps you need to take to inform yourself about your benefits. (You should, for example, begin by writing away immediately for a statement of the earnings credited to your Social Security account—see page 24.)

With preliminaries out of the way, you're now ready to calculate your life insurance needs. Chapter 3 will show you how, with a Life Insurance Planning Worksheet. We believe that the very process of filling out the Worksheet will help you to plan realistically for the future and make some decisions about your family's changing needs and lifestyles.

Once you know how much insurance you need to buy, if any, you're ready to start figuring out what kind of insurance to buy. Chapter 4 explains the basic types of policies available and the kinds of provisions they include. Chapter 5 tackles the long-standing and controversial question of which is better, term insurance or cash value insurance. After you decide which is better for you, your next basic choice is between a policy that pays dividends and one that doesn't. We devote Chapter 6 to issues related to this choice.

Then we move into the realm of life insurance costs. When you buy a typical consumer product, the cost of the purchase is fairly precise. Not so with a life insurance policy. It's a transaction that may involve multiple exchanges of money between you and the company over many years. Because several variables may affect the real cost of a policy, cost indexes with which to compare policies become highly important. The rates for similar policies can vary tremendously from one company to another. We explain the most commonly used cost indexes in Chapter 7. In Chapter 8, we explain further how to use these indexes when shopping and give additional suggestions about how to shop for a policy. We also suggest you give some consideration to nonprice factors such as an insurance company's financial stability and the quality of an agent's or company's service.

Chapter 9 is devoted to a brief discussion of some of the lesser-known types of policies you may encounter. Then, no matter what kind of policy you buy, you'll be faced with a decision about whether to add on certain options, known as riders. Chapter 10 discusses the three most common riders and gives our recommendations about them.

Your chances of understanding a life insurance policy are improving as the fine print gives way to more readable English. But to understand the significance of what the policy says, you need to interpret policy language. Chapter 11 provides the necessary background.

For those who already have some life insurance coverage, Chapter 12 discusses the knotty question of whether (and when) to drop one policy and replace it with another. We close Part I with Chapter 13, in which we report on the state of life insurance regulation and outline CU's views on some urgently needed improvements, particularly in the area of cost disclosure.

Part II of the book consists of comparative cost index Ratings of 478 life insurance policies—199 term and 279 cash value—from 110 companies. Each of the two groups of policies is listed in two ways: in order of cost from lowest to highest in twelve tables (covering combinations of age and face amount, with and without dividends), and summarized alphabetically by company. The results of CU's survey can help you shop for a policy. Also included is a brief introduction to CU's survey, conducted in 1979, and some of the procedures involved in its preparation.

Wisdom doesn't come easily in the life insurance marketplace. The number of variables and imponderables can be forbidding, and consumers have few reliable guides they can count on. CU hopes that this book will prove a useful reference tool for you, now and in the future, as you try to achieve and maintain the kind of protection you need at a cost you can afford.

Part I
What You Should Know About Life Insurance

Who Really Needs Life Insurance?

Most life insurance is sold to cover the breadwinner. But a number of policies are also sold that cover the breadwinner's spouse and even their children. In addition, some policies are sold on a "family plan" basis (see page 22), with some coverage for the breadwinner, the spouse, and the children. To get the maximum benefit from your insurance dollar, you have to ask yourself which of the possible configurations of coverage makes the most sense. In other words, who really needs life insurance?

The Single Person—Not Usually

The primary purpose of life insurance is to protect dependents against the financial consequences of the death of the breadwinner. It takes an income earner *plus* a child or some other necessarily dependent person to create a compelling need for life insurance. Unless a single person contributes to the support of one or more people, a single person does not usually need life insurance. Yet, insurance agents come up with a variety of reasons why people without dependents should buy life insurance. Consumers Union finds these reasons generally unconvincing.

One reason a single person is often urged to buy life insurance *now* is because someday there may be children to care for. Life insurance is "needed" as a hedge against the possibility that the prospective policyholder might later become uninsurable because of poor health. Unless there is a substantial family history of health problems, CU thinks that the purchase of life insurance before a person has dependents would be premature. What's more, a person who buys life insurance when it is not really needed would be hard pressed to determine rationally how much to buy.

A second argument is that a single person may want to carry life insurance to benefit a favorite charity or other cause. One may well wish to do this but, in CU's view, it doesn't constitute a *need* for life insurance.

A third reason sometimes heard is that people should pay their own funeral expenses. In our view, this is an individual decision. A small life insurance policy might be carried to cover final expenses but only until an adequate amount of money earmarked for that purpose is put away in savings or investments. Once that's done, every cent a person without dependents pays for life insurance normally can better be invested, or spent on more tangible things.

To be sure, life insurance can have other uses besides financial protection for dependents. It can be used as a tax shelter, a forced savings plan, a device to ensure the payment of debts, a tool to provide estate liquidity. It can be used to buy out the heirs of a business partner or to compensate a corporation for the death of a key executive. Any proficient life insurance agent can add to the list. But a consumer who would use life insurance for some of these purposes had best consult a knowledgeable attorney or an expert in estate planning. This book will concentrate on family financial protection, which is what leads the majority of people to buy life insurance.

The Breadwinner—Usually

There is a need for family financial protection when one or more persons must depend on another person for money to live on. Emphasis is on the word *must.* A family consisting of two working adults and no dependents often does not need any life insurance protection at all. Economic dependence in marriage has been decreasing. Many married women without children earn enough to support themselves in the event of their spouse's death. This number will presumably increase as barriers to the employment of women and to equal pay for equal work continue to fall.

Children change the picture. In many cases the arrival of a child removes one parent from the work force for a period of time. A couple earning two salaries often becomes, with the first child, a threesome living on one salary. Additional children add to the family's responsibilities and often continue to keep one of the parents at home. Even with changes in the patterns of family life for some people, this traditional approach is likely to persist for a great many others, at least while their children are young.

Children are necessarily dependent. They almost always rely on someone else's income to provide food, shelter, clothing, and general economic well-being. And because children may continue their education beyond high school, their economic dependence often stretches to their twenty-second year—sometimes beyond. Children, then, are the kind of financial responsibility that usually calls for the purchase of life insurance. Of course, a family with other financially dependent members—a spouse with a health problem that prevents him or her from working, for example—can also have a need for insurance protection.

If both parents are producing income that is vital to the family, both parents should be insured. In families with only one breadwinner, that person should be adequately insured before any thought is given to insuring the nonwage-earning spouse. And "adequate" insurance on the breadwinner may mean a larger amount than you'd think. Chapter 3 is devoted to helping families make a realistic calculation of the amount of coverage needed.

The Spouse—Sometimes

We have already said that where both parents contribute vital portions of family income, both should be insured. A hard look is in order, however, at the relative contributions of the two parents to family income. If both are working, but one is the family's economic mainstay, the urgent priority is adequate insurance on that person. If both incomes are vital, but one is larger than the other, both breadwinners should have life insurance, with their coverage amounts—usually called face amounts in the insurance industry—in rough proportion to their incomes.

In many families, one parent has the role of breadwinner and the other the role of homemaker. A parent who spends full time taking care of children and the home is making a vital contribution to the economic well-being of the family. In the event of death, of course, the homemaker can never truly be replaced. But the economically measurable services performed by a homemaker must be replaced, and it costs money—for babysitters, day care, housecleaners, and the like. In figuring life insurance needs, a family must consider, among other things, the additional expenses resulting from the homemaker's death. Should the family carry life insurance on the homemaker?

The answer is: Maybe. In cold financial terms, the death of a homemaker is a trade-off. In the short run, the death creates a cash drain, as well as an emotional one. There may be medical bills to pay; there probably will be funeral expenses. A housekeeper may be hired on a full-time or part-time basis. There may be a need for babysitters, or day-care facilities; this need may last for only a few months, or for years. In time, however, the death of a homemaker usually creates a long-run savings in terms of the money that would have gone for clothing, food, medical expenses, transportation, and so on. After some months or years, the savings will probably exceed the cash drain. How long it takes to reach that point will vary substantially from family to family. Should the family carry life insurance on the homemaker to tide it over until that point is reached? The answer depends on how you answer three other questions.

First, is the breadwinner adequately insured? Until this is accomplished, no insurance on the homemaker should be considered.

Second, in the event of the homemaker's death, are there adequate savings to help the family over the immediate cash-drain period? If there are, no life insurance on the homemaker may be needed.

Third, can the family afford the premium for insurance on the homemaker? A family that is hard pressed to pay for food, shelter, and medical care would not be wise to allocate resources for life insurance on the homemaker.

In summary, insurance for a homemaker makes most sense for a family that already has adequate insurance on the breadwinner, that does not have a huge financial cushion to fall back on, and that can pay the extra premium without its being a hardship.

If you decide to purchase life insurance on the homemaker, then an important factor to consider is the number of years until your youngest child will be reasonably self-sufficient. You can then calculate the cost of babysitting services or day-care facilities. (In early 1980, the cost of day care ran roughly $1,500 to $4,000 a year, but showed great regional variation. Many day-care centers have sliding fee scales, based on parents' income. It should also be noted that most expenses for day care are now tax deductible. For a person in the 25 percent tax bracket, for example, the true cost of day care might be only 75 percent of the apparent cost.) A decision must also be made as to how many days a week housekeeping services would be required, and a check made on the cost of such services in your area.

Children—Seldom

Although one or both parents often have good reason to be insured, their children seldom need life insurance. A favored argument of insurance agents is that a child's future insurance premiums will be reduced if insurance coverage is begun at a tender age. That's true, if the policy happens to be the kind that carries a level premium throughout the insured's life—which normally means a cash value policy. But that low, level premium is possible in the future only because money spent to buy insurance protection is wasted, year after year, during childhood, when no insurance is likely to be needed. From the standpoint of the family unit, the transaction is extremely uneconomical. And by the time the child reaches adulthood, it is likely that the face amount of the policy, purchased years earlier, would have become inadequate or even negligible because of inflation. If inflation should run, say, at 6 percent a year, a $50,000 policy purchased today would be worth less than $16,000 of today's dollars twenty years from now.

Insurance agents sometimes argue that coverage purchased on children guarantees their insurability as an adult. The suggestion is that children may become uninsurable because of poor health before they have a real need for life insurance. It's true that about 3 percent of all life insurance applicants are rejected for coverage for health reasons; another 5 percent or so are charged an extra premium as health risks. But these figures cover applicants of all ages, including those who develop illnesses late in life and those who have had chronic conditions since birth. The chance that a child will develop a serious health condition in the prime of life is remote and for most families the risk of a child's future uninsurability is a small one. Besides, the amount of insurance guaranteed when the child grows up may not be great. Typically, it's a multiple of the face amount of the initial policy—from one to six times the initial amount. So if you purchase your son or daughter a $10,000 life insurance policy with a guaranteed insurability rider (see Chapter 10), what you'll be guaranteeing, in most cases, is your child's right to buy up to $60,000 of insurance in the future—at the premium rates prevailing at that time for that particular insurance company.

An insurance agent may take the approach that one or two thousand dollars of insurance on a child costs little and at least pays for a funeral. But funeral costs are minimal compared with the cost of raising a child over a number of years. Tragic though the death of a child may be, it actually *reduces* the parents' financial responsibilities.

But what if the parents would have trouble paying for the funeral if their child died? In that event, they probably have many other things for which money is more urgently needed than for life insurance on the child—not the least of which might be adequate insurance for the breadwinner. Financially pressed families should not be spending their limited funds to insure against the risk of a child's death.

Even though parents may follow CU's advice and forgo purchasing insurance on a child, they may be surprised some years later to find that child returning home from college with an expensive life insurance policy. A college student who considers the purchase of life insurance should be wary of the policies aimed specifically at the college market (such policies are discussed in Chapter 9).

All Family Members, with One Policy—Rarely

One of the highly promoted items in the insurance agent's portfolio is a policy known as the family plan. It usually consists of a cash value form of coverage for the primary breadwinner and small amounts of term insurance on the other parent and the children. Typically, the policy is open-ended, covering additional children almost from birth at no additional premium.

In a typical family plan, because life insurance is purchased as a package, it is unlikely that coverage for parents will be allocated in accordance with the family's particular needs. And so, the purchase of a family plan policy may siphon off premium money from where it's most urgently needed—adequate coverage for the breadwinner. It is usually better, as well as more economical, to have a life insurance portfolio tailor-made for your family needs.

Social Security

When most people think of Social Security they think of retirement benefits. But Social Security is in fact an amalgam of several programs, and one of them—survivors benefits—is, in effect, life insurance.* For those who are eligible, Social Security survivors benefits can be a significant component of a life insurance program. Indeed, for a person who has had substantial earnings, Social Security survivors benefits can amount, over a period of years, to the equivalent of more than $200,000 of life insurance.

Nor is the survivors benefits program the only one to be considered in estimating life insurance needs. Of the four major programs that comprise the Social Security Administration—retirement benefits, survivors benefits, disability

---

*The Social Security Administration offers brochures that may also be useful to you in understanding Social Security and in planning your life insurance coverage. Among those available are "Social Security Information for Young Families," "Your Social Security," "Social Security Survivors Benefits," "Estimating Your Social Security Retirement Check," and "If You Become Disabled." All are free at local SSA offices.

benefits, and Medicare—all but Medicare may be directly relevant to life insurance planning.

Social Security Earnings

Each of the three applicable Social Security programs has its own eligibility standards, which are described later in this chapter. These standards tell you only whether you (or your survivors) will be eligible for any benefits. They don't tell you what the amount of those benefits will be. The amount of the benefits under each of the three programs is determined on the basis of the earnings credited to your Social Security account over the years.

Every two years or so, you should obtain from a local Social Security Administration office a special postcard, Form OAR-7004, entitled A Request for Statement of Earnings. Fill out the card and send it to the SSA, which in due course will send you back a statement of the earnings that you have been credited with. It's important to review the statement periodically because the SSA has set a time limit for correcting errors. According to the SSA, "Unless you report an error within 3 years, 3 months and 15 days . . . correction of our records may not be possible." So if you believe your earnings statement to be incorrect, be sure to inform the SSA promptly and in writing.

Getting your record of earnings straight is only the first step. Average earnings are used as the basis for calculating your benefit levels—the monthly dollar amounts you or your survivors receive. In years past, the Social Security law specified a complicated procedure for determining your average earnings. Now it has an even more complicated formula for determining your *average indexed yearly earnings* (AIYE). The indexing feature means that your earnings in past years are adjusted to reflect increases in average earnings over the years. The numbers used in the formula for indexing change every year. In Table 2–1 on pages 26–28, we present the indexing system in operation during 1980; if you die, become disabled, or reach age sixty-two in 1980, this procedure would apply to you.

You might think you could simply find out your AIYE by inquiring at a local Social Security Administration office. Logical, but unlikely. According to the SSA, such a service to the public would overload the system. The SSA needs its personnel and computer time to calculate AIYE data for people who are actually receiving or about to receive benefits. As a matter of policy, then, the SSA doesn't ordinarily make AIYE calculations for consumers who want to do advance planning.

Consumers Union believes it's very difficult to estimate effectively the amount of life insurance you need unless you have a good idea of prospective Social Security benefits. And you can't effectively estimate your probable Social Security benefits unless you have a good idea of your AIYE. You therefore have three choices: (1) You can go to an SSA office and hope to find an employee with the time, skill, and willingness to help you determine your AIYE. (2) You can rely on a life insurance agent to do the calculations for you. (3) You can fill out a form such as the one in Table 2–1 and get your approximate AIYE.

If, however, you've consistently earned the maximum wage taxed by Social Security, you may not need to fill out the form; we can give you a pretty good idea of what your 1980 AIYE is, based on earnings through 1979: Specifically, if you're twenty-nine or younger, it's $20,352. If you're thirty, it's $19,464. If thirty-five, it's $17,532. If forty, it's $16,020. If forty-five, it's $15,072. If fifty, it's $14,532. And if you're between fifty-one and sixty-two, it's $14,496. (As you can see, the Social Security law favors younger people

(Text continued on page 29)

Table 2–1
Calculating Your 1980 AIYE

To determine your approximate 1980 AIYE, start with Column 1 and circle the year you turned twenty-two, or 1951, whichever year is later. That circled year is your starting year. In Column 2, enter your actual earnings (in jobs where Social Security taxes were paid) for each year—enter a zero if earnings were zero—making an entry for every year from your starting year through 1979. Take each year's actual earnings in Column 2, or (from Column 3) the maximum Social Security earnings for that year—*whichever is less*—and multiply that dollar amount by the indexing factor in Column 4 for that year. For any year for which your actual earnings were zero, put a zero in Column 5. You now have your indexed earnings, year by year, in Column 5.

Column 1	Column 2		Column 3		Column 4		Column 5
Year	Your Actual Earnings	or	Social Security Maximum Earnings	×	Indexing Factor	=	Indexed Earnings for Year
1951	$_____		$ 3,600		3.771		$_____
1952	_____		3,600		3.550		_____
1953	_____		3,600		3.362		_____
1954	_____		3,600		3.345		_____
1955	_____		4,200		3.197		_____
1956	_____		4,200		2.988		_____
1957	_____		4,200		2.899		_____
1958	_____		4,200		2.873		_____
1959	_____		4,800		2.738		_____
1960	_____		4,800		2.634		_____
1961	_____		4,800		2.583		_____
1962	_____		4,800		2.460		_____
1963	_____		4,800		2.401		_____
1964	_____		4,800		2.307		_____

Column 1	Column 2		Column 3		Column 4		Column 5
Year	Your Actual Earnings	or	Social Security Maximum Earnings	×	Indexing Factor	=	Indexed Earnings for Year
1965	$_____		$ 4,800		2.266		$_____
1966	_____		6,600		2.138		_____
1967	_____		6,600		2.025		_____
1968	_____		7,800		1.895		_____
1969	_____		7,800		1.791		_____
1970	_____		7,800		1.706		_____
1971	_____		7,800		1.625		_____
1972	_____		9,000		1.480		_____
1973	_____		10,800		1.393		_____
1974	_____		13,200		1.314		_____
1975	_____		14,100		1.223		_____
1976	_____		15,300		1.144		_____
1977	_____		16,500		1.079		_____
1978	_____		17,700		1.000		_____
1979	_____		22,900		1.000		_____

Note: Under the Social Security law, when calculating average indexed yearly earnings (AIYE), you may subtract from your total number of years with indexed earnings the years—up to five of them—in which you had the lowest earnings or no earnings at all. (Omitting those years from your calculations will give you a higher average earnings figure and thus entitle you to higher benefits.) The only limitation is that what's left—the remaining calculation years —must amount to at least two years.

Accordingly, to calculate your approximate 1980 AIYE:

Step 1. Count the number of years for which you have entries in Column 5, above, and insert that total number of years with indexed earnings on Line 1 on page 28. (Remember, be sure to include years with zero earnings.)

(Table 2–1 continued on page 28)

(Table 2–1 continued from page 27)
Step 2. Figure out the number of years with indexed earnings you may subtract from the total indexed earnings on Line 1 below:

If the number of years on Line 1 is:	Then you may enter on Line 2:
1 or 2 years	nothing
3 years	1 year
4 years	2 years
5 years	3 years
6 years	4 years
7 or more years	5 years

Step 3. Subtract Line 2 from Line 1 to get the number of remaining calculation years, and enter this number on Line 3.

Step 4. In Column 5, cross out the years with lowest earnings or no earnings—but be sure not to cross out more years than the number indicated on Line 2. Then add up your indexed earnings for the remaining years in Column 5 and enter on Line 4 the total dollar amount of indexed earnings in the calculation years.

Step 5. Divide Line 4 by Line 3; enter the resulting average indexed yearly earnings—your approximate 1980 AIYE—on Line 5.

Line 1. Total number of years with indexed earnings (from Column 1) _____years.

Line 2. Total number of years you may subtract (from Step 2) _____years.

Line 3. Number of remaining calculation years (Line 1 minus Line 2) _____years.

Line 4. Total indexed earnings in calculation years (from Column 5) $_____.

Line 5. Average indexed yearly earnings—approximate 1980 AIYE (Line 4 divided by Line 3) $_____.

(Text continued from page 25)

over older ones.) You can get a workable estimate of your AIYE even if your exact age isn't among those listed above by interpolating (in effect, prorating) between the AIYE figures for the ages on either side of your age. But don't forget, you must have earned at least the Social Security maximum each year. If you've had some years in which you earned less than the Social Security maximum (most people have), you can calculate your approximate AIYE by using Table 2–1.

Keep in mind that the numbers given in Table 2–1 are for 1980. To estimate your benefits for later years, use the updating procedure outlined on pages 39–40.

Survivors Benefits

When you die, your survivors may well qualify for Social Security survivors benefits, which are usually paid out in monthly installments. These monthly payments aren't issued automatically; survivors must apply for them. The application will be granted if you've accumulated enough Social Security work credit over your lifetime to establish eligibility.

Work credit for survivors benefits involves an important distinction between being *fully insured* or *currently insured.* If you were fully insured (see Table 2–2 on page 30), your survivors would most likely receive benefits. If you were currently insured, your survivors would be eligible for benefits only under certain conditions (see Table 2–3 on page 31). To be currently insured, you have to work (at jobs where Social Security taxes were paid) for periods totaling at least one and one-half of the three years preceding your death.

Now you know whether you are fully insured, currently insured, or neither. To determine if your survivors would be eligible for benefits, see Table 2–3 on page 31.

(Text continued on page 31)

Table 2–2
Definition of Fully Insured

The table below shows how many years of work credit (in jobs where Social Security taxes were paid) a worker needs to be *fully insured* for the purpose of Social Security survivors benefits. If the precise year or age for which you want to know the years of work credit does not appear in the lists below, you can interpolate (in effect, prorate) the work credit figures for the years or ages above and below the year or age with which you're concerned.

A worker who was born before 1930 and dies in:	Needs this many years of work credit:
1977	6½
1979	7
1981	7½
1983	8
1987	9
1991 or later	10

A worker who was born after 1929 and dies at age:	Needs this many years of work credit:
28 or younger	1½
30	2
32	2½
34	3
36	3½
38	4
40	4½
42	5
46	6
50	7
54	8
58	9
62 or older	10

Table 2–3
Eligibility for Survivors Benefits

If survivors are not caring for dependent children and fit any of the definitions below, a worker must have been *fully insured* for them to receive survivors benefits:
- Widow or widower age sixty or over.
- Disabled widow or widower age fifty or over.
- Dependent parent age sixty-two or over.

If survivors fit any of the definitions below, a worker need only have been *currently insured* for them to receive survivors benefits:
- Widow or widower (regardless of age) who is caring for a child under the age of eighteen. (Note: The child must be entitled to survivors benefits in order for the parent to receive child-raising benefits.)
- Widow or widower (regardless of age) who is caring for a child (regardless of age) who becomes disabled before age twenty-two.
- Dependent children.
- Dependent grandchildren (under certain conditions).

At this point, you know if your survivors would be entitled to Social Security survivors benefits. What remains is to determine about how much money they can expect to receive in the event of your death. Table 2–4 on page 33 shows representative benefit levels as of January–May 1980.

With the exception of the lump-sum death benefit (see page 37), all Social Security benefits are paid in the form of monthly income. With survivors benefits, the duration of some of that monthly income is tied to the ages of surviving children, if any. Child-raising benefits for a surviving parent generally stop when the youngest child reaches eighteen. A dependent child's income usually continues until the child's eighteenth birthday, but children who are full-time students and unmarried will receive income until the end of the school semester in which they become twenty-two. There are some exceptions to these rules. One exception takes effect in the case of widowed parents with children who become disabled before their twenty-second birthday. If the parent must perform personal services for the child, both the parent's and the disabled child's incomes can continue indefinitely. Another exception applies to surviving spouses who become disabled within seven years after the worker's death or their youngest child's eighteenth birthday.

Most surviving parents face a period—from the youngest child's eighteenth birthday to their own sixtieth birthday—when they will receive no Social Security income for themselves. Of course, if a widow or widower reaches age sixty before the youngest child becomes eighteen, Social Security income is not interrupted.

CU suggests that you prepare a written record (see Table 2–5 on page 34) of your estimate of the Social Security benefit income that would be due your survivors.   You will be using this information when you fill out the Life Insurance Planning Worksheet in Chapter 3.

Survivors benefits, like all monthly benefits payable under Social Security, are exempt from federal income tax. Once you begin receiving monthly benefits, your benefits are adjusted each June to take inflation into account.

Retirement Benefits

Knowing your Social Security retirement benefits is useful when you're doing financial planning for your retirement years. Sometimes it's also relevant to life insurance planning.

If your spouse works and will be eligible for retirement benefits, you should estimate the amount to which your spouse is likely to be entitled. Your spouse could also be eligible for survivors benefits in the event of your death. In your planning, use the larger of the two benefits—since your

Table 2-4
Representative Survivors Benefits, January–May 1980

The monthly survivors benefits listed below, rounded to the nearest dollar, are payable at death. These figures are as of January–May 1980. A child receives benefits until age eighteen, or until age twenty-two if the child is a full-time student and unmarried. If a child is disabled before age twenty-two, benefits continue for the duration of the disability. Benefits for a widow or widower are shown below as starting at age sixty-five, but benefits can be taken at an earlier age. If begun at sixty-two, for example, benefits are reduced 17.1 percent from the amount shown below. If begun at sixty, benefits are reduced 28.5 percent from the amount shown. If a recipient of survivors benefits earns income, benefits may be reduced $1 for each $2 earned above a threshold level. That threshold may vary from year to year. In 1980 it was $3,720 for people under sixty-five, and $5,000 for people sixty-five and over.

Your AIYE	Surviving Parent and One Child	Surviving Parent and Two Children	One Surviving Child	Widow's or Widower's Benefit, Starting at Age 65	Family Maximum
$ 1,400	$183	$ 183	$122	$122	$ 183
2,400	265	265	132	177	265
4,800	361	361	180	241	361
6,600	433	482	216	289	482
8,400	505	613	252	337	613
10,200	577	707	288	385	707
12,000	649	771	324	433	771
14,400	737	860	369	492	860
16,200	771	900	386	514	900
18,000	805	939	402	537	939
20,400	850	992	425	567	992
22,200	884	1,031	442	589	1,031
22,900	897	1,046	448	598	1,046

Table 2–5
Social Security Benefits Record

The following Social Security benefits information should be computed and jotted down. You will need Social Security information for the Life Insurance Planning Worksheet in Chapter 3.

■ Monthly survivors benefits if the breadwinner of the family were to die now $_____.
■ Monthly survivors benefits for a child age eighteen to twenty-two who is a full-time unmarried student $_____.
■ Widow's or widower's monthly retirement benefits, if started at age sixty-five $_____.
■ Widow's or widower's monthly retirement benefits, if started at age sixty-two $_____.
■ Widow's or widower's monthly retirement benefits, if started at age sixty $_____.
■ Monthly disability benefits the family would receive if the breadwinner were to become disabled now $_____.

---

spouse will receive only the larger, not both.

If you're the only breadwinner in the family the nonworking spouse's possible future retirement benefits under Social Security shouldn't play a role in life insurance planning. Granted, the surviving spouse, heretofore a homemaker, might get a job after the breadwinner's death and might accumulate enough retirement benefits to exceed the survivors benefits. But you can't predict in advance that this will happen. Unless you know for a fact that retirement benefits will be greater, the prudent assumption is to plan on survivors benefits being the larger of the two.

Eligibility requirements for retirement benefits are shown in Table 2–6.

The amount of retirement benefits you're entitled to de-

Table 2–6
Eligibility for Retirement Benefits

A worker who reaches age 62 in:	Needs this many years of work credit:*
1977	6½
1978	6¾
1979	7
1980	7¼
1981	7½
1983	8
1987	9
1991 or later	10

*Work credit must be earned in a job where Social Security taxes are paid.

pends on your AIYE. Some sample benefit levels are shown in Table 2–7 on page 36.

If your spouse is not now near retirement age, any estimate you make of his or her retirement benefits will be very inexact. But CU believes that future retirement benefits are likely at least to equal those shown in Table 2–7. Use your spouse's current AIYE as the basis for estimating the retirement benefits. That figure should be updated periodically, using the procedure described on pages 39–40.

Disability Benefits

Social Security disability benefits are paid to workers who become disabled. Disabled means, in essence, that you are unable to work as a result of a medically determinable impairment that is expected to last for at least one year or to result in death. You cannot begin to receive Social Security

(Text continued on page 37)

Table 2–7
Representative Retirement Benefits, January–May 1980

The monthly retirement benefits listed below, rounded to the nearest dollar, are as of January–May 1980. Of course, the younger you are, the less precise these benefit estimates are, since actual retirement benefits will depend heavily on your future earnings. If you elect to start benefits between ages sixty-two and sixty-five, your monthly check would be between the amounts shown below. Because of the transition from the old benefit computation procedures in the Social Security law to the new ones, it is not practical to estimate benefits for people age sixty-three or older in 1980 by the methods in this chapter; if you are in this category, your local Social Security Administration office can help you estimate what your retirement benefits would be. If you work while drawing Social Security retirement benefits, those benefits will be reduced by $1 for each $2 you earn above a certain threshold level. In 1980 the threshold (for beneficiaries at least sixty-five years old) was $5,000. The threshold changes from year to year. For retired workers under age sixty-five, this threshold was $3,720 in 1980.

	Monthly Retirement Benefits	
Your AIYE	**Age 62**	**Age 65**
$ 1,400	$ 98	$122
2,400	141	176
4,800	192	240
6,600	231	289
8,400	269	336
10,200	308	385
12,000	346	432
14,400	393	491
16,200	411	514
18,000	429	536
20,400	453	566
22,200	471	589
22,900	478	597

Table 2–8
Eligibility for Disablity Benefits

If at the time of disablement a worker's age is:	The worker must be fully insured (see Table 2–2) and:
Less than 24	Have earned Social Security work credit in at least 1½ of the previous 3 years.
24 to 30	Have earned Social Security work credit for half the time between age 21 and the time the worker became disabled.
31 or older	Have earned Social Security work credit in 5 of the previous 10 years.

Note: A worker disabled by blindness needs enough Social Security work credit to be fully insured, as shown in Table 2–2; but the other requirements shown above do not apply.

disability benefits until your disability has lasted for five full months. To be eligible for disability benefits, you must be fully insured (as shown in Table 2–2) and also meet the requirements shown in Table 2–8, above.

Sample payment levels for disability benefits as of January–May 1980 are shown in Table 2–9 on page 38.

Death Benefit

The three programs described so far—survivors benefits, retirement benefits, and disability benefits—can all have a major impact on a family's finances. Less significant, but still worth knowing about, is the lump-sum death benefit to help cover funeral and burial expenses. The lump sum is up to

Table 2–9
Representative Disability Benefits, January–May 1980

The monthly disability benefits listed below, rounded to the nearest dollar, are as of January–May 1980. In addition to the benefits paid to a disabled person, each dependent of a disabled person is eligible to receive half the amount shown below. However, total payments cannot exceed the family maximum as shown in Table 2–4.

Your AIYE	Monthly Disability Payment
$ 1,400	$122
2,400	177
4,800	241
6,600	289
8,400	337
10,200	385
12,000	433
14,400	492
16,200	514
18,000	537
20,400	567
22,200	589
22,900	598

$255. The eligibility requirement is that the deceased person must have earned Social Security work credit in any six quarters (one and a half years) of the three years prior to death, or be fully insured under Social Security.

Undertakers often help make the arrangements for collecting this benefit. When that's not the case, arrangements for collection can be made with a local SSA office—but the benefit must be applied for within two years of the date of death. The money may go to the surviving spouse, to another person who paid for funeral and burial, or directly to the undertaker.

To Update Your Social Security Benefit Estimate

The formula given in this chapter for calculating your approximate AIYE will change from year to year. Benefit levels for a given AIYE may also change. Thus, any calculations you make based on the charts or forms in this chapter may have been accurate as of January–May 1980, but probably will be less so as the years pass.

Consumers Union hopes you will be able to obtain accurate and up-to-date information from the Social Security Administration or from your life insurance agent. If that proves not to be possible, you can do your life insurance planning by using the updating procedure described here. If your earnings since 1979 have grown at about the same rate as the average for all workers, this procedure should give you a reasonably good approximation of your current potential Social Security benefits. If your earnings have increased unusually quickly (or, conversely, at a much slower rate or not at all) since 1979, the approximation will be rough at best but better than none.

Calculate your 1980 approximate AIYE as in Table 2–1. Then, using Tables 2–4, 2–7, and 2–9, figure out 1980 benefit levels for survivors benefits, retirement benefits, and disability benefits (if applicable).

These benefits can now be adjusted to their approximate level for a person becoming eligible for benefits in some later year. The procedure is as follows:

Step 1. Multiply the monthly benefit amount from Table 2–4, 2–7, or 2–9 by the *average wage amount* for the year that is two years prior to the year for which you are calculating your AIYE. Thus, if you were calculating your 1983 AIYE, you would need the average wage amount for 1981.

You can obtain the average wage amount you need to

calculate your benefits by writing the Office of Public Inquiries, Social Security Administration, Baltimore, Maryland 21235 or by telephoning that office at 301-594-7700.

Step 2. Divide the amount obtained in Step 1 by $10,556. The result is a rough estimate of what your Social Security benefits would be if you died, retired at age sixty-two, or became disabled in the year for which you are making these calculations.

Let's say you're estimating your life insurance needs in the year 1983 and want to calculate Social Security survivors benefits. Let's say the SSA's Office of Public Inquiries tells you that using Tables 2–1 and 2–4, you figure your survivors would get $500 a month as of 1980. For 1983, you would use the average wage amount for two years earlier—1981. At this writing, of course, that average wage amount is not yet known, but let's say it's $13,600. As indicated above, you would multiply $500 by $13,600 and divide by $10,556. That would give you an estimated monthly survivors benefit (rounded to the nearest dollar) of $644, and you could use that figure in your life insurance planning.

How Much Life Insurance Do You Need?

Those quick-and-easy rules often cited for figuring out how much life insurance a person needs are usually close to worthless. It is wise to be skeptical of advisers who come up with such facile formulas as "life insurance coverage should be equal to six times annual income" and to be even more skeptical of those who would tailor insurance coverage to a person's maximum ability to pay premiums. One insurance agent some years ago counseled a Consumers Union shopper to spend on life insurance each year a basic sum equal to 6 percent of the breadwinner's gross income, plus another 1 percent for each dependent. The total was a burdensome 9 percent of income a year for the CU shopper who was married and had two children. This is not the way to plan a life insurance program. The idea is not to find the largest sum that a person can afford to pay for life insurance but rather to determine how much protection the family actually needs and to purchase that amount in the most economical way possible.

The Life Insurance Planning Worksheet on pages 46–47

can help you figure out step by step what your family's needs are. Before you proceed with the Worksheet, however, four factors need to be reckoned with. The first is the same for everybody: the assumption that the breadwinner may die tomorrow, or—if both parents work and contribute significantly to the family's support—that either breadwinner may die tomorrow. The adequacy of a life insurance policy can best be measured against the financial consequences of imminent death.

Needs can and do change significantly. The arrival of a child, a permanent disability to child or spouse, or an improvement in the family's standard of living, on the one hand, can boost insurance requirements. On the other hand, an inheritance or a financial success can sometimes reduce life insurance needs.

Typically, the financial responsibilities of a young breadwinner to his or her family increase rapidly for a number of years as children arrive and as rising income allows greater comforts. The family very probably will need to increase its life insurance coverage periodically during those years. But once family size and living standards stabilize, a breadwinner's financial responsibilities tend to decrease. Life insurance needs will generally level off. Whether they decrease in actual dollar coverage will depend to a large extent on the rate of inflation.

The second factor, which applies to families with only one breadwinner, will vary: Would the surviving parent go to work if the breadwinner died? It is necessary to consider three points here: (1) the importance that may be given to the surviving parent's staying home with the children while they're young; (2) how easily the surviving parent could find a job; and (3) how much the surviving parent could realistically expect to earn. It may be tempting to speculate about possibilities for financial support such as remarriage or assistance from relatives, but this kind of speculation can be hazardous. In planning life insurance, as little as possible should be left to chance.

The third factor has to do with those who own their home. Those who do should consider whether the house would be kept or sold after the breadwinner's death. If the house is to be sold, the equity (the house's current market value, minus the balance remaining on the mortgage, if any, and minus the capital gains tax on the sale) should be viewed as an asset. If the house is to be kept, the equity is irrelevant and should not be viewed as an asset for purposes of this Life Insurance Planning Worksheet. What's more, mortgage (if there is one) and property tax payments as well as maintenance expenditures would continue.

The fourth factor is concerned with the effects of inflation and of interest earnings on the amount of insurance that is needed. No one knows what inflation rates will be over the next year, five years, or twenty years. But considering the substantial inflation rates that have prevailed since 1973, it's important to take inflation into account in completing the Life Insurance Planning Worksheet. While the buying power of the estate presumably will decline over the years, the total number of dollars in the estate can be expected to grow, because a portion of the money left to survivors presumably will be earning interest.

The difference between how fast savings (or investments) grow and how fast prices rise is the critical point. If prices rise 5 percent a year, and the money left to survivors grows at 5 percent a year after taxes, there would be no need to take interest and inflation into account when planning for insurance because they would cancel each other out. In recent years, though, prices have been rising faster than many people's savings or investments have. In the early months of 1980, prices were rising at about a 15 percent annual rate while ordinary savings accounts were paying about 5¼ to 5½ percent before taxes.

It's difficult to do any long-range financial planning under the assumption of a permanent inflation rate of 10 or 15 percent per year. But it does seem prudent to assume that prices will increase faster than invested money—particularly money invested as conservatively as an insurance nest egg should be.

We have assumed that prices will rise 1 percent faster than the money you leave your survivors will grow. The inflation factors shown in Table 3–1 are approximations based on that assumption. (You will be referring to Table 3–1 when you calculate the Needs portion of the Worksheet.)

Having peered into the future and made some tentative assumptions and decisions, you can now begin to set life insurance objectives and to determine how much, if any, life insurance is needed. You can't compute your family's continuing needs to the penny, but you can make reasonable estimates based on reasonable assumptions. Remember that if both spouses' income go to support the family, the Worksheet should be filled out twice to determine each one's life insurance requirements.

Worksheet Directions

A. Life Insurance Already Owned. If you already have life insurance, enter as Item A the total face amounts of the policies. Include additional insurance purchased with dividends and any dividends that have been left with the company to accumulate at interest.* Do not count accidental death benefits (see Chapter 10). Deduct from face amounts the total of any loans outstanding against the policies. In-

---

*If these amounts are not listed on your most recent premium notice, the insurance agent or company can get the information for you.

clude group insurance if provided as a fringe benefit of a job, but bear in mind that changing jobs (or dropping membership in an organization through which life insurance is purchased) means the group insurance may lapse—unless it is converted to an individual policy, probably at a higher rate. Either way, your life insurance status should be reviewed.

B. Lump-Sum Pension Benefits. Enter lump-sum pension benefits that would be paid at your death. Do not include pension or Social Security retirement benefits payable as monthly income. They are taken into account in figuring out the Family Income Fund and the Retirement Fund (Items J and L).

C. Cash and Savings. Enter total deposits in savings accounts and checking accounts at current value. A certificate of deposit should be considered a savings account for this purpose.

D. Equity in Real Estate. (Remember to count as equity in real estate only those properties that would be sold.) Take the current estimated market value of your house and any other real estate (including undeveloped land) you may own, subtract any sums owed on mortgages, as well as the capital gains tax on the sale, closing or selling costs, and moving expenses, and enter the difference as Item D.

E. Securities. Enter the estimated market value of all stocks, money market funds, other mutual funds, and bonds you own. It might be wise to use average values over the past few years rather than current values, if market fluctuations have been severe. Speculative assets such as commodity holdings, stock options, and tax-shelter ventures should be valued conservatively.

Life Insurance Planning Worksheet

The Worksheet directions beginning on page 44 tell how to fill in the blanks. At three points the Worksheet directions call for the use of inflation factors to adjust for future price rises in the economy. You'll find these inflation factors in Table 3–1 on page 57.

Assets*

A. Life Insurance Already Owned	$_____
B. Lump-Sum Pension Benefits	_____
C. Cash and Savings	_____
D. Equity in Real Estate	_____
E. Securities	_____
F. Other Assets	_____
Total Assets	$_____

Needs

G. Final Expenses

1. Uninsured Medical Costs	$_____
2. Funeral Costs	_____
3. Probate Costs	_____
4. Estate Taxes	_____
Total Final Expenses	$_____

---

*Social Security benefits are not taken into account under Assets. They are included under Item J, Family Income Fund.

Needs *(continued)*

H. Repayment of Debts	$_____
I. Emergency Fund	_____
J. Family Income Fund	_____
1. Oldest Child	_____
2. Second Child	_____
3. Third Child	_____
4. Other Children	_____
5. Total of 1–4	_____
6. Total Family Income Fund	_____
K. Education Fund	_____
L. Retirement Fund	_____
M. Homemaking Expenses	_____
Total Needs	$_____

Insurance Needed (Total Needs minus Total Assets)

Total Needs	$_____
minus	
Total Assets	$_____
Additional Insurance Needed	$_____

F. Other Assets. Enter the value of any assets you own not included in Items A to E that survivors would plan to sell if you died. Such items might include jewelry, artwork, collectibles, a car, specialized equipment, an equity in a business. Any trust funds should be included here. Do not include questionable assets, such as royalties to be gleaned from as-yet-unpublished works and inheritances expected but not yet realized.

G. Final Expenses. At death, there may be medical expenses left over from a final illness, funeral and burial (or other disposition) costs, probate costs, and estate taxes to be dealt with. Together, these four items make up the cluster of costs termed Final Expenses:

G–1. Uninsured Medical Costs. If your health insurance includes major medical coverage, your survivors may be spared most of the burdensome hospital and doctor bills. Doctors and hospitals will probably bill your estate for any costs not covered by hospital and medical insurance. Even if you carry comprehensive health insurance, it's usually wise to expect at least $1,000 of additional costs. Check your health insurance coverage to make your own estimate for Item G–1.

*G–2. Funeral Costs.** Enter a reasonable figure for funeral and burial expenses. The average cost of a funeral and burial is about $2,000. But, by planning in advance or by making arrangements through a nonprofit memorial or funeral society, costs can be held down. (You may wish to write the

---

Funerals: Consumers' Last Rights by the Editors of Consumer Reports Books is the Consumers Union report on conventional funerals and burial, and some alternatives, including cremation, direct cremation, direct burial, and body donation.

Continental Association of Funeral and Memorial Societies, 1828 L Street, N.W., Washington, D.C. 20036 to see if there is such a society in your area. Or the association may provide other helpful information.) The lump-sum death benefit from Social Security (see page 37) should be considered when estimating funeral costs.

Death benefits are also available from the Veterans Administration. The survivor of a veteran who has served honorably in the armed forces is eligible to receive $300 from the VA. In addition, the veteran is entitled to free burial in a national cemetery. Spouses and minor children are also entitled to burial, provided the veteran is buried there. (If the spouse or child of the veteran dies first, he or she may be buried in a national cemetery if the veteran signs a paper confirming intent to be buried next to the spouse or child.) If a veteran is buried in a private cemetery, $150 is available from the VA for cemetery expenses in addition to the standard $300 death benefit. All veterans are also entitled to a headstone. Under certain conditions, members of the National Guard, Armed Forces Reserve, and Reserve Officers Training Corps also qualify for death benefits. Those who wish to have further information should contact their local VA office.

G–3. Probate Costs. Probate is the procedure by which a court validates a will and supervises the collection of assets, the payment of debts and taxes, and the distribution of the estate according to instructions in the will. If there is no will, assets are distributed according to a formula laid down in state law. But that formula may not be consistent with your wishes—and that's one reason why virtually everyone should have a will.

Probate procedures and costs can vary from state to state and even from county to county. The major components of probate costs are attorney's fees, executor's fees, appraisal fees, and court fees. In order to keep probate costs down, you might want to name a spouse or other family member as executor. Such a person might well perform the service without a fee, especially if he or she is a beneficiary of the estate. Many people name an attorney as executor. If you do, discuss with the attorney whether the work involved justifies both an executor's commission and a legal fee. The attorney may be willing to forgo one or the other.

If an attorney helped you draft your will, you might ask the attorney to estimate the probate costs your estate is likely to incur. Otherwise, you can estimate probate costs at about 4 percent of the value of your estate, not counting life insurance. (The proceeds of a life insurance policy with a named beneficiary go directly to that beneficiary and do not have to pass through probate.) Enter your estimated probate costs as Item G–3 on the Worksheet.

G–4. Estate Taxes. Your estate is the sum of the wealth you leave to your heirs. When an estate reaches a certain size, it's subject to federal estate tax and, in some cases, to a state tax as well. If your estate, including life insurance, comes to less than $161,563, it is ordinarily exempt from federal estate taxes. (In 1981 and thereafter the figure will rise to $175,625.)

In addition to the exemption, there is a substantial marital deduction. If part of your estate is going to your spouse, you may deduct from the taxable estate up to $250,000 or half the value of the estate, whichever is greater. (However, the deduction can't be greater than the amount you actually leave to your spouse.) So, if you leave everything to your spouse, you can probably bequeath at least $411,563 tax free. Beginning in 1981, that figure will rise to $425,625. For additional information about estate taxes, see Appendix IV.

Many people, of course, don't need to be concerned with estate taxes when estimating insurance needs and so can leave Item G–4 blank on the Worksheet. If your estate is likely to be large or complex, you should read Appendix IV and perhaps seek legal advice from an expert in estate taxes (who will also be able to help you arrive at a reasonable estimate for Item G–4).

Add your estimates for Items G–1 through G–4 and enter the total as Item G on the Worksheet.

H. Repayment of Debts. If you want to leave your survivors as free of debt as possible, you will probably want to provide for repayment of any outstanding balance on car loans, bank or finance company loans, loans from friends, and credit card or charge account installment debt. If you own a home, you may want to provide enough to pay off the outstanding balance on the mortgage. (The alternative is to include the cost of mortgage payments in the family budget when you calculate money needed for the Family Income Fund—Item J.) Enter the appropriate figure as Item H on the Worksheet.

I. Emergency Fund. You can't foresee every emergency, but it's reasonable to expect emergencies to occur—the need for a new furnace or a new roof for the house, or some unexpected medical bills. So include an emergency fund. We suggest $10,000 or six months' income, whichever is less. Enter the appropriate figure as Item I on the Worksheet.

J. Family Income Fund. Family household expenses typically eat up about 75 percent of a breadwinner's take-home pay. Review your present monthly income to determine what percentage goes for the support of the family, as distinct from what you use specifically for yourself. Items such as your life insurance premiums, transportation, clothing, and lunch money should be excluded, as should any surplus income put into savings, investments, etc. Family household expenses include everything else, from the family's food and shelter to its recreation.

If the family pays rent, plan on continuing rent payments in the future, including periodic rent increases. If the family owns a house and expects to keep it after your death, then the schedule of payments on the mortgage, if any, becomes part of the planning picture. The interest on the mortgage and the property taxes provide income tax deductions. (It might seem best to pay off the mortgage immediately at a saving of interest on the debt. Keeping the mortgage, however, means that it may be paid off with ever-cheapening dollars, because of inflation.) If the mortgage is covered by a separate life insurance policy, the monthly payment of principal and interest on the mortgage can be ignored in planning the family's life insurance coverage. But the payments for property taxes and insurance will continue. So will maintenance and repair expenses on the house. If the family expects to sell the house and move to rented quarters, provisions must be made for the expenses involved in selling the house and moving, for capital gains tax on the sale, and for the estimated rent.

If your children are attending a private or parochial school, the associated expenses are probably already a standard part of the family budget. If they attend public school, no special provision need be made to cover school costs. If, however, they are currently too young for school and you intend to send them to a private or parochial school, you should include the anticipated expenses when you calculate the Family Income Fund.

As discussed in Chapter 2, Social Security will probably provide a significant portion of the family's income until the youngest child turns eighteen, but there will be serious problems if the family tries to maintain its existing standard of living on Social Security alone. Part of the difference could be made up if the surviving spouse works, if there's monthly pension income, or if there's income from investments. But the main burden will probably go to life insurance.

To determine the total needed for the Family Income Fund, use the following procedure:

J–1. Take the number of years until the oldest child at home is eighteen: _____ years. Multiply by 12 to find the number of months until the oldest child reaches age eighteen: _____ months. Multiply this number by the amount of monthly income you anticipate the surviving family members would need to cover ordinary household expenses, at current price levels, if you died: $_____ per month. Subtract anticipated monthly Social Security benefits (see Chapter 2), salary (if any) of surviving spouse, and monthly pension benefits (if any): $_____. The remainder: $_____. If you have only one child, skip to J–5.

J–2. Now take the number of years from the time your oldest child at home turns eighteen until the second child turns eighteen (i.e., the difference in their ages): _____ years. Multiply by 12 to find the number of months in this period: _____ months. Multiply this number by the amount of monthly income you anticipate the surviving parent and all the children except the oldest (already covered in J–1) would need at current price levels, if you died: $_____ per month. Subtract anticipated monthly Social Security benefits (see Chapter 2), salary (if any) of surviving spouse, and monthly pension benefits (if any): $_____. The remainder: $_____. If you have only two children, skip to J–5.

J–3. Take the number of years from the time your second child turns eighteen until your third child does: _____ years. Multiply by 12 to find the number of months in this period: _____ months. Multiply this number by the amount of monthly income you anticipate the surviving parent and all the children except the oldest and the second child would need at current price levels, if you died: $_____ per month. Subtract anticipated monthly Social Security benefits (see Chapter 2), salary (if any) of surviving spouse, and monthly pension benefits (if any): $_____. The remainder: $_____. If you have only three children, skip to J–5.

J–4. If you have more than three children, continue in the same manner, until you reach the point where your youngest child turns eighteen.

J–5. Add up all the figures from J–1 to J–4 that you have filled in. You should be adding up as many figures as you have children. This gives a total, not adjusted for inflation, of: $_____. Round it off upward to the next $1,000. The total, not adjusted for inflation, is: $_____.

J–6. Take the total from J–5 and adjust it for inflation. Do this by multiplying it by an inflation factor from Table 3–1 on page 57. Choose a factor covering the number of years until your youngest child is fourteen, which will provide a reasonable approximation for the block of years involved. Total from J–5: $_____ multiplied by inflation factor _____ gives a Family Income Fund of $_____. Enter this figure as Item J on the Worksheet.

K. Education Fund. College tuition and other education costs have been soaring. According to data compiled by the Life Insurance Marketing and Research Association, an industry organization, the median cost of tuition, room, and board at state colleges averaged about $2,000 a year for state residents and $3,000 a year for out-of-state residents in 1979–1980. At private colleges and universities, the average was about $4,600, but it was as high as $8,000 at some institutions. None of those figures included travel, books, or pocket money, all of which can easily add another $1,000 to $2,000 to the yearly cost. Thus, at current prices, a four-year college education is likely to cost anywhere from $12,000 to $40,000. (A two-year program would cost about half as much, a one-year technical or vocational program even less.)

The amount of money projected for your family's Education Fund should be based on an estimate of total costs for postsecondary education, less Social Security benefits for the surviving child or children. The Social Security law provides vital financial aid to students in families whose breadwinner has died or has become totally disabled. It does so by prolonging survivors benefits until the age of twenty-two for full-time unmarried students in colleges and universities (as well as in high schools, vocational schools, and junior and community colleges). Otherwise, income ceases just before a survivor's eighteenth birthday (unless that child is disabled). Student monthly income from Social Security for a surviving child could run as high as $424.50 in 1980. A full-time student can get this money twelve months a year, including summer vacations, for a four-year period. Thus, the federal government could pay as much as $20,376 (at 1980 rates) toward educational expenses for some fatherless or motherless young people. With two or more survivors, including a spouse and a student, the family as a whole could receive a monthly total benefit as high as $990.60 and as low as $183 in 1980. In some cases, then, it may be to a family's advantage for the youngest child to continue in school, thus perpetuating the child's Social Security benefits. (Benefits would be reduced if surviving family members had more than a moderate amount of earnings.)

Parents should ask themselves how much money they are prepared to spend on a child's higher education. Because of fast-rising costs, though, that figure may have to be updated when you do your life insurance planning for the future, and over the years when you review your program. Many insurance companies and their agents can give you education cost figures based on annual surveys done by the Life Insurance Marketing and Research Association.

College students in families with low-to-moderate incomes may have good opportunities for loans, scholarships, and self-help programs, but don't include such funds in your calculations unless and until they are actually awarded.

Take the lump sum you anticipate would be needed (at current costs) for each child you think will continue schooling after age eighteen. Once you know how much of the bill Social Security will pay, subtract those benefits to get a corrected figure for each child's college or technical studies. Then adjust each figure separately for inflation, using Table 3–1. Use the inflation factor for the next-to-last year of each child's schooling. Finally, add these adjusted figures together and enter the sum as Item K on the Worksheet.

L. Retirement Fund. Ordinarily, once the youngest child turns eighteen or thereafter completes schooling, the surviving spouse will no longer receive Social Security benefits until at least age sixty. One of the decisions you must make in your life insurance planning is whether to provide income—and, if so, how much—for the surviving parent during the middle years between the end of child-raising and the survivor's retirement. In many families, paying for insurance on a breadwinner to provide a substantial lifetime income for the surviving parent will be more than the budget can stand. If it is anticipated that a survivor will be unable to be self-supporting, then, of course, that contingency will have to be taken into account. Otherwise, it normally should be assumed that the surviving parent will be self-supporting during the middle years. During the retirement years, however, that usually will not be the case.

Table 3–1
Accounting for Inflation and Interest

The inflation factors are approximations based on the assumption that prices will rise 1 percent faster than the money you leave your survivors will grow. Use the table for inflation factors for three items in the Worksheet. For the Family Income Fund (Item J), use the number of years until your youngest child is fourteen. For the Education Fund (Item K), use the number of years until your youngest child is in the next-to-last year of schooling. For the Retirement Fund (Item L), use the number of years until your spouse is seventy-two (or use twenty years, if smaller). For periods beyond twenty years, we suggest using the inflation factor for twenty years. Long-term historical precedent seems to justify an assumption that savings and investment returns will eventually catch up to the rate of inflation, if not exceed it.

Years Before Money Will Be Used	Inflation Factor
1	1.01
2	1.02
3	1.03
4	1.04
5	1.05
6	1.06
7	1.07
8	1.08
9	1.09
10	1.10
11	1.12
12	1.13
13	1.14
14	1.15
15	1.16
16	1.17
17	1.18
18	1.20
19	1.21
20	1.22

When your spouse reaches retirement age, some Social Security benefits will probably be available. But these will not be enough to provide for a comfortable retirement. Your spouse can choose either survivors benefits (which start again after retirement age) or retirement benefits, but not both. If your spouse has earned a good deal of money, the decision probably will be to select retirement benefits.

Which kind of benefits should you use in insurance planning? Ordinarily, you should begin by looking at the survivors benefits, because you *know* your spouse can get those. However, if your spouse is already working and is entitled to retirement benefits, check out both survivors and retirement benefits and use the higher of the two.

Figure out how much monthly income your spouse would need to live on, at current prices. From this figure, subtract the Social Security benefits (survivors or retirement), and pension benefits, if any, that your spouse would have coming. This leaves the monthly income total that you should provide.

Multiply this monthly income total by 12 to get a yearly total. Then multiply the yearly total by 20 to provide a fund large enough to last twenty years.* The reason we use twenty years is that a sum that size should suffice to purchase a lifetime income. Currently, it is more than enough to purchase a lifetime annuity. (Whether your spouse should turn to an annuity or to some other form of investment is a separate question, which your spouse can decide at retirement time.)

Finally, adjust the fund for inflation, using a factor from Table 3–1. Choose the factor for twenty years, or the factor

---

*If your spouse is unlikely to be self-supporting during the middle years (between the time your youngest child reaches eighteen or completes schooling and the time your spouse reaches retirement age), use a larger number of years in the calculation.

for the number of years until your spouse turns seventy-two, whichever is smaller. Enter the total as Item L on the Worksheet.

M. Homemaking Expenses. If you're a full-time or even a part-time homemaker, replacing some of your services could cost a substantial amount of money. Day-care costs ranged from about $1,500 to about $4,000 a year as of early 1980. A housekeeper or cleaning service can cost as much or more. Your death might also mean increased family expenses for eating out, babysitters, laundry service, and a variety of other goods and services. At the same time, your death would very probably reduce family expenses for such items as clothing, food, medical costs, and transportation. After a number of years, the savings in these areas would outweigh the added expenses. So, you may need to provide a fund for homemaking expenses for a limited number of years.

Based on your family situation and the ages of your children, try to make a realistic estimate of the economic impact your death might have, and include an appropriate figure as Item M on the Worksheet.

Needs Minus Assets = Insurance

At this point, you're ready to balance your survivors' assets against their needs. The extent by which the needs exceed the assets is the amount of life insurance you need.

Even though you've performed all the calculations in good faith, you may get discouraged because of the figure you come up with. The total the Worksheet calls for could seem out of your reach. But before you succumb to despair, it would be wise to learn something about the various types of life insurance and how they are priced (see Chapters 4, 5, and 7). Then, if it still seems as though you need more life insurance than you can afford, go back and check your Worksheet to see if you've been too extravagant in any of your assumptions. If that has not been the case, and you've been quite realistic in preparing the Worksheet, CU suggests buying as much protection as you can afford. That will mean concentrating on term insurance (see Chapter 4); its chief advantage is that it has lower initial premiums than cash value insurance. Term insurance offers the best opportunity, in CU's judgment, for most family heads to purchase adequate protection.

A closing word: Your needs and circumstances—and those of your family—may change rather frequently. So it's a good idea to review periodically all insurance coverage (not just life insurance, but automobile, medical, homeowner's or renter's, and disability as well as Social Security benefits). Selecting a fixed date every year and marking it on the calendar far in advance can help you remember to do an annual review.

The Basic Policy Types

There are many kinds of life insurance policies. Once you've figured out how much life insurance is needed, you'll be ready to consider what kind of policy to shop for.

Virtually all policies fall into one of two categories: *term insurance,* which provides insurance protection only, and *cash value insurance,* which combines insurance with savings. In this chapter, we will consider both categories, and some of the policies within each, to see how they work and what some of their advantages and disadvantages are.

Term insurance, as its name indicates, covers you for a specific term, usually one year or five years. When the term is over, so is your life insurance coverage—unless you've purchased *renewable term.* When you buy a renewable term policy, the company cannot later deny your right to renew the coverage, regardless of any changes in your health or occupation, until you reach an age specified in the policy. The premium for renewable term insurance rises at the beginning of each new term. The increasing premium reflects the increasing probability of death.

Renewable term policies usually run out at age sixty-five or seventy. A few companies sell term insurance that can be renewed up to age one hundred. But the premiums after retirement age would be prohibitively high for most buyers. (For example, one major company would charge $15,405 at age eighty for one year's coverage under a $50,000 renewable term policy.) Should there be a need for insurance after age sixty-five or seventy, a policyholder of a *convertible term* policy can convert the term policy to a cash value policy regardless of changes in health or occupation. The opportunity to convert, however, usually expires before the renewable term policy itself expires. All of the term policies rated in Chapters 15 and 16 are convertible to at least age sixty and renewable to at least age sixty-five.

With the vast majority of term policies you get no money back when the policy expires or if you don't renew.

Cash value insurance is usually a considerably more complicated product than term insurance. As its name indicates, it includes a cash value, often compared to a built-in savings account, within the life insurance policy. The cash value builds slowly in the first year or two and gradually accumulates to a substantial sum. At some specified point—sometimes age one hundred, ninety-five, or ninety; sometimes twenty years from the date of the policy's issue; sometimes at another date specified in the policy—the cash value becomes equivalent to the face amount of the policy. When that point is reached, the policyholder receives the amount of the cash value and the policy is terminated. The policy is said to *endow* at that point.

With most cash value policies, the annual premium stays level throughout the life of the policy. In effect, the buyer pays more than is needed to cover the statistical risk of death in the early years, and less than the amount needed to cover the statistical risk of death in later years. Thus a cash value policy is a vehicle that allows for the continuation of insurance into old age without the upward rise in annual premiums that accompanies renewable term insurance.

You are not entitled to withdraw money from the savings component of a cash value policy before the maturity date, unless you cancel the policy. But you can borrow against it, at whatever interest rate is guaranteed in the policy. In early 1980, most companies were charging 8 percent interest. Under many older policies, the rate is 5 or 6 percent.

The savings component of a cash value policy exists for the benefit of the policyholder and not the beneficiary. If the policyholder dies, the beneficiary receives no more than the face amount of the policy regardless of how much or how little money has accumulated in the savings component.*

Here are some of the basic term and cash value policies.

Basic Term Policies

Level renewable term insurance has a fixed face amount and a fixed annual premium during each term of coverage. With each renewal the annual premium is increased for the new term, according to your age at the time of renewal. The term of insurance coverage is usually one year or five years. The policy may be renewed up to, usually, age sixty-five or seventy, regardless of changes in your health or occupation. It cannot be canceled by the insurance company except for nonpayment of premium. At the time of renewal—in most insurance contracts—you have the right to reduce the amount of coverage and therefore the premium. No company will permit the amount of coverage to be increased

---

*If you borrow against the cash value and die before the loan is repaid, the amount outstanding plus interest is subtracted from the policy's face amount before payment is made to your beneficiary. If you should cancel your policy, the cash value of the policy at the time of cancellation—less any outstanding loans plus interest—is payable to you.

without the company's approval, which is often contingent upon a medical examination. Virtually all renewable term policies can be converted, without medical examination, to a cash value form of insurance. If you're going to convert, you must usually do so by age sixty, though the policy itself may be renewable to age sixty-five or seventy. Each policy specifies the deadline for conversion.

Renewable and convertible term insurance is Consumer Union's policy of choice for most buyers. Our reasons are set forth in detail in Chapter 5. The main reason, however, as discussed in Chapter 3, is: The lower initial premiums for term insurance help make adequate coverage possible during the child-raising years—a critical time for life insurance, in CU's opinion, when for many families income may be relatively low. With the convertibility privilege (a feature of almost all term policies), the policyholder has a way to continue coverage past age sixty-five or seventy, if necessary.

Level nonrenewable term insurance has a fixed face amount and a fixed annual premium during the term of coverage. The term may be five years, ten years, or some other period up to—in all but a few cases—the policyholder's sixty-fifth or seventieth birthday. The policy cannot be renewed but, as a rule, it can be converted (during some limited period) to a cash value policy despite changes in health or occupation.

Decreasing term insurance (also called reducing term, declining term, or mortgage term) is a term policy whose face amount gradually decreases and whose annual premium is fixed. Decreasing term policies are usually bought for ten, fifteen, twenty, twenty-five, or more years. Because this kind of insurance is often used to cover the outstanding balance on a home mortgage, the decrease in coverage sometimes follows the pattern of mortgage amortization, diminishing little during the early years and more steeply later. The pattern may look something like this:

If death occurs in year	Death benefit is
1	$30,000
5	28,470
10	25,470
15	21,150
20	14,520
40	2,520

Instead of following the pattern above, decreasing term may follow a simple step pattern, decreasing a fixed amount each year.

During its earliest years, a decreasing term policy offers perhaps the largest amount of coverage available for the relatively low size of the premium. Thus, decreasing term can be very attractive to the financially pressed family. However, the inflexibility of decreasing term makes it a poor choice as the primary policy for most breadwinners. Changing circumstances—for example, the birth of a child, an adoption, a new house, a divorce, or a remarriage—can change insurance needs. So can inflation. These problems, of course, can exist with all life insurance policies, including level term insurance (the kind CU recommends) and cash value policies. But the problems are most acute with decreasing term. Because the face amount declines inexorably, decreasing term offers no hedge at all against inflation or changing needs.

For this reason, the conversion privilege is particularly important with a decreasing term policy. A policyholder who fears becoming, or who is becoming, uninsurable may want to try to arrest the annual decrease in the amount of coverage by converting the policy to cash value insurance and thereby freezing the amount of coverage at its current level.

Most decreasing term policies are convertible only to a cash value policy.* Some decreasing term policies can be converted in amounts equal to only 80 percent, 75 percent, or less of their face amount at the time of conversion. Then even a person who can afford to convert to the maximum cash value policy may face a dilemma. If you convert, part of the protection is lost immediately; if you do not convert right away, the face amount will continue to decrease, and the amount that is convertible will be even less, in time.

CU believes that decreasing term may be appropriate if used to insure a homemaker when the family does not expect to have more children. In such a case, the decline in face amount may genuinely mirror a decline in insurance needs.

Basic Cash Value Policies

Whole life is the best known and most widely sold form of life insurance. Probably the most common type of whole life is *straight life*. With it, you pay premiums to age one hundred and the policy endows at age one hundred. Your premiums and the face amount remain fixed throughout the time the policy is in effect. If you live to age one hundred and have continued paying premiums, you will receive the full face amount of the policy at that time (less any loans outstanding), and the policy will terminate.

A number of variations are possible from the straight life model. Instead of endowing at age one hundred, the policy may endow at age ninety-five, ninety, or eighty-five. Such

---

*Policies that can be converted from decreasing term to level renewable term are quite rare, though that kind of convertibility would be a desirable feature for many buyers, since they could then arrest the coverage decline without going to a cash value form of insurance. One company offering such a conversion privilege is Occidental Life Insurance Company of California.

policies are sometimes called *endowment policies* (see page 70). However, that designation is often reserved for policies that endow earlier than age eighty-five. Generally the earlier a policy endows, the higher the annual premium.

Some whole life policies may also differ from the straight life model by having annual premium payments cease before the endowment year. A policy might endow at age one hundred but be *paid up* at age ninety-five, ninety, eighty-five, or even sixty-five. The shorter the premium payment period, the higher you can expect the annual premium to be. The ultimate is single-premium life insurance, where the buyer pays one very large premium and has a whole life policy paid up from then on. CU believes that, in most cases, paid-up-early policies tend to be poor buys; our reasons are explained in Chapter 9.

Insurance companies devised the whole life policy as a way to offer a level premium for a lifetime of coverage. (The advantages and disadvantages of level premiums are discussed in Chapter 5.) The level premium is one of whole life's major selling points.

As a selling device, some whole life policies have premiums for the first three years or so that are lower than subsequent premiums. Such policies are called Modified Whole Life, Modified Life, or sometimes Mod. (A numeral in the policy name—e.g., Modified 3—usually gives the number of years until the premium increases.)

All whole life policies today are cash value policies, but this was not always so. The cash value feature arose in the last century as a reform, to answer protests that people who had made high early-year payments and then dropped their policies had "forfeited" a good deal of money to the companies. As a result, "nonforfeiture" laws were passed.

If you surrender (i.e., terminate) a cash value policy before the maturity date, you have three options—often called *non-*

forfeiture options—to choose from (see Table 4-1). A schedule of these options is always included in a cash value policy. Here are the three nonforfeiture options:

1. You can take the money in cash. If you do so, there are several options of how to receive the money; these are called *settlement options.*

One settlement option is to take the money in a lump sum. Barring adverse tax consequences, this is often the best since you may be able to invest your money more profitably than the insurance company would invest it on your behalf.

A second settlement option is to leave all of the cash value on deposit with the insurance company to earn interest. The interest rate can vary and will be what the company pays at the time.

A third settlement option is to take the money in installments of a fixed size, for as long as the money—including interest earned—lasts.

A fourth settlement option is to take the money, including interest earned, in a fixed number of installments. The company will then calculate the size of each installment accordingly.

A fifth settlement option is to take the money, including interest earned, in the form of an annuity. Most companies offer lifetime annuities with a guaranteed payment period of at least ten or twenty years.

2. You can take a reduced amount of paid-up cash value insurance. The amount of paid-up insurance you get is based on the amount of cash value you accumulated and your age at the time. Interest on the cash value more than covers the cost of the protection, so that the cash value in paid-up policies continues to grow. In the event of your death, the policy pays the reduced death benefit to the beneficiary. If you survive to age one hundred, the policy endows at that time, but at the reduced face amount.

Table 4–1
Nonforfeiture Options on Surrender of Policy

This table illustrates the three nonforfeiture options available to you should you decide to surrender (terminate) your cash value policy. The figures given are for the whole life policy of one major company and assume a male buyer thirty years old and a face amount of $50,000. CU has not made a detailed study of nonforfeiture options and cannot say whether the figures given below are average, above average, or below average. They are given to illustrate the kind of choices involved and the order of magnitude of the dollar figures.

Years Since Policy Was Bought	Cash Value*	Paid-Up Insurance	Extended Term Insurance (Full Face Amount)
5	$ 2,250	$ 6,400	12½ years
10	7,300	16,150	19½ years
15	11,550	22,550	20 years
20	16,150	27,950	19½ years
25	20,550	32,500	18 years
30	24,950	36,300	16½ years

*Cash value settlement options are described on page 68.

3. You can take extended term insurance. The length of your protection period under this provision depends on your age at the time you cash in the policy, and on the amount of cash value that has accumulated. The term policy has the same face amount as the original policy.

In the event you should terminate a cash value policy, a decision about which option to take should be made only after careful study. The choices can vary significantly in their consequences for your financial well-being.

Endowment policies — those actually labeled as such—are cash value policies with the emphasis on savings instead of on insurance protection. Endowment comes not at age one hundred but at the date you select when buying the policy —often well within your life expectancy. The term "endowment policy" is often reserved for policies that endow earlier than age eighty-five. Two fairly common versions are twenty-year endowment (in which the policy matures twenty years after purchase) and endowment at age sixty-five. At the maturity date, you receive the face amount of the policy. If death occurs before the maturity date, your beneficiary receives the face amount.

Premiums for endowment policies run very high. Generally speaking, the earlier a policy endows, the more rapidly cash values build up within it, and the higher the annual premium. For example, a $50,000 twenty-year endowment policy bought by a thirty-five-year-old man might well carry a premium of more than $2,100 a year. What the policyholder gets in exchange for this premium is of questionable value. To be sure, the face amount received at the end of the endowment period would exceed the sum of the premiums paid in. But the relevant comparison here is how much more money could be made if the savings component of the premium—that is, the total premium minus a portion sufficient to pay for the insurance protection—were invested elsewhere. Usually it's a good deal more. That fact probably accounts for the declining popularity of endowments. As of 1978, only about 4 percent of policies sold were endowments. Viewed as investments, endowment policies are unspectacular. Viewed purely as life insurance, they involve unnecessarily large cash outlays.

In 1978, approximately 51 percent of individual life insurance policies purchased were in the form of whole life, of which more than two-thirds were straight life. Another 5 percent were modified whole life, and about 4 percent were endowment policies. About 19 percent were term policies. Another 10 percent involved a combination of whole life and term. Thus, the policies discussed in this chapter, singly and in combination, account for about 89 percent of all policies sold. The remaining 11 percent represent various other forms of policies, some of which are discussed in Chapter 9.

Term Versus Cash Value

More people buy cash value insurance than any other form of life insurance. Why? Well, as we suggested in the Introduction, life insurance is sold, not bought. It's usually the insurance agent who seeks out the buyer, not the other way around. And it's the agent who usually steers the buyer to a particular type and size of policy.

Some critics of the life insurance industry attribute the sales pressure behind cash value insurance to the large commissions it usually pays to the insurance agent. Insurance companies, the critics say, weight their commissions in favor of cash value policies because the high premiums for such policies put extra funds at a company's disposal to use for investment.

It is true that agents generally make higher commissions by selling cash value policies than by selling term. According to a 1979 report of the Federal Trade Commission, the average first-year commission on the sale of a whole life policy (the most common type of cash value policy) was $273 in 1974, while the average first-year commission on the sale of a level term policy was then $98. This was true even though the average term policy was for more than double the face amount of insurance—$46,430 as against $19,560 for the average whole life policy. This is not to imply that an agent's only interest in whole life is for the commission. Most life insurance agents are taught by their companies to believe wholeheartedly in the virtues of cash value policies and to stress protection-plus-savings in their sales presentations. But the fact that an agent may be sincere in advising you to buy a cash value policy doesn't necessarily mean that the agent is right. Let us, then, examine the pros and cons of the arguments you are likely to hear in favor of cash value policies.

"Cash value premiums stay level, while term premiums rise every term of coverage." This is true, but whether a level premium is seen as an advantage or disadvantage depends on your point of view. There's a certain advantage to the level premium when it comes to ease of budgeting, but you pay a price for it. After all, with a cash value policy an insurance company is offering that fixed premium while still covering the increasing likelihood of death over time. In order to do this without losing money, the insurance company sets the annual premium of the policy higher than necessary to cover the likelihood of death in the early years and lower than necessary in the later years.

The term insurance premium starts out as only a fraction of the cash value premium—ranging initially from approximately a tenth to a half of the cash value premium, depending on a person's age at the time the policy is bought. It is true that with term insurance the year will eventually come when the term premium is higher than the cash value premium would have been, but the crossover point may not come until thirty years or so after the purchase.

The upward slope of term premiums over the years can be

viewed as a disadvantage: It may make coverage more difficult to afford during middle age and close to impossible to maintain after retirement age. Consumers Union, however, views this slope as an advantage: The term premium structure makes protection easier to afford during the early years when children are in the home and income may be relatively low—precisely the time when life insurance coverage is most needed. A large number of families are underinsured. In early 1979, the average American family had about $35,100 in life insurance, including group insurance. But that amount would be grossly inadequate for many families, especially families with young children at home.

Another observation may be made about the increase in term insurance premiums over the years. For most people, it's not unrealistic to expect income to rise with time (especially in view of inflation). The rise in term insurance premiums may parallel, to some extent, a rise in ability to pay higher premiums.

"Term insurance is temporary, whereas cash value insurance is permanent." In fact, as already noted, term policies can be bought with a conversion privilege that allows them to be converted to cash value policies during a stated time period (often up to age sixty). Most commonly, conversion requires that buyers pay the cash value premium for their age at the time of conversion. This is called *attained age conversion.* For example, $100,000 of coverage bought at age twenty-five in the form of five-year renewable and convertible term insurance might cost, at the outset, about $240 per year. To convert that policy to a whole life policy at age forty-five might mean an annual premium in the neighborhood of $1,200.

Some policies allow for either attained age or *original age conversion.* In the latter, the new contract is drawn up as if the buyer had selected a cash value policy from the outset so the annual premium is lower, being based on the original age. Roughly, to accomplish an original age conversion, the buyer must usually pay the difference between the term premiums totaled and what the premiums for the cash value policy would have been over the years until conversion, plus interest of 5 or 6 percent a year. Either way, conversion can be expensive. Conversion clauses are discussed further in Chapter 11.

CU recommends buying renewable term insurance with the conversion privilege, in order to maintain flexibility. But we doubt that most people would choose to convert their term policies, because for most people it doesn't make sense to carry life insurance in the retirement years. For that same reason, we regard the "permanence" of cash value policies as a minor virtue. Adequate life insurance is highly desirable during the income-earning years. Adequate retirement funds are highly desirable in later years. In CU's judgment, the two are independent of each other and should be planned for separately.

Many people cash in their policies at retirement. To hang on to an insurance policy past retirement normally makes little sense. There is no longer a loss of income to insure against. The premiums spent on life insurance during retirement could better be spent, in most cases, in other ways. Often, to continue holding a policy amounts, in effect, to a gamble that an insured spouse will die soon enough to add to the survivor's otherwise inadequate retirement resources.

There might be an exception to this reasoning if you had a serious health problem at the time of retirement and realistically had a short life expectancy. Other exceptions might include an older person who still has dependents and a comparatively wealthy person who needs insurance to provide estate tax liquidity. In such cases, it might well be the rational course to hold on to an insurance policy. This does not mean, however, that a cash value policy has to be bought at the outset.

Although a whole life policy makes it possible to carry life insurance into retirement, it isn't necessarily a wise thing to do. Suppose you had a $50,000 whole life policy with a cash value, at age sixty-five, of $32,500. You might be better off cashing it in. If the money isn't needed immediately, it could be invested. At the interest rates prevailing in early 1980, you could turn that $32,500 into $50,000 within five years, and $75,000 within ten years. (In this example, we assume that you are in the 33 percent tax bracket.) Interest rates (12–14 percent before taxes on high-grade corporate bonds) may well drop, but the idea would still merit consideration.

To repeat, the need for life insurance after retirement is rare. For most people, what's needed in retirement is not life insurance but adequate retirement income. And, frankly, neither term nor cash value policies can ensure that. It requires separate financial planning.

"But at least a cash value policy can contribute substantially to a retirement nest egg. Money spent on term goes down the drain." This argument is commonly used by life insurance agents. It is fallacious.

To begin with, money spent on term premiums buys exactly what it purports to buy: protection against the financial consequences of the policyholder's death. If the policyholder dies while a policy is in force, the policyholder would have paid much less money in premiums with term insurance than with cash value. If you knew you were going to die within a few years of buying a policy, you would probably buy term insurance, since its premiums are substantially lower than those for cash value policies in the early years. Your beneficiaries would get the same amount of money (the face amount), and your premium outlay would have been lower:

In this situation, it is cash value buyers who might be said to have thrown their premium money down the drain.

The person who buys a cash value policy and then, for any of a number of reasons, drops it would also have been better off buying term. Most agents advise against dropping policies once bought—advice that may be right on many occasions, wrong on others. Agents are less free, however, in giving the corresponding advice: You should not buy a cash value policy unless you are quite certain that you will not be dropping the policy early. With cash value policies, you incur a substantial front-end load of expenses (including a sizable agent's commission). The return for this investment, in the form of significant cash value, takes years to develop.

The Federal Trade Commission, in 1979, calculated the rate of return on the average whole life policy as *minus* 8.36 percent over the first five years, 1.43 percent over ten years, 4.12 percent over twenty years, and 4.45 percent over thirty years.* The FTC calculations showed the lowest projected rates of return to be minus 30.07 percent over the first five years, minus 3.35 percent over ten years, 1.52 percent over twenty years, and 1.79 percent over thirty years. The FTC's highest projected returns for five, ten, twenty, and thirty years were 0.58 percent, 5.55 percent, 7.61 percent, and 7.75 percent, respectively. To repeat, a cash value policy should not be bought by anyone who doubts his or her determination or need to keep the policy in force for many years.

But, an insurance agent might interject, term insurance is the kind of life insurance "you have to die to beat." Again, this is a fallacy, for it ignores the importance of the time

---

*The figures cited—for a male buyer, age thirty-five, in 1977—are for participating (dividend-paying) policies. Those for nonparticipating policies are even lower. The figures are based on a hypothetical cost for the insurance protection offered by the policies and assume that dividends are paid as illustrated.

value of money—or, to put it more simply, interest. The difference between term premiums and the higher cash value premiums can be put into a savings account or otherwise invested and left to accrue at compound interest. It is quite possible to build up a sizable nest egg in this way—very often a more sizable one than the cash value in a cash value policy.

In industry parlance, the strategy described above is "buying term and investing the difference." It has been debated for years, and people on both sides of the argument have compiled many statistics. CU considers the question of the investment merits of term versus cash value insurance important enough to have made detailed actuarial tests on the subject. But we do not base our advocacy of term insurance solely on a buy-term-and-invest-the-difference philosophy. Investment considerations are secondary to insurance protection for the family. And where insurance needs are great and income is limited, the purchase of term insurance may be the only way to afford adequate protection. In cases where truly adequate coverage appears to be a goal out of reach, term insurance will at least allow a family to come closer to meeting its insurance needs than it could with whole life or other cash value insurance.

That said, let us return to the question of the investment merits of term versus cash value insurance. As a result of CU's 1973 study of life insurance costs, we were able for the first time to single out with reliability the low-cost policies in the life insurance marketplace. We were thus able to compare low-cost term insurance with low-cost cash value insurance. And we were able, at last, to provide a more precise answer to the long-standing question: How much must a term buyer earn on investments after taxes to come out ahead with a buy-term-and-invest-the-difference strategy?

When we compared the lowest-cost term policies with the

lowest-cost whole life policies, we found that the term buyer would need an aftertax return of between 5 and 6 percent to come out ahead.* Our 1979 survey tended to confirm this conclusion. Earning 5 to 6 percent after taxes on one's investments year after year is not necessarily an easy task. Yet some people do that well; some people do even better.

The percentages given above are based on studies that assume a thirty-five-year-old male buyer who holds his policy to age sixty-five. Those interested in our method of calculation can find details in Appendix II.

If one compares high-cost term policies with high-cost whole life policies, it appears that the term buyer would need only a 2.5 percent return after taxes to come out ahead. Most people could easily surpass that rate.

In terms of investment strategy, we would say that the lowest-cost whole life and term policies are at a virtual standoff. (Detailed information on the rate of return on the savings component of cash value policies can be found in Chapter 17.) But for most people investment strategy ought not to be the primary consideration in life insurance buying. And it would be mere self-delusion for most people to think they can build up an adequate retirement nest egg either by purchasing a cash value policy *or* by buying term and investing the difference.

Retirement planning requires consideration of present and future inflation. If inflation averages even a mere 4 percent in the last twenty years of this century, it will take $2.19 in the year 2000 to buy what $1.00 bought in 1980. An 8 percent inflation rate would hike that figure to $4.66. At 12 percent, it would be $9.65.

---

*We use aftertax figures for the term policyholder's savings because the savings in the cash value portion of a whole life policy are largely tax-sheltered. This aspect of whole life is explained later in this chapter.

Planning for adequate retirement income, especially for anyone who cannot count on help from a pension, is likely to require a program of savings and investments. The money going into such a program probably will have to be substantially more than the difference between term and cash value premiums. And the accumulated retirement fund will have to be far more than any ordinary person would accumulate in the cash value of a life insurance policy.* Without such resources, a retired person or a couple might be reduced to trying to scrape by only on Social Security benefits—a difficult existence indeed.

"People who buy term won't invest the difference between term and cash value premiums; they'll spend it. Cash value insurance is a valuable aid to willpower, a means of forced savings." Cash value insurance is indeed a forced savings vehicle, and CU believes that people who need life insurance and can afford to save, but who genuinely lack the willpower to save, should consider the purchase of cash value insurance. But while some life insurance agents seem to think that almost everyone lacks willpower, CU would apply that description much more sparingly. We do not believe, for example, that the term buyer is obliged to invest the difference and that failure to do so is a sign of lack of willpower. The term buyer who prefers to spend the difference is not necessarily squandering it. What's important is adequate insurance protection and separate provision for retirement.

There are, we agree, some people who find saving impossible. Many of them could benefit by the use of some sort of forced savings plan. Among such plans that might merit

---

*A $25,000 whole life policy, for example, if purchased around age thirty, might build up cash values of about $15,000 at age sixty-five. But inflation, meantime, will probably reduce the purchasing power of that $15,000 to less than half of what it was when the policy was purchased.

consideration are payroll deduction plans, thrift plans, and cash value insurance.

With payroll deduction plans, available at many work places, a certain amount is automatically deducted from an employee's paycheck. The money may be deposited in the employee's credit union account. Or the employer may invest the money on the employee's behalf in United States Government EE bonds. Contingent on their being held to maturity (eleven years), EE bonds were paying 7 percent annual interest before taxes in 1980 (an improvement over past years but still not a particularly high rate of return). If they were cashed in before the maturity date, a lesser rate would be paid. With this kind of plan, then, there is not only an automatic saving mechanism but also a built-in incentive to hold on to the savings for a period of time. Interest on EE bonds is exempt from state and local taxes, but not from federal income tax.

Thrift plans, offered to employees as a fringe benefit by many large firms, are similar to payroll deduction plans but usually more advantageous because the employer may match a portion of the employee's contribution to the plan. One common method is for the employer to contribute one dollar for each two dollars the employee contributes, up to a certain limit. The money may be invested in any of several ways: in stocks, in savings certificates, in government or corporate bonds—or, often, in the company's own stock. Many times a number of choices is offered, with employees permitted to choose from among them, and to change to another plan from time to time. The employer's contribution and any income from investments are taxable—but not until the money is withdrawn.

Comparing cash value insurance with these other forced savings methods is difficult because—as with many investment vehicles—it's impossible to say with certainty what the return will be on a cash value policy. First of all, it varies from policy to policy. Second, it varies with the length of time a policy is held. Third, for some policies, it depends on dividend payments that can't be precisely predicted in advance. And fourth, the annual premium pays for both insurance protection and savings, wound inextricably together, and so the return on the savings portion can be calculated only by making certain statistical assumptions.

Under reasonable assumptions, the usual conclusion is that after several years of building up cash values, a good cash value policy returns between 5 and 6 percent on the savings portion. Under the same assumptions, the rates of return on some other cash value policies, however, may be only around 2.5 to 4 percent.

The rate of return on the savings component of cash value policies may seem inferior to that of the other forced savings vehicles discussed above. But the cash value in an insurance policy is substantially tax-sheltered. You do not have to pay income taxes on the interest earned on the cash value unless the cash value upon surrender of the policy exceeds the sum of the premiums paid in.* Even then, only that portion of the cash value that exceeds the sum of the premiums is taxable. What's more, by buying cash value insurance you delay your rendezvous with the Internal Revenue Service during all the years the cash value builds up. If the policy is cashed in after retirement, you will most likely be paying the taxes when you are in a lower tax bracket. In contrast, someone who has a savings account in a bank or credit union must pay taxes on the interest as it is credited to the account, whether it is actually withdrawn or not.

---

*In the case of a participating policy, which pays dividends to the policy-holder, the sum of the premiums is reduced by the sum of any dividends received. Participating and nonparticipating policies are discussed in Chapter 6.

Because of the tax wrinkle, CU judges the return on a low-cost cash value policy to be at least equal to that of most other forced savings methods, though probably not up to a good thrift plan. And cash value insurance has an advantage over the other forced savings methods in that the reluctant saver may be less likely to skip payments than with other methods. If a policyholder fails to keep up with the life insurance premium payments, the family's security may be impaired. Thus, there is a strong inducement to keep up the premium payments and thereby, without "saving" as such, keep adding to the policy's cash value.

But the savings in a life insurance policy cannot be taken out and spent with impunity. When a policyholder borrows against the cash value, the amount that would be paid to the beneficiary is reduced accordingly. Assuming the amount of insurance bought in the first place is the amount that is needed (or less), reducing it is normally undesirable. An exception to this reasoning may be the policyholder who borrows against cash value, only to reinvest the borrowed money at a higher rate of interest than must be paid on the loan. In times of high interest rates (such as early 1980, when this book went to press), many policyholders choose to do this. Interest must be paid on the loan (unless, of course, the policyholder terminates the policy—which would totally eliminate the insurance protection).

Some savings, even in the form of cash value insurance, is better than no savings. In sum, depending on family circumstances, cash value insurance may be an appropriate forced savings vehicle.

"Cash value insurance is also a substantial tax shelter." It certainly is and—for those in high tax brackets—purchase of cash value insurance as a tax shelter deserves consideration. Whether this and other tax shelters of the wealthy ought to

exist is a subject that is beyond the scope of this book. But under tax law as it stands, people with income that needs sheltering should (in consultation with their lawyer, accountant, or financial adviser) consider cash value insurance along with other possibilities such as tax-exempt bonds.

The shelter of a cash value insurance policy, as mentioned earlier, derives from two factors. First, no income tax is paid on the interest earned on the cash value except insofar as the cash value upon surrender exceeds the sum of premiums paid over the years (minus any dividends received). Second, if a policy is surrendered at retirement, the tax that has to be paid upon surrender is incurred at a time when the former policyholder may well be in a lower tax bracket than before retirement.

Most wealthy people can afford the premium outlay to protect their family adequately by either route—term or cash value insurance. But those who have to pay a large percentage of their investment return in taxes have more difficulty succeeding with a strategy of buying term and investing the difference. To make a 5 percent aftertax return, a married person with a $15,000 taxable income (after deductions and exemptions) would need a gross return of roughly 6.4 percent. But a person with a $100,000 taxable income would need roughly a 12.5 percent gross return.

"A cash value policy is sheltered not only from taxes, but from creditors as well." This is true: Creditors would have a hard time getting at the funds in the cash value of a life insurance policy. For people who tend to get deeply in debt, this factor is an advantage of cash value insurance over term insurance plus a separate arrangement for savings. However, many of these same people need the low initial premium outlay of term insurance to enable them to protect their families adequately.

"Cash value policies offer features unavailable with term policies." This argument, too, is correct. A frequently cited example, previously discussed, is that the cash value in a policy can be borrowed against if need be, and at a favorable rate of interest. (The loan rates for recent policies have gone up substantially from 5 percent a few years ago to 8 percent in 1980. Such increases, of course, have not affected loan rates set in older policies, which remain unchanged. And even 8 percent was attractive when the prime rate, in early 1980, was in the neighborhood of 15–20 percent.)

Another example is that the cash value may be used by the insurance company to pay for an automatic loan that in turn pays the premium if a policyholder neglects (perhaps because of illness, unemployment, or extended travel) to pay it. No such device is available to the term policyholder, who must apply for reinstatement if a premium is missed. That reinstatement may not be forthcoming if there has been a change in health. For this reason, it is especially important for term policyholders to pay their premiums on time.

A third example of useful features is that dividends on some cash value policies can be used to purchase additional insurance without proof of insurability. (Rates for such additions, however, may not always be favorable and should be examined carefully.) A fourth example is that certain riders (see Chapter 10) are normally available only with cash value policies.

In short, there's no question that a cash value policy is a more versatile financial instrument than a term policy. CU believes, however, that versatility is less important than adequate protection for the family.

"Term may be needed to help provide adequate coverage, but it should be purchased in conjunction with cash value insurance." Agents often sell a package in which term insurance

is attached as a rider to cash value (usually whole life) insurance. Most of the insurance protection in these packages usually resides in the term rider. One serious problem here is that the rider may not be renewable up to retirement age and in some cases isn't renewable at all. CU recommends that buyers of term insurance (whether in the form of a separate policy or a rider) purchase the kind that is renewable to at least age sixty-five.

That problem aside, there would appear to be no objection to the purchase of whole life and term in combination—if that combination meets the family's financial needs. Except for families that need forced savings, or a tax shelter, CU judges term insurance to be more likely to meet the family's needs. Buyers who do need both term and whole life should generally purchase individually tailored policies instead of prepackaged combinations.

The arguments discussed in this chapter are the ones you are most likely to hear in favor of cash value insurance. In trying to provide answers to these arguments, CU does not wish to induce an adversary relationship between insurance buyers and the agents who serve them. The reasoning of an informed and thoughtful agent is worth listening to. Unfortunately, with the huge turnover of life insurance agents in the industry the consumer cannot always count on agents to be truly well informed. In some cases, they are merely indoctrinated. Cash value insurance such as whole life should certainly be purchased if it meets your family's needs. But, as we've said, CU believes renewable, convertible term is the life insurance of choice for most people who need insurance.

Par Versus Nonpar

Life insurance dividends differ significantly from the dividends most people are more familiar with—the dividends paid to stockholders. Dividends on stock holdings represent a share of a company's profits. Dividends on a life insurance policy are a partial refund by the company of the premiums you've already paid.

Policies that pay dividends are called *participating* policies, or *par* policies for short. Policies that don't pay dividends are called *nonparticipating* policies, or *nonpar* for short.

Mutual life insurance companies, which are corporations without stockholders, usually stick to offering par policies. Some stock life insurance companies offer only nonpar policies, while others offer both par and nonpar. A few stock life insurance companies offer only par policies.

When a company designs any policy, par or nonpar, it sets the premiums high enough to provide some cushion against unfavorable events. Mortality might be higher than the company's actuaries assume. Company expenses might be higher. Or return on company investments might be lower.

On a nonpar policy, the die is cast once the policy is issued. If mortality, expenses, or investment return shows unfavorable results, the company may take a smaller profit or a loss. If these factors are favorable, there will be extra money that would constitute additional profit.

On a par policy, there is a larger cushion against these contingencies. To put it another way, the premium for a par policy will normally be higher than the premium for a comparable nonpar policy. If the company experiences the assumed level of mortality, expenses, and investment return, then dividends will theoretically be paid as illustrated at the time of sale. If the company does better than expected, dividends should be higher. If the dividends are substantial enough, then the par policyholder is better off than a comparable nonpar policyholder, even though the par policyholder probably pays higher premiums. In recent decades, par policies studied by Consumers Union have in fact been a better buy, on average, than nonpar policies.

If you're shopping for a par policy, the agent will provide you with an illustration of what dividends might be paid to you. The illustration will normally be accompanied by a disclaimer (often required by state regulations) that the illustration is "neither an estimate nor a guarantee." Rather, it simply describes the insurance company's current dividend scale. Any projected cost figures you're shown will be based on the dividends in this illustration.

Dividends usually begin to be paid at the end of the first or second year a par policy is in force. They usually grow in amount as the years pass.

You can do several things with dividends. If you have a term policy, you usually have three choices. You can take the dividends in cash, use them to reduce your annual premiums, or leave them with the company to accumulate at a stated rate of interest (often somewhere in the neighborhood of bank passbook savings account rates). If you have a cash value policy, you usually have at least one additional option: using dividends to buy paid-up additional cash value insurance. Unfortunately, the amount of additional insurance a dividend will buy in this way is usually small.

Some companies offer more than the standard four dividend options on cash value policies. Dividends can sometimes be used, for example, to buy one-year term insurance. Used this way, the dividends can add significantly to your total amount of coverage. A few companies let you buy as much one-year term insurance as the dividends will purchase. This is called the *term addition option.* Somewhat more common is the *fifth dividend option.* With it, part of the dividend is used to purchase one-year term in an amount equal to the cash value of the policy. The rest of the dividend usually must be left with the company to accumulate at interest.

Dividends are not taxed when they're paid to you. That's because the Internal Revenue Service considers life insurance dividends to be refunds of your previous overpayments on premiums. But dividends could still affect your taxes if you should terminate a cash value policy. Then you would be taxed on the amount, if any, by which the cash value exceeds the premiums paid, less the dividends you've already received. This method of calculation is consistent with the IRS's view of dividends as a partial return of premiums. If you leave your dividends with the insurance company to accumulate at interest, you're taxed on the interest.

Choosing Between Par and Nonpar

Should you choose a par or a nonpar policy? CU generally recommends par, particularly for those people who are buying a cash value policy. For term policies, the choice is less crucial, since dividends on term policies tend to be comparatively modest.

One argument in favor of nonpar policies is that their cost is guaranteed. If you have a particular need to know in advance what your life insurance cost will be, year by year, you may well prefer a nonpar policy. You might also want a nonpar policy if you think there's going to be a prolonged and severe economic downturn. A serious, long-lasting depression could cause a drop in some insurance companies' investment return, making less money available for dividends for par policies. Similarly, dividends might be lower if mortality rates were to rise substantially (an unlikely event) or if company expenses were to soar.

When you evaluate par against nonpar policies, you will naturally be reflecting on the fact that par policies usually have higher premiums than nonpar policies. You might ask yourself whether you'd be better off with nonpar, since you could earn interest on the difference between the par premiums and the nonpar premiums. (This line of reasoning recalls the dispute over whether it pays to "buy term and invest the difference." Here the question is whether it pays to "buy nonpar and invest the difference.") The answer depends to an extent on how much interest you assume you're forgoing when you pay the higher premiums for a par policy. CU now uses in most calculations the 5 percent interest rate recommended by the National Association of Insurance Commissioners, a group of state regulators. CU's Ratings shown in Chapters 15 and 17 are based on the 5 percent assumption (CU interprets this as an aftertax rate). In general, par policies appear to be a better buy than nonpar policies, according to our Ratings tables.

If you assume a higher interest rate, then the difference between par and nonpar policies would narrow. But even at 8 percent—quite a high aftertax rate to assume—par policies still look a shade better (at least they did in two studies—based on 1973 data—of which CU is aware). One study found par policies to be a better buy in roughly three-quarters of the cases when a 4 percent interest rate was assumed, but in only a little better than half the cases when an 8 percent interest rate was assumed. (These figures were based on a face amount of $100,000 and a twenty-five-year-old male buyer.)

Advocates of nonpar policies may respond that par policies may seem to be the better buy, but that the actual costs of par policies could prove higher than the costs projected at the time of sale. That's true. The dividend scales on which cost illustrations are based are companies' current dividend scales. If dividends fall below the illustrations, par policies could end up being more costly than the buyer expected. However, most major companies during the past two decades have generally been paying dividends that significantly exceed the dividend illustrations made at the time of sale. That could change. But dividends would have to fall substantially to make nonpar policies, in general, a better buy than par.

We should note that the median cost for par and nonpar policies, as projected at the time of sale, is often fairly close together. However, par policies that are lower in cost than the median are more widely distributed in price than nonpar policies, which tend to cluster around the median. Thus, there are often significantly better buys among par policies. But just any par policy is not necessarily a good buy. It's important to comparison-shop for the lowest-priced among the pars available.

The point can be demonstrated by looking at our Ratings for $100,000 of cash value insurance, issued to a thirty-five-year-old male. The lowest in projected cost among the nonpars was "The Competitor," issued by Time Insurance Company. There were sixty-seven par policies that were lower in projected cost than the lowest-cost nonpar policy. Similarly, for $25,000 of cash value insurance for a thirty-five-year-old male, there were eighty-three par policies that were lower in projected cost than the lowest-priced nonpar policy.

Are Dividends Allocated Fairly?

Let's say a life insurance company has generally experienced the mortality, expenses, and investment income that it assumed at the time its policies were issued. It then has some "divisible surplus"—as they say in the industry—to share with participating policyholders. The question is how shall this pie be sliced.

Making sure that policyholders get their fair share is a major job to which many actuaries devote much of their time. Many companies are extremely conscientious about trying to do the job fairly. And the process is not simple.

CU doubts that the objective of fairness is always achieved. There's a temptation to give more generous dividends to more recent policyholders. The dividends paid to recent buyers can then be illustrated to new sales prospects as the company's "current" dividend scale, which may spur sales. But it's hardly fair to longtime policyholders, whose dividends may cease growing or grow more slowly than they would under another formula.

Policyholders are vulnerable to unfair treatment for several reasons. First, there are absolutely no requirements for continuing cost disclosure on life insurance products after the time of sale. Second, policyholders may not know how the dividends they're being paid compare with those illustrated to them at the time of sale, unless they kept careful records. Even if the dividends being paid do equal or exceed the illustrations, longtime policyholders still have no way to judge whether the dividends received represent their fair share of the divisible surplus. Third, longtime policyholders don't know what dividends are being paid to more recent policyholders. Fourth, dividend allocation formulas are often kept secret (and in any event are too complex for most lay people to understand). Fifth, because of the way dividend formulas work, it's generally more costly to a company to increase dividends on older policies than on newer policies —so there's an economic incentive to "throw the older policyholders to the wolves," to quote Joseph M. Belth, professor of insurance at Indiana University.

Belth has documented several cases of apparent abuses with respect to dividend practices. He suggests that such abuses are quite common among both mutual and stock companies that issue participating policies. One company, for example, did not increase its dividend scale for some twenty years, from the late 1950s to the late 1970s, during a period when interest rates and company investment return were generally rising.

CU published an article entitled "What's Happening to Life-Insurance Dividends?" in the November 1976 issue of CONSUMER REPORTS. In that article we discussed several ways in which companies can allocate higher dividends to newer policyholders than to older ones. Policies are commonly divided into groups, called blocks, according to the time they were issued. Older blocks may be allocated a greater share of expenses, on the grounds that their average face amount is lower. Newer blocks may be allocated a greater share of investment income, on the grounds that the company has been earning a higher rate of interest on premium money recently received. Or certain tax factors may be allocated differently among the blocks. Any of these practices can be defended. But they can also be abused.

As we said, there may be a tendency for some companies to choose those methods of dividend allocation that have a favorable impact on the "current" dividend scale shown to sales prospects. This curtails the ability of consumers to make accurate comparisons of policy costs.

There is also a potential problem in the possibility that a company might flip-flop from one allocation method to another, depending on which method would produce the best marketing results at a particular time. Such switching would surely be unfair to companies that may have regularly shared divisible surplus according to a consistent formula for all policyholders. CU believes the whole area of dividend allocation deserves careful attention from life insurance regulators. Up to now, it has received relatively little.

How Reliable Are Dividend Illustrations?

As we said earlier in the chapter, dividend illustrations are normally accompanied by a disclaimer that they are neither estimates nor guarantees. The inevitable question is: How reliable are the illustrations as predictors of future dividend payments? The answer is: Not very.

In the decades since the end of World War II, most major par companies have paid substantially more than the dividends illustrated at the time of sale. But the consumer has had no way of knowing in advance *how much more* each company would pay than the amount illustrated. CU surveyed the historical cost of $15,000 whole life policies issued in 1953 by sixty-nine major life insurance companies. During the period 1953 to 1973, all sixty-nine companies paid dividends equal to or greater than those they had illustrated in 1953. Two companies, Integon Life Insurance Company and Security Life and Accident Company, paid only what they illustrated. The other sixty-seven companies exceeded their illustrations—but by wildly varying amounts. Over the twenty-year period, the total of dividends paid by Equitable Life Assurance Society of the United States, for example, exceeded its illustration by only 7 percent; Teachers Insurance and Annuity Association of America exceeded its illustration by a whopping 153 percent.

When you go shopping for a life insurance policy, you'll probably use a cost index. (How to use cost indexes and how to comparison-shop for life insurance is explained in Chapters 7 and 8.) If you're buying a participating policy, the cost index you're shown will be based on the illustrated dividends. But, as we've seen, the dividends illustrated provide only an uncertain gauge of the dividends that will actually be paid.

When buying a par policy, you can never entirely remove this element of uncertainty. But there are a couple of things you can do to hedge against it to some degree. For one thing, you can ask the agent to provide you with a figure called the *equivalent level dividend.* This figure will tell you to what extent a par policy's cost index is dependent on future dividend payments. (The lower the cost index, the lower the projected cost.) Say the cost index is $4.05 per $1,000 of coverage. If the equivalent level dividend is $1.25, that means the cost index of the insurance would rise to $5.30 if no dividends whatever were paid. Therefore, if you are considering two par policies that have about the same cost index, you might prefer the one with the lower equivalent level dividend—the one that is less dependent on dividend performance.

Another thing you might wish to do, if you're buying a par policy, is to buy from a company that has provided insurance at a low cost in the past. This involves looking at historical cost indexes based on dividends actually paid, rather than at current cost indexes, which are based on dividends now being illustrated.

For various reasons (among them logistical difficulties and budget), CU has never done a historical cost study as extensive as our cost studies on policies currently being offered. One source for information on historical cost indexes is a trade periodical called *Best's Review* (Life/Health Edition), published by the A. M. Best Company. (It may be hard to find *Best's Review* in your local library; you will probably need a large library or one with a collection specializing in finance or insurance.) Each year, *Best's Review* publishes an article entitled "20-Year Dividend Comparisons." The article usually runs in the December issue. Despite the article's name, it includes information not only on dividends paid over the previous twenty years, but also on each policy's total cost over that period.

There are three drawbacks to using the *Best's* article as a reference source. First, the *Best's* article usually covers only sixty to seventy companies; the company you're interested in may not be included. Second, the article shows information on one or perhaps two policies per company—and those policies may not be representative of the company's full line. Third, the article includes information on some companies' preferred risk policies (see page 111) but no information on their standard policies.

Even if the *Best's* data were perfect, you can't count on the assumption that a company's historical performance will necessarily predict its future performance. Company management, philosophy, and financial results can change over the years. So there will always be an element of uncertainty in buying a par policy.

Despite the uncertainty, CU believes that you should give serious consideration to buying participating insurance. If you do decide to buy a par policy, and you are deciding between two policies that look similar in cost based on illustrated dividends, you might then want to use historical cost information—if available—as a tie breaker.

Deciphering the Price

No one wants to choose an insurance policy by guesswork, by reacting to advertisements, or by succumbing to the most persistent and persuasive sales agent. Yet, in the absence of a usable tool for comparing the real prices of life insurance policies, this is what countless consumers have done. Studies have repeatedly shown that life insurance prices are hard to understand and compare, even for the astute shopper. In 1940, a government report stated:

> It is ... very difficult for a prospective policyholder to compare costs as between policies or between companies, or even to determine the cost of any one particular policy. The policyholder who attempts to make the determination will quickly find himself in a maze of technical terms and obliged to make numerous adjustments for variable factors which might affect the cost.

Things have improved somewhat in recent years. A widely used cost index has been developed. Consumers have had access to buying guidance, including Ratings of hundreds of policies, published by CONSUMER REPORTS in 1974 and

1980. Still, many buyers remain in the dark, and life insurance agents and companies don't always help matters. Frequently, the price they quote is the annual premium, which is only the crudest kind of indicator of the price. This is especially discouraging because there is a tremendous range in policy prices. For example, let's assume a thirty-five-year-old man wants to buy $100,000 of participating insurance. The difference between the highest- and lowest-cost term policies rated in Chapter 15 (including forgone interest at 5 percent) is about $13,000 over twenty years. In the case of cash value policies rated in Chapter 17, the corresponding difference is more than $33,000. These are the extremes, but they illustrate how important it is to shop around.

Ideally, of course, you want to know exactly how much a life insurance policy will cost. But the true cost is impossible to calculate in advance because no one knows how long you'll live or when you might surrender the policy. Instead, you must settle for some kind of index—a measure of what the policy would cost if you were to die or were to surrender the policy at some specified time. The time most often used for cost comparisons is twenty years, but looking at other periods can also be useful. There are a number of cost-comparison indexes. Of these, Consumers Union suggests the use of the interest-adjusted net cost and net payment indexes.

Before explaining how these indexes work, we need to identify the elements they have to measure. Four major elements affect the price of life insurance: (1) annual premium; (2) dividends, if any; (3) cash value, if any; and (4) time.

The annual premium is the obvious element in the price structure. But someone who considers the annual premium alone could buy a policy that appears cheap but is in fact comparatively expensive in the long run. Dividends, which can make a tremendous difference in the price, are considered in some detail in Chapter 6. That leaves the two other major elements in the price structure of life insurance: cash value and time.

Cash Value

One-year renewable and five-year renewable term insurance policies do not have a cash value.* Cash value policies—by definition—do have cash value, and the amount must be taken into account when calculating the cost of a policy. In its simplest form, the cost of a cash value policy can be measured in two ways: one, if you were to die while the policy is in effect; the other, if you were to surrender the policy.

The simplest way of measuring costs (though not, as we'll see, the best way) is the following: If you die, the cost of the policy can be roughly expressed as the sum of the premiums paid, minus—if it's a participating policy—any dividends received. Insurance companies refer to this as *net payment.* If you surrender the policy, the cost is roughly the sum of premiums paid, minus dividends, if any, and also minus the cash value received upon surrendering the policy. The final figure is the *net cost,* or surrender cost.

At the time a cash value policy is purchased, you cannot know whether death will occur while the policy is in force. Nor can you know whether you will surrender the policy at some time and obtain its cash value. So, if you buy a cash value policy you will want to look for one that would prove low in cost according to some measure of both net payment and net cost. As already noted, the problem doesn't arise with most term policies: Since there is no cash value, there's no difference between the net cost and net payment.

With some policies, the cash value builds up comparatively rapidly; with others, it is meager for quite a few years, then rises in the later years. A policy with a cash value table

---

*Some longer-term term policies have a substantial cash value.

that slopes sharply upward in the later years may look good in long-term cost comparisons; but people holding such policies will be at a disadvantage if they unexpectedly have to cash them in during the early years. For this reason, CU advises shoppers to compare costs using both a twenty- and ten-year cost index. As noted earlier, cost comparisons are often made for a twenty-year period only, but it should be easy to get ten-year indexes from the agent or company.

It's also possible that the slope of the cash value curve may fall off once the twentieth year—the traditional point for policy illustrations—has passed. CU provides in Part II cost and rate of return information extending beyond the twentieth year in order to alert consumers to this possibility. But consumers can't normally obtain this kind of long-term information for themselves.

Unlike dividends, cash values are guaranteed. In each cash value policy, there is a table listing the guaranteed cash value for selected years after purchase. In some policies, cash value figures are given for the entire face amount of the policy. In other policies, the figures may be expressed per $1,000 of coverage. In the latter case, to find out the cash value that would be received if a policy were cashed in after a specific number of years, multiply that cash value figure by the number of thousands of dollars in the face amount of the policy. For example, consider a $25,000 whole life policy for which the seventeenth-year cash value is listed as $224 per $1,000 of coverage. To figure the cash value after seventeen years, simply multiply $224 by 25; the cash value would be $5,600.

Time
Since life insurance is usually purchased to be held for many years, time becomes an especially important element in calculating its cost. Consider the example of two policies that

appear on the surface to be identical in cost. The sum of the premiums over, say, twenty years is the same for both. So is the sum of the dividends. The cash value tables are identical. It is nevertheless possible that one of the two policies is a distinctly better buy. Suppose one of the policies has more generous dividends in the early years; that policy is a better buy, other things being equal. By the same token, with two term policies, suppose one of the policies has lower premiums in the early years of the contract. Even though the sum of all the premiums is the same, again, that policy is a better buy. The reason is the same in both cases: time. You can earn interest on money—whether it is money you don't have to pay in premiums or money you receive in dividends—while it is in your possession.

Until the 1970s, calculations of the so-called net cost of a life insurance policy failed to consider the time value of money. Under the *traditional method* of calculating net cost, all the premiums to be paid over the period evaluated (usually twenty years) are added together. From the total are subtracted the sum of the dividends (if any) expected over that period and the cash value (if any) to be received if the policy were cashed in at the end of the period. The final figure is the *net cost.* * Dividing the net cost by the number of years in the period gives the average net cost per year, or the *net cost index.*

---

*Often, with a cash value policy, the net cost, as calculated by the traditional method will be a negative number (the cash value may be larger than the sum of the premiums paid). Some life insurance agents say this proves that life insurance costs nothing over the long run. Such an assertion, in CU's judgment, is misleading. If you had put your money in a bank account instead of buying life insurance, you'd be earning interest. Over the years, that interest could be substantial. So of course cash value insurance costs something. And it should, because it provides certain benefits —the chief one being protection for your family when you die.

In 1970 the Joint Special Committee on Life Insurance Costs* introduced a cost computation method that does consider the element of time. It is called the *interest-adjusted method.* Under this method, the first step is to assume an interest rate based on a reasonable estimate of long-term returns on a conservative savings vehicle. By recommendation of the National Association of Insurance Commissioners, a group of state regulatory officials, 5 percent is now the rate commonly used. The second step is to take the first year's premium, multiply it by the interest rate—in this case, 5 percent—and add the result to the premium, then add to that the second year's premium, then add 5 percent interest on the total so far, and continue for however many years an illustration is desired (usually twenty years). The same procedure is used with the dividends, if any; they are accumulated with interest for the same number of years. The accumulated dividends, if any, are then subtracted from the accumulated premiums. Then the cash value, if any, is subtracted at the end. Next, divide the resulting figure by the number of thousands of dollars in the face amount of the policy. That final figure is the *interest-adjusted net cost,* which measures the cost of a policy if it should be surrendered prior to the death of the policyholder.

It has been said that the interest-adjusted net cost is the "true cost" of a life insurance policy. A case could be made for that point of view, but only under exceptional circumstances: *if* a policyholder keeps a policy exactly twenty years, *if* the interest rate the policyholder could earn is indeed exactly 5 percent (or whatever interest rate is used in the calculation), and *if* dividends are paid exactly as illustrated.

---

*The committee was created by the American Life Convention, the Life Insurance Association of America, and the Institute of Life Insurance. These three groups subsequently merged to form what is now the industry's dominant trade group, the American Council of Life Insurance.

These assumptions won't necessarily come true; in fact, it would be unrealistic to assume they would. But certainly the interest-adjusted net cost is a step closer to reality than the traditional net cost is. Used conscientiously and consistently, the interest-adjusted net cost method can enable a buyer to make realistic cost comparisons.

To facilitate cost comparisons, you need only divide the interest-adjusted net cost by a constant to get the *interest-adjusted net cost index,* also known as the surrender index. The index equals the amount of money you'd need to put aside each year (in an account bearing the interest rate under analysis) to accumulate a sum equal to the interest-adjusted net cost. The constant you use varies according to the period under analysis and the interest rate. For a twenty-year analysis at a 5 percent interest rate, the constant is 34.719. As noted earlier, most cost analyses cover a twenty-year period, but a ten-year comparison is also desirable to see what would happen if a policy were terminated early. The ten-year constant for a 5 percent interest rate is 13.207.

The interest-adjusted net cost index is an artificial number in the sense that no particular cash outlay will equal the index. But it is a useful indicator of how much a life insurance policy costs in comparison with other policies. Note that the index should be used only to compare similar policies (for example, term with term, whole life with whole life, participating with participating, nonparticipating with nonparticipating).

For term insurance, it is sufficient to compare interest-adjusted net cost indexes. When shopping for a cash value policy, however, the buyer should compare the *interest-adjusted net payment index* as well as the interest-adjusted net cost index. (For term policies, the two are the same.)

The *interest-adjusted net payment,* which measures the cost of a policy that is held until the policyholder dies, is the accumulation of a policy's premiums at a stated rate of interest minus the accumulation of the dividends, if any, at that interest rate. Dividing the resulting figure by the same constant as that used in computing the interest-adjusted net cost index—34.719 for twenty years and 13.207 for ten years—gives you the interest-adjusted net payment index.

When shopping for insurance, it is important to get price quotations on an interest-adjusted basis on several companies' policies, and to compare both twenty-year and ten-year indexes. Be sure, of course, that identical riders, or options, are included in each policy. When comparing the indexes, place little or no weight on differences of less than 10 percent. Where the difference is that small, nonprice factors (see Chapter 8) should generally determine your buying decision. If the difference is more than 10 percent, other things being equal, it would be best to buy the policy with the lowest cost indexes.

The single most important index for the life insurance shopper is the twenty-year interest-adjusted net cost index. It is CU's primary measure of whether a policy is low cost or high cost. Indeed, when we rated cash value policies (see Chapter 17), we gave more weight to net cost than to net payment for several reasons. First, most buyers very probably will cash in their policies, rather than die while the policies are in force. Second, CU believes that most cash value policyholders who reach retirement age would be well advised to cash in their policies at that time, for their own financial benefit. Third, the cash value is present in the policy as a potential asset, whether the buyer actually chooses to use it or not. For all of these reasons, CU believes the primary measure of merit for a cash value policy should be one that reflects the cash value.

However, since buyers of cash value policies do not know in advance when they will cash in those policies or whether they will live until the maturity date, they should try to select a policy that ranks low in cost according to both the interest-adjusted net cost and net payment indexes for twenty and ten years (for sample calculations, see Table 7–1). Because the interest-adjusted net cost and net payment indexes are the same for most term policies (which have no cash value), the term shopper should look for a policy that ranks low in cost according to both the twenty-year and ten-year interest-adjusted net cost indexes. But no matter what type of policy you're shopping for, priority should be given to the twenty-year index.

Use of the interest-adjusted index grew in the 1970s and it appears that the index is now readily available to most life insurance buyers. As of early 1980, thirty states had regulations requiring that insurance companies furnish consumers with interest-adjusted indexes. In a few states, the disclosure is mandatory; in most, it is on request. The indexes have been gaining public recognition as a result of publication of guides for insurance shoppers by such organizations as Consumers Union and a few state insurance departments.

When shopping for life insurance, ask for the interest-adjusted indexes for any policy you're considering. State law may or may not require the company or agent to give them to you. But we would suggest that refusal to provide the indexes is an invitation to shop elsewhere.

Instead of waiting to be contacted by a life insurance agent, you should actively seek out the companies you wish to ask for price quotations. It will be necessary to be selective: With hundreds of life insurance companies in the business, it would be difficult to comparison-shop them all. Simply contacting the large companies won't necessarily result in finding an economical policy because they don't always offer the best buys. The Ratings in Part II of this book may help to determine which companies you wish to contact.

Table 7-1
How the Interest-Adjusted Method Works

The figures below are for a $25,000 whole life policy issued to a twenty-eight-year-old woman (or a twenty-five-year-old man) by a hypothetical life insurance company. We assume that the premiums are paid at the beginning of each policy year and the dividends are paid at the end of each policy year. Below the table are our calculations for the interest-adjusted net cost index and the interest-adjusted net payment index (at 5 percent for both twenty and ten years) for the policy.

Year	Premium	Dividend	Cash Value	Sum of Premiums	Accumulated Premiums at 5% Interest*	Sum of Dividends	Accumulated Dividends at 5% Interest*
1	$400	$ 0	$ 0	$ 400	$ 420	$ 0	$ 0
2	400	5	50	800	861	5	5
3	400	10	110	1,200	1,324	15	15
4	400	20	180	1,600	1,810	35	36
5	400	30	260	2,000	2,321	65	68
6	400	40	350	2,400	2,857	105	111
7	400	50	450	2,800	3,420	155	167
8	400	60	560	3,200	4,011	215	245
9	400	70	680	3,600	4,631	285	327
10	400	80	900	4,000	5,283	365	423
11	400	90	1,100	4,400	5,967	455	534
12	400	100	1,300	4,800	6,685	555	660
13	400	110	1,500	5,200	7,439	665	803
14	400	120	1,800	5,600	8,231	785	963
15	400	130	2,100	6,000	9,063	915	1,141
16	400	140	2,400	6,400	9,936	1,055	1,338

17	400	150	2,700	6,800	10,853	1,205	1,554
18	400	160	3,000	7,200	11,816	1,365	1,792
19	400	170	3,300	7,600	12,826	1,535	2,051
20	400	180	3,600	8,000	13,888	1,715	2,333

*For convenience, the numbers are rounded to the nearest dollar.

Calculations for Table 7-1

Interest-adjusted net cost: The accumulated premiums ($13,888) minus the accumulated dividends ($2,333) and minus the cash value ($3,600) = $7,955 over twenty years.

Interest-adjusted net cost index: For a twenty-year period, the interest-adjusted net cost ($7,955) divided by the constant for twenty years (34.719) = $229. To get the index per $1,000 of coverage, divide the index for the total amount of coverage ($229) by the number of thousand dollars of coverage (25) = $9.16. For a ten-year period, the interest-adjusted net cost ($3,960) divided by the constant for ten years (13.207) = $300. To get the index per $1,000 of coverage, divide the index for the total amount of coverage ($300) by the number of thousand dollars of coverage (25) = $12.

Interest-adjusted net payment: The accumulated premiums ($13,888) minus the accumulated dividends ($2,333) = $11,555 over twenty years.

Interest-adjusted net payment index: For a twenty-year period, the interest-adjusted net payment ($11,555) divided by the constant for twenty years (34.719) = $333. To get the index per $1,000 of coverage, divide the index for the total amount of coverage ($333) by the number of thousand dollars of coverage (25) = $13.32. For a ten-year period, the interest-adjusted net payment ($4,860) divided by the constant for ten years (13.207) = $368. To get the index per $1,000 of coverage, divide the index for the total amount of coverage ($368) by the number of thousand dollars of coverage (25) = $14.72.

Shopping for a Policy

Once the type and amount of coverage are decided, cost becomes a prime factor in shopping for a policy. After all, the product in its essence is a trading of present dollars for future dollars. The relationship between the two is crucial to the merits of any policy.

But cost is not the only significant criterion. Consumers Union believes there is one other factor, in addition to a policy's cost index, to which you should give priority when shopping for a policy: a company's financial stability. Insolvencies among life insurance companies are rare, but they do happen. If the company that sold you a policy should get into serious financial difficulties, a number of unfortunate things could happen to you or to your beneficiaries. If you were to die, payment to your survivors might be delayed. (CU knows of no cases in which financial troubles caused death claims to go unpaid.) If you were to cash in the policy, you might conceivably have to settle for a reduced cash value. With a participating policy your dividends could be sorely affected. Even if another company took over the foundering company's policies, you might still have problems—with red tape or strict interpretation of policy clauses. In short, you don't want to buy life insurance from a company likely to encounter serious financial difficulties.

Your most reliable guide to the financial stability of insurance companies is, in CU's opinion, *Best's Insurance Reports,* published by the A. M. Best Company. *Best's* gives letter grades (from A+ to C) to hundreds of life insurance companies. According to *Best's,* both A+ and A are equated with "excellent," B+ with "very good," B with "good," C+ with "fairly good," and C with "fair." In October 1977, in his monthly newsletter, *The Insurance Forum,* insurance professor Joseph M. Belth pointed out one of the problems with *Best's* system: that "life insurance buyers generally may not distinguish between the A+ and A ratings, especially since the word 'Excellent' follows both of them." CU recommends that you give first consideration to companies with an A+ rating in *Best's*—a list of about 200 companies. If that category proves inadequate, you can then widen your considerations to include the approximately 250 additional companies rated A in *Best's.* The insurance policies surveyed by CU and rated in Part II of this book all come from A+ or A companies.

Once you've selected the companies whose policies you want to consider and compare, you're ready to begin shopping for the best buy in a policy that meets your needs. A uniform method of price comparison is an essential tool when shopping for insurance. Comparisons should be made only among policies with the same face amount and the same features. (For three common options, see Chapter 10.)

As stressed in Chapter 7, CU favors using the interest-adjusted method to compare life insurance policies. Any company worthy of consideration ought to be able to provide, when you request it, the interest-adjusted net cost index

Table 8–1
Using Term Insurance Cost Indexes

If you're shopping for a term life insurance policy at levels other than $25,000 and $100,000, or if you're female, CU's Ratings of term policies in Chapter 15 won't apply directly. However, the table below can help you judge whether the twenty-year interest-adjusted index of a term policy you're offered is higher or lower than the average of those analyzed by CU. The indexes below are per $1,000 of coverage per year. Figures for males are from CU's 1979 survey and are based on a renewable convertible $100,000 term policy including a waiver of premium (see page 141). Figures for females are from a 1978 survey by the Wisconsin Insurance Department and are based on a renewable convertible $50,000 five-year term policy without waiver of premium.

	Lowest Cost	Median Cost	Highest Cost
Par Term/Net Cost Index			
Age 25 Male	$ 1.63	$ 3.07	$ 4.26
Age 35 Male	3.60	5.61	9.23
Age 45 Male	8.71	13.50	16.79
Nonpar Term/Net Cost Index			
Age 25 Male	$ 2.44	$ 2.96	$ 5.43
Age 35 Male	4.37	5.41	8.70
Age 45 Male	10.53	12.84	17.31
Par Term/Net Cost Index			
Age 25 Female	$ 1.60	$ 3.18	$ 6.87
Age 35 Female	2.81	4.95	15.00
Age 45 Female	6.22	10.65	17.56
Nonpar Term/Net Cost Index			
Age 25 Female	$ 2.38	$ 3.54	$ 7.03
Age 35 Female	2.97	5.37	15.74
Age 45 Female	5.35	10.81	17.64

for a policy—plus an interest-adjusted net payment index with a cash value policy. There are two possible ways to express that index: as a figure for the total face amount of the policy and as a figure per $1,000 of coverage. The index for each policy under consideration should be expressed the same way. (It's easy to approximate a conversion from one mode to the other; simply divide or multiply by the number of thousands of dollars in the face amount.)

Women usually get a lower rate than men. Since women as a group live longer than men, many life insurance companies charge women the premiums they charge men three years younger. Some companies give women a larger price differential. There are still a few companies, however, that charge the same rates to both sexes. If you're a woman, you'll naturally want to know how much less you'll be paying. But remember the size of the differential is less important than the policy's cost index. You might be better off buying from a company that sells low-cost insurance whether or not it has substantially lower rates for females than for males.

Don't be influenced too much by the name of a policy. While some *preferred risk* policies, sometimes referred to simply as preferred policies, really do offer substantial advantages, others do not. Such policies are issued to people a company regards as unusually good risks—those who stand a less-than-average chance of dying in the near future. Some companies issue preferred policies only to people in excellent health and safe occupations. But a few companies use the word "preferred" as a sales gimmick and will apply it to almost anybody. The same caution goes for other policy labels. Some *special* policies are bargains; others are costly. Some *executive* policies would be best avoided by consumers, executive or not, and so on. For those who don't smoke, a nonsmoker's policy might be a good buy—but not necessarily. How, then, can a good price be recognized?

Table 8–2
Using Cash Value Insurance Cost Indexes

If you're shopping for a cash value life insurance policy at an amount other than $25,000 or $100,000, or if you're female, CU's Ratings of cash value policies in Chapter 17 won't apply directly. However, the table below can help you judge whether the twenty-year interest-adjusted index of a cash value policy you're offered is higher or lower than the average of those analyzed by CU. The indexes below are per $1,000 of coverage per year. Figures for males are from CU's 1979 survey and are based on a $100,000 cash value policy including a waiver of premium (see page 141). Figures for females are from a 1978 survey by the Wisconsin Insurance Department, which computed net cost figures only, and are based on a $50,000 cash value policy without waiver of premium.

	Lowest Cost	Median Cost	Highest Cost
Par Cash Value/Net Cost Index			
Age 25 Male	$ 0.14	$ 2.62	$ 6.63
Age 35 Male	0.12	4.34	9.64
Age 45 Male	2.00	9.00	16.43
Nonpar Cash Value/Net Cost Index			
Age 25 Male	$ 2.10	$ 3.59	$ 6.54
Age 35 Male	4.15	5.97	9.45
Age 45 Male	9.50	11.66	16.21
Par Cash Value/Net Cost Index			
Age 25 Female	$ 0.30	$ 2.55	$12.28
Age 35 Female	1.00	4.05	16.63
Age 45 Female	0.96	7.53	24.58
Nonpar Cash Value/Net Cost Index			
Age 25 Female	$ 1.23	$ 3.81	$ 9.67
Age 35 Female	2.92	5.71	10.90
Age 45 Female	6.39	10.43	18.38

	Lowest Cost	Median Cost	Highest Cost
	Par Cash Value/Net Payment Index		
Age 25 Male	$ 6.07	$10.49	$14.49
Age 35 Male	8.63	14.81	19.93
Age 45 Male	13.57	22.22	29.34
	Nonpar Cash Value/Net Payment Index		
Age 25 Male	$ 6.58	9.84	13.75
Age 35 Male	11.62	14.77	19.09
Age 45 Male	20.67	23.15	28.55

CU's Ratings presented in Part II of this book should help. Even though the companies can change their rates from year to year, the Ratings can be used as a starting point when comparison shopping for a policy. But, as noted in Chapter 7, CU suggests you attach little significance to cost differences of less than 10 percent. While individual policies may move up or down the price ladder, the ladder itself (that is, the range of costs from highest to lowest) moves much more slowly. For that reason, we've distilled from our 1979 cost study some yardsticks to help you recognize a low-cost or high-cost policy. These yardsticks are presented in Tables 8-1 and 8-2. Table 8-1 shows the lowest, median, and highest cost indexes for term policies. Table 8-2 provides similar benchmarks for cash value policies. (Figures for males and females in these tables were based on somewhat different types of policies and were obtained a year apart.)

Looking for a Bargain

A few bargains in life insurance deserve special mention.

Savings bank life insurance (SBLI), offered by mutual savings banks in Massachusetts, New York, and Connecticut, is quite an economical purchase, in part because the savings banks offer the insurance on a walk-in basis with no overhead for a full marketing apparatus in support of a field force of agents. Because of political pressure from the commercial life insurance lobby, the face amount limits on SBLI have been kept rather low. In early 1980, the ceiling was $53,000 in Massachusetts and $30,000 in New York. In Connecticut, the limit on individual policies was $10,000, but it was scheduled to increase to $15,000 in 1981. People with accounts at Connecticut savings banks can also purchase $20,000 (or, in 1981, $30,000) of depositors group term life insurance.

Policies include both term and cash value types. As a rule, only those who live or work in Massachusetts, New York, or Connecticut are eligible for that state's SBLI. Resident college students also qualify, so an eligible student who needs insurance (see Chapter 1) should consider SBLI when shopping for a policy. Summer residents and nonresident traveling salespeople, however, usually cannot qualify. CU contested in court the limitations set on the size of SBLI policies but lost. CU has also been in litigation since 1974 to win permission for out-of-staters to buy SBLI. When this book went to press, that lawsuit had not been resolved.

Group insurance plans may be available where you work. Often group life insurance comes automatically in a policy covering all the employees of a company. Company plans usually consist of group term insurance and are often low priced. They are, of course, an even better deal if your employer pays part or all of the premium. An employee may be given the choice of taking the policy or not, or of buying more than the minimum amount of coverage. For many people, it's wise to buy all the on-the-job group coverage offered, but not without making some price comparisons. The interest-adjusted net cost index per $1,000 of coverage should be compared with those of other policies. Group plans are subject to price increases, and to possible cancellation. In many cases, if a policyholder leaves the job through which the group coverage was obtained, he or she must either give up the policy or convert it to an individual policy (often, a cash value policy) at a higher premium. And sometimes the face amount of that individual policy may be lower than the group policy's face amount was. Information about conversion may be found in the group contract. Check its provisions carefully to see what the rules are if you want to convert your group coverage to an individual policy.

Group insurance may also be available through a professional or trade association, a club, a fraternal organization, or a religious group to which you belong. In addition to sponsoring group insurance, such organizations may also have an arrangement with an insurance company by which members may purchase individual policies. These policies are often claimed to be low cost; in CU's experience they may or may not be.

Should the lack of guarantees dissuade someone from buying group insurance? Not necessarily. An organization whose plan has a history of successful operation will in all probability merit confidence. A newer or untried group plan needn't be passed up entirely if its rates are low. But it may not be wise to rely on group insurance for all of the family's insurance protection.

Veterans' insurance, over the years, has been considered a bargain. Any discussion of low-cost life insurance used to begin with advice to veterans not to drop their GI life insurance. Veterans of World Wars I and II were allowed to keep up to $10,000 of their armed forces insurance coverage as a term policy or cash value at low rates and with what have proved to be high dividends. Veterans who entered service during the Korean War could also keep their insurance at

115

low rates. Veterans who served in the military in Vietnam, however, were not given the same benefit. Under a special law, a group insurance plan underwritten by a large number of private insurance companies was inaugurated in 1966.

Coverage for active members of the armed forces was increased in 1974 to $20,000 and veterans were allowed to continue their coverage without a physical examination by applying within 120 days of their discharge for Veterans Group Life Insurance. The continuation takes the form of a nonparticipating five-year nonrenewable term policy. The premium for $20,000 of coverage (lesser amounts can also be selected) is $3.40 per month for veterans age thirty-four and younger and $6.80 per month for those thirty-five and older. The effect is that today's veterans can share some of the benefits enjoyed by their predecessors—but only for five years. After that, if they want to keep their policies, they must convert to a cash value form of insurance and pay commercial rates.

One-year renewable and convertible term insurance is often the most favorably priced type of term to buy if you're buying $100,000 or more. It's possible that one-year term is underwritten a bit more carefully—that is, companies may take a longer look at the health of a person who elects to buy insurance coverage for a year at a time. Whatever the reason for the rate differential, it's worthwhile for anyone who is in the market for a large purchase of life insurance to look into one-year renewable and convertible term.

There are two additional considerations to keep in mind when shopping for life insurance:
■ Watch for breakpoints. These are the face amounts at which size discounts begin to apply; they vary with each company (and may even vary from policy to policy). Those

who calculate their insurance needs at, say, $95,000 would often be better off buying a policy for $100,000. The reason: Companies give buyers of policies of a certain size what amounts to a quantity discount on the price. With many companies, breakpoints may occur even at $10,000 and $25,000 as well as at $100,000. If you're unsure about breakpoints, ask the agent or company how much insurance you'd need to buy to get a favorable rate.

■ Pay premiums annually if you can afford to. Some companies impose heavy carrying charges on semiannual, quarterly, or monthly installment payments. For instance, two semiannual premiums sometimes equal 104 percent of one annual premium: The policyholder pays half the annual premium at the beginning of each policy year and, in effect, borrows the other half for six months. That's the equivalent of an Annual Percentage Rate of approximately 17 percent. (The cost of paying premiums other than annually is further discussed in Chapter 11.)

If You're Considered a High Risk

If you have a serious health problem or have other serious insurability problems, everything we've said about the importance of shopping around becomes doubly important. Companies vary greatly in how they assess the impact of such conditions as cancer, cardiovascular complications, diabetes, epilepsy, high blood pressure, or even overweight. A condition that one company might consider sufficient reason to reject you for coverage might be cause, in another company's view, only for charging you an extra premium. (If you're charged an extra premium for insurance, you are said to be a *substandard risk,* and the policy issued you is said to be substandard, or "rated.") Similarly, a problem that might cause one company to classify you as a substandard risk might be dismissed as not serious by underwriters at another

117

company, who would classify you as a standard risk.

Naturally, you'll be interested in knowing how you're classified. However, remember that your classification is not your ultimate concern; getting the insurance at a reasonable cost is. There are some companies that will classify you as "standard" and then proceed to charge you rates higher than those you might have paid as a substandard risk with another company. The only way to avoid this is to shop around and compare the interest-adjusted costs for various policies. Some companies boast in their advertising that they'll insure anyone, regardless of health status. People with health problems may turn to such a company, relieved that they'll be spared the ordeal of medical examinations, questions about their health, and uncertainty. Buying insurance on such a basis is often stepping into a trap. Companies that take on all comers frequently charge sky-high rates or look for a contractual loophole when it comes time to pay a claim.

If you have a health problem, you should, of course, rely on group insurance to the greatest extent possible. And if you leave the group, do your best to convert the group policy to an individual one.

After shopping around with a sizable number of companies, if you find out you don't qualify for conventional life insurance, you may want to resort to buying graded-death-benefit life insurance. This type of insurance coverage pays only a fraction of the specified death benefit if you die of natural causes within a few years of purchase. (The fraction paid may start out simply as a refund of premiums with interest; typically, it rises as the years pass.) If you live a specified number of years after buying the policy (six or seven years, in some cases), the policy would pay off in full.

Assessment of your health is probably the largest element, but not the only element, in the process of *underwriting*— the assessment of how large a risk you represent to the insurance company. Two other significant elements that may be considered by underwriters are your occupation and (believe it or not) your lifestyle.

Some occupations that may raise underwriter eyebrows are: aerialist, aviator, blaster, chemical worker, coal miner, welder, window cleaner, handler of radioactive materials, or worker in certain potentially hazardous industries (e.g., asbestos worker). This is an abbreviated list and, in any event, the list varies from company to company. If you're in a hazardous occupation, the magic words, once more, are "shop around."

In the realm of lifestyle, the chief concern is excessive drinking. In years past, underwriters were concerned with such matters as adultery, cohabitation, divorce, or homosexuality, but most companies today give these factors little if any weight. When you apply for life insurance, you may be advised that the company might order from an independent firm an "investigative report" or "credit report" on you. Such reports may at times include information (usually gathered from neighbors, co-workers, or acquaintances) about your morals and behavior. If you are turned down for life insurance as a result of an investigative or credit report, the insurance company is obliged to tell you so and to reveal the name of the firm providing the information. Under the Fair Credit Reporting Act, you must be given the right to correct any erroneous information in your file.

As noted in Chapter 1, about 3 percent of all applicants for life insurance are rejected, and another 5 percent or so are classified as substandard risks. In the vast majority of these cases, health is the problem. (Of course, some people in poor health or hazardous occupations do not apply for insurance.) If you find yourself regarded as a high risk, don't despair. With persistence and astute comparison shopping, you may be able to purchase adequate coverage at affordable rates.

Nonprice Factors

A life insurance contract is purely a financial transaction and cost differences are critical in making a buying decision. Still, CU believes that in addition to a company's financial stability, there are several nonprice factors you may well want to consider.

Policy language. It's a good idea, if not an enjoyable pastime, to read through a life insurance policy before making a final decision whether to buy it. All policies aren't written in legalistic language any longer or printed in tiny type. Other things being equal, a policy that is easy to read and to understand obviously is to be preferred. But no matter how inviting the language or the type size, the meaning is what counts. Chapter 11 provides you with some guidelines for evaluating policies.

Agent service. If you know a life insurance agent who has served you—or someone you know—well in the past, and whose advice you would respect and trust, this should clearly be a factor in your decision. You might decide that service from a particular agent makes it worthwhile passing up a lower-priced policy of another company. Be aware, however, that many agents change companies rather frequently. This is especially true of the newer agents. According to *Probe,* an industry newsletter, fewer than fifteen out of every hundred agents recruited by a typical life insurance company will still be working for that company four years later.

State licensing. You should, CU believes, buy your life insurance from a company that's licensed to do business in your state. That way, should you have a problem with the company, your state insurance department (see Appendix III) is better equipped to help you. CU considers a request to the state insurance department for help to be the first logical recourse for a consumer with a problem that can't be resolved through direct dealings with the company. The quality of the help you receive may well vary from state to state and you may sometimes need to turn to other potential sources of aid such as your state attorney general's office and state or local consumer protection offices.

Historical cost. The interest-adjusted indexes (see Chapter 7) will give you an idea of how costly a company's policy is projected to be. If you're buying a participating policy, however, you may also want to give some weight to how that company's policies have ranked in cost in the past. Suggestions for looking at historical cost are given in Chapter 6.

Social responsibility. If a life insurance company has been found guilty of discrimination in employment, or has bribed public officials, or has otherwise demonstrated a lack of corporate social responsibility, you might not be disposed to buy from that company.

Other Types of Policies, from A to V

Most life insurance needs can be met—and met well—with the kinds of policies described in Chapter 4. Some consumers, however, may be interested in—or may be urged to buy —other types of policies. To describe all available policies here would be impossible, owing both to the complex nature of some and to the great number of variables. The policies described in this chapter include those that Consumers Union thinks you might be likely to encounter during a life insurance agent's sales presentation. Some of these policies might be genuinely useful to consumers with special needs. Others should definitely be avoided.

Adjustable life bridges cash value and term coverage. The product was introduced in 1971. When CU reported on it, in the August 1978 issue of CONSUMER REPORTS, it was being offered by only two major companies, Bankers Life Company (of Iowa) and Minnesota Mutual Life Insurance Company. That was still true in late 1979. But some major firms reportedly were considering introducing the product in 1980.

The policy is "adjustable" in two major ways. You can switch back and forth between term and cash value. And you can increase or decrease, within limits, the face amount of the policy. The lowest-premium protection you can buy under the plan is ten-year term (Bankers Life) or five-year term (Minnesota Mutual). Pay a higher premium without increasing the face amount and you get a longer term of coverage—to a specific age, such as fifty-three or seventy-eight. (Such long-term term policies have a considerable cash value, though less than a whole life policy with the same face amount would have. While the cash value in a whole life policy usually builds up steadily, the cash value in a long-term term policy usually declines toward the end of the term.) Add still more to the premium—again, without adding to the face amount—and it's a conventional whole life policy. Pay more yet, and it's a whole life policy that is paid up earlier and accumulates cash value faster.

Suppose you buy a $100,000 adjustable life policy in its term mode. After a few years, if you can afford a higher premium and want to start accumulating substantial cash values, you can change the policy over to a cash value form. Should you later suffer a financial pinch, you can reduce the premium, thus switching the policy back to term. Whatever cash value you've accumulated stays in the policy.

You can also, within limits and restrictions, increase or decrease the face amount. It's not too unusual for a policyholder of a conventional policy to be able to decrease the face amount. *Increasing* the face amount, however, without evidence of insurability, is a privilege a policyholder can normally get only by purchasing, at extra cost, a guaranteed insurability rider (see Chapter 10).

With both companies, you can increase the face amount to help compensate for inflation every three years. Your premium is increased proportionately. CU views this as a useful feature, since this increase can be made regardless of changes in your health or occupation. The cost-of-living adjustment is limited to 20 percent of the face amount each three years. With Minnesota Mutual, you must use the privilege each time you are eligible or you forfeit it.

In addition, both the Bankers Life and Minnesota Mutual adjustable life policies examined by CU allow you to buy a guaranteed insurability rider, even if your policy is in a term mode. That's unusual, because most companies will sell a guaranteed insurability rider only with cash value policies.

All of this flexibility is an advantage to the consumer, CU judges, but that advantage is offset by the fact that an adjustable life policy is likely to be more costly than a conventional policy. According to CU's 1978 study of adjustable life, both adjustable life policies then available were more expensive in the whole life mode than most whole life policies in CU's 1973 survey, and more expensive in the term mode than most one-year term policies in the 1973 survey. (During the five-year interval, life insurance prices, in general, had not risen and, if anything, had declined.) Unless or until the cost comes down, CU suggested that most people would be better off forgoing adjustable life. (Three policies called "adjustable life" are included in CU's Ratings in Part II, but only one —Minnesota Mutual's—fits the description given here and that policy was rated as if it were a conventional cash value policy with a fixed faced amount.)

CU did suggest, however, that certain consumers with special needs might want adjustable life. People who normally consider cash value insurance for its tax shelter might want to consider adjustable life if they have sharply fluctuating incomes. Young heads of families who expect to need increasing amounts of insurance might be interested in adjustable life, because of the cost-of-living increases and the guaranteed insurability rider offered in connection with the term mode. Finally, if a wealthy parent insists on purchasing life insurance for a child, an adjustable life policy might make sense. The parent could purchase it in a cash value mode, and the child could later convert it to a term mode, using the accumulated cash value to help keep premiums down. (As discussed in Chapter 1, CU normally discourages the purchase of insurance on children.)

Campus life insurance. Some companies specialize in marketing life insurance to college students or in selling parents policies for their college student children. Fidelity Union Life Insurance Company of Dallas, Texas, has maintained a large campus sales force, with a record of selling policies to about one of every twenty graduating seniors. Its sales tactics have been heavily criticized in several quarters, including the March 1977 issue of CONSUMER REPORTS. And Fidelity Union's "CollegeMaster" policies frequently involve a loan obligation that CU believes college students would usually do better to avoid. Sales tactics of other firms on campus have also been criticized by CU and others.

Several companies sell campus policies primarily through the mail, usually to the parents of college students. Most of these policies start out as term insurance, then convert (sometimes automatically) to cash value insurance at a specified time (such as age twenty-five). CU's objections to these policies are that they are often not needed and if needed are often high priced compared with most policies available in the marketplace. Moreover, for college students who may actually need life insurance, these policies often do not provide adequate coverage. Companies that push campus policies also tend to steer students toward cash value insurance when a conventional term policy (assuming they need insurance at all) might better serve their interests.

Cost-of-living insurance, available from only a few companies (often through a rider added to a conventional cash value policy) is designed to help insurance coverage keep up with the effects of inflation. Several arrangements are possible for boosting the policy's coverage. One is to allow the policyholder to buy one-year term insurance each year in the amount necessary to compensate for the increase in the cost of living after the policy was purchased. A second possible arrangement is to have the face amount of the basic policy itself increased in line with living costs. Usually the premium is increased proportionately.

With cost-of-living insurance there is a limit to how much supplementary coverage can be obtained. Often the rule is that the amount of supplementary coverage can't exceed the amount of coverage in the original policy. Thus, the policyholder could double the original coverage. This would happen in the event of a 100 percent increase in the cost of living.

The seriousness of inflation in recent years makes some kind of cost-of-living insurance appear increasingly desirable. It is to be expected that both the number of such plans on the market and the number of buyers will grow. CU judges the option well worth considering if it affords access to one-year term insurance at a reasonable price. (CU considers the price to be reasonable if there is only a small charge for the option, apart from the cost of the additional term insurance itself.)

Credit life is a special type of life insurance, which may be offered to you when you buy on credit or take out a loan. The policy is designed to pay off the loan, plus interest, if you die. Issuers of credit life argue that it's an advantage to consumers, who would have the peace of mind of knowing that their survivors won't have the car (or freezer, or furniture, or whatever) repossessed. CU thinks credit life benefits chiefly the people who sell it (such as car dealers, banks, loan companies, and department stores). It reduces their bad-debt costs. What's more, they get a handsome commission for selling it. Not only that, they make still more money by charging interest on the premium, which is lumped in with the original loan. The rewards to the buyer of credit life, in CU's view, are less substantial.

As CU reported in the July 1979 issue of CONSUMER REPORTS, credit life tends to be overpriced compared with conventional life insurance products. We judged it a decent buy only for people in poor health and people over fifty who live in a state where the maximum permitted premium rate for credit life is relatively low.

Rather than make separate insurance arrangements for each debt, CU suggests you plan your overall life insurance coverage so that your present and reasonably foreseeable debts are covered, along with other needs.

Debit insurance, also known as "home service insurance," "industrial insurance," and "monthly debit ordinary insurance," is a poor deal, which you should avoid if you possibly can. With this type of life insurance, an agent comes to your home weekly or monthly to collect the premium. The face amount is usually small, and the insurance is usually sold to poor or lower-middle-income people, often members of minority groups.

The trouble with debit insurance is that the cost per $1,000 of coverage is very high, compared with costs for other methods of payment. Companies that continue to sell debit insurance claim that it provides valuable coverage for people who would otherwise have to go uninsured, since they couldn't scrape together the premiums necessary for other forms of payment. The companies argue that the high cost per $1,000 of coverage is the natural result of the low face amounts and the method of premium collection.

A debit insurance policy traditionally is sold as burial insurance, and it is a far cry from what most families, rich or poor, need to protect themselves in case of a breadwinner's death. CU believes that families unable to afford life insurance in less costly forms should consider whether they want to spend their limited resources on life insurance at all. If so, CU suggests they seek a small, low-cost term policy—for example, Savings Bank Life Insurance, where available.

Deposit term is a modified form of term insurance, usually involving a first-year premium higher than that for the rest of the years in the term. The amount by which the first-year premium exceeds the premium for the next few years is the so-called deposit. Usually, the premium drops in the second year and stays constant until the end of the tenth year. At that point, the policy may be renewable as term (at higher premiums), it may be renewable only as cash value insurance, or it may be surrendered for its cash value. A deposit term policy usually has no cash value in the first few years. Around the fifth year or so, cash values become available. The cash value at the end of the tenth year is sometimes described to buyers as a return of their "deposit," plus "interest." This description is misleading, as explained on the following page.

The argument made in favor of deposit term is that the higher first-year premium encourages policyholders to hang on to their policies and not to let them lapse early. When policies do not lapse, expenses are lowered for the company, which can therefore presumably charge a lower rate for the insurance. It's a nice rationale, but there are a couple of drawbacks to the system.

One major drawback is that the price savings doesn't seem

to have materialized. CU checked cost indexes on a limited number of deposit term products sold by moderately large companies. (So far as CU knows, none of the twenty largest companies sells the product.) The indexes turned out to be average or worse. Other studies CU has seen tend to buttress that judgment. Another major drawback is that the product leaves the consumer without flexibility: If you drop the policy in the first five years or so, you typically forfeit all or a substantial part of the "deposit."

An agent who tries to sell you deposit term on the basis of the "high interest rate" you earn on the "deposit" may be engaging in a deceptive sales practice. First of all, there is no true deposit, as such. Furthermore, the "rate of return" on the so-called deposit (in the form of cash value available at the end of ten years) can distract attention from the price of the underlying term insurance, which is sometimes quite high.

CU would not rule out the possibility that a deposit term product could be attractively priced. But we urge consumers to examine the renewability features and check the cost indexes carefully against those of level renewable term policies. And even if a low-cost deposit term product should be found, the buyer should weigh any cost advantage against the lack of flexibility the policy entails.

Economatic policies are a variation on participating whole life policies. They were developed in large part to compete with the lower premium outlay of nonpar policies. Economatic policies are sold under a variety of names and with some differences in the policy provisions. Essentially, they work as follows. Say you want to buy $100,000 of cash value insurance. With an economatic policy, you buy a package that includes a dividend-paying whole life policy with a face amount of, perhaps, $65,000. Each year, the dividends are used to buy a combination of one-year term insurance (which makes up most of the $35,000 gap in the early years) and paid-up additional cash value insurance (which is added to the original policy). Gradually, the paid-up additions fill the coverage gap so that less one-year term is needed each succeeding year. After twenty years or so, you have a whole life policy for the full $100,000. At that point, you can begin to receive your dividends in cash or apply them to buy more insurance.

One disadvantage of economatic plans is that the full face value may not be guaranteed in the early years, possibly leaving you underinsured for that period. The dividends may fall below the levels illustrated, so that you might wind up insured for less than you intended. Some companies provide substantial or partial guarantees against such an eventuality. Others don't. Another drawback of economatic plans is that they require you to give up flexibility in the use of dividends, at least for a number of years. The dividends *must* be used to purchase the one-year term and paid-up additions.

On balance, however, CU thinks that the advantages of an economatic plan often outweigh the risks. Economatics offer you a way to get the favorable long-term net cost associated with some participating policies while keeping your annual premium close to what you'd expect for a nonpar policy.

Because the full face value of economatic plans is not guaranteed from the date of purchase, we did not include such plans in our Ratings of participating cash value policies (see Chapter 17). CU's consulting actuaries, however, evaluated a sampling of economatic policies—a dozen issued by eight major companies (see Table 9-1). Generally, we found that the twenty-year interest-adjusted net cost indexes were slightly lower than those for the same company's conventional whole life plan. In the case of two companies, Northwestern Mutual Life Insurance Company and Prudential

Table 9–1
Economatic Versus Participating Whole Life

The figures below, from CU's 1979 cost survey, are for a $100,000 policy (including waiver of premium), purchased by a thirty-five-year-old male. The indexes are twenty-year interest-adjusted net cost indexes. Companies are listed in order of cost, as measured by the indexes for the economatic policies.

Company	Net Cost Index		Annual Premium	
	Economatic	Whole Life	Economatic	Whole Life
Phoenix Mutual (nonsmokers)	$213	$229	$1,497	$2,062
Northwestern Mutual	225	327	1,416	2,004
Phoenix Mutual (standard)	265	303	1,549	2,136
New England Mutual (preferred)	272	295	1,297	1,628
Prudential (preferred)	284	410	1,384	2,125
Massachusetts Mutual	312	318	1,381	1,620
Prudential (standard)	314	460	1,413	2,175
New York Life	320	343	1,421	2,019
New England Mutual (standard)	329	377	1,354	1,710
Equitable Life Assurance Society	341	350	1,472	2,014
Metropolitan Life (preferred)	418	430	1,428	1,815
Metropolitan Life (standard)	475	508	1,485	1,893

Note: Based solely on the twenty-year interest-adjusted net cost index, a comparison of the economatic plans listed above with the 156 cash value participating policies rated in Chapter 17 (for a thirty-five-year-old male buying $100,000 worth of insurance) would have resulted in the following rankings for the economatics: Phoenix Mutual (nonsmokers), #2; Northwestern Mutual, #3; Phoenix Mutual (standard), #6; New England Mutual (preferred), #6; Prudential (preferred), #6; Massachusetts Mutual, #17; Prudential (standard), #18; New York Life, #19; New England Mutual (standard), #24; Equitable Life Assurance Society, #27; Metropolitan Life (preferred), #70; and Metropolitan Life (standard), #97.

Insurance Company of America, the economatic plan was substantially lower in net cost than the same company's conventional plan. But you can't assume an economatic is necessarily a good buy in cash value insurance. The two Metropolitan Life economatics we studied showed up poorly in comparison with most participating cash value policies evaluated. So, some good buys can be found among economatics—but you have to shop carefully. Also note that policy labels can be confusing. Some policies that are economatics are not so labeled. On the other hand, "Economaster" policies in Part II are not economatics.

Family income plans are designed to provide a family with a specific monthly income for a specific time period. They may be sold as a rider on a cash value policy or they may be sold as a separate policy.

Here's how they work: Suppose that a married man purchases, at the beginning of 1980, a monthly income plan that offers $400 a month income to his family until the year 2000. If he dies immediately, his family gets the full twenty years of monthly income, a total of $96,000 in 240 monthly installments. If he dies one month before the end of the year 2000, his family gets only one month's benefit, or $400. If he dies after the year 2000, his family gets no monthly income. This plan is really just a form of decreasing term insurance.

As noted above, other variations are available in which the family income plan is a rider on a cash value policy. There can be a lump-sum death benefit at the end of the monthly payout period or at the beginning, or part of the benefit may be paid out at the end and part at the beginning. Here, the payment schedule is essentially the same as if the buyer had purchased a cash value insurance policy *plus* a decreasing term policy.

There is also a *family maintenance plan;* with it, the family gets monthly payments for a fixed number of years, regardless of when the insured dies. This is in essence a combination of cash value insurance (which provides a lump-sum benefit) and level term insurance (which provides the monthly income). A family maintenance plan costs more than a family income plan for the same reason that a level term policy costs more than a decreasing term policy with the same initial benefits.

Flexible premium nonpar is a new type of policy, which was first introduced in the late 1970s. It is similar to participating insurance, despite its name. In 1979 it was being offered by large stock companies such as Aetna Life Insurance Company and Travelers Insurance Company.

If you buy a flexible premium nonpar policy, you don't get dividends. But the exact price of your insurance isn't fixed, either. Instead—assuming the company holds down expenses, or experiences lower-than-projected mortality or better-than-expected investment returns—you may receive a reduction of your annual premiums. Under some plans, your premiums can also be *increased* if the company does less well than expected. These policies have a limit on how high your premiums can go; they may also have a limit on how low the premiums can go.

If you think a policy of this type is worth considering, you can obtain the interest-adjusted index for a flexible premium nonpar policy and compare it with those for participating policies shown in CU's Ratings in Part II. (No flexible premium nonpar policies are included in Part II.) You might want to ask the agent or company for an index under each of three assumptions: that premiums stay constant; that they go down the maximum amount possible (if there is a limit); and, if it's permitted under the policy, that they go up the maximum amount possible.

Joint life, as its name implies, insures the lives of two people. But it normally pays only one death benefit—when the first person dies. This type of coverage is most commonly sold to a husband and wife, in an amount sufficient to cover a mortgage, or to two members of a business partnership.

Some joint life policies have a clause permitting a surviving policyholder to purchase a new policy, as an individual, without proof of insurability. Some policies also have a "grace period" clause providing that the surviving policyholder is covered for ninety days after the death of the other. (In other words, the policy pays twice the stated death benefit if the two deaths occur within three months of each other.) The claimed advantage of joint life is that it is cheaper than insuring two lives separately. (CU has not evaluated this claim.)

If you consider joint life, you should be aware of possible pitfalls. If trouble develops between marriage or business partners, the question of who owns the policy can become a hassle. Also, once the first death has occurred, the surviving policyholder, if he or she has become ill (and therefore can't get insurance from another company), may be stuck with whatever rates the issuing company is then charging for individual coverage.

A variation on joint life is *contingent life,* the chief difference being that each insured person receives a separate contract. So far as CU knows, contingent life is currently being offered only in the form of cash value insurance, and only by a few relatively small companies.

Limited payment life is a cash value policy with increased premium rates so that the policy will be paid up for the full face amount in a relatively few years. The idea is to pay for a lifetime of insurance coverage with money earned during high-income years. The shorter the payment period, of course, the higher the annual premium is likely to be. The annual premiums on one large company's $50,000 participating policy purchased for a thirty-five-year-old male in 1979 were about $993 for whole life, about $1,190 for a paid-up-at-age-sixty-five policy, and about $1,493 for a twenty-payment (paid-up-at-age-fifty-five) policy. The ultimate in limited payment life insurance is single-premium life. The same company's premium in 1979 for a $50,000 participating single-premium policy for a man at age thirty-five was $17,992.

Anyone who dies while still making payments under a limited payment plan will have paid more premiums than under a straight life plan because the same amount of insurance could have been purchased for a smaller premium outlay. The person who dies one year after having completed payments under such a plan—or two years after, or five years after—will also have paid more than necessary for life insurance coverage. When does the break-even point come? Not for many years—and, with some policies, probably never. Policyholders, after all, stop paying premiums after a while, but they are still living without the income they could have gained by investing the extra money paid out for those high premiums years before.

Some people in high tax brackets may wish to consider limited payment life insurance as a tax shelter (they should consult with their tax advisers), and there may be other rare circumstances that justify its purchase. In most circumstances, however, CU believes that limited payment life insurance is inappropriate.

Minimum deposit plans are not actually a type of policy but rather a way of paying premiums. Under such a plan, some premiums are paid with borrowed money. Certain policies are designed with the minimum deposit plan in mind. To provide collateral for the necessary loans, the cash value is higher than customary at the beginning of the contract. In some minimum deposit plans, the dividends are automatically used to buy one-year term insurance. This insurance is equal in face amount to the amount of cash value serving as collateral that year. This way, the death benefit remains the same because the borrowed cash value is compensated for by the additional insurance purchased with the dividends. In other minimum deposit plans, it is up to the policyholders to choose how they want to use the dividends.

A major drawback of minimum deposit plans (for many buyers) is that it is often difficult to keep a plan in force for more than twenty years. After twenty years or so the interest burden on the loan often makes it hard to keep up the combined premium and interest payments.

Tax advantages are central to the concept of this type of plan, since the interest paid on the large loans involved is—to a considerable extent—tax-deductible. Current federal tax law holds that the interest paid on the policy loans is tax-deductible if the policyholder has paid four of the first seven annual premiums with unborrowed money. For the typical consumer, however, paying four large premiums could be difficult. With the tax consequences factored in, minimum deposit plans can be competitive in cost with term insurance, but, by and large, only for people in high tax brackets.

This conclusion is consistent with actuarial tests performed by CU's consultants in 1974 on two minimum deposit plans. The two plans were compared with term insurance, since minimum deposit insurance is normally sold as an alternative to term insurance.* For buyers in the 50 per-

---

*The comparison was done on a twenty-year interest-adjusted basis (discussed in Chapter 7), with tax advantages factored in as if they were received by the policyholder each year in cash.

cent tax bracket, minimum deposit plan insurance appeared to be an excellent alternative to term insurance. For buyers in the 33 percent tax bracket, it was generally comparable to a low-cost term policy. For buyers in tax brackets below 33 percent—which includes most consumers—conventional term policies appeared to be preferable.

Complicated insurance policies involving tax considerations require thorough analysis and should be bought only after consultation with a qualified accountant, lawyer, or financial adviser. Tax laws and regulations are subject to change. What's tax-deductible this year may not be deductible some years hence. Beware of an insurance agent who presses the minimum deposit plan without fully explaining the contract and without suggesting that counsel be sought.

Policyholders can arrange to have an existing whole life policy maintained by borrowing the money to pay the premiums from the policy at the policy loan rate—provided there is enough cash value in the policy. But the insurance company won't always let policyholders buy additional term insurance with the dividends from an existing policy. Unless the policyholder can make such use of the dividends—exercising the fifth dividend option—their amount of coverage will slowly decrease. (The fifth dividend option allows the policyholder to buy one-year term insurance, usually in an amount not exceeding the cash value, with the dividends of a cash value policy.)

No minimum deposit plans as such are included in CU's Ratings in Part II.

Split life is a combination of term insurance and deferred annuities. Such packages are now sold under a variety of names by quite a few companies. It's often claimed that the combination provides a better rate of return than is available with conventional cash value insurance. We suspect that the claim is true in some instances, not true in others.

More to the point, in CU's opinion, is a comparison of this approach with the alternative of buying term insurance and investing the difference in some other way. If you're saving up for retirement, a deferred annuity may or may not be the best way to do it. If you are going to go the annuity route, you owe it to yourself to comparison-shop for annuities, just as you would for life insurance. It's not necessarily true that a package deal of term-plus-annuity will give you a better price than you could obtain by purchasing a term insurance policy from one company and an annuity from another.

Variable life insurance policies were first promoted in the 1970s. Rules governing the sale of this type of insurance were issued in late 1976 by the Securities and Exchange Commission, but as of early 1980 only one company (a subsidiary of Equitable Life Assurance Society of the United States) was selling variable life insurance policies. As of early 1980, forty-five states—all but Alaska, Hawaii, Maine, Minnesota, and Montana as well as the District of Columbia—had approved them for marketing.

The reason the SEC is involved is that variable life policies bear a close resemblance to securities. Equitable Life Assurance Society's variable life policy works this way: Buyers pay a fixed annual premium and are guaranteed a certain minimum death benefit payable to their beneficiaries. The actual death benefit of the policy could vary, depending on how well the insurance company invested policyholders' premiums. In addition, the cash value also is variable, and there is no guaranteed minimum cash value.

Insofar as it's a way of investing in securities through an intermediary, a variable life policy resembles shares in a mutual fund. Indeed, the mutual fund industry has repeatedly said that variable life vendors should be subject to all the restrictions, regulations, and disclosure requirements governing sellers of mutual funds. While there's no reason to think that insurance companies would do badly in the investment line, their investment track records are not as easy to ascertain as those of mutual funds. A prospective buyer might prefer an established mutual fund to a variable life insurance policy simply because of the ready availability of a previous record of investment performance.

This, however, is not a book on investments. From an insurance standpoint, the important thing is that a family be adequately protected. Therefore, CU recommends that variable life, when available, be purchased only by people whose families would have adequate insurance coverage should the variable life policy end up paying no more than its guaranteed minimum. This might mean using variable life, if at all, as a supplement to other types of insurance. Or it might mean purchasing a variable life policy whose minimum guaranteed death benefit is at least equal to the coverage needs of the family.

Riders

Riders are options that can be added to a policy, for a fee, at the policyholder's discretion. If you decide to purchase a rider, you should make sure the cost of the option is added on to the annual premium of each policy you're considering when you do your comparison shopping for life insurance. In this chapter we will look at three of the riders most commonly suggested by life insurance agents or companies. They are: accidental death benefit, waiver of premium in the event of disability, and guaranteed insurability.

Accidental Death Benefit

The accidental death benefit is also commonly known as double (or triple) indemnity. Almost every company offers an accidental death benefit that provides for payment of twice the face amount in case of accidental death. For the extra amount to be paid, the death must normally occur within ninety days of the accident. Some accidental death benefit clauses provide triple benefits if the fatal accident occurs on a common carrier: bus, train, or regularly scheduled commercial plane. The annual cost of the accidental death benefit rider is often between seventy-five cents and one dollar for every $1,000 of accidental death protection purchased. On a $100,000 policy with accidental death benefits, then, the cost of the rider might be about $75 to $100 a year. The common carrier death benefit would add a slight additional cost.

For most people, Consumers Union does not recommend the accidental death benefit at any price. The chances of a policyholder's dying by accident are small: According to one authority, only about 6 percent of all life insurance policyholders die that way. But regardless of percentages, it doesn't make sense for policyholders to bet they're going to die by accident. A family needs protection in full against its breadwinner's death, no matter what the cause. A person who *needs* the accidental death benefit doesn't have enough basic life insurance; if a person doesn't need the accidental death benefit, then it is a superfluous expense. (For the same reason, CU discourages the purchase of airline flight insurance.)

William Sheppard, former insurance commissioner of Pennsylvania, put it this way: The accidental death benefit is "probably a good gamble if you're a steeplejack or a member of some other hazardous profession, or if you travel a lot. But it's just that—it's a gamble, it's not really insurance. For the average consumer, it isn't a good buy." CU suggests that consumers who can't resist the gamble should at least be sure their coverage is adequate without the rider.

Waiver of Premium

A waiver-of-premium rider, available with most policies, provides that in the event the policyholder becomes totally disabled, the insurance company will keep the policy in force without the policyholder being obligated to pay premiums. The provision usually states that a policyholder who is less than sixty years of age and who has been disabled for six months does not have to pay premiums for the ensuing period of disability. (Often, the provision is retroactive to the beginning of the disability.) Sometimes the cost of the waiver provision is built into the annual premium. More often the waiver is optional at an extra price. CU's studies have shown large price differences for this rider from policy to policy. On $10,000 five-year renewable term policies for a male age thirty-five, for example, the waiver comprised anywhere from less than 1 percent to more than 12 percent of the total premium. The cost depends on age, sex, specific terms of the waiver benefit, and the pricing decision made by the company.

Waiver-of-premium clauses vary considerably from company to company, and so they must be read with particular care. Of prime importance is the definition of total disability. With many policies, a policyholder is considered totally disabled if rendered unfit by an injury or an illness for the work the policyholder has always done, or work for which the policyholder is "suited by training and experience." Some definitions, however, contain a clause providing that unless the policyholder is unfit for any work at all, premiums must be paid to keep the policy in force. Some policies use an intermediate definition.

The age requirements for eligibility are also important. The clause usually applies to an illness or an injury sustained before age sixty. But with some policies the age limit is only fifty-five; with some, sixty-five. Assuming costs are equal, the latter would be the better buy. With some policies, full benefits are paid if the disability occurs before age sixty, and reduced benefits are paid if the disability occurs between ages sixty and sixty-five. Check also whether the waiver benefit, once it has been triggered by a disability, continues for life (or until recovery) or only for a specified period.

At age sixty-five, if not sooner, the waiver clause ceases to apply altogether. With some policies, the premium increment that financed the rider will then drop off, resulting in a lower total annual premium. With other policies, the premium remains the same even though the waiver clause is no longer in effect. Neither alternative is inherently preferable; it depends on how the benefit was priced from the outset.

With most policies, there is an elimination period of six months between the time a disability begins and the time the waiver-of-premium rider takes effect. Occasionally, the elimination period is only four months. Assuming costs are equal, a shorter elimination period is advantageous for the buyer.

Term insurance policy buyers should be especially careful about how the waiver-of-premium rider is worded. With some term policies, the policyholder, once disabled, can't convert to a cash value policy and keep the waiver in effect. From the insurance company's standpoint there is some sense to this. If the policyholder converts to a cash value policy while disabled and the premiums are waived, the company must, in effect, pay the higher premiums. However, becoming disabled is one very good reason why a person might *want* to exercise the right to convert to a cash value policy. A policyholder would then benefit, at no additional cost, from the buildup of cash value. Some insurance companies will let the policyholder convert with the waiver in effect. Their waiver-of-premium riders are therefore better for the consumer—but of course this advantage may be reflected in a higher price.

The waiver-of-premium rider is, in effect, a miniature disability income insurance policy. When the family breadwinner is laid up by illness or injury for much more than six months, the financial consequences can be horrendous. It may be cold comfort then if the life insurance bill is paid but there isn't enough money for current living expenses. Social

143

Security disability benefits (see Chapter 2) will help considerably.

If additional income is needed—and it probably would be —separate disability insurance can supply it. Disability insurance is a highly desirable and often neglected part of a breadwinner's insurance portfolio.

Because most families lack adequate disability coverage— and because in some cases the waiver-of-premium rider can be purchased very economically—the waiver-of-premium rider may deserve consideration. Whether you should purchase the waiver-of-premium rider depends on how extensive your other disability insurance is. If your present disability coverage is fully adequate, the rider is probably not needed. If your disability coverage is inadequate, upgrading it might be a better (but costlier) solution than purchasing the rider.

Beware of any disability income contract—whether a rider on a life insurance policy or a separate disability policy—that the insurance company can choose to renew or not renew from year to year as it sees fit. The protection should be guaranteed renewable.

For women, purchasing waiver of premium may not be an easy thing to do. According to a Michigan task force on sex discrimination in insurance, some companies will sell the rider only to unmarried women. Others refuse to sell it to women who work at home, even though the companies may at times offer the rider to self-employed men who work at home. It is true that women, statistically, are disabled more frequently than men are. But, in CU's opinion, this justifies at most a rate differential—not the unavailability of benefits to women. In various states, task forces on sex discrimination were established by state insurance departments in the early 1970s. Some of those states are now following up the recommendations of their task forces with remedial legislation or regulation. The process, however, is a slow one. For those faced with discrimination, the available routes for recourse are shopping around for the best price possible, exerting heightened pressure on state insurance agencies, and filing lawsuits.

Guaranteed Insurability

Guaranteed insurability is usually available only with cash value policies* and can normally be purchased only by people in their twenties and early thirties. It guarantees the policyholder the right to buy additional cash value insurance at standard rates, regardless of changes in health or occupation. The additional insurance can be purchased at various times—usually every three years—until age forty or thereabouts. The maximum amount of additional insurance that you can buy under the rider is specified in the rider itself. You can usually buy less than the amount specified, subject to some minimum.

For those who have less insurance than they expect ultimately to need—parents who plan to have more children, for example—the guaranteed insurability rider merits consideration. (Some riders specifically allow the purchase of more insurance upon the birth of a child; others allow such purchase only at the scheduled times.)

Here's an example of how the rider would work. If you bought $25,000 of cash value insurance, the rider would guarantee you the right to buy another $25,000 at each of several option dates in the future. There may be up to six (or, with some companies, seven) option dates, depending on your age at time of original purchase. Thus, you could buy

---

*One exception of which CU is aware: Term policies issued by Occidental Life Insurance Company of California. It allows the purchase of the rider. The company also allows purchase of term insurance under the rider.

up to another $175,000 worth of insurance, regardless of changes in your insurability. The dates are often spaced three years apart, coming, for example, at the policy anniversaries nearest ages twenty-five, twenty-eight, thirty-one, thirty-four, thirty-seven, and forty. The price you pay for the additional insurance is based on your age at the time you exercise the option to buy.

Reserving this future insurance usually costs about $1.50 per year for each $1,000 of coverage guaranteed at each option date. The price of the rider does not, of course, include—nor does it guarantee—the price of any additional insurance you may choose to buy under provisions of the rider. In the example given above, the cost of the rider itself would usually be about $37.50 per year for a $25,000 policy.

CU can see potential value in a new form of contract that would be sold for a modest price to guarantee later availability of life insurance—without the necessity of buying insurance before it's needed. At the very least, CU would like to see the guaranteed insurability rider sold in conjunction with term policies, rather than only with cash value policies as is the case with most companies at present.

How to Read
a Life Insurance Policy

Like many other legal contracts, life insurance policies have developed a well-deserved reputation over the years for being virtually unreadable by many of the individuals most affected by them. Not only was the "fine print" a frequent deterrent, but tortuous sentences of unrelieved, obscure legalese often were open to interpretation, meaning different things to different readers—or perhaps meaning nothing at all.

Today, you have a better chance of understanding policy language than you did in years past. That's largely because a number of states have passed laws in an effort to ensure that policies will be written understandably. These states turned to the Flesch Readability Scale as a measure of clear writing and mandated that insurance policies meet a minimum Flesch readability score.

The Flesch Readability Scale was developed by reading expert Rudolf Flesch in 1943. By assigning numerical values to the length of sentences and numbers of syllables in a text, and then using a mathematical formula, the Flesch readability score for that text can be determined. The higher the score, the more readable the text. Normally, scores range from 0 (very difficult) to 100 (very easy).* Here are two sample sentences, each with its Flesch score: "Damn the torpedoes—full speed ahead." (Admiral David Farragut; 74.) "If the insured dies during the initial term or a renewal term of this policy, an amount of money called the insurance proceeds will be payable to the beneficiary." (Excerpt from a life insurance policy; 34.)

Of course, a high Flesch score does not necessarily mean that the material is perfectly readable, since sentence length and numbers of syllables are not the only elements of readability. Consider, for example, this sentence with a Flesch score of 81: "There are some orts that usually go into the garbage that could be saved and used the next day." Despite the relatively high Flesch score, you don't know precisely what the sentence means unless you know that an ort is a morsel of food left at a meal. (The Editors of Consumer Reports Books trust that readers of *The Consumers Union Report on Life Insurance* will resist any temptation to apply the Flesch Readability Scale to this book.)

Massachusetts was the first state to clamp down on the policy language problem. In 1977, it passed a law requiring that all life insurance policies sold in the state, beginning with July 1, 1979, have a score of at least 50 on the Flesch Readability Scale. Since most major national companies sell in Massachusetts, the state law had a nationwide effect. (The Massachusetts Insurance Department granted extensions to

---

*The Flesch Readability Scale is described in Flesch's book, *The Art of Readable Writing.* Briefly, the first step involves determining the average number of words in a sentence—its length (L)—and the average number of syllables per hundred words (S). These are established by sampling an appropriate cross-section of the work being analyzed. Next, the average numbers L and S are used in the following formula: If $X = 1.015L$ and $Y = 0.846S$, then $206.835 - (X + Y) =$ Flesch readability score.

some companies unable to comply with the starting date.)

In 1977, Minnesota passed a law requiring that all policies sold in that state, starting January 1, 1980, have a minimum Flesch score of 40. By late 1979, nine other states had passed laws or regulations governing life insurance policy readability, which were to take effect in 1980 or later. (The nine were Arkansas, Connecticut, Maine, Nebraska, New Jersey, North Carolina, Ohio, Oregon, and South Carolina.) Most of the state rules called for a minimum Flesch score of 40; Connecticut's called for 45, and Maine's 50. More states were expected to pass similar legislation, modeled to some extent on a prototype regulation, approved by the National Association of Insurance Commissioners in June 1978, calling for a minimum Flesch score of 40.

Consumers Union thinks the readability laws and regulations, on balance, are good news for consumers. Such requirements should make it easier for you to read and understand the provisions of a life insurance policy. The policy may still not be simple to read. You'll have to plow through some language that can be sleep-inducing. That chore can pay off for you, though, especially if you read actively to catch subtleties of policy language that could affect your interests if you buy the particular policy.

In late 1979, CU wrote to fifteen life insurance companies for samples of their term and whole life policies: Aetna Life Insurance Company, Continental Assurance Company, Equitable Life Assurance Society of the United States, Federal Kemper Life Assurance Company, INA Life Insurance Company, Indianapolis Life Insurance Company, Massachusetts Savings Bank Life Insurance, Metropolitan Life Insurance Company, Midland National Life Insurance Company, Nationwide Life Insurance Company, New England Mutual Life Insurance Company, Northwestern Mutual Life Insurance Company, Prudential Insurance Company of

America, State Mutual Life Insurance Company, and Teachers Insurance and Annuity Association of America. The fifteen companies were chosen to include a balance of large and medium-sized companies and to include some that did well and some that did poorly in CU's Ratings.

We reviewed twenty-nine policies in all, comparing the major provisions and noting differences and similarities among them. Based on that survey, we prepared this chapter in which we analyze most of the provisions you'll find in a typical life insurance policy. (If you have questions about clauses in your policy that are not covered here, direct your inquiries to company headquarters—see *Definitions,* page 152.) As a reference point, we use language from sample policies of Metropolitan Life, a representative large company. Sample policies of other companies are cited where there are significant variations.

Basic Provisions

In this section, we look at basic provisions that are found in renewable and convertible term policies or in both term and cash value policies. Later in this chapter, we analyze some provisions peculiar to cash value policies.

Specifications. Some of the most important information comes at the very beginning of most life insurance policies —the information that you (or the agent) specify. These specifications will include the name of the insured (you), the issue date of the policy, your age and sex, and the policy classification (standard, preferred, or substandard; see Chapter 8). They will include the face amount and the type of insurance you buy (e.g., term, whole life). They will also include the name of the owner of the policy, which may or may not be you, depending on your estate tax planning (see Appendix IV).

Perhaps the most important specification is the beneficiary. The beneficiary clause names the person or persons who'll receive the proceeds when you die. If more than one beneficiary is named, the clause should stipulate how the money will be shared. A common practice is to name your spouse as primary beneficiary and your children as secondary, or contingent, beneficiaries. That way the children get the money in case your spouse dies with or before you (in an accident, for example). If you don't make any provision for a secondary beneficiary, and if your primary beneficiary dies before you do, your insurance proceeds would be distributed, along with the rest of your estate, according to the terms of your will. If you do not have a will, then your estate, including your insurance proceeds, would be probated in accordance with the laws of your state. Thus, your insurance proceeds might not go to the people you wanted, or might not be divided in the way you wanted.

The beneficiary clause of your life insurance policy should be coordinated with your will. If your will is a recent one you may want to use its beneficiary clause verbatim in your life insurance policy. Otherwise, it might be a good idea to check the wording of your policy's beneficiary clause with your attorney, if you have one.

If you become divorced or separated, or if there has been a death in the family, it's wise to review the beneficiary clause of the life insurance policies you own. (Your agent should be able to help you do this; otherwise, write directly to the company headquarters.) It has happened that a person has remarried and neglected to update the beneficiary clause; upon the policyholder's death, all the insurance money went to the previous spouse, none to the present spouse. Unwritten wishes don't count: It is important to make sure your beneficiary clause is up to date.

After you purchase a policy, you should double-check

151

when the document is delivered to make sure all the specifi-cations are correct and in accordance with what you wanted.

Definitions. Metropolitan Life put some basic definitions in a section entitled "Understanding This Policy." The section is largely self-explanatory and is not quoted here. Like com-parable sections of many policies, it refers you to your agent if you need service. If you don't know who your agent is, or have none, you can address requests to company headquar-ters. That address is often given on the first or last page of your policy; if not, you can find it in *Best's Insurance Reports* (Life/Health Edition), available at many libraries.

Premiums and reinstatement. The sample Metropolitan Life policy's clause on premiums read as follows:

Premium Payment—The benefits provided by your policy de-pend on the payment of premiums when due. Premiums are payable while the insured is alive, on or before their due dates as shown in the premium schedule. . . . Premiums may be paid at our Home Office or any other office we designate or to your sales representative. . . . You may change the frequency of payment with our approval.

The next paragraph described the grace period, which permits one month for late premium payments—a standard industry practice. The grace period allows for mail delays and occasional forgetfulness. Some consumers routinely wait until well into the grace period to pay their premiums, thus perhaps gaining extra interest on their savings or invest-ments. This practice is perfectly legal; but, it leaves less of a hedge against absentmindedness or erratic postal service.

The provision in the Metropolitan Life policy concerning reinstatement follows:

Reinstatement—If you have stopped paying premiums, you may reinstate the policy while the insured is alive if you:

1. Request reinstatement within 5 years of the due date of the first unpaid premium;

2. Provide evidence of insurability satisfactory to us; and

3. Pay all overdue premiums to the date of reinstatement with compound interest at the rate of 6% a year.

This language generally reflects standard industry practice. However, there are exceptions: Our sample Prudential and Teachers Insurance and Annuity Association policies allowed only three years for reinstatement rather than five.

Some companies provide a short period (usually fifteen to thirty-one days) after the end of the grace period during which a policy can be reinstated without evidence of insurability and, in some cases, without payment of any interest.

Those who fall far behind in payments are sometimes allowed "reinstatement by redate," which restores coverage without payment of all past-due premiums. This privilege—in effect, a change in the starting date of a policy—may not be mentioned in the text of the policy.

Dividends (for participating term policies). Under the heading "Payments During Insured's Lifetime," the Metropolitan Life policy clause discussed dividends as follows:

Every year we determine an amount to be paid to our policyholders as dividends. We will determine the share, if any, for this policy and credit it as a dividend at the end of the policy year. We do not expect that any dividend on this policy will be paid until 2 years from its [issue] date.

You may choose to use dividends in any one of these ways:

1. Dividend Accumulations—To be left with us to earn interest at the rate we set from time to time.

2. Premium Payment—To be applied toward the payment of premiums.

3. Cash—To be paid to you by check.

Your choice may be made on the application for your policy or in writing at a later date. If no choice has been made, we will provide dividend accumulations unless you make a different choice within 3 months after a dividend is credited. If a dividend check has not been cashed within one year, a choice of dividend accumulations will be deemed to have been made.

Any dividends left with us to earn interest, together with any current dividend, will be paid to you by check if this policy is not renewed on a renewal date. Any dividends left with us to earn interest will be paid to you by check after the end of the grace period of an unpaid premium.

At any time you can withdraw dividends left with us to earn interest.

There are several noteworthy items in this passage about dividends. First, the laconic phrase "Every year we determine" the amount of dividends to be paid is a revealing one, touching as it does on the fact that dividend-determination formulas remain entirely internal company business, with little or no disclosure to consumers, and relatively little regulatory supervision. CU's views on the implications for consumers of company secrecy about dividend formulas are found in Chapter 6.

Second, you'll note that the policy provides a choice of what to do with your dividends (leave them to accumulate, use them to reduce your annual premiums, or take them in cash). That's standard practice for term insurance policies. Cash value policies, by contrast, normally have a fourth dividend option, which is the use of dividends to buy paid-up additional cash value insurance. Some policies also offer additional dividend options. Seven of our eight sample participating term policies provided the standard three dividend options. Prudential also provided the fourth option—with the proviso that paid-up additions must be in the form of an endowment policy maturing at age seventy. CU can't get very excited about this option: We believe endowment policies are usually poor buys (see page 70).

Third, you'll note that Metropolitan Life will automatically keep your dividends to accumulate at interest, unless instructed otherwise by you. The same provision was in most of the other participating term policies we looked at. But not all companies follow this practice. Nationwide Life would pay you dividends in cash unless instructed otherwise. Prudential would use them to buy the little endowment policies mentioned above.

The practice of automatically keeping dividends to accumulate at interest, unless otherwise instructed, can be defended on grounds of administrative convenience. But CU believes the practice serves, in effect, to maximize the funds available to insurance companies for investment. In CU's view, consumers would be better off, on balance, if more companies paid dividends in cash unless otherwise instructed.

Policies generally specify a minimum interest rate at which dividends will accumulate. CU doesn't view this as a major factor because companies usually pay a higher rate than the specified minimum. Some major companies were paying about 6½ percent interest in early 1980, as compared with a guaranteed minimum of about 2½ to 4 percent. In any case, CU suggests that policyholders shouldn't leave their dividends to accumulate.*

Renewals. The key questions concerning the renewability feature are whether the policy can be renewed, and for how long. Some term policies can't be renewed after the initial

---

*For the 38 percent of policyholders who leave dividends to accumulate, we note what the minimum interest rate on dividend accumulations would be, based on eight sample policies: 4 percent at Massachusetts Savings Bank Life Insurance; 3½ percent at Northwestern Mutual; 3 percent at Equitable Life Assurance Society, Indianapolis Life, Metropolitan Life, and Prudential; 2½ percent at Nationwide Life and New England Mutual.

term; they can only be converted to a cash value policy. It's not enough that a term policy is renewable. You should also check how long it can be renewed—until what age or for how many renewals. In CU's Ratings in Part II, we include only policies that can be renewed at least up to age sixty-five. Not all term policies can be renewed that long. Nationwide Life's one-year term, for example, could be renewed only nine times, though the same company's five-year term could be renewed up to age sixty-five. CU views renewability to age sixty-five or seventy as an important provision.

Some policies can be renewed even longer. There were among our sample policies some that offered term insurance renewable to age one hundred. In many cases, though, the cost of the term insurance for elderly people would be well beyond their reach. For example, Federal Kemper would charge a ninety-five-year-old man about $56,800 to insure his life for $100,000 for one year.

Table of renewal premiums. The table of renewal premiums tells you what your premiums will be each time you renew your term policy. With a five-year term policy, the premium will change every five years; if it's a one-year term policy, the premium will change every year. In either case, look in the column marked "age at renewal" to see how old you'll be when the premium changes, then read across to see how much you'll pay in premiums if you continue your coverage. Some policies make it even easier for you. Instead of your age at renewal, they provide a series of actual dates in the left-hand column, e.g., November 1, 1989, November 1, 1990, and so forth.

Reading across, you'll see that you have a choice regarding payment frequency. With most companies, you can pay annually, semiannually, or quarterly. The policy makes it clear how much you will pay in each case. When you pay other than annually, you're in effect taking out what amounts to a loan on a portion of the premium and paying a finance charge. As with many installment contracts, that charge can be hefty. It is usually worth your while to make every effort to pay annually. (According to the 1979 *Life Insurance Fact Book,* published by the industry's leading trade association, only 19 percent of policyholders pay premiums annually.)

Many companies let you pay monthly if you wish. Some let you make monthly payments through an automatic payment plan coordinated with your bank; these plans are designated as "Check-O-Matic," "Auto-Check," or the like. If for some reason you do pay monthly, an automatic payment plan might be a bit cheaper than mailing in the check yourself. Reason: Some companies give you a discount from their regular monthly rates, reflecting the lower costs for automatic collection.

Joseph M. Belth, professor of insurance at Indiana University, published in the December 1978 issue of his monthly newsletter, *The Insurance Forum,* an analysis of how the implicit finance charges vary among companies. The variations are so striking that CU suggests you take the implicit finance charge into account when purchasing a policy, if you think you're likely to pay other than annually.

Belth looked at the implicit rate, expressed as Annual Percentage Rate (APR),* for a sample of policies from fifteen

---

*Belth used three formulas, one for semiannual, one for quarterly, one for monthly premiums:

$$APR = \frac{200\ (2S\text{-}A)}{A\text{-}S} \qquad APR = \frac{1200\ (4Q\text{-}A)}{5A\text{-}2Q} \qquad APR = \frac{3600\ (12M\text{-}A)}{13A+42M}.$$

Where APR is the annual percentage rate expressed as a percentage, A is the annual premium, S is the semiannual premium, Q is the quarterly premium, and M is the monthly premium. Because the formulas are approximations, Belth suggests that the results should be carried out only to the nearest tenth of a percentage point.

major life insurance companies. He found that the APR for paying semiannually varied from 5.0 percent (Equitable Life Assurance Society) to 14.2 percent (Connecticut Mutual Life Insurance Company). The APR for paying quarterly ranged from 4.9 percent (Equitable Life Assurance Society) to 28.7 percent (United Benefit Life Insurance Company). For regular monthly premiums, the charge ranged from 4.9 percent (Equitable Life Assurance Society) to 29.3 percent (American National Insurance Company). And for a monthly automatic payment plan, the charge varied from 4.3 percent (Aetna) to 12.4 percent (United Benefit).

To sum up: Pay annually if you possibly can. If you doubt your ability to budget one large annual premium payment, then check the policy to find out how much it will cost you to pay in installments. Take this charge into account when you comparison-shop for life insurance policies.

Conversion. Most term policies can be converted to cash value policies under certain conditions. CU views convertibility as a desirable feature: It provides flexibility in case your life insurance needs change. Because conversion clauses vary considerably, you should carefully read the conversion clause of any term policy you consider buying. The Metropolitan Life conversion clause read in part:

Conversion at End of Final Renewal Term—If all due premiums have been paid to the end of the final renewal term, you may then convert the policy, without evidence of insurability, to a new policy on the life of the insured.

The new policy will be on the Whole Life plan in the same underwriting class as this policy. . . . The new policy must be for at least $10,000 but not more than the Face Amount of Insurance of this policy. The premium will be determined by the insured's age on the date of conversion. . . .

Other Conversion—At any time while your policy is in force

with all due premiums paid, you may convert it without evidence of insurability to a new policy on the life of the insured. To do so, send us a written request and this policy.

The amount of life insurance provided by the new policy may not be more than the Face Amount of Insurance of this policy. The date of the new policy may be either the date of this policy or the date of conversion. The new policy may be on any life or endowment plan (but not a term plan) in an amount which we regularly issue at the insured's age on the date of the new policy. . . . Premium rates will be those in effect on the date of the new policy. We will determine the amount of any other payment required by reason of the conversion.

The Metropolitan Life policy is unusual in that it spelled out in a table of conversion premiums (discussed below) the exact premium you'd pay if you converted the policy at the end of the final renewal term. Other than that, the Metropolitan Life clause is relatively standard in its description of *attained age conversion.* Under this arrangement, the premium you pay if you convert is based on your age at the date of conversion.

There is, however, another kind of conversion, called *original age conversion.* With it, the premium you pay is based on your age at the issue date of your original term policy. You pay the company the money it would have received—as well as interest on that money—if you had elected the cash value insurance from the outset. In other words, you pay the difference between what the term premiums were (adjusted for any dividends) and what the cash value premiums would have been, as well as interest on that difference.

From the consumer's viewpoint, there's an advantage in having a choice—at the time the conversion is to take place—between attained age and original age conversion: One method of conversion is likely to be cheaper for you than the other.

If you're planning to convert your term policy to a cash value policy and you're given a choice between original age and attained age conversion, you'll have to do some figuring to see which basis is better for you. If you choose attained age, your annual premium will be higher, but you probably won't have to make a large lump-sum payment to the company. (If you are considering a conversion on an attained age basis, you may find it useful to make a comparison similar to the one shown in Appendix II.)

If you use an original age basis, your annual premium will be lower, but you'll probably have to pay a large lump sum to convert the policy. We suggest that you start by computing the amount of the lump sum you'll have to pay. Because you most likely will have to withdraw the money from your savings account or from other investments, estimate how much interest on that money you'd be giving up each year in the future. Then, see how that lost interest compares with your annual premium savings from using an original age basis for conversion.

CU examined the conversion clauses of our sample term policies. About half of them did not allow original age conversion while the rest did. Generally, those that did allow original age conversion required the payment of the difference in premiums as well as payment of 6 percent compound interest on that difference, plus adjustments for past dividends payable under the cash value policy. Several policies also required that the conversion take into account the cash value on the new policy. Equitable Life Assurance Society required that the conversion fee be not less than the cash value of the new policy.

Metropolitan Life's policy allowed original age conversion but gave no details (such as the interest rate you'd have to pay). In an interview with CU, Metropolitan Life's representative said that a policyholder who wants to effect an original age conversion would have to contact the company to find out how to do it.

Prudential's system for computing the original age conversion charge differed from others CU looked at. The company reserved the right to charge the greater of two sums. One sum was based on the accumulated difference in premiums, using 6 percent interest, as is common practice. The second sum was based on the cash value of the new contract, increased by "not more than 14 percent," pius an adjustment for the cost of any extra benefits under the new contract. "We will compare the amounts we compute in 1 and 2 above," said the Prudential policy. "The charge to be paid will never be more than the larger of the two. It may be less."

CU believes that it is extremely difficult for consumers to estimate the potential cost of converting their term policies to cash value policies—with almost any company, and especially with companies using a complex clause like Prudential's or a vague clause like Metropolitan Life's.

Original age conversion offers a possible advantage over attained age conversion in the event you want to buy a term policy now, but think it's likely you'll want to switch to a cash value policy later. An original age conversion clause allows you to lock in the premium-and-dividend structure of a cash value plan you find attractive. To get that advantage, you may even want to purchase your term policy from a company that charges a bit more than its competitors, if the cash value policies offered by that company look attractive to you. CU believes that's a sensible approach, because it takes into account the possibility that for some buyers conversion could become a desirable feature.

Preset conversion premiums. The Metropolitan Life policy provided a table that tells you how much you'd pay if you converted your term policy on an attained age basis to a whole life plan at the end of the final renewal term. For example, if you converted at age sixty-six, your annual premium on a $100,000 whole life policy would be $8,595 per year. Instead of converting at the preset rate, you also have the option of choosing to convert on an attained age basis at whatever premium the company is then charging. That premium rate may be higher or lower than the preset rate. The preset premiums, however, are offered only at ages sixty-six to seventy. If you were to convert earlier on an attained age basis you would have no choice: You would have to pay whatever premium the company was then charging.

This approach appears to be unusual in the industry. Of the sample policies we checked, only Metropolitan Life's had preset conversion rates at any age. CU views optional preset conversion premiums as an advantage for the consumer because they facilitate planning. We would like to see this kind of option offered at additional ages, and by more companies. From the consumer's point of view, it would be ideal to have —at any age—a choice of either the preset rates or the rates in effect at the time the conversion actually is to take place. And because preset rates are probably based on conservative actuarial assumptions, we believe it might be possible for companies to offer such a choice. However, no company whose sample policy we reviewed made such an offer.

Ownership and beneficiary. This section of the policy tells how you can change the ownership of the policy, or change your designation of the beneficiary. Any transfer of ownership of your policy, which is most often done for tax reasons, requires careful planning, as explained in Appendix IV.

Incontestability. If you misstate something material (such as the extent of a health problem) on the policy application, the company can legitimately deny all or part of an insurance claim—but only for a limited time. To avoid endless fights and litigation, it's in everyone's interest for there to be a time limit on such contests. Custom and regulation set the limit at two years. (However, if you made a mistake regarding your age in filling out the application, the death benefit will be adjusted, as explained below.)

Age and sex: Metropolitan Life's sample policy stated:

If the insured's age or sex on the date of the policy is not correct as shown in the policy specifications, we will adjust the benefits under this policy. The adjusted benefits will be those which the premium paid would have bought at the correct age and sex.

CU believes that this language (or similar provisions) is just about universal. Companies require proof of death when a death claim is submitted. Most people submit a death certificate as proof of the policyholder's death. If the age (or sex) stated in the death certificate differs from that shown on the policy and the discrepancy favors the company, the company may reduce benefits, as stated above. Should the beneficiary wish to contest the age stated in the death certificate, it would be useful to have a proof of age at hand to help resolve a possible dispute with the company. (It would be wise, therefore, for a policyholder to keep a valid proof of age on file with important papers.)

Suicide. The suicide clause is almost universal. Here's the one from Metropolitan Life's sample policy:

Suicide—The insurance proceeds will not be paid if the insured commits suicide, while sane or insane, within 2 years from the date of the policy. Instead, we will pay the beneficiary an amount equal to all premiums paid, without interest.

In examining the clause in fifteen sample policies, CU found only one company, Northwestern Mutual Life Insurance, whose suicide clause differed materially. That company used a one-year limit, rather than two.

Payment when insured dies. The clause in the Metropolitan Life policy read as follows:

> If the insured dies during the initial term or a renewal term of this policy, an amount of money, called the insurance proceeds, will be payable to the beneficiary. The insurance proceeds are the total of:
> - The Face Amount of Insurance. PLUS
> - Any insurance on the insured's life which may be provided by riders to this policy.
> - Any dividends left with us to earn interest.
> - Any dividend which we may credit at death.
> - Any part of a premium paid for coverage beyond the policy month in which the insured dies. MINUS
> - Any premium due (not more than one month's part of the premium).
> We will pay the insurance proceeds to the beneficiary after receipt of proof of death and a proper written claim.

The essence of the clause is that, if you've paid your premiums, the company will pay the death benefit when you die, provided the beneficiary submits proof of death and fills out a claim form. Usually, neither step is difficult. Most companies pay death claims promptly, and there is generally a minimum of red tape.

The beneficiary should normally expect to get any needed forms and help from the agent who serviced the policy or directly from the company headquarters. If the policy proceeds aren't received within a month after the claim is filed, the beneficiary should certainly contact company headquarters, and the beneficiary may also want to bring the matter to the attention of his or her state insurance department (see Appendix III).

Settlement options. Every policy spells out in detail the settlement options available to the beneficiary. They are the same five settlement options available to a policyholder who cashes in a policy, as described in Chapter 4. The policy itself specifies the *minimum* amount to be paid under each option. Currently, companies are paying substantially more than the guaranteed minimum, but CU believes that the minimums are still worth looking at before buying a policy.

After the policyholder's death, the right to select a settlement option normally belongs to the beneficiary. However, a policyholder can specify a settlement option in advance, either on an advisory or a binding basis. It is normally wise to leave a beneficiary as wide a range of choice as possible by making no such specification. A policyholder who decides to select a particular settlement plan should try not to word the specification so rigidly that it might some day cause serious problems for a beneficiary.

In deciding which option to use after the policyholder has died, the beneficiary should consider the interest rate paid by the insurance company on any money left with it. (Technically, this is called the rate of interest on the unliquidated proceeds.) If that interest rate is low, it's almost always to a beneficiary's advantage to take the death benefit in a lump sum and invest it. If the company's interest rate on unliquidated proceeds is reasonably high, then the beneficiary may want to consider choosing one of the other settlement options. At the time that the question of settlement options is being decided by the beneficiary, the beneficiary should check with the company to find out exactly how much would be paid under each of the settlement options being considered.

CU checked two settlement options for each of fifteen sample policies. We found differences of up to 20 percent in the guaranteed monthly payments. This finding underlines the importance of giving the beneficiary flexibility, and the

---

Table 11–1
Twenty-Year Payments on a
Lifetime Annuity Settlement Option

Shown below are the guaranteed minimum monthly payments for twenty years on a $100,000 life insurance policy with a sixty-year-old female beneficiary and a lifetime annuity settlement option.

Company	Guaranteed Minimum Monthly Payment
State Mutual	$500
Aetna	492
New England Mutual	484
Massachusetts SBLI	483
Northwestern Mutual	483
Metropolitan Life	467
Indianapolis Life	465
Continental Assurance	462
Midland National	457
Equitable Life Assurance Society	452
Federal Kemper	447
Nationwide Life	439
Teachers Insurance and Annuity Association	399
INA	*
Prudential	*

*INA and Prudential do not offer a lifetime annuity settlement option with twenty years certain payments; they do offer one with ten years certain.

---

importance of the beneficiary's getting informed advice about which option to take.

One option we looked at was a lifetime annuity with a guaranteed payment period of twenty years. (If the beneficiary dies before twenty years are up, the remaining payments

Table 11–2
Twenty-Year Fixed Payment Settlement Option

Shown below are the guaranteed minimum monthly payments for twenty years on a $100,000 life insurance policy.

Company	Guaranteed Minimum Monthly Payment
Massachusetts SBLI	$590
Equitable Life Assurance Society	576
INA	575
Northwestern Mutual	575
Prudential	575
State Mutual	575
Aetna	551
Continental Assurance	551
Indianapolis Life	551
Metropolitan Life	551
New England Mutual	551
Midland National	539
Federal Kemper	527
Nationwide Life	527
Teachers Insurance and Annuity Association	527

go to the beneficiary's heirs. If the beneficiary lives longer than twenty years, payments continue for the life of the beneficiary, then stop.) We assumed that the beneficiary was a female who was sixty years old when the insured died. Table 11–1 on page 166 shows the range of payments we found.

The other option CU looked at was simply twenty years of fixed installment payments. Here again we found variations among the guaranteed values specified in our fifteen sample policies. The range of payments is shown in Table 11–2, on page 167.

CU doesn't think guaranteed minimum settlement options should be a major factor in life insurance buying decisions, because we think most beneficiaries would be better off taking the proceeds in a lump sum. However, we do think the variations among companies in settlement options show that beneficiaries should get good advice—including advice as to federal income tax consequences—before deciding how to take the proceeds.

Additional Provisions of Cash Value Policies

Many of the policy provisions we've discussed earlier in this chapter apply to cash value, as well as to term, policies. We'll discuss here a few provisions found *only* in cash value policies.

Table of values. Every cash value policy has a table—called variously table of values, table of nonforfeiture values, table of nonforfeiture and loan values, or by some similar name—that shows how much money or paid-up insurance would be available if and when a policyholder should choose to terminate a policy. As discussed in Chapter 4, there are three basic surrender (nonforfeiture) options: First, you can take the full amount of the cash value in cash. (All of the settlement options are normally available; you can take the money in a lump sum, or as an annuity, or in installments, or leave it with the company to accumulate at interest.) Second, instead of taking the cash value in money, you can elect to use it to buy a specified amount of paid-up cash value insurance. The third surrender option available to you is to take extended term insurance.

Accordingly, the policy's table of nonforfeiture values (under whatever name) lists three columns of numbers, usually year by year for the first twenty years, and thereafter at selected ages (such as sixty and sixty-five). The three columns in the table of values show the cash value of the policy, the reduced face amount of paid-up cash value insurance that could be bought with the policy's cash value, and the term (both in years and days) of paid-up term insurance for which you can extend the policy with the same face amount as the cash value policy had.

Table 11–3 (on pages 170–171) shows a typical table of values based on a Metropolitan Life sample policy for $25,000 of whole life insurance, with an issue date of July 1, 1979, for a thirty-five-year-old male. As of July 1, 1999 (after twenty years), the cash value of the policy would be $7,575. This sum could be used to buy $14,575 of paid-up whole life insurance. In other words, the policyholder would thereafter be insured for $14,575 and would not have to pay any more premiums. If the original policy were held for thirty years (to age sixty-five) rather than twenty, the cash value would be $12,675. That would buy $18,950 of paid-up insurance at that time.

We wondered how much difference there would be in the amount of paid-up insurance that a fixed amount of cash value would buy. So we did a comparison involving thirteen of our sample policies, based on a thirty-five-year-old male buyer who holds a policy until age sixty-five, then elects paid-up insurance. Our comparison showed that the paid-up insurance per $100 of cash value varied from a high of $192 to a low of $134. Those two extremes were for nonparticipating policies.

The best participating policies in this respect offered $159 of paid-up insurance per $100 of cash value. But some par policies would also pay dividends on the paid-up insurance itself. Without knowing the dividend scales involved, however, all CU can say is rather obvious: A given amount of

Table 11-3
A Typical Table of Values, $25,000 Whole Life Policy

The following table of values, based on one from Metropolitan Life, is applicable to a policy without paid-up additions, dividend accumulations, or policy loan. The Metropolitan Life policy stated: "On request, we will provide values for dates not shown."

DATE OF POLICY—JULY 1, 1979

PLAN—WHOLE LIFE

FACE AMOUNT OF INSURANCE IS $25,000

INSURED'S AGE AND SEX—35 MALE

Value Date	Guaranteed Cash Value	Reduced Paid-Up Insurance	Extended Term Insurance Years	Days
JAN. 1, 1980	$ 0	$ 0	0	60
JULY 1, 1980	0	0	0	60
JULY 1, 1981	25	100	0	99
JULY 1, 1982	275	900	2	244
JULY 1, 1983	625	1,950	5	112
JULY 1, 1984	1,000	3,025	7	176
JULY 1, 1985	1,375	4,025	9	53
JULY 1, 1986	1,775	5,025	10	194

Value Date	Guaranteed Cash Value	Reduced Paid-Up Insurance	Extended Term Insurance Years	Days
JULY 1, 1987	$ 2,175	$ 5,950	11	221
JULY 1, 1988	2,575	6,825	12	157
JULY 1, 1989	3,000	7,725	13	55
JULY 1, 1990	3,425	8,550	13	252
JULY 1, 1991	3,850	9,325	14	34
JULY 1, 1992	4,300	10,100	14	162
JULY 1, 1993	4,750	10,825	14	252
JULY 1, 1994	5,200	11,500	14	310
JULY 1, 1995	5,675	12,200	14	359
JULY 1, 1996	6,150	12,850	15	15
JULY 1, 1997	6,625	13,450	15	11
JULY 1, 1998	7,100	14,025	14	351
JULY 1, 1999	7,575	14,575	14	308
At age 60	10,100	17,050	14	2
At age 65	12,675	18,950	12	279

paid-up insurance that pays dividends is preferable to the same amount of paid-up insurance that doesn't pay dividends. As a rough guide in shopping for a policy, we suggest viewing it as a disadvantage if the amount of paid-up insurance per $100 of cash value (at age sixty-five) is less than $150—particularly if the policy you are considering is nonpar.

If you were to elect extended term insurance, you would remain covered for the full face amount of the policy for a specified length of time. During this period, you pay no premiums. With the table of values shown in Table 11–3, for example, a thirty-five-year-old man who bought $25,000 of whole life and paid annually until age fifty-five could receive fourteen years and 308 days of extended term coverage without paying premiums.

The amount of extended term insurance available with a cash value policy typically begins to decline when the policyholder is in his or her fifties, because the probability of death is increasing rapidly enough to more than offset the increasing cash value. With the table of values shown in Table 11–3, the turning point is at age fifty-four.

Cash values and policy loans. The sample Metropolitan Life whole life policy read in part as follows:

Policy Loan—You can get cash from us by taking a policy loan. If there is an existing loan you can increase it. The most you can borrow is the cash value at the end of the current policy year less any unpaid premiums for that year and loan interest to the end of that year. A loan may not be taken if extended term insurance is in effect. . . .

Loan interest is charged daily at a rate we set from time to time. The rate will not be increased more than once a year, and no increase will add more than a rate of 1% to the prior rate. The effective rate will never be more than 8% a year. When a loan is made, we will inform you of the rate and if any rate increase is to be made within 40 days. We will mail a notice to you at least 30 days before we make any rate increase which will apply to an existing loan.

Loan interest is due at the end of each policy year. Interest not paid within 31 days after it is due will be added to the loan principal. It will be added as of the due date and will bear interest at the same rate as the rest of the loan principal.

Loan Repayment—You may repay all or part (but not less than $20) of a policy loan at any time while the insured is alive.

Policy Termination—Your policy will terminate whenever the amount of your policy loan plus loan interest is more than the sum of:

1. The guaranteed cash value;
2. The cash value of any insurance bought with dividends; and
3. Any dividends left with us to earn interest.

We will mail notice to you at least 31 days before termination. . . . You can prevent termination by making sufficient repayment of the loan.

Deferment—We may delay paying the cash value for up to 6 months from the date we receive a request for payment. If we delay for 30 days or more, interest will be paid from the date we receive the request at the rate we set from time to time. We also may delay making a policy loan for up to 6 months from the date you request the loan except for a loan to pay a premium.

In general, this clause is representative of those found throughout the industry. It contains a couple of phrases whose import is more theoretical than real. There's very little likelihood that you'd experience a six-month delay in withdrawing your cash value or obtaining a policy loan. That clause—similar to the delay clause used by some banks and savings institutions—is meant to protect against a Depression-style "run on the bank."

We found a six-month deferment clause in most of our sample policies, but not in the policies that were issued by

Equitable Life Assurance Society, Massachusetts Savings Bank Life Insurance, Midland National, and Nationwide Life. CU knows of one case in which a small company invoked the deferment clause, but we believe such instances are rare.

We also doubt that you should put much faith in the hint that your policy loan rate might be less than the maximum specified in the policy. (In early 1980, this was usually 8 percent.) In practice, most companies routinely charge the maximum permitted under the policy.

Most of our sample whole life policies contained an automatic premium loan clause. Under this clause, if you fall behind in premium payments, you are automatically given a policy loan—to make the payment and keep the policy in force—if there's sufficient cash value in the policy. Of our sample policies that had automatic premium loans, all but one provided the feature only if the policyholder had requested it—either when the policy was purchased or later. One company, Teachers Insurance and Annuity Association, had an automatic premium loan that became operative unless the policyholder had requested otherwise in writing. Thus, for most of the sample policies, the feature wasn't truly "automatic." You had to ask for it if you wanted it.

Dividends on cash value policies. The clause describing the payment of dividends is similar in many respects to that in term policies (see page 153). However, while term policies usually give you only three options regarding dividend use (take them in cash, use them to reduce the annual premium, or leave them to accumulate), cash value policies normally give you four. The fourth option you get with a cash value policy is that you can use your dividends to buy paid-up additional cash value insurance.

Some cash value policies offer an additional dividend option, allowing you to use your dividends to buy one-year term insurance. CU views this as a valuable option. Unfortunately, relatively few companies offer it. Some companies, however, will make the option available at no extra cost if you ask. Of the nine participating whole life policies we examined, all offered only the four standard dividend options, and all specified that dividends would be used to buy paid-up additions unless the policyholder elected otherwise. CU thinks this standard industry practice is regrettable, even if it's a convenient way for companies to sell extra insurance.

Sometimes paid-up additions are sold at "net rates," i.e., there are no commission charges. That tends to lower the costs. However, the trouble with paid-up additional insurance, in CU's view, is that it's single-premium insurance (see page 135) and thus has a high initial outlay. The amount of additional paid-up insurance your dividends will buy is likely to be small. As we said earlier, we believe companies should pay dividends in cash unless otherwise instructed.

CU thinks the differences in sections and clauses among policies are worth your attention. Reading a life insurance policy may be less fun than reading a best-selling novel but the time you invest may pay off.

Before you buy any life insurance policy, CU suggests you obtain a sample policy and read it through, keeping in mind the issues raised in this chapter. Some agents may try to shrug off your request for a sample policy, pointing out that you get a ten-day "free look" anyway, once the policy's delivered. It's true that in most states you can cancel a policy within ten days and obtain a full refund of your money. However, this procedure is a nuisance and, in practice, many consumers will decide to stick with a purchase once they've paid for it, rather than go through the trouble and possible embarrassment of undoing it.

The time to do your comparison shopping, CU believes, is before you buy your policy. That means you should obtain and consider both complete price information about the policy and a copy of the policy itself before you pay out any money.

Should You
Switch Policies?

Deciding which life insurance policy to buy isn't easy. Deciding whether to drop an existing policy and replace it with a new one can be even harder. If you already have a policy and you're considering replacement, this chapter can help you make that difficult decision.

To the question of whether you should switch, many people in the life insurance industry have a simple answer: Don't. They think that a policy, once purchased, should never be replaced. Consumers Union does not subscribe to that view. We think replacement—purchasing a new policy and at the same time discontinuing a previously held policy —can sometimes make sense. But when an agent or company suggests you switch policies, we think you should be given information about the costs involved. In some states, the replacing company is obliged to meet limited disclosure requirements. (Illegal, however, is the practice of "twisting"— inducing a policyholder to switch policies on the basis of misleading information.)

Many industry representatives believe that companies, instead of selling life insurance to people who are already covered by another company, should concentrate on selling life insurance to people who have no coverage—or at least to people who don't have enough. To do otherwise, it's argued, would mean the sort of internecine competition that only weakens the industry and raises expenses for all companies. Ultimately, the argument goes on, the consumer is harmed, because increased expenses mean higher prices.

Such reasoning against intercompany raiding has a certain plausibility—at least from the industry's viewpoint. But CU doesn't believe it should be taken too seriously by consumers. After all, the same argument could be made for any service business. Carried to its extreme, the argument against companies raiding one another's turf is tantamount to an agreement to stifle competition.

This is not to suggest that switching policies is necessarily desirable from the consumer's viewpoint. Indeed, anyone considering such a move should proceed cautiously. There are at least three reasons why the replacement of one policy by a new one should be carefully weighed.

When you replace one life insurance policy with another, you have to pay a new front-end load, including a commission (if an agent sold you the policy), other sales expenses, and administrative costs. The new front-end load may be reflected in higher premiums, delayed dividend payments, and/or delayed buildup of cash value. If you're reasonably satisfied with your existing policy and its price is fairly close to that of the replacement policy, it's rarely in your interest to pay a second front-end load. For that reason, agents who sell replacement policies are often suspected of pursuing their own interests, and not the consumer's needs.

A second argument against replacements is that the new policy is likely to have higher premiums because you're older than when the original policy was issued. In the case of cash value policies, this argument makes some sense because the premium stays constant from year to year and is based on age at the time of purchase. In the case of one-year or five-year renewable term policies, it's less clear, since term premiums normally increase with age anyway. However, the premium for an existing term policy at a given age may sometimes be lower than the premium for a newly purchased term policy at that age, particularly if the existing term policy is replaced in the middle of its term.

Third, if you replace your policy, you lose important protection afforded by the suicide clause and the incontestability clause of the old policy. These clauses are discussed in Chapter 11. Essentially, they mean that your beneficiaries may not get the full death benefit if you should commit suicide within two years of purchasing the new policy, or if you should die within two years of purchasing the new policy and the insurance company were to find out that you had made important misstatements in the application for the new policy. (It would not matter if the misstatements were made inadvertently or under an assumption that they were true at the time.)

Industry people who oppose switching policies will point to the three considerations just discussed as justification for not switching and, for many policyholders, these reasons may well be valid. But what the people who decry replacement fail to appreciate—or at least to acknowledge—are the huge variations in cost among policies. If your present policy happens to be a high-cost one, it may very well pay you to switch, despite the cautions discussed earlier. Thus, before you decide either way—to switch or not to switch—you need to know the cost of your present policy so that you can compare it with the cost of a possible replacement. Knowing the cost of your present policy may also be useful if you're considering whether to convert a term policy to a cash value one.

Determining the cost of your present policy can be difficult. In none of the fifty states are there regulations requiring that the cost of a policy be disclosed to a policyholder at any time after it has been sold. (Recommendations for such disclosure are discussed briefly in Chapter 13.)

Given the current regulations, CU believes the best way to estimate the cost of your policy is to obtain or calculate an interest-adjusted net cost index for the next twenty years, using the present—the year you begin your analysis—as the starting point. You can ask your agent or company to provide you with the index, but not all agents or companies are able or willing to do so. Table 12–1 can help you make your own calculations for a policy under analysis. The procedure in Table 12–1 is applicable only to policies with a level face amount. For other kinds of policies, CU knows of no simple procedure to make such comparisons.

Making the Replacement Decision

Once you know the twenty-year interest-adjusted net cost index for your existing policy, you are in a position to compare the cost of the policy with that of a possible replacement. Bear in mind that the interest-adjusted net cost index will tell you whether your policy is high or low in cost for its type. You can begin by comparing your policy's cost against the cost of similar policies shown in Part II.

If your policy seems to be low in cost compared with those of similar policies shown in CU's Ratings, there's probably little reason to consider a replacement (other things being equal). If your policy appears to be high in cost compared with available alternatives, then switching deserves your serious consideration. We suggest that differences of less than 10 percent in the twenty-year index should be regarded as insignificant for this purpose. You probably should not consider

(Text continued on page 185)

Table 12–1
Calculating a Twenty-Year Interest-Adjusted
Net Cost Index for an Existing Policy

Step 1. Write on each line below the annual premiums on the policy for the next twenty years. These are shown in the basic policy. Accumulate the premiums at 5 percent interest, as shown below. (If the premium remains constant, you needn't go through all the procedures in Step 1. Just multiply the premium by 34.719 and enter the result as the total for Step 1, on the next page.)

Line 1. First-year premium of _____ multiplied by 2.653 = _____.

Line 2. Second-year premium of _____ multiplied by 2.527 = _____.

Line 3. Third-year premium of _____ multiplied by 2.407 = _____.

Line 4. Fourth-year premium of _____ multiplied by 2.292 = _____.

Line 5. Fifth-year premium of _____ multiplied by 2.183 = _____.

Line 6. Sixth-year premium of _____ multiplied by 2.079 = _____.

Line 7. Seventh-year premium of _____ multiplied by 1.980 = _____.

Line 8. Eighth-year premium of _____ multiplied by 1.885 = _____.

Line 9. Ninth-year premium of _____ multiplied by 1.796 = _____.

Line 10. Tenth-year premium of _____ multiplied by 1.710 = _____.

Line 11. Eleventh-year premium of_____ multiplied by 1.629 = _____.

Line 12. Twelfth-year premium of_____ multiplied by 1.551 = _____.

(Table 12–1 continued on page 182)

181

(Table 12–1 continued from page 181)
Line 13. Thirteenth-year premium of _____ multiplied by 1.477 = _____.
Line 14. Fourteenth-year premium of _____ multiplied by 1.407 = _____.
Line 15. Fifteenth-year premium of _____ multiplied by 1.340 = _____.
Line 16. Sixteenth-year premium of _____ multiplied by 1.276 = _____.
Line 17. Seventeenth-year premium of _____ multiplied by 1.215 = _____.
Line 18. Eighteenth-year premium of _____ multiplied by 1.157 = _____.
Line 19. Nineteenth-year premium of _____ multiplied by 1.102 = _____.
Line 20. Twentieth-year premium of _____ multiplied by 1.050 = _____.
Line 21. Add up your figures from Line 1 through Line 20. The total = _____.

The total for Step 1 is the number entered on Line 21: _____.
It represents your accumulated premiums at 5 percent.

Step 2. If your policy is a participating policy, you also need information on illustrated dividends. At the time you bought the policy, you may have been provided with a table of illustrated dividends. If you still have the table it may be possible to use it for Step 2, but chances are it's out of date and incomplete. Your calculations would be more accurate if you asked the company for an illustration of dividends for the next twenty years. CU warns that the information will not be easy to get. But we know of no other way you can make the calculations you should do for a rational comparison. Be persistent. If you obtain the necessary dividend figures, accumulate them much as you did the premiums.

Line 1. First-year dividend of _____ multiplied by 2.527 = _____.

Line 2. Second-year dividend of _____ multiplied by 2.407 = _____.

Line 3. Third-year dividend of _____ multiplied by 2.292 = _____.

Line 4. Fourth-year dividend of _____ multiplied by 2.183 = _____.

Line 5. Fifth-year dividend of _____ multiplied by 2.079 = _____.

Line 6. Sixth-year dividend of _____ multiplied by 1.980 = _____.

Line 7. Seventh-year dividend of _____ multiplied by 1.885 = _____.

Line 8. Eighth-year dividend of _____ multiplied by 1.796 = _____.

Line 9. Ninth-year dividend of _____ multiplied by 1.710 = _____.

Line 10. Tenth-year dividend of _____ multiplied by 1.629 = _____.

Line 11. Eleventh-year dividend of _____ multiplied by 1.551 = _____.

Line 12. Twelfth-year dividend of _____ multiplied by 1.477 = _____.

Line 13. Thirteenth-year dividend of _____ multiplied by 1.407 = _____.

Line 14. Fourteenth-year dividend of _____ multiplied by 1.340 = _____.

Line 15. Fifteenth-year dividend of _____ multiplied by 1.276 = _____.

Line 16. Sixteenth-year dividend of _____ multiplied by 1.215 = _____.

Line 17. Seventeenth-year dividend of _____ multiplied by 1.157 = _____.

Line 18. Eighteenth-year dividend of _____ multiplied by 1.102 = _____.

Line 19. Nineteenth-year dividend of _____ multiplied by 1.050 = _____.

(Table 12–1 continued on page 184)

(Table 12–1 continued from page 183)

Line 20. Twentieth-year dividend of _____ multiplied by
1.000 = _____.

Line 21. Add up your figures from Line 1 through Line 20.
The total = _____.

The total for Step 2 is the number entered on Line 21: _____.
It represents your accumulated dividends at 5 percent.

Step 3. Using the cash value figures stated in the policy (and terminal dividend, if any), complete the following calculations:

Line 1. Enter the current cash value, if any (plus the terminal dividend, if any), of the policy: _____.

Line 2. Multiply amount from Line 1 by 2.653: _____.

Line 3. Enter the cash value, if any (plus the terminal dividend, if any), that the policy will have in twenty years: _____.

Line 4. Subtract Line 2 from Line 3 and enter the difference (if any), which represents the interest-adjusted increase in cash value over the next twenty years: _____.

The total for Step 3 is the number entered on Line 4: _____.
It represents the interest-adjusted increase in cash value.

Step 4. To calculate the interest-adjusted net cost index (for twenty years at 5 percent), proceed as follows. Let P be the total of accumulated premiums, which is the total for Step 1. P = _____.
Let D be the total of accumulated dividends, which is the total for Step 2. D = _____. Let C be the interest-adjusted increase in cash value (if any), which is the total for Step 3. C = _____.
The interest-adjusted net cost index is: $\dfrac{(P\text{-}D)\text{-}C}{34.719}$.

Step 4, then, provides the twenty-year interest-adjusted net cost index on the policy under analysis: _____. (If you wish to have the index expressed per $1,000 of coverage, divide the figure for Step 4 by the number of thousands of dollars in the face amount of the policy.)

(Text continued from page 180)
replacement unless the price advantage is substantial. In a few cases, nonprice considerations—better options, for example—may make a switch to a new policy, even if more costly, advantageous.

The four basic types of replacements are: (1) replacing one term policy with another; (2) replacing a term policy with a cash value policy; (3) replacing one cash value policy with another; and (4) replacing a cash value with a term policy. If you do decide on a replacement policy—no matter which type—remember not to drop the old policy until the new one is in force.

Replacing term with term. Replacing one term policy with another is less complex than the other alternatives. In doing so, you aren't concerned with any long-term buildup of cash values. The comparative costs of the two policies can be fairly well established by looking at the twenty-year interest-adjusted indexes. If the proposed replacement appears to be much less costly than your current policy, you should certainly consider a switch. (The advice in this paragraph does not apply to those rare long-duration term policies that have a cash value.)

Replacing term with cash value. Replacing a term policy with a cash value policy can normally be done through the term policy's conversion clause. But, if you've decided you want cash value insurance, the company that issued your term policy may not offer the best buy in a cash value policy. To help find out, ask the agent or company for the interest-adjusted index for the cash value policy you would obtain by converting your term policy. Then compare that index with the indexes for other cash value products available to you, keeping in mind CU's suggestion that differences of less than

10 percent be disregarded. If the company declines to assist you or takes an inordinately long time to comply with your request, you can go back to Table 12–1 and attempt the analysis yourself. You may still have to rely on your company to provide you with new figures for dividends or cash value. If the company refuses to provide you with even this limited information, CU suggests you write your state insurance department (see Appendix III) to complain.

Based on CU's thinking about the relative merits of term and cash value, there are three reasons why you might consider it advantageous to switch from term to cash value. One would be that you have entered a higher tax bracket and are interested in a tax shelter. Should that be the case, you and your beneficiaries may be enjoying a higher standard of living than you had when you purchased the term policy. Thus, you might want to add insurance—perhaps a cash value policy in addition to your existing term coverage. But if your coverage needs are not affected by the change in tax bracket, then a switch might be appropriate.

Another reason for switching from term to cash value might be that you have decided you really need forced savings and that you consider a cash value insurance policy to be the best available forced savings vehicle for you. If that should be the case, be sure you plan to keep the new policy in force for the long haul. As Chapter 17 shows, rates of return on most cash value policies are low until they've been in force for at least twenty years or so.

A third reason for switching to cash value coverage might be that you now perceive you'll have a need for insurance coverage past the age when your term policy will end. In this situation, your choices are to convert your existing coverage to cash value insurance or to buy a new cash value policy. (You might also consider buying a new term policy—replacing term with term—renewable to an advanced age.) If you decide to convert, check to see whether you have a choice between original age conversion and attained age conversion. (These alternatives are described in some detail in Chapter 11.)

Replacing a term policy with a cash value policy will result in an increase in your annual premiums for some years to come. So make sure the switch to cash value still allows you to give your family adequate insurance protection without unduly straining the family budget. If you can do this, and have a reason for wanting cash value coverage, go ahead—but proceed cautiously. A new policy would have to be chosen with great care, since cash value policies vary more widely in cost than term policies do.

Replacing cash value with cash value. The classic objections to replacement strike with particular force if you're contemplating replacing one cash value policy with another. You'd have to pay another hefty front-end load. And you're older, so your new premium would probably be higher. Still, if your current whole life or other cash value policy is high in cost, and if the proposed replacement is low in cost and provides equal or better coverage, the switch could be worthwhile. Such a situation is most likely to arise with policies issued quite a few years ago, especially nonparticipating policies.

Replacing cash value with term. Since CU recommends term insurance for most buyers, you might think we'd be all in favor of replacing cash value policies with term policies. Not necessarily so. Once you've bought a cash value policy, assuming it was a reasonably good one, it often pays to hold on to the policy. In effect, the company amortizes its front-end load during the early years of the policy's life. So, it will take some time before cash values and dividends begin to accumulate to the point of compensating for the sizable premiums you've already paid out. If you switch the policy soon after purchase, you risk taking a substantial loss. If you've already paid in for a number of years, you might be approaching a time when dividends and cash value buildup start to justify your substantial investment. In other words, don't pay for the meal and then leave before the main course.

There are two exceptions to this general advice. First, some cash value policies are poor investments. With these policies you may well be considerably better off buying term insurance and investing the difference you save on the lower premiums. If you want to make a calculation to test this point, you can use a procedure for doing so that is shown in Appendix II.

A second exception: You may need to replace a cash value policy, even though it means taking a loss, if you simply can't afford the annual outlay the policy requires. Sometimes, the situation can be salvaged by borrowing against the cash value of the existing policy to help pay the premiums and then purchasing supplementary term coverage. This can be done only if sufficient cash value has accumulated in the existing policy. If that solution is not feasible, CU suggests you replace the cash value policy with a renewable term policy.

In any decision you make about replacement that involves cash value, remember not to focus exclusively on net cost, but to consider net payment as well. Net cost, as we note in Chapter 7, measures the cost if you surrender a policy. Net payment measures the cost if you continue to hold it, or if you die while holding it. For term policies, the two are the same. But for cash value policies, there's a substantial difference between the two. To calculate net payment, use Table 12–1, omitting Step 3 and reformulating Step 4 accordingly:

$$\frac{(P-D)}{34.719}.$$

Let us emphasize that you should never drop a policy (assuming you need insurance protection) until the new policy is paid for, in force, and delivered to you. Otherwise, you could be left without coverage.

A few other cautions are also in order. Don't forget to check out the financial stability of the company you might switch to (see page 109). Compare the language of both policies as we suggest in Chapter 11, to make sure the difference in cost isn't accompanied by a diminution in the quality of the contract. Take into consideration the kind of agent service you've been getting. Discuss the proposed switch with the agent for your existing policy as well as with the one for the policy you're actively considering. After you've done all that, and you still are convinced the switch is in your interest, go ahead and make the switch.

Demystifying the Life Insurance Marketplace

The primary aim of this book is to help consumers plan and buy the life insurance protection they need. For many, the process is complex and complicated. Despite Consumers Union's best efforts to clarify and simplify in this book, figuring out the right answers remains difficult. Indeed, it's sometimes difficult even to know the right questions to ask. CU believes the life insurance marketplace could benefit from demystification. For a purchase so vitally important to so many people, there should be an easier way.

Legislation has not yet provided adequate answers. Extending over almost a century, a series of laws including the McCarran-Ferguson Act of 1944 have eschewed federal involvement and reserved to the states the responsibility for regulating the life insurance industry. Thus, it is the state insurance departments and their commissioners (some states call them by other titles) that have been responsible for helping consumers with the complexities and complications of the life insurance marketplace. How well are the states doing their job?

Not very well, according to a 1979 report on state regulation of the insurance industry, published by the General Accounting Office. The GAO report said there were "serious shortcomings in State laws and regulatory activities" designed to protect insurance consumers. CU agrees—and we assume a number of readers of this book will also agree.

The GAO report criticized the state insurance departments for failing to maintain independence from the industry they are supposed to be regulating. It noted that the state insurance departments had failed to maintain "an arms-length relationship between the regulators and the regulated," and that a "common and longstanding criticism of insurance departments is that they are overly responsive to the insurance industry at the expense of its consumers."

The Wall Street Journal put it more succinctly in 1973 in a front-page article headlined: "The States' Regulation of Insurance Companies Often Viewed as Farce." According to the article, the number of people staffing the state insurance departments about doubled from 1945 to 1973. Over that same period, however, there was a fourfold increase in one area of the departments' jurisdiction—the number of life insurance companies. And these companies experienced a tenfold increase in the dollar amount of life insurance sold.

"We have two kinds of people," one regulator told the newspaper, "youngsters who don't know what they're doing yet and who will go to work in the industry just as soon as they learn, and older guys who have come here to retire and draw a paycheck at the same time."

Apparently, the situation didn't improve much after 1973. Understaffing and underfunding continued to be problems emphasized by the 1979 GAO report. "In general," the report said, "the number of individuals on insurance department staffs with relevant professional training is small, departments spend little to upgrade staff skills, and salary levels are low in relation to the salaries of similar professionals elsewhere."

Not surprisingly, many insurance department employees either come from the insurance industry or go into it after serving in the insurance department. The phrase commonly used by critics to describe the process is "the revolving door." Where there is a revolving door —and the phenomenon is by no means limited to regulation of the insurance industry—CU believes there may be a subtle influence on regulators' attitudes and ways of thinking. (In late 1979, CU completed a survey to determine the whereabouts of the fifty state insurance commissioners who were the immediate predecessors of the incumbents. In all, CU learned that nineteen previous state commissioners had found employment in the insurance industry after leaving office.)

Historically, when regulators are too comfortable with those they are assigned to regulate, it is the consumer who inevitably is the loser. CU believes that there is enough evidence of deficiency in state regulation of the insurance industry to justify at the least the holding of Congressional hearings to consider a possible repeal or modification of the McCarran-Ferguson Act, thus allowing the federal government to intervene. One insurance executive, asked if he would prefer state or federal regulation, replied, "Would you rather be regulated by fifty monkeys or by King Kong?" Perhaps there's no perfect solution, but CU thinks the question of jurisdiction over the insurance industry deserves the spotlight of public attention.

The staff of the Federal Trade Commission in 1979 criticized cost disclosure practices of the life insurance industry. In January 1980, President Carter commended to the state governors the model state regulation prepared by the FTC, which was "designed to provide meaningful disclosure of life insurance costs." President Carter commented that "Americans spend over $30 billion a year on life insurance premium payments. Yet too often, consumers lack the basic cost information they need to find the best policy at the lowest price." CU itself could hardly have summed up the consumer's quandry more clearly.

The FTC report, President Carter said, concluded that whole life insurance policies "not held to maturity pay a relatively low rate of return on their cash values, and that consumers are not getting the information they need to understand the true costs of their policies. The result is billions of dollars a year in unnecessary costs to consumers."

What Consumers Need

In CU's judgment, the greatest consumer need in life insurance is improved cost disclosure—both to buyers of new policies and to current policyholders. If the states had instituted adequate requirements in this regard, the case for federal regulation would be less powerful than it now appears.

Some progress in cost disclosure was made during the 1970s. An industry committee developed the interest-adjusted index, the National Association of Insurance Commissioners recommended its use, and, increasingly, states have adopted it. Since CU's 1974 report on life insurance, the number of states making provisions for consumers to obtain the index has grown from two to twenty-nine. (The NAIC model leaves it up to the states whether this information is to be provided automatically or only at the request of the consumer; the vast majority of states have chosen the latter.)

In states that have adopted the NAIC model, consumers are furnished—in most states, on request—with the net cost index (and for cash value policies, the net payment index as well) for both ten and twenty years. Consumers buying participating policies are furnished—in most states, on request —with the equivalent level dividend (see page 95), a figure that reveals the extent to which the cost index is based on future dividend payments.

But the NAIC model does not go far enough in meeting the needs of consumers. A number of authorities on life insurance have offered suggestions for a broader and better system of disclosure. Among them is Joseph M. Belth, professor of insurance at Indiana University. CU's seven suggestions for improving cost disclosure, summarized below, include several that have been advocated by Belth.

1. The cost-disclosure information that is now furnished only on request under the NAIC model should be furnished automatically. Purchase of a policy should not be permitted until a prospective buyer has seen the information on indexes, along with a brief and clear summary of the significance of the indexes. (The summary provided should be uniform for all companies.) The importance of cost disclosure can clearly be seen by scanning CU's Ratings in Part II. Take, for example, the case of a forty-five-year-old man buying $100,000 of participating cash value insurance. If he had bought the lowest-cost commonly available standard risk policy shown in Chapter 17 for that age and face amount (Central Life Assurance Company's "Maximum Life"), his projected cost over the next twenty years, including forgone interest at 5 percent, would have been $22,567. If he had bought the highest-cost policy (Fidelity Life Association's "Ordinary Life"), his projected cost would have been $57,043. That's a difference of more than $34,000. (Both costs are based on the calculation of the interest-adjusted net cost index and on the assumptions that the policyholder surrenders the policy after twenty years and that dividends are paid as illustrated.)

2. All policyholders should receive automatically year-by-year disclosure of the ongoing cost of their insurance protection.

3. Rate of return information for the savings component of cash value policies should be provided both at the time of sale and each year thereafter. Again, CU's Ratings in Part II illustrate the importance of this information. Consumers deal with the interest-adjusted index *only* when they're buying life insurance, a relatively rare event. CU believes that well-prepared, adequately explained rate of return information will help consumers make knowledgeable choices about life insurance policies. Certainly, buyers would appreciate at a glance the contrast between the 6.12 percent rate of return over a period of nineteen years projected by the Central Life policy and the 0.84 percent rate of return over the same period projected by the Fidelity Life policy. And they could also roughly compare the 6.12 percent, which is substantially tax-sheltered, with the rate they may be getting on other investments. (The reasons why the comparison is rough are explained in Chapter 17.)

Ongoing disclosure of the yearly rate of return would be a great help to long-time policyholders. If the yearly rate of return were very poor, they could easily recognize that fact and might then want to evaluate the pros and cons of switching policies (see Chapter 12).

4. The Annual Percentage Rate (APR) for the added cost of paying premiums on other than an annual basis should be disclosed automatically. The 81 percent of policyholders who pay other than annually have no way of knowing how much they are paying for the privilege. In 1978, Belth computed the APRs for fifteen major companies. For people who pay their premiums monthly, he found a range of from 4.9 percent to 29.3 percent.

5. For those consumers who wish the data, complete year-

by-year information concerning premiums, cash values, and dividends should be available both to prospective buyers and to longtime policyholders.

6. For those consumers who wish the data, cost indexes and other information should be available for periods longer than the traditional twenty years. The importance of this recommendation can again be illustrated by CU's Ratings in Part II. A thirty-five-year-old man who wanted to purchase $25,000 of nonparticipating cash value insurance might have considered two policies—"Preferred Executive Whole Life" from Life and Casualty Insurance Company of Tennessee, and "Executive Life Paid Up at 95" from Kansas City Life Insurance Company. Based on the twenty-year index, he would have been likely to pick the former. But with cost information going beyond the traditional twenty years, he would have probably picked the latter.

The importance of looking beyond the traditional twenty years is also shown by CU's yield figures in Chapter 17. The Ratings show that while the rate of return on the savings component of most cash value policies continues to rise as time goes on, the rate of return on some policies declines after the twentieth year.

7. Regulators should carefully scrutinize dividend practices, an area that has been little examined. As noted in the November 1976 issue of CONSUMER REPORTS, the formulas by which dividends are computed are often considered company secrets. Regulators haven't turned over many rocks to see what was underneath, but CU thinks it's time they did. The formulas may be skewed. For example, some companies selling participating policies have improved their dividend formulas on newer issues, while keeping dividend formulas unchanged on policies issued years ago. This may be grossly unfair to longtime policyholders, whose interests are being sacrificed in the rush for new business. Such older policy-

holders may never know they are being treated unfairly.

Questionable dividend practices are also of concern because they may distort the price comparisons made by current buyers. By raising dividends on recent business only (which costs the company relatively little), a company can develop attractive dividend scales for sales illustrations that may make the company look better in cost comparisons than it deserves to.

CU anticipates that insurance companies will protest that to provide broad and thorough disclosure, as outlined above, would be so expensive that the cost of insurance would have to go up. CU would be hard to convince on this point. Similar arguments were made against the interest-adjusted index in the early 1970s. Yet since that step to cost disclosure was made, cost indexes on newly sold policies have generally gone down, not up. In large part, that is an effect brought about by rising interest rates. But CU thinks increased price competition on new sales may also have played a part in the decline.

The importance of reforms in cost disclosure might be brought home to consumers by an analogy between car buyers and buyers of life insurance. Suppose that car buyers were never told the price of a car, just the monthly payment. And suppose that the monthly payment turned out to be roughly the same for most cars. It would hardly be a surprise to find many a Rolls-Royce, Mercedes-Benz, and Jaguar on the road, with rarely a Chevrolet in sight. Suppose further that what the buyers didn't know, and weren't told, was that the Rolls-Royce payments, say, were on twenty-year loans rather than three-year loans, that the Mercedes payments covered interest only, and that the Jaguar payments were for leases, not for purchases.

Absurd? Of course. And absurd is the only word to describe the way many consumers must decide which life insurance policy to buy—without full understanding of a policy's projected cost. Agents and companies rarely educate consumers on how to take advantage of what cost information there is available. And much of the insurance industry is reluctant to disclose additional cost data. Because cost information is limited, many buyers focus solely on the premium. That's how, in the life insurance industry, companies can sell as many policies at Rolls-Royce prices as at Chevrolet prices.

One wonders how consumers would react if General Motors said that it would cost too much to figure out the price of a Chevrolet, and that all the consumer really needs to know is the monthly payment.

If it weren't so serious, it might almost be funny. The life insurance industry offers a purely financial product. Yet, faced with demands to disclose in detail the price of its product, large segments of the industry are still able to duck disclosure and evade the obligation to provide comprehensive and comprehensible cost information.

Part II
Consumers Union's Ratings of Life Insurance Policies

Introduction
to CU's Ratings

To prepare the Ratings of life insurance policies that are presented in Part II, Consumers Union undertook in 1979 a comparative survey of prices in the industry. CU's insurance survey differs in significant respects from others that may be available to consumers. To begin with, it includes an unusually large number of companies. We sent a detailed questionnaire to 172 companies in the United States and Canada.* To be included, a company had to be among the 160 largest companies as determined by any of the four following measures: (1) assets, (2) individual insurance in force, (3) individual total sales in 1977, and (4) total individual premium income in 1977. A company also needed to have at least an A rating for financial stability from the A.M. Best Company, publisher of *Best's Insurance Reports.*

---

*Among these 172 companies is National Life Insurance Company (Montpelier, Vermont), which was inadvertently omitted from our 1979 survey as published in CONSUMER REPORTS in February and March 1980. Our consulting actuaries subsequently analyzed National Life's 1979 policies, however, and CU's Ratings for them are included in Part II.

201

We received 114 responses (of which 110 proved usable). Included were replies from the twenty largest United States life insurance companies and forty-six of the fifty largest as listed by *Fortune* magazine. The combined respondents represented at least 75 percent of individual life insurance sales in the United States.

As far as we know, all other cost surveys published in popular media have relied on the accuracy of the data as submitted by the companies. Unfortunately, such data are not always reliable. Indeed, our experience has taught us that it's necessary to check the accuracy of the data submitted by the companies against the insurers' own rate books—which we also asked each company to submit. CU's consulting actuaries found one or more errors in 82 percent of the returns—that is, 95 out of the 114 companies responding to our questionnaire supplied inaccurate information. The errors were painstakingly corrected through followup correspondence and telephone calls. CU saw no evidence that such errors were an attempt to improve a company's standing. More often than not, the errors made the companies look worse. They were simply clerical or technical mistakes.

Some published surveys are confined to a single age, such as thirty-five. CU developed data for three ages, twenty-five, thirty-five, and forty-five, to give buyers cost information close to their age. We also showed cost figures for two face amounts, $25,000 and $100,000.

Unlike the alphabetical guides put out by some state insurance departments and industry groups, CU ranks policies in order of projected cost, from lowest to highest.

In our 1979 cost survey, we have made what we regard as an improvement in our cost-ranking method. In 1974, we simply ranked companies according to twenty-year interest-adjusted net cost. Now, we take into account the net cost at three intervals. That gives you a better idea of how good a buy a policy would prove to be if you held it for a shorter or a longer time than the twenty-year period customarily used in such comparisons. It is unusual to be able to take long-range figures into account because they are rarely made available by the industry.

Instead of analyzing costs over the traditional ten- and twenty-year periods and the less common thirty-year span, we looked at nine-, nineteen-, and twenty-nine-year periods (in addition to the twenty-year index). Industry critics have charged that, through certain actuarial manipulations, some companies were fudging their figures to make themselves look good at the traditional ten- and twenty-year comparison points. We wanted to protect our results against such manipulation, if it existed. As it turned out, if manipulation is practiced by the companies responding to our questionnaire, our use of nontraditional comparison points was unable to uncover evidence of it. There was, however, a definite advantage in looking past the twentieth year, where policy illustrations traditionally stop. Some policies that looked attractive over a nineteen- (or twenty-) year period appeared less attractive when viewed over a twenty-nine- (or thirty-) year time span. Consumers do not regularly have such long-range cost and yield figures available, but CU believes that they ought to be made available. (In Chapter 13, we suggest regulatory changes to accomplish this.)

Normally, one would expect the yield on a cash value policy to continue rising after the twentieth year. After all, the front-end load (including agent's commission and sales costs) has almost certainly been amortized by then. Yet, CU found many cash value policies on which the twenty-nine-year yield was less than the nineteen-year yield. This finding seemed to us to be possible evidence that some companies may have specifically designed their policies to look attractive at the traditional twenty-year point. Whether such a practice constitutes manipulation CU is not prepared to say, but we think this finding deserves to be scrutinized by those charged with regulating the insurance industry.

Other things being equal, CU believes that buyers of cash value policies who are using CU's Ratings in Chapter 17 should give preference to policies listed in that chapter whose yield does not decline after the twentieth year.

In our Ratings, we accorded the greatest importance to our nineteen-year measure. The twenty-nine-year results are relatively speculative in the case of participating policies because current dividend scales extended so far into the future may not prove close to the mark. The nine-year scores were also given subordinate weight; CU believes that our readers, having made an informed purchase, will be less likely than most buyers to terminate their policies so early.

Policies Not Included in CU's Survey

The policies shown in CU's Ratings by no means constitute all the policies issued by companies included in our survey. We requested companies to submit data on all of their basic term and cash value policies, within some broad limits. (We excluded, for instance, all policies with a face amount that varied from year to year.)

After receiving the companies' submissions, we narrowed our analysis to those policies that met our criteria. For example, we included only term policies that were renewable to at least age sixty-five and convertible to at least age sixty. We included only cash value policies that endowed, or were paid up, at age eighty-five or later.

Some companies chose not to submit data on certain of their policies, although, as it turned out, some of those policies would have met our criteria. So, if you're in doubt about what policies a company offers, write to the company headquarters or ask an insurance salesperson.

Companies Not Included in CU's Survey

In 1974, CU characterized one or more policies issued by twenty-four companies as "unusually expensive." Of those companies, twenty-one were invited to participate in the 1979 survey, and thirteen did. Seven of the twenty-one companies ignored CU's original letter and followup letter and questionnaire. They were: Capitol Life Insurance Company, Equitable Life Insurance Company, Fidelity and Guaranty Life Insurance Company, Great Southern Life Insurance Company, Ohio State Life Insurance Company, Philadelphia Life Insurance Company, and Western and Southern Life Insurance Company. One company, Business Men's Assurance Company of America, declined to participate in our survey, saying it was revising its life insurance portfolio.

Among the 114 companies that did fill out CU's questionnaire, four were eventually excluded from the survey: Life Insurance Company of Georgia refused to comply with CU's request for a copy of its rate book, so we could not check the accuracy of its figures. (All the other 113 companies complied with this request and sent us rate books.) Farmers New World Life Insurance Company made errors in the data it sent us, as did most companies. But the actuaries at Farmers were too "overloaded" to help correct the errors. Puritan Life Insurance Company completed only a small part of the questionnaire.

Connecticut Savings Bank Life Insurance was not included because state laws limit the size of its policies to less than $25,000—the minimum face amount used in CU's survey. (In Massachusetts and New York, the regulations concerning savings bank life insurance permit policies somewhat larger than $25,000.)

CU's Ratings
of Term Policies

The tables in this chapter show comparative cost index Ratings for 199 term policies evaluated by Consumers Union in 1979. These policies are renewable to at least age sixty-five and convertible to at least age sixty. Twelve tables cover combinations of age (twenty-five, thirty-five, and forty-five), and face amount ($25,000 and $100,000), with and without dividends (par and nonpar). To make best use of the tables, select the one closest to your situation.

The twenty-year interest-adjusted net cost index is included in all tables because comparable indexes on policies you're considering should be readily available to you. Thus, the tables can be used to compare the indexes of policies you're offered with the indexes in CU's Ratings. Remember that the difference between a high-cost and a low-cost policy can mean thousands of dollars to you.

The Ratings give, in addition to the cost index, the first year's premium for each policy. Note that the rates shown in the tables are for males. Rates for females are generally lower at all ages, because women as a group live longer than men. Traditionally, insurance surveys have covered only men because men bought most policies. That is changing, but men still account for about 75 percent of sales.

You may find you're charged a different premium from the one shown in our Ratings for other reasons.

■ The tables show 1979 rates, and rates can change. Recently, most rate changes have been downward.

■ Our actuaries adjusted some premiums to account for the fact that some companies calculate your age based on your nearest birthday, while others use your last birthday.

■ The tables show annual premiums; if you pay more frequently, the total premiums for the year are higher.

■ Premiums and indexes shown in CU's tables all include waiver of premium in the event of disability. In some policies, the waiver was standard and its cost was automatically included in the premium. It was easier to add the cost of the waiver for policies that didn't include it than to subtract its cost from policies that did.

Ratings order was determined as follows: Policies were grouped by their performance on the nineteen-year interest-adjusted net cost index. Within these groups, they were ranked according to their performances over nine years and twenty-nine years, weighted equally. Ties were broken by listing tied policies in order of increasing twenty-year interest-adjusted index. Remaining ties were broken by listing policies according to the amount of the initial premium.

Some policies are available only to people in certain groups, geographic areas, or occupations. Restrictions on availability are recorded in the footnotes to the Ratings.

The tables are a guide to—but not a substitute for—comparison shopping. In light of variations in policy language and other nonprice factors and, on par policies, of uncertainty of dividend illustrations, CU suggests you give little weight to differences of less than 10 percent in the cost index.

Term Insurance Policies
Type: Nonparticipating   Amount: $25,000   Age: 25

Listed in order of increasing cost, based primarily on 19-year cost index (see p. 207). All are men's policies; rates for women are generally lower. All are renewable to at least age 65, and convertible to at least age 60. If a company has several listings, check length of term or see Notes. Abbreviations include LIC (Life Insurance Co.), and LAC (Life Assurance Co.). All data are based on 1979 rates and include waiver of premium in event of disability.

Best ● ◑ ○ ● Worst

Company	Term (years)	Initial premium	20-year	Cost Indexes 9-year	19-year	29-year	Notes
Old Line LIC of America	5	$68	$ 84	●	●	●	
Sun LIC of America	1	76	87	●	●	●	
Continental Assurance Co.	1	73	88	●	●	●	
Provident Life & Accident Ins. Co.	1	76	89	●	●	●	
Provident Life & Accident Ins. Co.	5	77	90	●	●	●	
IDS LIC	1	78	90	●	●	●	
Southwestern LIC	1	72	92	●	●	●	
Beneficial LIC	1	77	92	●	●	●	
Columbus Mutual LIC	1	82	92	●	●	●	
Safeco LIC	1	76	93	●	●	●	
Southwestern LIC	5	76	93	●	●	●	
Connecticut General LIC	1	79	93	●	●	●	
Monarch LIC	5	79	93	◑	●	◑	
Security-Connecticut LIC	5	88	95	◑	◑	◑	
United Investors LIC	1	82	96	●	◑	◑	

Company			Rating 1	Rating 2	Rating 3
J.C. Penney LIC	1	79	98	◑	◑	●
Lincoln National LIC	5	87	97	◑	◑	◑
Lincoln National LIC	1	87	98	◑	◑	◑
Colonial LIC of America	5	89	98	◑	◑	◑ (B)
Security-Connecticut LIC	1	88	99	◑	◑	◑
Standard Ins. Co.	5	88	99	◑	◑	◑
American States LIC	3	90	99	◑	◑	◑
First Colony LIC	1	82	100	◑	◑	◑
North American Co. for Life & Health Ins.	1	83	100	◑	◑	◑
North American Co. for Life & Health Ins.	5	84	100	◑	◑	◑
All American Life & Casualty Co.	5	87	100	◑	◑	◑
U.S. LIC in the City of N.Y.	5	87	100	◑	◑	◑
Jefferson Standard LIC	5	86	101	◑	◑	◑
Federal Kemper Life Assurance Soc.	1	87	101	◑	◑	◑
Federal Kemper Life Assurance Soc.	5	89	101	◑	◑	◑
Dominion LAC	5	91	101	◑	◑	◑
Security Life & Accident Co.	5	89	102	◑	◑	◑
Dominion LAC	1	91	103	◑	◑	◑
Life & Casualty Ins. Co. of Tenn.	1	85	104	◑	◑	◑
Imperial LAC of Canada	5	93	106	◑	◑	◑
Northwestern National LIC	5	94	107	◑	◑	◑
IDS LIC	5	92	105	○	◑	◑
Farm Bureau (Iowa)	5	96	106	◑	◑	◑
Kansas City LIC	5	93	107	○	◑	◑
Great-West LAC	5	99	107	○	◑	◑
Home Beneficial LIC	5	95	107	○	◑	○

A – Available only to "preferred risks."
B – Available only to nonsmokers.
C – Available only in Massachusetts.
D – Available only in New York.
E – Available only to Lutherans.
F – Available only to people in certain jobs.
G – Available only to members of a fraternal organization.

Ratings of Term Policies (Nonpar/$25,000/25 Years) *continued*

Company	Term (years)	Initial premium	20-year	Cost Indexes			Notes
				9-year	19-year	29-year	
Occidental LIC of California	1	$95	$110	○	○	○	
Colonial LIC of America	5	96	110	○	○	○	
Travelers Ins. Co.	5	98	110	○	○	○	
Hartford LIC	5	97	111	○	○	○	
National LAC of Canada	1	100	112	○	○	○	
National LAC of Canada	5	100	112	○	○	○	
Sun LAC of Canada	5	101	112	○	○	○	
Life & Casualty Ins. Co. of Tenn.	5	94	113	○	○	○	
North American LAC	5	100	113	○	○	○	
Connecticut General LIC	5	104	113	○	○	○	
Safeco LIC	5	100	114	○	○	○	
National Life & Accident Ins. Co.	5	96	115	○	○	○	A
Liberty LIC	5	98	115	○	○	○	
Aetna LIC	1	101	115	○	○	○	
Manufacturers LIC	1	104	115	○	○	○	
Aetna LIC	5	106	115	○	○	○	
Allstate LIC	6	100	118	○	○	○	
Equitable LIC of Iowa	5	107	118	○	○	○	
J.C. Penney LIC	5	102	121	◑	○	○	
United Benefit LIC	5	105	121	◑	○	○	
Fireman's Fund American LIC	5	110	120	●	◑	○	
Canada LAC	1	111	123	●	●	○	
Canada LAC	5	112	123	◑	◑	○	
Fidelity Union LIC	5	104	125	○	◑	◑	

Company	Term (years)	Initial premium	20-year	9-year	19-year	29-year
Anchor National LIC	1	111	126	◐	◐	○
Southland LIC	5	108	127	◑	◑	◑
Anchor National LIC	5	114	129	◑	◑	◑
Midland National LIC	5	113	132	◐	◐	◐
American National Ins. Co.	5	115	132	◑	◑	◑
Commonwealth LIC	5	119	135	◑	◑	◑
Franklin LIC	5	122	137	◑	◑	◑
Bankers Life & Casualty Co.	5	122	139	●	●	●
Monumental LIC	5	128	143	●	●	●
Nationwide LIC	5	126	144	●	●	●

Type: Nonparticipating   Amount: $25,000   Age: 35

Listed in order of increasing cost, based primarily on 19-year cost index (see p. 207). All are men's policies; rates for women are generally lower. All are renewable to at least age 65, and convertible to at least age 60. If a company has several listings, check length of term or see Notes. Abbreviations include LIC (Life Insurance Co.) and LAC (Life Assurance Co.). All data are based on 1979 rates and include waiver of premium in event of disability.

Best ●   ◐   ○   ◑   ● Worst

Company	Term (years)	Initial premium	20-year	Cost Indexes 9-year	19-year	29-year	Notes
Sun LIC of America	1	$82	$143	●	●	●	
Security-Connecticut LIC	5	95	147	●	●	●	

A – Available only to "preferred risks."
B – Available only to nonsmokers.
C – Available only in Massachusetts.
D – Available only in New York.
E – Available only to Lutherans.
F – Available only to people in certain jobs.
G – Available only to members of a fraternal organization.

Ratings of Term Policies (Nonpar/$25,000/35 Years) *continued*

Company	Term (years)	Initial premium	20-year	Cost Indexes			Notes
				9-year	19-year	29-year	
Columbus Mutual LIC	1	$ 85	$148	●	●	●	
IDS LIC	1	87	149	●	●	●	
Provident Life & Accident Ins. Co.	1	87	150	●	●	●	
Continental Assurance Co.	1	86	151	◕	◕	◕	
Provident Life & Accident Ins. Co.	5	94	151	●	●	◕	
Old Line LIC of America	5	91	152	●	●	◕	
Connecticut General LIC	1	89	156	●	◕	◐	
Safeco LIC	1	91	159	◕	◐	◐	
Beneficial LIC	1	89	160	◐	◐	◐	
Colonial LIC of America	5	103	156	◐	◐	◐	B
Security-Connecticut LIC	1	95	159	◐	◐	◐	
Standard Ins. Co.	5	100	160	◐	◐	◐	
Southwestern LIC	1	90	161	◐	◐	◐	
Southwestern LIC	5	99	161	◐	◐	◐	
American States LIC	3	100	161	◐	◐	◐	
United Investors LIC	1	93	162	◐	◐	◐	
J.C. Penney LIC	1	95	163	◐	◐	◐	
Monarch LIC	5	98	163	◐	◐	◐	
Farm Bureau (Iowa)	5	107	163	◐	◐	◐	
Lincoln National LIC	1	92	164	◐	◐	◐	
Lincoln National LIC	5	99	164	◔	◐	◐	
Federal Kemper Life Assurance Soc.	5	104	164	◔	◐	◐	
Dominion LAC	5	106	164	◔	◔	◐	
Great-West LAC	5	107	164	◔	◔	◐	

Dominion LAC	1	101	465	◐	◐	●	●
Federal Kemper Life Assurance Soc.	1	95	167	○	●	○	○
All American Life & Casualty Co.	5	103	168	◐	◐	◐	○
U.S. LIC in the City of N.Y.	5	103	168	●	◐	●	○
First Colony LIC	1	95	169	●	○	●	○
Jefferson Standard LIC	5	105	169	◐	●	●	○
Security Life & Accident Co.	5	107	170	◐	◐	●	○
Imperial LAC of Canada	5	110	171	◐	●	●	◐
Life & Casualty Ins. Co. of Tenn.	1	101	173	●	●	◐	●
Manufacturers LIC	1	112	169	○	◐	●	●
Northwestern National LIC	5	110	171	○	○	●	◐
North American Co. for Life & Health Ins.	1	97	174	◐	●	◐	○
North American Co. for Life & Health Ins.	5	105	174	◐	●	◐	○
IDS LIC	5	109	174	○	○	◐	○
Home Beneficial LIC	5	108	177	○	○	○	○
Kansas City LIC	5	112	177	○	○	○	○
North American LAC	5	117	177	○	○	○	○
National LAC of Canada	1	109	178	○	○	○	○
National LAC of Canada	5	116	178	○	○	○	○
Occidental LIC of California	1	111	179	○	○	○	○
Aetna LIC	5	112	179	○	○	○	○
Safeco LIC	5	118	179	○	○	○	○
Colonial LIC of America	5	119	180	○	○	○	○
Sun LAC of Canada	5	115	181	○	○	○	○
Travelers Ins. Co.	5	117	183	○	○	○	○
Connecticut General LIC	5	124	183	○	○	○	○

A – Available only to "preferred risks."
B – Available only to nonsmokers.
C – Available only in Massachusetts.

D – Available only in New York.
E – Available only to Lutherans.
F – Available only to people in certain jobs.

G – Available only to members of a fraternal organization.

Ratings of Term Policies (Nonpar/$25,000/35 Years) *continued*

Company	Term (years)	Initial premium	20-year	Cost Indexes			Notes
				9-year	19-year	29-year	
Aetna LIC	1	$109	$185	○	○	○	
Hartford LIC	5	117	185	○	○	○	
Canada LAC	1	118	186	○	○	○	
Fireman's Fund American LIC	5	123	186	○	○	○	
Liberty LIC	5	122	188	○	○	○	
National Life & Accident Ins. Co.	5	123	188	○	○	○	A
Equitable LIC of Iowa	5	127	188	○	○	○	
Canada LAC	5	129	189	○	○	○	
United Benefit LIC	5	126	191	○	○	○	
Anchor National LIC	1	120	192	○	○	○	
Life & Casualty Ins. Co. of Tenn.	5	121	194	○	◐	○	
J.C. Penney LIC	5	125	197	○	◐	○	
Southland LIC	5	136	200	◐	◐	○	
Allstate LIC	6	118	204	○	◐	◐	
Bankers Life & Casualty Co.	5	152	204	◐	◐	○	
Fidelity Union LIC	5	133	205	◐	◐	○	
Anchor National LIC	5	132	206	◐	◐	◐	
Commonwealth LIC	5	139	206	◐	◐	◐	
American National Ins. Co.	5	138	207	◐	◐	◐	
Midland National LIC	5	135	211	◐	◐	◐	
Franklin LIC	5	149	217	●	◐	◐	
Monumental LIC	5	146	221	●	◐	◐	
Nationwide LIC	5	149	225	●	◐	◐	

Type: Nonparticipating   Amount: $25,000   Age: 45

Listed in order of increasing cost, based primarily on 19-year cost index (see p. 207). All are men's policies; rates for women are generally lower. All are renewable to at least age 65 and convertible to at least age 60. The 29-year cost index has not been calculated for policies issued at age 45 because most policies are not renewable after the age of 65 or 70. If a company has several listings, check length of term or see Notes. Abbreviations include LIC (Life Insurance Co.) and LAC (Life Assurance Co.). All data are based on 1979 rates and include waiver of premium in event of disability.

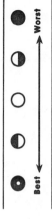

Best ● ◐ ○ ◑ ● Worst

Company	Term (years)	Initial premium	Cost Indexes 20-year	Cost Indexes 9-year	Cost Indexes 19-year	Notes
Sun LIC of America	1	$145	$310			
Security-Connecticut LIC	5	183	315			
IDS LIC	1	154	323			
Provident Life & Accident Ins. Co.	1	154	325			
Provident Life & Accident Ins. Co.	5	182	329			
Continental Assurance Co.	1	152	331			
Manufacturers LIC	1	171	333			
Columbus Mutual LIC	1	150	344			
Old Line LIC of America	5	186	337			
Farm Bureau (Iowa)	5	197	339			
Safeco LIC	1	156	341			
J.C. Penney LIC	1	169	341			

A – Available only in New York.
B – Available only to nonsmokers.
C – Available only in Massachusetts.
D – Available only to "preferred risks."
E – Available only to Lutherans.
F – Available only to people in certain jobs.
G – Available only to members of a fraternal organization.

Ratings of Term Policies (Nonpar/$25,000/45 Years) continued

Company	Term (years)	Initial premium	20-year	Cost Indexes 9-year	19-year	Notes
Southwestern LIC	1	$166	$342	◕	◑	
Standard Ins. Co.	5	190	345	◕	◑	
Great-West LAC	5	192	345	◕	◕	
Connecticut General LIC	1	162	346	◕	◑	
Dominion LAC	5	195	349	◕	◑	
Beneficial LIC	1	162	351	◕	◑	
American States LIC	3	187	351	◕	◑	
Southwestern LIC	5	192	352	◑	◑	
Security-Connecticut LIC	1	157	353	◕	◕	
United Investors LIC	1	163	356	◕	◑	
Dominion LAC	1	167	357	◕	◕	
First Colony LIC	1	170	363	◕	◑	
Northwestern National LIC	5	201	365	◕	◑	
Jefferson Standard LIC	5	199	368	◑	◑	
Monarch LIC	5	202	368	◕	◑	
Federal Kemper Life Assurance Soc.	1	170	370	◕	◑	
Life & Casualty Ins. Co. of Tenn.	1	178	370	◕	◑	
Imperial LAC of Canada	5	199	372	◕	◑	
Colonial LIC of America	5	194	373	◕	◑	B
Federal Kemper Life Assurance Soc.	5	194	373	◕	◑	
Security Life & Accident Co.	5	201	373	◕	◑	
All American Life & Casualty Co.	5	202	374	◑	◑	
U.S. LIC in the City of N.Y.	5	202	374	◑	◑	
Lincoln National LIC	1	166	382	◑	◑	

Safeco LIC	5	212		●
IDS LIC	5	209		●
National LAC of Canada	1	177		◐
Lincoln National LIC	5	195	●	○
North American LAC	5	206	●	○
National LAC of Canada	5	207	◐	○
Connecticut General LIC	5	219	○	○
Anchor National LIC	1	194	○	○
Kansas City LIC	5	209	○	○
Fireman's Fund American LIC	5	218	○	○
Occidental LIC of California	1	178	○	○
Canada LAC	5	227	○	○
Aetna LIC	1	190	○	○
Canada LAC	1	189	○	○
Occidental LIC of California	5	215	○	○
Sun LAC of Canada	5	219	○	○
Home Beneficial LIC	5	215	○	○
J.C. Penney LIC	5	236	○	○
Bankers Life & Casualty Co.	5	243	○	○
National Life & Accident Ins. Co.	5	220	○ A	○
United Benefit LIC	5	223	○	○
Travelers Ins. Co.	5	223	○	○
North American Co. for Life & Health Ins.	1	176	○	○
North.American Co. for Life & Health Ins.	5	208	○	○
Aetna LIC	5	211	○	○
Hartford LIC	5	218	○	○

A – Available only in New York.
B – Available only to Lutherans.
C – Available only in Massachusetts.
D – Available only to "preferred risks."
E – Available only to nonsmokers.
F – Available only to people in certain jobs.
G – Available only to members of a fraternal organization.

Ratings of Term Policies (Nonpar/$25,000/45 Years) *continued*

Company	Term (years)	Initial premium	Cost Indexes 20-year	Cost Indexes 9-year	Cost Indexes 19-year	Notes
Southland LIC	5	$231	$405	○	○	
Equitable LIC of Iowa	5	226	406	○	○	
Liberty LIC	5	220	407	○	○	
Colonial LIC of America	5	223	414	○	○	
Life & Casualty Ins. Co. of Tenn.	5	234	417	○	○	
Fidelity Union LIC	5	240	410	◐	○	
Commonwealth LIC	5	240	414	◐	○	
American National Ins. Co.	5	240	422	◐	○	
Midland National LIC	5	250	423	◐	○	
Nationwide LIC	5	265	441	◐	◐	
Franklin LIC	5	266	442	◐	◐	
Monumental LIC	5	263	443	◐	◐	
Allstate LIC	6	241	444	◐	◐	

Type: Participating   Amount: $25,000   Age: 25

Listed in order of increasing cost, based primarily on 19-year cost index (see p. 207). All are men's policies; rates for women are generally lower. All are renewable to at least age 65, and convertible to at least age 60. If a company has several listings, check length of term or see Notes. Abbreviations include LIC (Life Insurance Co.) and LAC (Life Assurance Co.). All data are based on 1979 rates and include waiver of premium in event of disability.

Best ● ◐ ○ ◑ ● → Worst

Cost Indexes

Company	Term (years)	Initial premium	20-year	9-year	19-year	29-year	Notes
Massachusetts SBLI	5	$ 52	$54	●	●	●	C
Teachers Ins. & Annuity Assoc. of America	5	65	55	●	●	●	F
New York SBLI	5	76	78	◐	◐	●	D
USAA LIC	5	92	79	◐	◐	●	F
New England Mutual LIC	5	75	80	◐	◐	●	A
Prudential Ins. Co. of America	5	95	81	◐	◐	●	
Penn Mutual LIC	1	76	87	◐	◐	◐	B
Pan-American LIC	1	70	88	◐	◐	◐	A
Home LIC	5	96	89	◐	◐	◐	
Aid Association for Lutherans	1	81	91	◐	◐	◐	E
State Farm LIC	5	86	91	◐	◐	◐	
Penn Mutual LIC	1	77	92	◐	◐	◐	
Manhattan LIC	5	78	92	◐	◐	◐	A
Woodmen of the World Life Ins. Soc.	5	90	92	●	◐	◐	G
Confederation LIC	1	82	93	●	◐	◐	
State Mutual LAC of America	5	104	91	○	◐	◐	B
New England Mutual LIC	5	84	92	◐	◐	◐	
Metropolitan LIC	5	110	87	◐	◐	○	
Acacia Mutual LIC	5	86	95	◐	◐	◐	B
Security Benefit LIC	5	86	97	○	○	◐	
Confederation LIC	5	86	97	○	○	○	
State Mutual LAC of America	5	105	97	○	○	○	

A – Available only to "preferred risks."
B – Available only to nonsmokers.
C – Available only in Massachusetts.
D – Available only in New York.
E – Available only to Lutherans.
F – Available only to people in certain jobs.
G – Available only to members of a fraternal organization.

Ratings of Term Policies (Par/$25,000/25 Years) *continued*

Company	Term (years)	Initial premium	20-year	Cost Indexes 9-year	19-year	29-year	Notes
New York LIC	5	$ 95	$ 98	○	○	○	
Union Central LIC	5	113	98	○	○	○	
National LIC	5	107	99	◑	◑	◑	B
Lutheran Mutual LIC	5	110	99	○	○	○	
Minnesota Mutual LIC	1	81	100	○	○	○	
Mutual LIC of New York	5	98	100	○	○	○	
Mutual Benefit LIC	1	108	100	○	○	○	
Manhattan LIC	5	84	100	○	○	◑	
Massachusetts Mutual LIC	5	117	101	◑	○	○	
Acacia Mutual LIC	5	92	103	○	○	◑	
National LIC	5	108	102	◑	◑	◑	
Pan-American LIC	5	88	104	○	◑	●	A
Connecticut Mutual LIC	5	101	104	◑	◑	●	
Knights of Columbus	5	108	104	◑	◑	◑	G
Connecticut Mutual LIC	1	95	105	◑	◑	◑	
Union Mutual LIC	5	134	105	◑	◑	◑	
Equitable Life Assurance Soc. of the U.S.	5	94	107	◑	◑	◑	
American Family LIC	5	101	107	◑	●	●	
Pacific Mutual LIC	5	105	108	◑	◑	●	
Phoenix Mutual LIC	5	97	110	◑	●	●	B
Guardian LIC of America	5	111	111	●	●	●	A
Mutual Trust LIC	5	116	111	◑	●	●	
Ohio National LIC	5	110	112	◑	◑	●	

Company	Term (years)	Initial premium	20-year		Cost Indexes		Notes
				9-year	19-year	29-year	
Phoenix Mutual LIC	5	100	113		◐	◐	◐	
Bankers Life Co.	5	106	113		◐	◐	◐	
Guardian LIC of America	5	115	116		◐	◐	◐	
Indianapolis LIC	5	113	118		◐	◐	◐	

Type: Participating   Amount: $25,000   Age: 35

Listed in order of increasing cost, based primarily on 19-year cost index (see p. 207). All are men's policies; rates for women are generally lower. All are renewable to at least age 65, and convertible to at least age 60. If a company has several listings, check length of term or see Notes. Abbreviations include LIC (Life Insurance Co.) and LAC (Life Assurance Co.). All data are based on 1979 rates and include waiver of premium in event of disability.

Best ● ◐ ○ ◐ ● Worst

Company	Term (years)	Initial premium	20-year	Cost Indexes			Notes
				9-year	19-year	29-year	
Massachusetts SBLI	5	$ 62	$ 95	●	●	●	C
Teachers Ins. & Annuity Assoc. of America	5	93	104	●	●	●	F
Prudential Ins. Co. of America	5	125	122	◐	◐	●	
New York SBLI	5	98	137	◐	◐	◐	D
USAA LIC	5	119	138	◐	◐	◐	F
Penn Mutual LIC	1	85	143	◐	◐	◑	B

A – Available only to "preferred risks."
B – Available only to nonsmokers.
C – Available only in Massachusetts.
D – Available only in New York.
E – Available only to Lutherans.
F – Available only to people in certain jobs.
G – Available only to members of a fraternal organization.

Ratings of Term Policies (Par/$25,000/35 Years) *continued*

Company	Term (years)	Initial premium	20-year	Cost Indexes 9-year	Cost Indexes 19-year	Cost Indexes 29-year	Notes
New England Mutual LIC	5	$101	$144	◐	◐	◐	A
State Mutual LAC of America	5	127	149	●	●	●	B
Confederation LIC	1	89	151	●	●	●	
Penn Mutual LIC	1	90	153	●	●	●	
Pan-American LIC	1	85	154	●	●	●	A
State Farm LIC	5	105	156	○	●	●	
National LIC	5	127	149	○	◐	◐	B
Home LIC	5	120	155	○	◐	◐	
Aid Association for Lutherans	1	88	156	◐	●	○	E
New York LIC	5	119	157	○	●	◐	
Confederation LIC	5	99	159	◐	●	○	
Manhattan LIC	5	100	159	○	●	◐	A
Acacia Mutual LIC	5	106	159	●	●	○	B
Metropolitan LIC	5	145	155	○	●	○	
National Life of Vermont	5	132	160	○	○	◐	
Union Central LIC	5	121	163	◐	○	○	
Mutual LIC of New York	5	122	167	○	○	◐	
Lutheran Mutual LIC	5	134	162	○	○	○	
Woodmen of the World Life Ins. Soc.	5	119	163	○	○	○	G
American Family LIC	5	121	164	○	○	○	
Massachusetts Mutual LIC	5	147	165	○	○	○	

New England Mutual LIC	5	114	**166**	○	○	○	
Acacia Mutual LIC	5	115	**169**	○	○	○	
Mutual Benefit LIC	1	126	**169**	○	○	○	
State Mutual LAC of America	5	132	**170**	○	○	○	
Connecticut Mutual LIC	5	114	**171**	○	○	○	
Minnesota Mutual LIC	1	99	**171**	○	○	○	
Connecticut Mutual LIC	1	102	**171**	○	○	○	
Phoenix Mutual LIC	5	113	**171**	○	○	○	B
Security Benefit LIC	5	114	**174**	○	○	○	
Manhattan LIC	5	108	**176**	○	○	○	
Pan-American LIC	5	107	**174**	◐	◐	◐	A
Bankers Life Co.	5	125	**174**	○	○	○	
Mutual Trust LIC	5	148	**179**	○	◐	◐	
Knights of Columbus	5	140	**178**	◐	◐	◐	G
Phoenix Mutual LIC	5	122	**181**	◐	◐	◐	
Union Mutual LIC	5	173	**181**	◐	◐	◐	
Equitable Life Assurance Soc. of the U.S.	5	123	**182**	◐	◐	◐	
Ohio National LIC	5	131	**183**	◐	◐	◐	
Guardian LIC of America	5	138	**184**	◐	◐	◐	A
Pacific Mutual LIC	5	135	**185**	◐	◐	◐	
Indianapolis LIC	5	143	**195**	◐	◐	●	
Guardian LIC of America	5	144	**195**	◐	◐	●	

A – Available only to "preferred risks."
B – Available only to nonsmokers.
C – Available only in Massachusetts.

D – Available only in New York.
E – Available only to Lutherans.
F – Available only to people in certain jobs.

G – Available only to members of a fraternal organization.

Type: Participating   Amount: $25,000   Age: 45

Listed in order of increasing cost, based primarily on 19-year cost index (see p. 207). All are men's policies; rates for women are generally lower. All are renewable to at least age 65, and convertible to at least age 60. The 29-year cost index has not been calculated for policies issued at age 45 because most policies are not renewable after the age of 65 or 70. If a company has several listings, check length of term or see Notes. Abbreviations include LIC (Life Insurance Co.) and LAC (Life Assurance Co.). All data are based on 1979 rates and include waiver of premium in event of disability.

Cost indexes symbols: Best ● ◑ ○ ◐ ● Worst

Company	Term (years)	Initial premium	Cost indexes 20-year	9-year	19-year	Notes
Massachusetts SBLI	5	$126	$232	●	●	C
Teachers Ins. & Annuity Assoc. of America	5	194	232	●	●	F
Prudential Ins. Co. of America	5	219	272	◑	◑	F
USAA LIC	5	216	279	◑	◑	D
New York SBLI	5	195	291	◑	◑	B
National LIC	5	222	306	○	○	B
Penn Mutual LIC	1	148	313	○	○	B
State Mutual LAC of America	5	232	321	○	○	B
New York LIC	5	226	324	○	○	
Confederation LIC	1	153	327	○	○	A
New England Mutual LIC	5	195	331	◐	◐	
Penn Mutual LIC	1	158	334	◐	◐	A
Pan-American LIC	1	166	339	◐	◐	A
Acacia Mutual LIC	5	195	344	●	◐	B

Company						Notes
American Family LIC	5	214	345	●	◐	
Confederation LIC	5	188	348	◐	◑	
Mutual LIC of New York	5	228	328	○	◐	
National LIC	5	236	335	○	◐	
State Farm LIC	5	204	343	○	◐	
Home LIC	5	224	344	○	◐	
Manhattan LIC	5	191	345	○	◐	A
Aid Association for Lutherans	1	160	364	◐	○	E
Woodmen of the World Life Ins. Soc.	5	215	354	○	○	G
Acacia Mutual LIC	5	206	356	○	○	
Minnesota Mutual LIC	1	176	358	○	○	
Security Benefit LIC	5	231	371	○	○	
Phoenix Mutual LIC	5	205	372	○	○	B
Bankers Life Co.	5	209	372	○	○	
Mutual Benefit LIC	1	212	374	○	○	
State Mutual LAC of America	5	248	374	○	○	
Massachusetts Mutual LIC	5	259	375	○	○	
Lutheran Mutual LIC	5	237	376	○	○	
Connecticut Mutual LIC	5	224	381	○	○	
New England Mutual LIC	5	221	383	○	○	
Connecticut Mutual LIC	1	182	384	○	○	
Union Central LIC	5	218	384	○	○	
Metropolitan LIC	5	267	380	◐	○	
Manhattan LIC	5	208	382	●	○	
Guardian LIC of America	5	250	382	●	○	A
Mutual Trust LIC	5	275	386	◐	○	

A – Available only to "preferred risks."
B – Available only to nonsmokers.
C – Available only in Massachusetts.
D – Available only in New York.
E – Available only to Lutherans.
F – Available only to people in certain jobs.
G – Available only to members of a fraternal organization.

Ratings of Term Policies (Par/$25,000/45 Years) *continued*

Company	Term (years)	Initial premium	Cost Indexes 20-year	Cost Indexes 9-year	Cost Indexes 19-year	Notes
Pan-American LIC	5	$208	392	○	◑	A
Equitable Life Assurance Soc. of the U.S.	5	233	389	◑	◑	
Ohio National LIC	5	239	390	◑	◑	
Phoenix Mutual LIC	5	224	391	◑	◑	
Knights of Columbus	5	256	391	◑	◑	G
Union Mutual LIC	5	300	392	◑	◑	
Pacific Mutual LIC	5	264	405	◑	◑	
Guardian LIC of America	5	265	408	◑	◑	
Indianapolis LIC	5	261	431	◑	◑	

Type: Nonparticipating   Amount: $100,000   Age: 25

Listed in order of increasing cost, based primarily on 19-year cost index (see p. 207). All are men's policies; rates for women are generally lower. All are renewable to at least age 65, and convertible to at least age 60. If a company has several listings, check length of term or see Notes. Abbreviations include LIC (Life Insurance Co.) and LAC (Life Assurance Co.). All data are based on 1979 rates and include waiver of premium in event of disability.

Best ← → Worst

Company	Term (years)	Initial premium	Cost Indexes 20-year	Cost Indexes 9-year	Cost Indexes 19-year	Cost Indexes 29-year	Notes
All American Life & Casualty Co.	4	$212	$244	●	●	●	
U.S. LIC in the City of N.Y.	4	212	244	●	●	●	

Company				Rating 1	Rating 2	Rating 3
United Benefit LIC	1	203	245	●	●	●
All American Life & Casualty Co.	1	212	247	●	●	●
U.S. LIC in the City of N.Y.	1	212	247	●	●	●
North American Co. for Life & Health Ins.	1	201	249	●	●	●
Old Line LIC of America	1	204	249	●	●	●
North American Co. for Life & Health Ins.	5	205	249	●	●	●
Fireman's Fund American LIC	1	206	251	●	●	●
Occidental LIC of California	1	202	253	●	●	●
Anchor National LIC	1	203	254	●	●	●
Northwestern National LIC	1	208	254	●	●	●
Sun LIC of America	1	212	255	●	●	●
Federal Kemper Life Assurance Soc.	1	205	256	●	●	●
United Investors LIC	1	217	257	●	●	●
Equitable LIC of Iowa	1	224	258	●	●	●
Monarch LIC	1	218	259	●	●	●
First Colony LIC	1	215	262	●	●	●
American Health & Life Ins. Co.	1	201	263	●	●	● A
Columbus Mutual LIC	1	227	262	◐	●	◐
Midland National LIC	1	206	265	●	◐	●
Federal Kemper Life Assurance Soc.	5	225	267	◐	◐	◐
Security-Connecticut LIC	5	240	268	◐	◐	◐
Aetna LIC	1	220	270	●	●	●
Provident Life & Accident Ins. Co.	1	218	272	●	◐	◐
Provident Life & Accident Ins. Co.	5	221	272	◐	◐	◐
Security-Connecticut LIC	1	240	272	○	◐	●
Continental Assurance Co.	1	212	273	◐	◐	◐

A – Available only to "preferred risks."
B – Available only to nonsmokers.
C – Available only in Massachusetts.
D – Available only in New York.
E – Available only to Lutherans.
F – Available only to people in certain jobs.
G – Available only to members of a fraternal organization.

Ratings of Term Policies (Nonpar/$100,000/25 Years) continued

Company	Term (years)	Initial premium	20-year	Cost Indexes 9-year	19-year	29-year	Notes
National LAC of Canada	1	$215	$273	●	◐	◐	
Time Ins. Co.	1	214	277	●	◐	◐	
Hartford LIC	1	221	276	◐	◐	◐	
Jefferson Standard LIC	1	230	279	◐	◐	◐	
Southland LIC	1	226	280	◐	◐	◐	
Safeco LIC	1	223	281	●	◐	◐	
Kansas City LIC	1	226	281	◐	◐	◐	
State Mutual LAC of America	1	229	281	◐	◐	◐	B
IDS LIC	1	232	281	◐	◐	◐	
Great-West LAC	1	258	282	○	◐	●	
J.C. Penney LIC	1	233	286	◐	◐	◐	
Commonwealth LIC	1	215	287	◐	◐	◐	
Liberty LIC	1	226	287	◐	◐	◐	
Old Line LIC of America	5	230	289	◐	◐	◐	
Connecticut General LIC	1	239	290	◐	◐	◐	
Southwestern LIC	1	214	291	◐	◐	◐	
Lincoln National LIC	1	252	292	◐	◐	◐	
Dominion LAC	1	247	293	◐	◐	◐	
Lincoln National LIC	5	253	293	◐	◐	◐	
Dominion LAC	5	247	295	◐	◐	◐	
Durham LIC	1	241	296	◐	◐	◐	
Imperial LAC of Canada	1	245	297	○	◐	◐	
Great-West LAC	5	258	283	○	◐	◐	
American States LIC	3	257	288	○	◐	◐	

Company				Rating			Notes
American Health & Life Ins. Co.	4	229	291	◐	◐	◐	
American States LIC	1	254	291	○	◐	○	
Midland National LIC	5	221	292	◐	◐	◐	
Manufacturers LIC	1	253	295	◐	◐	◐	
Southwestern LIC	5	229	296	◐	◐	○	
IDS LIC	5	249	298	◐	○	○	
Monarch LIC	5	244	301	◐	○	○	
Franklin LIC	1	231	306	○	○	○	
North American LAC	5	256	302	○	○	○	
Colonial LIC of America	5	267	302	○	○	○	B
Hartford LIC	5	276	305	○	○	○	
All American Life & Casualty Co.	5	269	306	○	○	○	
U.S. LIC in the City of N.Y.	5	269	306	○	○	○	
Jefferson Standard LIC	5	249	307	○	○	○	
North American LAC	1	247	308	○	○	○	
Beneficial LIC	1	249	309	○	○	○	
State Mutual LAC of America	1	250	309	○	○	○	A
Sun LAC of Canada	1	270	310	○	○	○	
Monumental LIC	1	251	314	○	○	○	
Standard Ins. Co.	1	270	314	○	○	○	
Colonial LIC of America	1	285	315	○	○	○	
Fidelity Union LIC	1	261	317	○	○	○	
Life & Casualty Ins. Co. of Tenn.	1	254	318	○	○	○	
National Life & Accident Ins. Co.	5	255	320	○	○	○	A
United Benefit LIC	5	267	321	○	○	○	
Monumental LIC	5	260	328	○	○	○	

A – Available only to "preferred risks."
B – Available only to nonsmokers.
C – Available only in Massachusetts.
D – Available only in New York.
E – Available only to Lutherans.
F – Available only to people in certain jobs.
G – Available only to members of a fraternal organization.

Ratings of Term Policies (Nonpar/$100,000/25 Years) *continued*

Company	Term (years)	Initial premium	20-year	Cost Indexes		
				9-year	19-year	29-year
Canada LAC	1	$283	$332	○	○	○
Imperial LAC of Canada	5	288	332	○	○	○
Connecticut General LIC	5	307	334	○	○	○
Occidental LIC of California	5	262	336	○	○	○
Allstate LIC	6	280	339	○	○	○
Life & Casualty Ins. Co. of Tenn.	5	277	342	○	○	○
Kansas City LIC	5	287	343	○	○	○
Security Life & Accident Co.	1	314	346	◑	◑	◔
Sun LAC of Canada	5	297	345	◔	◑	◔
Security Life & Accident Co.	5	295	349	◔	◑	◔
Colonial LIC of America	5	292	350	◔	◑	◔
Travelers Ins. Co.	5	302	350	◔	◑	◔
Paul Revere LIC	5	303	352	◔	◑	◔
Northwestern National LIC	5	307	356	◑	◑	◑
Standard Ins. Co.	5	317	359	◑	◑	◑
American National Ins. Co.	1	293	361	◑	◑	◕
Home Beneficial LIC	5	320	368	◑	◕	◕
Canada LAC	5	327	371	◕	◕	◕
National LAC of Canada	5	324	372	◕	◕	◕
J.C. Penney LIC	5	315	384	◕	●	◕
Farm Bureau (Iowa)	5	352	393	●	●	◕
Safeco LIC	5	339	395	●	●	◔
Equitable LIC of Iowa	5	367	413	●	●	●
Aetna LIC	5	380	414	●	●	●

Notes

Company	Term (years)	Initial premium	20-year	9-year	19-year	29-year
Fireman's Fund American LIC	5	380	422	●	●	●
Fidelity Union LIC	5	341	423	●	●	●
Southland LIC	5	370	447	●	●	●
American National Ins. Co.	5	398	466	●	●	●
Franklin LIC	5	417	477	●	●	●
Anchor National LIC	5	425	484	●	●	●
Bankers Life & Casualty Co.	5	457	524	●	●	●
Nationwide LIC	5	473	543	●	●	●

Type: Nonparticipating   Amount: $100,000   Age: 35

Listed in order of increasing cost, based primarily on 19-year cost index (see p. 207). All are men's policies; rates for women are generally lower. All are renewable to at least age 65, and convertible to at least age 60. If a company has several listings, check length of term or see Notes. Abbreviations include LIC (Life Insurance Co.) and LAC (Life Assurance Co.). All data are based on 1979 rates and include waiver of premium in event of disability.

Best → Worst
● ◐ ○ ◑ ●

Company	Term (years)	Initial premium	Cost Indexes 20-year	Cost Indexes 9-year	Cost Indexes 19-year	Cost Indexes 29-year	Notes
All American Life & Casualty Co.	4	$238	$437	●	●	●	
U.S. LIC in the City of N.Y.	4	238	437	●	●	●	
United Benefit LIC	1	232	444	●	●	●	
All American Life & Casualty Co.	1	225	449	●	●	●	
U.S. LIC in the City of N.Y.	1	225	449	●	●	●	

A – Available only to "preferred risks."
B – Available only to nonsmokers.
C – Available only in Massachusetts.
D – Available only in New York.
E – Available only to Lutherans.
F – Available only to people in certain jobs.
G – Available only to members of a fraternal organization.

Ratings of Term Policies (Nonpar/$100,000/35 Years) continued

Company	Term (years)	Initial premium	20-year	Cost Indexes 9-year	19-year	29-year	Notes
Fireman's Fund American LIC	1	$232	455	●	●	●	
Security-Connecticut LIC	5	271	457	●	●	●	
Equitable LIC of Iowa	1	236	463	●	●	●	
Great-West LAC	1	260	463	●	●	●	
Northwestern National LIC	1	238	466	●	●	●	
Great-West LAC	5	284	467	●	●	●	
North American Co. for Life & Health Ins.	1	234	468	●	●	●	
Old Line LIC of America	1	229	469	●	●	●	
Columbus Mutual LIC	1	239	470	●	●	●	
Security-Connecticut LIC	1	256	473	●	●	●	
United Investors LIC	1	235	478	●	●	●	
First Colony LIC	1	233	480	●	●	●	
Sun LIC of America	1	238	481	●	●	●	
Occidental LIC of California	1	234	484	●	●	●	
Aetna LIC	1	260	484	●	●	●	
Anchor National LIC	1	234	485	●	●	●	
North American Co. for Life & Health Ins.	5	265	468	●	◐	◐	
Monarch LIC	1	242	481	●	◐	◐	
Federal Kemper Life Assurance Soc.	1	236	487	●	◐	◐	
Federal Kemper Life Assurance Soc.	5	275	483	◐	◐	◐	
American States LIC	3	300	490	●	◐	●	
American Health & Life Ins. Co.	1	217	494	◐	◐	◐	A
Manufacturers LIC	1	281	501	◐	◐	●	
State Mutual LAC of America	1	263	509	◐	◐	◐	B

IDS LIC	1	271	511	◐	◑	◐
American States LIC	1	296	511	○	◑	●
Midland National LIC	1	256	512	◐	◑	◐
Kansas City LIC	1	270	513	◐	◑	◐
Continental Assurance Co.	1	265	514	◐	◑	◐
Southland LIC	1	268	514	◐	◑	◐
Provident Life & Accident Ins. Co.	1	260	515	◐	◑	◐
J.C. Penney LIC	1	274	515	◐	◑	◐
Provident Life & Accident Ins. Co.	5	289	517	◐	◑	◐
Jefferson Standard LIC	1	264	518	◐	◑	◐
Hartford LIC	1	263	521	◐	◑	◐
Hartford LIC	5	293	525	◐	◑	◐
Safeco LIC	1	275	532	◐	◑	◐
Imperial LAC of Canada	1	286	532	◐	◑	◐
National LAC of Canada	1	246	533	◐	◑	◐
Dominion LAC	1	282	535	◐	◑	◐
Connecticut General LIC	1	277	538	◐	◑	◐
Liberty LIC	1	275	543	◐	◑	◐
Durham LIC	1	283	543	◐	◑	◐
Colonial LIC of America	1	290	525	◐	◑	○
Lincoln National LIC	1	270	534	◐	◑	○
Lincoln National LIC	5	300	535	◐	◑	○
Old Line LIC of America	5	316	537	◐	◑	◐
All American Life & Casualty Co.	5	326	530	○	◑	○
U.S. LIC in the City of N.Y.	5	326	530	○	◑	○
Colonial LIC of America	5	320	534	○	◑	○
						B

A—Available only to "preferred risks."
B—Available only to nonsmokers.
C—Available only in Massachusetts.
D—Available only in New York.
E—Available only to Lutherans.
F—Available only to people in certain jobs.
G—Available only to members of a fraternal organization.

Ratings of Term Policies (Nonpar/$100,000/35 Years) *continued*

Company	Term (years)	Initial premium	20-year	Cost Indexes 9-year	19-year	29-year	Notes
Dominion LAC	5	$314	$539	○	○	●	
North American LAC	5	315	539	○	○	●	
IDS LIC	5	311	544	○	○	◐	
North American LAC	1	296	548	●	○	◐	
Time Ins. Co.	1	264	550	◐	○	◐	
Commonwealth LIC	1	279	551	◐	○	○	
Life & Casualty Ins. Co. of Tenn.	1	308	555	○	○	○	
Monumental LIC	1	292	565	○	○	●	
Southwestern LIC	1	283	566	○	○	●	
Fidelity Union LIC	1	315	557	○	○	◐	
Sun LAC of Canada	1	296	564	○	○	○	
American Health & Life Ins. Co.	4	300	564	○	○	○	
State Mutual LAC of America	1	290	565	○	○	○	A
Midland National LIC	5	318	567	○	○	○	
Southwestern LIC	5	321	567	○	○	○	
Standard Ins. Co.	1	286	569	○	○	○	
National Life & Accident Ins. Co.	5	350	573	○	○	●	A
Monarch LIC	5	317	577	○	○	○	
Beneficial LIC	1	296	578	○	○	○	
United Benefit LIC	5	339	578	○	○	○	
Jefferson Standard LIC	5	325	580	○	○	○	
Canada LAC	1	310	582	○	○	○	
Security Life & Accident Co.	1	319	585	○	○	○	
Imperial LAC of Canada	5	344	587	○	○	○	

Allstate LIC	6	340	627	○	○	○
American National Ins. Co.	1	364	602	◐	○	○
Standard Ins. Co.	5	363	603	◐	○	○
Connecticut General LIC	5	387	610	◐	○	○
Northwestern National LIC	5	370	613	◐	○	○
Kansas City LIC	5	361	614	◐	○	○
Life & Casualty Ins. Co. of Tenn.	5	366	614	◐	○	◐
Franklin LIC	1	299	630	○	○	○
Sun LAC of Canada	5	355	620	◐	◐	○
Monumental LIC	5	349	622	◐	◐	○
Security Life & Accident Co.	5	366	622	◐	◐	○
Farm Bureau (Iowa)	5	396	622	◐	◐	○
Travelers Ins. Co.	5	369	629	◐	◐	○
Paul Revere LIC	5	347	634	◐	◐	○
Occidental LIC of California	5	379	635	◐	◐	○
National LAC of Canada	5	389	635	◐	◐	○
Canada LAC	5	396	637	◐	◐	○
Safeco LIC	5	413	655	◐	◐	○
J.C. Penney LIC	5	408	660	◐	◐	○
Colonial LIC of America	5	385	631	◐	◐	◐
Home Beneficial LIC	5	370	647	◐	◐	◐
Aetna LIC	5	404	673	◐	◐	◐
Fireman's Fund American LIC	5	432	683	◐	◐	◐
Equitable LIC of Iowa	5	449	694	●	◐	◐
Southland LIC	5	486	740	●	●	◐
Fidelity Union LIC	5	457	743	●	●	◐

A – Available only to "preferred risks."
B – Available only to nonsmokers.
C – Available only in Massachusetts.

D – Available only in New York.
E – Available only to Lutherans.
F – Available only to people in certain jobs.

G – Available only to members of a fraternal organization.

Ratings of Term Policies (Nonpar/$100,000/35 Years) *continued*

Company	Term (years)	Initial premium	Cost Indexes 20-year	9-year	19-year	29-year	Notes
American National Ins. Co.	5	$493	$766	●	●	●	
Bankers Life & Casualty Co.	5	577	782	●	●	●	
Anchor National LIC	5	500	791	●	●	●	
Franklin LIC	5	526	798	●	●	●	
Nationwide LIC	5	568	870	●	●	●	

Type: Nonparticipating   Amount: $100,000   Age: 45

Listed in order of increasing cost, based primarily on 19-year cost index (see p. 207). All are men's policies; rates for women are generally lower. All are renewable to at least age 65, and convertible to at least age 60. The 29-year cost index has not been calculated for policies issued at age 45 because most policies are not renewable after the age of 65 or 70. If a company has several listings, check length of term or see Notes. Abbreviations include LIC (Life Insurance Co.) and LAC (Life Assurance Co.). All data are based on 1979 rates and include waiver of premium in event of disability.

Best ●➡○ ⊙ ◐ ● ➡Worst

Company	Term (years)	Initial premium	Cost Indexes 20-year	9-year	19-year	Notes
Great-West LAC	5	$555	$1053	●	◐	
Great-West LAC	1	462	1054	●	●	
Security-Connecticut LIC	5	572	1056	●	●	
All American Life & Casualty Co.	4	505	1069	●	●	

U.S. LIC in the City of N.Y.	4	505	1069	●	●
Northwestern National LIC	1	481	1077	●	●
United Benefit LIC	1	453	1078	●	●
All American Life & Casualty Co.	1	459	1103	●	●
U.S. LIC in the City of N.Y.	1	459	1103	●	●
Security-Connecticut LIC	1	484	1104	●	●
Fireman's Fund American LIC	1	470	1112	●	●
Aetna LIC	1	490	1113	●	●
Old Line LIC of America	1	472	1136	●	●
First Colony LIC	1	475	1138	●	●
Manufacturers LIC	1	506	1145	●	●
Sun LIC of America	1	489	1149	●	●
United Investors LIC	1	480	1163	●	◐
American States LIC	3	590	1109	◐	◐
American States LIC	1	581	1138	◐	◐
Anchor National LIC	1	491	1140	◐	◐
Occidental LIC of California	1	490	1152	◐	◐
Southland LIC	1	531	1166	◐	◐
J.C. Penney LIC	1	542	1176	●	◐
Columbus Mutual LIC	1	480	1195	●	◑
Equitable LIC of Iowa	1	478	1209	●	◑
North American Co. for Life & Health Ins.	5	560	1212	●	◑
North American Co. for Life & Health Ins.	1	454	1214	●	◑
American Health & Life Ins. Co.	1	422	1244	●	◑ (A)
Monarch LIC	1	479	1277	●	◑
IDS LIC	1	531	1187	◑	◑

A – Available only to "preferred risks."
B – Available only to nonsmokers.
C – Available only in Massachusetts.
D – Available only in New York.
E – Available only to Lutherans.
F – Available only to people in certain jobs.
G – Available only to members of a fraternal organization.

Ratings of Term Policies (Nonpar/$100,000/45 Years) continued

Company	Term (years)	Initial premium	Cost Indexes 20-year	9-year	19-year	Notes
Kansas City LIC	1	$523	$1192	◑	◑	
Federal Kemper Life Assurance Soc.	1	493	1197	◑	◑	
Old Line LIC of America	5	649	1203	◑	◑	B
State Mutual LAC of America	1	511	1204	◑	◑	
Continental Assurance Co.	1	519	1206	◑	◑	
Monumental LIC	1	593	1208	◑	◑	
Jefferson Standard LIC	1	525	1213	◑	◑	
Provident Life & Accident Ins. Co.	1	528	1214	◑	◑	
Federal Kemper Life Assurance Soc.	5	586	1221	◑	◑	
Midland National LIC	1	525	1226	◑	◑	
Provident Life & Accident Ins. Co.	5	640	1229	◑	◑	
Life & Casualty Ins. Co. of Tenn.	1	571	1237	◑	◑	
Safeco LIC	1	517	1238	◑	◑	
Imperial LAC of Canada	1	533	1241	◑	◑	
Liberty LIC	1	550	1263	◑	◑	
Dominion LAC	1	542	1267	◑	◑	
Hartford LIC	1	523	1268	◑	◑	
Connecticut General LIC	1	546	1275	◑	◑	
National LAC of Canada	1	487	1277	◑	◑	
Durham LIC	1	559	1284	◑	◑	
North American LAC	1	557	1293	◑	◑	
Dominion LAC	5	659	1253	○	◑	
IDS LIC	5	671	1263	○	◑	
Midland National LIC	5	705	1277	○	◑	

North American LAC	5	658	1280	○	◐	
National Life & Accident Ins. Co.	5	684	1280	○	◐	A
Fidelity Union LIC	1	551	1293	○	◐	
Southwestern LIC	1	588	1293	○	◐	
All American Life & Casualty Co.	5	627	1306	◐	○	
U.S. LIC in the City of N.Y.	5	627	1306	◐	○	
Hartford LIC	5	646	1308	◐	○	
Lincoln National LIC	1	541	1333	◐	○	
Colonial LIC of America	1	532	1349	○	○	
Standard Ins. Co.	1	593	1323	○	○	
Lincoln National LIC	5	647	1325	○	○	
Commonwealth LIC	1	560	1326	○	○	
Farm Bureau (Iowa)	5	758	1326	○	○	
Time Ins. Co.	1	570	1330	○	○	
Security Life & Accident Co.	1	600	1331	○	○	
Southwestern LIC	5	691	1332	○	○	
State Mutual LAC of America	1	569	1338	○	○	A
Standard Ins. Co.	5	725	1343	○	○	
Beneficial LIC	1	587	1344	○	○	
Sun LAC of Canada	1	581	1347	○	○	
United Benefit LIC	5	698	1362	○	○	
American Health & Life Ins. Co.	4	668	1373	○	○	
Jefferson Standard LIC	5	701	1375	○	○	
Imperial LAC of Canada	5	694	1376	○	○	
Connecticut General LIC	5	760	1384	○	○	
American National Ins. Co.	1	591	1389	○	○	

A – Available only in New York.
B – Available only to nonsmokers.
C – Available only in Massachusetts.
D – Available only to "preferred risks."
E – Available only to Lutherans.
F – Available only to people in certain jobs.
G – Available only to members of a fraternal organization.

Ratings of Term Policies (Nonpar/$100,000/45 Years) continued

Company	Term (years)	Initial premium	Cost Indexes 20-year	9-year	19-year	Notes
Northwestern National LIC	5	$735	$1390	○	○	
Life & Casualty Ins. Co. of Tenn.	5	747	1390	○	○	
Monarch LIC	5	733	1399	○	○	
Colonial LIC of America	5	685	1401	○	○	B
Canada LAC	1	596	1404	○	○	
Kansas City LIC	5	740	1407	○	○	
Monumental LIC	5	779	1374	◐	○	
Safeco LIC	5	788	1410	◐	○	
J.C. Penney LIC	5	793	1414	◐	○	
Canada LAC	5	788	1426	◐	○	
Allstate LIC	6	751	1427	◐	○	
National LAC of Canada	5	754	1430	●	○	
Security Life & Accident Co.	5	744	1433	●	○	
Occidental LIC of California	5	768	1454	●	○	
Sun LAC of Canada	5	769	1461	●	○	
Fireman's Fund American LIC	5	812	1466	●	○	
Paul Revere LIC	5	770	1471	●	○	
Travelers Ins. Co.	5	780	1478	◐	○	
Home Beneficial LIC	5	799	1514	●	◐	
Southland LIC	5	865	1560	●	◐	
Equitable LIC of Iowa	5	844	1564	●	◐	
Colonial LIC of America	5	800	1566	●	◐	
Aetna LIC	5	798	1572	●	◐	
Franklin LIC	1	624	1575	◐	◐	

Company			Term (years)			
Bankers Life & Casualty Co.	5	939	1543	●	◐	◐
Fidelity Union LIC	5	886	1563	●	◐	◐
American National Ins. Co.	5	899	1625	●	◐	◐
Franklin LIC	5	994	1696	●	●	●
Nationwide LIC	5	1028	1731	●	●	●

Type: Participating   Amount: $100,000   Age: 25

Listed in order of increasing cost, based primarily on 19-year cost index (see p. 207). All are men's policies; rates for women are generally lower. All are renewable to at least age 65, and convertible to at least age 60. If a company has several listings, check length of term or see Notes. Abbreviations include LIC (Life Insurance Co.) and LAC (Life Assurance Co.). All data are based on 1979 rates and include waiver of premium in event of disability.

Best → Worst

Company	Term (years)	Initial premium	Cost Indexes 20-year	9-year	19-year	29-year	Notes
Teachers Ins. & Annuity Assoc. of America	5	$258	$163	●	●	●	F
Metropolitan LIC	1	216	192	●	◐	●	A
USAA LIC	1	182	223	●	●	●	F
New England Mutual LIC	1	195	236	●	●	●	A
Security Benefit LIC	1	211	238	◐	●	●	
Metropolitan LIC	5	314	204	●	●	●	A

A– Available only to "preferred risks."
B– Available only to nonsmokers.
C– Available only in Massachusetts.
D– Available only in New York.
E– Available only to Lutherans.
F– Available only to people in certain jobs.
G– Available only to members of a fraternal organization.

Ratings of Term Policies (Par/$100,000/25 Years) *continued*

Company	Term (years)	Initial premium	20-year	Cost Indexes 9-year	19-year	29-year	Notes
Beneficial LIC	1	$214	$256	●	◐	●	
Manhattan LIC	1	225	257	●	●	●	A
Equitable Life Assurance Soc. of the U.S.	1	232	257	●	◐	●	
Penn Mutual LIC	1	242	259	●	●	●	B
Metropolitan LIC	1	273	261	●	●	●	
Pan-American LIC	1	204	264	◐	●	●	A
Confederation LIC	1	226	270	●	●	◐	B
Pacific Mutual LIC	1	214	271	●	●	●	
State Farm LIC	1	245	273	●	●	●	
Midland Mutual LIC	1	236	275	●	●	●	A
New England Mutual LIC	5	255	275	●	●	●	
Mutual LIC of New York	1	223	276	●	●	●	
Penn Mutual LIC	1	218	278	●	●	●	
Minnesota Mutual LIC	1	218	281	◐	●	●	
Knights of Columbus	1	256	282	●	●	●	G
Central LAC	1	219	284	●	●	●	
Southern Farm Bureau LIC	1	250	285	○	●	●	
National LIC	1	274	276	◐	●	◐	B
Confederation LIC	5	243	286	●	●	●	B
Manhattan LIC	5	233	287	●	●	○	A
New England Mutual LIC	1	229	288	●	◐	○	
New York LIC	1	222	289	◐	●	◐	
National LIC	1	227	289	○	●	◐	

Metropolitan LIC	5	371	275		◐	●	◐	
Prudential Ins. Co. of America	5	343	286		◐	○	●	F
USAA LIC	5	369	296		○	○	○	G
Woodmen of the World Life Ins. Soc.	1	261	297		○	○	○	
Indianapolis LIC	1	232	299		○	○	○	G
Woodmen of the World Life Ins. Soc.	5	297	302		○	○	○	
Mutual Benefit LIC	1	261	305		○	○	○	
Acacia Mutual LIC	5	274	305		○	○	○	B
Union Central LIC	1	254	307		○	○	○	
Ohio National LIC	1	255	307		○	○	○	
Provident Mutual LIC	1	262	311		○	○	○	
Bankers Life Co.	1	287	312		○	○	○	
Acacia Mutual LIC	1	273	315		○	○	○	B
Manhattan LIC	1	259	317		○	○	○	
New York LIC	5	304	318		○	○	○	
State Farm LIC	5	297	316		◐	○	○	
State Mutual LAC of America	5	369	317		◐	○	○	B
Mutual Trust LIC	1	263	323		○	◐	○	
Manhattan LIC	5	256	322		○	◐	○	
New England Mutual LIC	5	289	322		○	◐	○	
Pan-American LIC	5	275	325		◐	◐	○	A
Aid Association for Lutherans	1	289	325		○	◐	○	E
Security Benefit LIC	5	284	329		○	◐	○	
Guardian LIC of America	1	257	330		◐	◐	○	A
Connecticut Mutual LIC	5	315	327		◐	◐	○	A

A – Available only to "preferred risks."
B – Available only to nonsmokers.
C – Available only in Massachusetts.
D – Available only in New York.
E – Available only to Lutherans.
F – Available only to people in certain jobs.
G – Available only to members of a fraternal organization.

Ratings of Term Policies (Par/$100,000/25 Years) continued

Company	Term (years)	Initial premium	20-year	Cost Indexes 9-year	19-year	29-year	Notes
Connecticut Mutual LIC	1	$289	$330	◑	◑	◑	
Home LIC	5	359	332	◑	◑	◑	
Acacia Mutual LIC	5	299	335	◑	◑	◑	
State Mutual LAC of America	5	373	341	◑	◑	◑	
Union Central LIC	5	398	346	◑	◑	◑	
Acacia Mutual LIC	1	297	347	◑	◑	◑	
Guardian LIC of America	1	270	352	●	◑	◑	
Bankers LIC of Nebraska	5	342	350	●	◑	◑	
National LIC	5	390	359	●	◑	◑	B
Lutheran Mutual LIC	5	410	365	●	●	◑	
National LIC	5	394	372	◑	●	◑	
Pacific Mutual LIC	5	360	373	●	●	●	
Mutual Trust LIC	5	405	384	●	●	◑	
Union Mutual LIC	5	511	391	●	●	●	
Knights of Columbus	5	407	393	●	●	●	G
Phoenix Mutual LIC	5	341	395	●	●	●	
Guardian LIC of America	5	399	398	●	●	●	A
American Family LIC	5	378	403	●	●	●	
Ohio National LIC	5	395	403	●	●	●	
Bankers Life Co.	5	379	407	●	●	●	
Phoenix Mutual LIC	5	355	409	●	●	●	
Guardian LIC of America	5	414	418	●	●	●	
Indianapolis LIC	5	407	426	●	●	●	

Type: Participating   Amount: $100,000   Age: 35

Listed in order of increasing cost, based primarily on 19-year cost index (see p. 207). All are men's policies; rates for women are generally lower. All are renewable to at least age 65, and convertible to at least age 60. If a company has several listings, check length of term or see Notes. Abbreviations include LIC (Life Insurance Co.) and LAC (Life Assurance Co.). All data are based on 1979 rates and include waiver of premium in event of disability.

Best ● ◐ ○ ◑ ● Worst

Company	Term (years)	Initial premium	20-year	9-year	19-year	29-year	Notes
Teachers Ins. & Annuity Assoc. of America	5	$373	$360	●	●	●	F
Metropolitan LIC	1	252	373	●	●	●	A
USAA LIC	1	210	408	●	●	●	F
New England Mutual LIC	1	228	440	●	●	●	A
Metropolitan LIC	5	436	394	◐	●	●	A
Security Benefit LIC	1	270	463	●	◐	◐	
National LIC	1	330	474	◐	◐	●	B
Prudential Ins. Co. of America	5	466	451	○	◐	●	A
Manhattan LIC	1	277	470	◐	◐	◐	A
Penn Mutual LIC	1	248	481	◐	◐	◐	B
Beneficial LIC	1	255	485	◐	◐	◐	
Equitable Life Assurance Soc. of the U.S.	1	268	487	◐	◐	◐	
Pan-American LIC	1	252	491	◐	◐	◐	A
Midland Mutual LIC	1	253	491	◐	◐	◐	

A – Available only to "preferred risks."
B – Available only to nonsmokers.
C – Available only in Massachusetts.
D – Available only in New York.
E – Available only to Lutherans.
F – Available only to people in certain jobs.
G – Available only to members of a fraternal organization.

Ratings of Term Policies (Par/$100,000/35 Years) *continued*

Company	Term (years)	Initial premium	20-year	Cost Indexes 9-year	Cost Indexes 19-year	Cost Indexes 29-year	Notes
Confederation LIC	1	$254	$495	◕	◕	◕	B
Pacific Mutual LIC	1	258	497	●	●	●	
Southern Farm Bureau LIC	1	308	513	●	●	◕	
Knights of Columbus	1	288	517	●	●	●	G
Penn Mutual LIC	1	271	523	●	●	●	
State Farm LIC	1	288	523	◕	●	◕	
Confederation LIC	5	294	526	◕	●	●	B
Mutual LIC of New York	1	270	532	◑	●	●	
National LIC	1	341	516	○	●	◑	
USAA LIC	5	445	521	○	●	○	F
Metropolitan LIC	1	310	523	◕	●	○	
Central LAC	1	273	532	◑	●	○	
Minnesota Mutual LIC	1	271	542	◑	●	◑	A
New England Mutual LIC	5	357	530	○	●	●	B
Acacia Mutual LIC	5	348	537	○	●	●	
New England Mutual LIC	1	282	545	◑	●	○	
Indianapolis LIC	1	297	545	○	○	○	A
Manhattan LIC	5	320	548	◑	○	◑	
Woodmen of the World Life Ins. Soc.	1	303	550	○	○	○	G
State Mutual LAC of America	5	461	552	○	○	◑	B
New York LIC	5	399	554	○	○	◑	
New York LIC	1	282	561	◑	○	○	
Ohio National LIC	1	296	557	○	○	○	
Bankers Life Co.	1	325	558	○	○	○	

National LIC	5	473	560	◑	○	◑	◑	B
Acacia Mutual LIC	1	329	568	○	○	○	○	B
Mutual Benefit LIC	1	325	575	○	○	○	○	
Pan-American LIC	5	328	575	○	○	○	○	A
Union Central LIC	1	329	581	○	○	○	○	
Provident Mutual LIC	1	325	590	○	○	○	○	
Metropolitan LIC	5	508	546	◑	○	○	◑	
State Farm LIC	5	374	576	◑	○	○	◑	
Acacia Mutual LIC	5	383	578	◑	○	○	◑	
Aid Association for Lutherans	1	316	584	○	○	○	◑	E
Woodmen of the World Life Ins. Soc.	5	411	586	◑	○	○	○	G
Connecticut Mutual LIC	1	316	595	○	◑	○	◑	
Manhattan LIC	1	332	595	◑	◑	○	○	
Home LIC	5	455	596	○	◑	○	◑	
Mutual Trust LIC	1	309	604	◑	◑	○	◑	
Connecticut Mutual LIC	5	367	590	◑	◑	◑	◑	
Bankers LIC of Nebraska	5	367	593	◑	◑	◑	◑	
National LIC	5	491	603	●	◑	◑	◑	
Union Central LIC	5	438	606	◑	◑	◑	◑	
Acacia Mutual LIC	1	364	610	◑	◑	◑	◑	
Manhattan LIC	5	352	614	◑	◑	◑	◑	
Lutheran Mutual LIC	5	506	615	◑	◑	◑	◑	
New England Mutual LIC	5	411	619	◑	◑	◑	◑	
Guardian LIC of America	1	322	621	◑	◑	◑	◑	A
State Mutual LAC of America	5	481	629	◑	◑	◑	◑	
American Family LIC	5	460	632	◑	◑	◑	◑	

A – Available only to "preferred risks."
B – Available only to nonsmokers.
C – Available only in Massachusetts.
D – Available only in New York.
E – Available only to Lutherans.
F – Available only to people in certain jobs.
G – Available only to members of a fraternal organization.

Ratings of Term Policies (Par/$100,000/35 Years) *continued*

Company	Term (years)	Initial premium	20-year	9-year	19-year	29-year	Notes
				Cost Indexes			
Security Benefit LIC	5	$397	$636	◐	◐	◐	
Phoenix Mutual LIC	5	405	640	◐	◐	●	
Guardian LIC of America	1	342	671	◐	◐	●	
Bankers Life Co.	5	453	648	●	◐	◐	
Mutual Trust LIC	5	533	658	●	◐	◐	
Pacific Mutual LIC	5	478	679	◐	●	◐	
Phoenix Mutual LIC	5	443	678	●	●	◐	
Knights of Columbus	5	536	687	●	●	◐	G
Ohio National LIC	5	480	688	●	●	◐	
Guardian LIC of America	5	508	689	●	●	◐	A
Union Mutual LIC	5	665	696	●	●	●	
Guardian LIC of America	5	531	736	●	●	●	
Indianapolis LIC	5	527	737	●	●	●	

Type: Participating   Amount: $100,000   Age: 45

Listed in order of increasing cost, based primarily on 19-year cost index (see p. 207). All are men's policies; rates for women are generally lower. All are renewable to at least age 65, and convertible to at least age 60. The 29-year cost index has not been calculated for policies issued at age 45 because most policies are not renewable after the age of 65 or 70. If a company has several listings, check length of term or see Notes. Abbreviations include LIC (Life Insurance Co.) and LAC (Life Assurance Co.). All data are based on 1979 rates and include waiver of premium in event of disability.

Best ● ◐ ○ ◐ ● Worst

Company	Term (years)	Initial premium	Cost Indexes 20-year	Cost Indexes 9-year	Cost Indexes 19-year	Notes
Teachers Ins. & Annuity Assoc. of America	5	$774	$ 871	●	●	F
USAA LIC	1	435	970	●	●	F
Metropolitan LIC	1	455	988	●	●	A
New England Mutual LIC	1	461	1071	◑	●	A
Metropolitan LIC	5	793	1040	◑	◔	A
Prudential Ins. Co. of America	5	841	1052	◑	◔	
USAA LIC	5	833	1085	◑	◑	F
National LIC	1	613	1086	◑	◑	B
Security Benefit LIC	1	564	1118	◑	◑	
Manhattan LIC	1	533	1119	◑	◑	A
Pan-American LIC	1	510	1126	◑	◑	A
Southern Farm Bureau LIC	1	615	1151	◑	◑	
Penn Mutual LIC	1	501	1162	◑	◑	B
Pacific Mutual LIC	1	506	1166	◑	◑	
Midland Mutual LIC	1	498	1170	◑	◑	B
Confederation LIC	1	504	1179	◑	◑	
Beneficial LIC	1	501	1193	◑	◑	
Equitable Life Assurance Soc. of the U.S.	1	549	1208	◑	◑	
Acacia Mutual LIC	5	672	1220	◑	◑	B
Penn Mutual LIC	1	542	1246	◑	◑	
State Farm LIC	1	594	1251	◑	◑	
Knights of Columbus	1	572	1263	◑	◑	G
Confederation LIC	5	640	1263	◑	◑	B
Minnesota Mutual LIC	1	560	1274	◑	◑	

A – Available only to "preferred risks."
B – Available only to nonsmokers.
C – Available only in Massachusetts.
D – Available only in New York.
E – Available only to Lutherans.
F – Available only to people in certain jobs.
G – Available only to members of a fraternal organization.

Ratings of Term Policies (Par/$100,000/45 Years) *continued*

Company	Term (years)	Initial premium	Cost Indexes 20-year	Cost Indexes 9-year	Cost Indexes 19-year	Notes
Mutual LIC of New York	1	$ 559	$1279	◐	◐	
Central LAC	1	543	1291	◐	◐	
National LIC	5	852	1189	○	◐	B
National LIC	1	657	1196	○	◐	
New York LIC	5	828	1221	○	◐	
State Mutual LAC of America	5	881	1237	○	◐	B
Manhattan LIC	5	684	1266	○	◐	A
Acacia Mutual LIC	5	716	1270	○	◐	
New England Mutual LIC	5	733	1280	○	○	A
New England Mutual LIC	1	565	1315	◐	○	
Indianapolis LIC	1	558	1346	◐	○	
New York LIC	1	593	1309	○	○	
Woodmen of the World Life Ins. Soc.	1	585	1310	○	○	G
Acacia Mutual LIC	1	604	1347	○	○	B
Union Central LIC	1	596	1350	○	○	
Ohio National LIC	1	566	1355	○	○	
Bankers Life Co.	1	608	1355	○	○	
Provident Mutual LIC	1	661	1365	○	○	
Mutual Benefit LIC	1	636	1368	○	○	
Metropolitan LIC	1	621	1369	○	○	
Pan-American LIC	5	691	1397	○	○	A
Acacia Mutual LIC	1	649	1399	○	○	
National LIC	1	909	1303	◐	○	
State Farm LIC	5	771	1325	◐	○	
Woodmen of the World Life Ins. Soc.	5	795	1353	◐	○	G
Home LIC	5	871	1353	◐	○	

Company						Note
American Family LIC	5	831	1355	○	◐	
Manhattan LIC	1	659	1383	○	◐	
Aid Association for Lutherans	1	598	1416	◐	○	E
Connecticut Mutual LIC	1	636	1444	◐	○	
Manhattan LIC	5	752	1417	◐	◐	
Metropolitan LIC	5	990	1422	◐	◐	
Security Benefit LIC	5	864	1425	◐	◐	
Connecticut Mutual LIC	5	805	1435	◐	◐	
Bankers Life Co.	5	792	1442	◐	◐	
Phoenix Mutual LIC	5	775	1444	◐	◐	
State Mutual LAC of America	5	945	1451	◐	◐	A
Guardian LIC of America	1	644	1455	◐	◐	
Mutual Trust LIC	1	627	1466	◐	◐	
Lutheran Mutual LIC	5	920	1471	◐	◐	
New England Mutual LIC	5	837	1486	◐	◐	
Union Central LIC	5	828	1493	◐	◐	
Bankers LIC of Nebraska	5	754	1515	◐	◐	
Phoenix Mutual LIC	5	850	1519	◐	◐	
Guardian LIC of America	1	699	1572	●	◐	A
Guardian LIC of America	5	954	1482	●	◐	
Mutual Trust LIC	5	1039	1485	●	◐	
Ohio National LIC	5	910	1515	●	◐	
Knights of Columbus	5	1001	1539	●	◐	G
Union Mutual LIC	5	1173	1540	●	◐	
Pacific Mutual LIC	5	997	1561	●	◐	
Guardian LIC of America	5	1015	1589	●	◐	
Indianapolis LIC	5	999	1679	●	●	

A– Available only to "preferred risks."
B– Available only to nonsmokers.
C– Available only in Massachusetts.
D– Available only in New York.
E– Available only to Lutherans.
F– Available only to people in certain jobs.
G– Available only to members of a fraternal organization.

Alphabetical Summary of Term Policies

If you're considering a particular term insurance policy and you want to get a rough idea of its relative merit, you can use this alphabetical summary of all companies whose policies are included in Chapter 15. It's important to remember that you're shopping for the best possible policy, and not necessarily the best company. Some companies offer policies that may be excellent buys at certain ages and at certain face amounts, but not as good buys at other ages or face amounts. For example, the preferred one-year term policy of New England Mutual Life Insurance Company did quite well in Consumers Union's analyses of $100,000 policies at all three ages. But the same company's five-year term was rated only an average buy for a thirty-five- or forty-five-year-old man buying $25,000 of insurance.

Very few companies did consistently well at all ages and face amounts. Among companies selling participating term insurance, Teachers Insurance and Annuity Association of America was consistently at the top of CU's Ratings. Other companies whose par policies were consistently better than average in nineteen-year net cost were Penn Mutual Life Insurance Company and USAA Life Insurance Company. Among companies selling nonparticipating term policies, those of Sun Life Insurance Company of America were most consistently near the top of the Ratings. Other companies selling nonpar term policies that rated well at a variety of ages and face amounts were (in alphabetical order): Continental Assurance Company, First Colony Life Insurance Company, Old Line Life Insurance Company of America, Security-Connecticut Life Insurance Company, and United Investors Life Insurance Company.

Three companies managed the dubious distinction of having their term policies rank near the bottom of the nineteen-year Ratings at all ages and face amounts: Guardian Life Insurance Company of America, Nationwide Life Insurance Company, and Union Mutual Life Insurance Company.

Prices can change from year to year. The symbols in this table, based on 1979 rates, show roughly how each policy ranked compared with other similar policies, as measured by the nineteen-year interest-adjusted net cost index. This gives a good basic idea of a policy's comparative cost, in CU's view. A more complete idea of comparative cost can be obtained by looking at the detailed information about a policy in the tables in Chapter 15.

Summary Table of Term Policies

Listed alphabetically by company. Judgments are based on 19-year cost index (see p. 207), using rates for men. Types indicated are Participating (P) and Nonparticipating (N). If a company has several list- ings, check length of term or see Notes. In addition to standard abbreviations, the following are used: LIC (Life Insurance Co.) and LAC (Life Assurance Co.). All data are based on 1979 rates and include waiver of premium in event of disability.

Best → ⊙ ◐ ○ ◑ ● ← Worst

Company	Term (years)	Type	Age 25 $25M	Age 25 $100M	Age 35 $25M	Age 35 $100M	Age 45 $25M	Age 45 $100M	Notes
Acacia Mutual LIC	1	P		◐		⊙		○	
Acacia Mutual LIC	1	P		○		○		○	B
Acacia Mutual LIC	5	P	◐	◐	○	○	◐	◐	
Acacia Mutual LIC	5	P	○	◐	◐	○	◐	◐	B
Aetna LIC	5	N	○	●	○	○	○	◐	
Aetna LIC	1	N	○	◐	◐	●	○	◐	
Aid Association for Lutherans	1	P	◐	◐	◐	⊙	◐	◐	E
All American Life & Casualty Co.	1	N		⊙	◐	⊙	◐	⊙	
All American Life & Casualty Co.	5	N	◐	◐	◐	●	○	◐	
All American Life & Casualty Co.	4	N		⊙	◐	◐	●	⊙	
Allstate LIC	6	N	○	○	◐	○	○	○	
American Family LIC	5	P	●	●	◐	●	◐	○	
American Health & Life Ins. Co.	4	N	◐	◐	○	○	◐	◐	
American Health & Life Ins. Co.	1	N	◐	⊙	○	◐	◐	◐	A
American National Ins. Co.	5	N		◐		●		○	

American National Ins. Co.	1	N							
American States LIC	1	N							
American States LIC	3	N							
Anchor National LIC	5	N							
Anchor National LIC	1	N							
Bankers Life & Casualty Co.	5	N							
Bankers Life Co.	5	P							
Bankers Life Co.	1	P							
Bankers LIC of Nebraska	5	P							
Beneficial LIC	1	P							
Beneficial LIC	1	N							
Canada LAC	5	N							
Canada LAC	1	N							
Central LAC	1	P							
Colonial LIC of America	5	N							
Colonial LIC of America	5	N							B
Colonial LIC of America	1	N							
Columbus Mutual LIC	1	N							
Commonwealth LIC	5	N							
Commonwealth LIC	1	N							
Confederation LIC	1	P							
Confederation LIC	1	P							B
Confederation LIC	5	P							
Confederation LIC	5	P							B

A – Available only to "preferred risks."
B – Available only to nonsmokers.
C – Available only in Massachusetts.
D – Available only in New York.
E – Available only to Lutherans.
F – Available only to people in certain jobs.
G – Available only to members of a fraternal organization.

Summary Table of Term Policies *continued*

Company	Term (years)	Type	Age 25		Age 35		Age 45		Notes
			$25M	$100M	$25M	$100M	$25M	$100M	
Connecticut General LIC	5	N	○	○	○	○	○	○	
Connecticut General LIC	1	N	◉	◐	◉	◐	◐	◐	
Connecticut Mutual LIC	1	P	◐	◐	○	◐	○	◐	
Connecticut Mutual LIC	5	P	◐	◐	○	◐	○	◐	
Continental Assurance Co.	1	N	◉	◐	◉	◐	◉	◐	
Dominion LAC	1	N	◐	◐	◐	◐	◐	●	
Dominion LAC	5	N	◐	◐	◐	◐	◐	◐	
Durham LIC	1	N		◐		◐		◐	
Equitable Life Assurance Soc. of the U.S.	1	P					◐		
Equitable Life Assurance Soc. of the U.S.	5	P	◐	●			○		
Equitable LIC of Iowa	5	N		◉	◐	●		◐	
Equitable LIC of Iowa	1	N	◐	●	◐	●	◐	◐	
Farm Bureau (Iowa)	5	N	◐	●	◐	◐	◐	◐	
Federal Kemper Life Assurance Soc.	5	N	◐	◐	◐	◉	◐	◐	
Federal Kemper Life Assurance Soc.	1	N	◐	●	◐	●	○	◐	
Fidelity Union LIC	5	N	◐	○	◐	○	◐	◐	
Fidelity Union LIC	1	N	○		○			○	
Fireman's Fund American LIC	5	N	○	●	○	◉	○	◉	
Fireman's Fund American LIC	1	N	◐	◉	◐	●	●	●	
First Colony LIC	1	N		○	○	◉	●	◐	
Franklin LIC	1	N	◐	●	◐	○	◐	●	
Franklin LIC	5	N	◐	●	◐		◐	●	
Great-West LAC	5	N	◐	◐	◐	◉	◐	◉	

Company										Note
Great-West LAC	1	N								
Guardian LIC of America	1	P								
Guardian LIC of America	1	P								A
Guardian LIC of America	5	P								
Guardian LIC of America	5	P								A
Hartford LIC	5	N								
Hartford LIC	1	N								
Home Beneficial LIC	5	N								
Home LIC	5	P								
IDS LIC	5	N								
IDS LIC	1	N								
Imperial LAC of Canada	5	N								
Imperial LAC of Canada	1	N								
Indianapolis LIC	1	P								
Indianapolis LIC	5	P								
J.C. Penney LIC	1	N								
J.C. Penney LIC	5	N								
Jefferson Standard LIC	5	N								
Jefferson Standard LIC	1	N								
Kansas City LIC	5	N								
Kansas City LIC	1	N								
Knights of Columbus	1	P								G
Knights of Columbus	5	P								G
Liberty LIC	5	N								

A – Available only in New York.
B – Available only to nonsmokers.
C – Available only in Massachusetts.
D – Available only to "preferred risks."
E – Available only to Lutherans.
F – Available only to people in certain jobs.
G – Available only to members of a fraternal organization.

Summary Table of Term Policies *continued*

Company	Term (years)	Type	Age 25 $25M	Age 25 $100M	Age 35 $25M	Age 35 $100M	Age 45 $25M	Age 45 $100M	Notes
Liberty LIC	1	N		◐		●		●	
Life & Casualty Ins. Co. of Tenn.	1	N	◐	○	◐	○	◐	○	
Life & Casualty Ins. Co. of Tenn.	5	N	○	◐	○	○	○	○	
Lincoln National LIC	5	N	◐	◐	◐	◐	◐	◐	
Lincoln National LIC	1	N	◐	◐	◐	●	◐	●	
Lutheran Mutual LIC	5	P	○	●	○	◐	○	◐	
Manhattan LIC	5	P	○	◐	○	◐	○	◐	A
Manhattan LIC	5	P	◐	○		○	○	○	
Manhattan LIC	1	P		◐		◐		◐	A
Manhattan LIC	1	P	○	◐	◐	●	●	●	
Manufacturers LIC	5	P	◐		●		○		
Massachusetts Mutual LIC	5	P	⊙		⊙		⊙		C
Massachusetts SBLI	5	P	◐		◐		○		
Metropolitan LIC	5	P	◐	◐	○	○		◐	A
Metropolitan LIC	5	P	⊙	⊙	⊙	⊙		⊙	
Metropolitan LIC	1	P	◐	●	●	●		○	A
Metropolitan LIC	1	P	◐	◐	◐	◐		◐	
Midland Mutual LIC	1	P	◐		◐		○		
Midland National LIC	5	N		◐		○		◐	
Midland National LIC	5	N		●		○		◐	
Midland National LIC	1	N		●		◐		◐	
Minnesota Mutual LIC	1	P	○	◐	○	○	○	◐	

Company				Rating	Class	Note
Monarch LIC				1	N	
Monarch LIC				5	N	
Monumental LIC				5	N	
Monumental LIC				1	N	
Mutual Benefit LIC				1	P	
Mutual LIC of New York				1	P	
Mutual LIC of New York				5	P	
Mutual Trust LIC				5	P	
Mutual Trust LIC				1	P	
National Life & Accident Ins. Co.				5	N	A
National LAC of Canada				5	N	
National LAC of Canada				1	N	
National LAC of Canada				1	N	
National LIC				1	P	
National LIC				1	P	B
National LIC				5	P	
National LIC				5	P	B
Nationwide LIC				5	N	
New England Mutual LIC				1	P	
New England Mutual LIC				1	P	A
New England Mutual LIC				5	P	
New England Mutual LIC				5	P	A
New York LIC				1	P	
New York LIC				5	P	
New York SBLI				5	P	D

A – Available only to "preferred risks."
B – Available only to nonsmokers.
C – Available only in Massachusetts.
D – Available only in New York.
E – Available only to Lutherans.
F – Available only to people in certain jobs.
G – Available only to members of a fraternal organization.

Summary Table of Term Policies *continued*

Company	Term (years)	Type	Age 25 $25M	Age 25 $100M	Age 35 $25M	Age 35 $100M	Age 45 $25M	Age 45 $100M	Notes
North American LAC	1	N						◐	
North American LAC	5	N		○		○	○	◐	
North American Co. for Life & Health Ins.	1	N	◐	⊙	◐	⊙	◐	●	
North American Co. for Life & Health Ins.	5	N	◐	●	○	●	◐	◐	
Northwestern National LIC	1	N	◐	⊙	◐	●		⊙	
Northwestern National LIC	5	N		◐	◐	○	◑	○	
Occidental LIC of California	1	N	○	◐	○	◐	●	●	
Occidental LIC of California	1	N							
Occidental LIC of California	5	N		○			○	○	
Ohio National LIC	1	P		○	◐	○	○	◐	
Ohio National LIC	5	P	◐	●		●		◐	
Old Line LIC of America	1	N	⊙	●	⊙	●	◐	●	
Old Line LIC of America	5	N	◐	◐	◑	●	◐	●	
Pacific Mutual LIC	5	P	◐	●		◐	◐	●	
Pacific Mutual LIC	1	P	◐	◐		○	◐	●	
Pan-American LIC	5	P	◐	◐	○	○	◐	○	A
Pan-American LIC	1	P	◐	◐	◐	◐	◐	◐	A
Paul Revere LIC	5	N	◐	◑				○	
Penn Mutual LIC	1	P	◐	◐	◐	◐	◐	◐	
Penn Mutual LIC	1	P	◐	●	◐	◐	◑	◐	B
Phoenix Mutual LIC	5	P	◐	◐	○	◐	○	◐	
Phoenix Mutual LIC	5	P	◐	●		◐	○	◐	B
Provident Life & Accident Ins. Co.	5	N	⊙	◐	⊙	◐	⊙	◐	

Company		
Provident Life & Accident Ins. Co.	1	N
Provident Mutual LIC	1	P
Prudential Ins. Co. of America	5	P
Safeco LIC	5	N
Safeco LIC	1	N
Security Benefit LIC	5	P
Security Benefit LIC	1	P
Security-Connecticut LIC	5	N
Security-Connecticut LIC	1	N
Security Life & Accident Co.	5	N
Security Life & Accident Co.	1	N
Southern Farm Bureau LIC	1	P
Southland LIC	1	N
Southland LIC	5	N
Southwestern LIC	1	N
Southwestern LIC	5	N
Standard Ins. Co.	1	N
Standard Ins. Co.	5	N
State Farm LIC	1	P
State Farm LIC	5	P
State Mutual LAC of America	5	P
State Mutual LAC of America	5	P — B
State Mutual LAC of America	1	N — A

A—Available only to "preferred risks."
B—Available only to nonsmokers.
C—Available only in Massachusetts.
D—Available only in New York.
E—Available only to Lutherans.
F—Available only to people in certain jobs.
G—Available only to members of a fraternal organization.

Summary Table of Term Policies *continued*

Company	Term (years)	Type	Age 25 $25M	Age 25 $100M	Age 35 $25M	Age 35 $100M	Age 45 $25M	Age 45 $100M	Notes
State Mutual LAC of America	1	N		◐		◐	◐		B
Sun LAC of Canada	1	N		○		○		○	
Sun LAC of Canada	5	N	○	◑	○	○	○	○	
Sun LIC of America	1	N	◉	●	◉	●	●	◉	
Teachers Ins. & Annuity Assoc. of America	5	P	◉	●	◉	●	●	◉	F
Time Ins. Co.	1	N		◐		○		○	
Travelers Ins. Co.	5	N	○	○	○	○	○	◐	
Union Central LIC	1	P		○		○		○	
Union Central LIC	5	P	○	◐	○	◐	◐	○	
Union Mutual LIC	5	P	◑	●	◐	●		●	
United Benefit LIC	1	N		◉		○		○	
United Benefit LIC	5	N	○	○	○	○		◐	
United Investors LIC	1	N	◐	●	◐	●		●	
U.S. LIC in the City of N.Y.	1	N	◐	●	◑	◉	○	◉	
U.S. LIC in the City of N.Y.	5	N	◐	○	◐	◉	◐	●	
U.S. LIC in the City of N.Y.	4	N		◉		◉	◐	●	
USAA LIC	1	P	◑	●	◑	◉		◐	F
USAA LIC	5	P	◑		◐	○	◉	◐	F
Woodmen of the World Life Ins. Soc.	5	P	○	○				○	G
Woodmen of the World Life Ins. Soc.	1	P	○	○		○		○	G

A – Available only to "preferred risks."
B – Available only to nonsmokers.
C – Available only in Massachusetts.
D – Available only in New York.
E – Available only to Lutherans.
F – Available only to people in certain jobs.
G – Available only to members of a fraternal organization.

CU's Ratings of Cash Value Policies

The tables in this chapter show comparative cost index Ratings for 279 cash value insurance policies evaluated by Consumers Union in 1979. All are cash value policies with the premium payment period extending to age eighty-five or later and with endowment at age eighty-five or later. Twelve tables cover combinations of age (twenty-five, thirty-five, and forty-five), and face amount ($25,000 and $100,000), with and without dividends (par and nonpar). To make best use of the tables, select the one closest to your situation.

The tables show the rate of return on the savings component of each policy. As far as CU knows, rate of return figures have been previously published only in academic or insurance industry circles, and for far fewer policies. With information on rate of return, you can make a rough comparison between yields on cash value policies* and yields on other investment vehicles such as passbook accounts, certifi-

---

*As we explain in Chapter 5, the yield on the savings component of a cash value policy is tax-deferred and at least partially tax-exempt.

cates of deposit, and municipal bonds. (The accuracy and usefulness of such comparisons are often questioned by people within the life insurance industry because the insurance rate of return figure is dependent on certain actuarial assumptions, as explained below.) You can also compare potential rate of return of a cash value policy with that of a term policy combined with investment income. (The more that actual dividends deviate from those illustrated at the time of sale, the rougher the comparison.) If you buy a low-cost term policy—but not one of the *very* lowest in cost—your investment income will need to match or exceed the yields shown in CU's Ratings for cash value policies to make it worthwhile to "buy term and invest the difference."

A yield figure is provided in our Ratings for nine years, nineteen years, and twenty-nine years. A glance at the tables will show that the yields are paltry or even appear as minus figures over nine years but increase as time passes. When a cash value policy is held for as long as twenty-nine years, the investment yields are good on some policies but remain quite poor on others. There are even policies whose yield declines between the nineteenth and twenty-ninth years. As we state in Chapter 14, CU believes that buyers of cash value policies who are using our Ratings in this chapter should give preference—other things being equal—to the policies whose yield does not decline in the third decade.

The yields shown played no part in the Ratings order, though they correlate closely with the interest-adjusted cost indexes. We show the yields because an average annual rate of return is a figure that consumers are used to. You should understand, however, that the size of the yields shown depends on certain actuarial assumptions. The method used in calculating the yields—called the Linton method after its developer, Albert Linton—assumes that a portion of the cash value premium goes to pay for insurance protection, and a portion goes for savings. But how much of the premium goes for insurance protection and how much for savings? That's a crucial question. The bigger the insurance protection component of the premium, the smaller the savings component. And the smaller the savings component, the higher the apparent yield on the savings.

The protection element in a cash value policy is measured by the cost of term insurance (which is, after all, pure protection). But whose term insurance rates should be used as the standard? If you want to show that the savings element of a cash value policy has a high investment yield, you can assume that the insurance protection part of the premium is the same as for *costly* term insurance. Thus, your investment in the savings component is small, and the return seems high when calculated against it. If you want to show that the yield on the cash value savings element is poor, you can assume that the insurance component is the same as for very inexpensive term insurance. As one actuary said to CU, "Show me the yield you want to illustrate, and I'll tell you what term rates to use."

CU's calculations, performed using the Linton-yield computer program of the Federal Trade Commission, make what we consider to be reasonable assumptions. The hypothetical term insurance rates used in our calculations are the "low-cost" term rates developed for this purpose by the Society of Actuaries, a professional organization. We think this procedure provides a fair way to separate the insurance-protection component of cash value policies from the savings component. (Although the term rates developed by the Society of Actuaries are hypothetical, there are, in fact, term policies on the market that are priced as low or lower.)

More important, the assumptions used are the same for all companies. Some in the insurance industry may complain that the investment yields shown are too low; that is, we should have assumed a higher-cost insurance component to show better yields on the savings component. But the differences among companies are striking, and hard to argue away. And these differences would remain no matter what assumptions went into the calculation. For example, for a thirty-five-year-old man who bought a $100,000 participating cash value policy from the Aetna Life Insurance Company, our study projected a twenty-nine-year yield of 3.69 percent. As a comparison, for a participating policy for the same age and face amount purchased from Teachers Insurance and Annuity Association of America, we showed a yield of 8.07 percent.

No economatic plans were included in our Ratings of cash value policies because the full face amount of economatics, typically, is not guaranteed from the time of purchase. As reported in Chapter 9, CU's consulting actuaries evaluated a dozen economatic policies from eight companies and found some good buys—and some mediocre ones. (See page 129 for more information about economatic policies.)

The twenty-year interest-adjusted net cost index is included in all tables because comparable indexes on policies you're considering should be readily available to you, particularly if you ask for them. Thus, the tables can be used to compare the indexes of policies you're offered with the indexes in the Ratings. Remember that the difference between a high-cost and a low-cost policy can mean hundreds of dollars to you—even thousands over twenty years or so.

The range of cost indexes for cash value insurance is huge. Let's say you are a thirty-five-year-old man shopping for a $100,000 participating cash value policy. The Ratings show that the top-ranked policy generally available to standard risks, Central Life Assurance Company's "Maximum Life," had a twenty-year interest-adjusted net cost index of $303. That worked out to a theoretical cost, over twenty years, of

$10,520. The bottom-ranked policy, Fidelity Life Association's "Ordinary Life," had an index of $964, which amounted to a theoretical cost of $33,469 over twenty years. The cost difference would have been $22,949.

The Ratings give, in addition to the cost index, the first year's premium for each policy. Note that the rates shown in the tables are for males. Rates for females are generally lower at all ages, because women as a group live longer than men. Traditionally, insurance surveys have covered only men because men bought most policies. That is changing, but men still account for about 75 percent of sales.

You may find you're charged a different premium than the one shown in our Ratings for other reasons.

■ The tables show 1979 rates, and rates can change. Recently, most rate changes have been downward.

■ Our actuaries adjusted some premiums to account for the fact that some companies calculate your age based on your nearest birthday, while others use your last birthday.

■ The tables show annual premiums; if you pay more frequently, the total premiums for the year are higher.

■ Premiums and indexes shown in CU's tables all include waiver of premium in the event of disability. In some policies, the waiver was standard and its cost was automatically included in the premium. It was easier to add the cost of the waiver for policies that didn't include it than to subtract its cost from policies that did.

The Ratings order was determined as follows: First, policies were grouped by their performance on the nineteen-year interest-adjusted net cost index. Within these groups, they were ranked according to their performance on nine-year net cost, twenty-nine year net cost, and nineteen-year net payment, all weighted equally. Ties were broken by listing the tied policies in order of increasing twenty-year interest-adjusted net cost index. Any remaining ties were broken by listing the policies according to the amount of the initial premium for a policy. As we explain in Chapter 7, we gave more weight to net cost than to net payment for several reasons. First, most buyers very probably will cash in their policies before they die. Second, CU believes that most cash value policyholders who reach retirement age will be well advised to cash in their policies at that time, for their own financial benefit. Third, the cash value is present in a policy as a potential asset, whether the buyer actually uses it or not. For all of these reasons, CU believes the primary measure of merit for a cash value policy should be the one that reflects the cash value.

Some policies are available only to people in certain groups, geographic areas, or occupations. Restrictions on availability are recorded in the footnotes to the Ratings.

Use the tables in Part II as a guide to—but not as a substitute for—your own comparison shopping. In light of variations in policy language and other nonprice factors and, on par policies, of the uncertainty of dividend illustrations, CU suggests that you give little weight to differences of less than 10 percent in the cost index.

Cash Value Insurance Policies
Type: Nonparticipating Amount: $25,000 Age: 25

Listed in order of increasing cost, based primarily on 19-year cost index (see p. 267). All of the rates are for men's policies; rates for women at the same age are generally lower. Where company and policy listings are the same, difference is indicated by footnote. In addition to standard abbreviations, the following are used: LIC (Life Insurance Co.), and LAC (Life Assurance Co.). All data are based on 1979 rates and include waiver of premium in event of disability.

Best ◀————————▶ Worst

Company and policy	Annual premium	Cost Indexes 20-yr	Cost Indexes 9-yr	Cost Indexes 19-yr	Cost Indexes 29-yr	Net payment index	Yields 9-yr	Yields 19-yr	Yields 29-yr
Continental Assurance Co. Economiser	$187	$77	◐	●	●	●	-1.78%	5.10%	5.63%
Provident Life & Acc. Ins. Co. Whole Life Paid Up—90	262	82	●	●	●	●	3.51	4.76	4.14
Continental Assurance Co. Maximiser II	231	84	◐	●	●	●	0.88	4.59	4.58
Equitable LIC of Iowa Life Paid Up at 95	267	85	●	●	●	◐	2.62	4.58	4.00
Old Line LIC of Amer. Bus. Whole Life	301	87	●	●	●	○	6.94	4.52	3.59
Allstate LIC Exec. Plan [B]	249	94	◐	◐	◐	◐	0.03	3.99	3.98
Time Ins. Co. Whole Life	249	95	◐	◐	◐	◐	-0.89	3.89	3.88
Home Beneficial LIC Life Paid Up at 95	249	97	◐	◐	◐	◐	0.16	3.86	4.04
Amer. States LIC Whole Life	253	100	◐	◐	◐	◐	-0.28	3.74	3.78
Allstate LIC Exec. Plan	254	100	◐	◐	◐	◐	-0.63	3.69	3.78
Kansas City LIC Exec. L 95 Guaranteed Cost	254	101	◐	◐	◐	◐	-0.84	3.64	3.79
Federal Kemper Life Assurance Soc. OL—4	253	104	◐	◐	◐	◐	1.21	3.54	3.73

[A] Available only to "preferred risks."
[B] Available only to nonsmokers.
[C] Available only in Massachusetts.
[D] Available only in New York.
[E] Available only to Lutherans.
[F] Available only to people in certain jobs.
[G] Available only to members of a fraternal organization.

Ratings of Cash Value Policies (Nonpar/$25,000/25 Years) continued

Company and policy	Annual premium	Cost Indexes 20-yr.	9-yr.	19-yr.	29-yr.	Net payment index	Yields 9-yr.	19-yr.	29-yr.
Fidelity Union LIC Presidents Pfd. Life	$271	$105	◐	◐	◐	◐	−0.06%	3.50%	3.45%
Monarch LIC Ordinary Life-NP	280	109	◐	◐	◐	◐	−0.39	3.37	3.37
Colonial LIC of Amer. Life Paid Up at 92	261	110	◐	◐	◐	◐	−1.09	3.23	3.60
Manufacturers LIC Permanent Economic Protection	261	110	●	◐	◐	◐	−1.03	3.26	3.62
Life & Casualty Ins. Co. of Tenn. Pfd. Exec. Whole Life	305	98	●	○	○	○	4.10	4.10	3.39
All Amer. Life & Casualty Co. Bus. Whole Life	313	100	●	○	○	○	5.98	4.09	3.28
U.S. LIC in the City of N.Y. Bus. Whole Life	313	100	●	○	○	○	5.98	4.09	3.28
Southwestern LIC Exec. 85	311	106	●	○	○	○	3.40	3.71	3.10
National Life & Acc. Ins. Co. Exec. Whole Life A	313	106	●	◐	◐	◐	3.83	3.78	3.08
Lincoln National LIC Whole Life B	254	107	○	◐	◐	◐	−1.87	3.30	3.84
Southwestern LIC Special Exec. 95	269	107	○	◐	◐	◐	−1.75	3.34	3.45
Lincoln National LIC Whole Life	258	111	○	◐	◐	◐	−2.35	3.07	3.69
Occidental LIC of Calif. Guaranteed Whole Life	307	98	●	◐	◐	◐	0.40	3.99	3.31
Travelers Ins. Co. Ordinary Life	293	105	○	◐	◐	◐	0.93	3.61	3.14
Home Beneficial LIC Whole Life	299	111	○	◐	◐	◐	0.01	3.44	3.18
Provident Life & Acc. Ins. Co. Whole Life	319	108	●	◐	◐	◐	3.93	3.77	2.94
J.C. Penney LIC Value Select—Whole Life	252	114	○	○	◐	◐	−2.86	2.86	3.53
Dominion LAC Whole Life	254	115	○	○	◐	◐	−2.93	2.80	3.54
IDS LIC Whole Life	265	115	○	○	○	◐	−2.48	2.89	3.33
Paul Revere LIC Exec. Life to 95	266	115	○	○	○	◐	−1.86	2.97	3.44
Amer. National Ins. Co. Life Paid Up at 90	274	119	○	○	○	◐	−1.68	2.74	3.24
Midland National LIC Whole Life	227	120	○	○	○	●	−8.60	1.85	3.52
United Investors LIC Whole Life	270	120	○	○	○	◐	0.04	2.68	3.17

Policy		Circles						1	2	3
Durham LIC Life Paid Up at 90	302	○	○	◑		○	114	1.08	3.32	3.10
Jefferson Standard LIC Life Paid Up at 90	302	○	○	◑		○	114	1.08	3.32	3.10
Durham LIC Life Paid Up at 95	264	◐	◑	◑		◑	115	-4.41	2.87	3.36
Monumental LIC LP at 95 Exec.	302	◑	◑	◑		○	116	1.16	3.25	3.06
Commonwealth LIC Life Paid Up at 95	259	●	◑	◑		◑	118	-3.21	2.63	3.37
National Life & Acc. Ins. Co. Exec. Life Plus Ⓐ	261	◑	◑	◑		◑	118	-3.20	2.62	3.34
Travelers Ins. Co. Presidential Whole Life—4	260	◑	◑	○		◑	121	-3.79	2.42	3.24
Jefferson Standard LIC Life Paid Up at 95	277	○	◑	◑		○	121	-2.06	2.71	3.24
Colonial LIC of Amer. Endowment at 98 Ⓑ	261	◐	○	◑		◑	122	-3.74	2.41	3.29
Sun LIC of America L96	272	○	◑	◑		○	114	-4.99	2.99	3.21
IDS LIC Select Whole Life	323	◑	○	●		◑	119	3.37	3.26	2.81
Liberty LIC Liberty Protection 95 (LPU at 95)	330	◑	◑	●		◑	119	2.99	3.29	2.64
Monarch LIC Accelerator 95	312	○	◑	◐		○	121	1.56	3.03	2.77
Aetna LIC Whole Life	276	◑	○	◑		○	122	-2.92	2.60	3.07
Franklin LIC Pfd. 95	277	○	◑	◑		○	123	-3.20	2.56	3.03
Southland LIC Exec. Pfd. Whole Life	321	◑	◑	◑		◑	115	0.59	3.32	2.87
J.C. Penney LIC Exec. Select Life Paid Up at 90	328	◑	◑	◑		◑	120	1.89	3.12	2.69
First Colony LIC Whole Life	294	○	○	◑		○	113	-7.03	3.13	2.97
Security-Connecticut LIC Bus. Whole Life	303	◑	◑	◑		○	115	-1.48	3.25	2.83
Commonwealth LIC Whole Life	323	◑	◑	◑		○	118	-0.11	3.22	2.81
Colonial LIC of Amer. Whole Life Ⓑ	332	◑	◑	◑		○	120	-0.75	3.16	2.75
Colonial LIC of Amer. Endowment at 98	267	◑	○	◑		◑	128	-4.41	2.09	3.08
INA LIC Whole Life	268	◑	○	◑		◑	129	-4.47	2.07	3.06
United Benefit LIC Ordinary Life	268	◑	○	◑		◑	130	-4.71	1.98	2.95
Hartford LIC Whole Life	271	○	○	◑		◑	132	-4.81	1.90	2.95

Ⓐ Available only to "preferred risks."
Ⓑ Available only to nonsmokers.
Ⓒ Available only to people in certain jobs.
Ⓓ Available only in New York.
Ⓔ Available only to Lutherans.
Ⓕ Available only in Massachusetts.
Ⓖ Available only to members of a fraternal organization.

Ratings of Cash Value Policies (Nonpar/$25,000/25 Years) *continued*

Company and policy	Annual premium	Cost indexes 20-yr.	Cost indexes 9-yr.	Cost indexes 19-yr.	Cost indexes 29-yr.	Net payment index	Yields 9-yr.	Yields 19-yr.	Yields 29-yr.
National LAC of Canada Exec. Ordinary Life	$275	$136	◑	◑	○	◕	−5.54%	1.68%	2.81%
Colonial LIC of Amer. Cash Flo [B]	276	137	◑	◑	○	◕	−5.32	1.66	2.79
Nationwide LIC W.L.P.U. at 95	289	125	◑	◑	○	○	−3.49	2.50	2.93
Safeco LIC Pfd. Life/Exec. Life	289	127	◑	◑	○	○	−3.63	2.41	2.86
Amer. National Ins. Co. Life Paid Up at 95	284	129	◑	◑	○	○	−2.65	2.27	2.94
Connecticut General LIC OL Plus	276	131	◑	○	○	◕	−4.99	2.05	2.41
United Benefit LIC Life Paid Up at 90	312	132	○	◑	◑	○	−0.03	2.44	2.58
Time Ins. Co. Exec. Special	321	142	◔	◑	◑	○	1.85	2.21	2.36
Amer. Health & Life Ins. Co. Freedom Whole Life—Level	307	127	◑	◑	◑	○	−1.55	2.71	2.78
Northwestern National LIC Whole Life Non Par	298	130	◑	◑	◑	○	−3.21	2.44	2.78
Great-West LAC Life at 90	297	142	◑	◑	◑	○	−4.02	1.72	2.60
Security Life & Acc. Co. Whole Life 10	301	147	◑	◑	◑	○	−1.87	1.52	2.31
Aetna LIC Life Paid Up at 95	333	149	◑	●	◑	◑	0.85	1.95	2.17
Colonial LIC of Amer. Whole Life	338	127	◑	◑	◑	◑	−1.23	2.93	2.60
Liberty LIC Liberty Exec. Pfd. (WL)	317	137	◑	◑	◑	◑	−2.03	2.30	2.52
Monumental LIC LP at 90 Exec.	328	141	◑	◑	◑	◑	−2.57	2.20	2.38
Connecticut General LIC Ordinary Life	309	144	●	◑	◑	◑	−6.04	1.75	2.28
Bankers Life & Casualty Co. Exec. Ordinary Life	326	146	◑	◑	◑	◑	−0.97	1.98	2.27
Imperial LAC of Canada Whole Life	286	147	●	◑	◑	○	−6.29	1.19	2.49
Colonial LIC of Amer. Economiser [B]	345	133	○	◑	●	●	−1.70	2.71	2.45
North Amer. Co. for Life & Health Ins. Life Paid Up at 95	352	147	◔	◑	●	●	0.65	2.24	2.03
Bankers Life & Casualty Co. Life Paid Up at 95	351	171	◑	●	●	●	−0.70	1.09	1.66
INA LIC Exec. Whole Life	353	173	◑	●	●	●	−0.64	1.02	1.61

Type: Nonparticipating   Amount: $25,000   Age: 35

Listed in order of increasing cost, based primarily on 19-year cost index (see p. 267). All of the rates are for men's policies; rates for women at the same age are generally lower. Where company and policy listings are the same, difference is indicated by footnote. In addition to standard abbreviations, the following are used: LIC (Life Insurance Co.) and LAC (Life Assurance Co.). All data are based on 1979 rates and include waiver of premium in event of disability.

Best ● ◑ ○ ◑ ● Worst

Company and policy	Annual premium	Cost Indexes 20-yr.	9-yr.	19-yr.	29-yr.	Net payment index	Yields 9-yr.	19-yr.	29-yr.
Continental Assurance Co. Economiser	$316	$141	◑	●	●	●	−1.72%	3.93%	4.66%
Continental Assurance Co. Maximiser II	357	145	◑	●	●	◑	0.63	3.92	4.05
Provident Life & Acc. Ins. Co. Whole Life Paid Up—90	388	147	●	●	◑	◑	2.32	3.96	3.64
Equitable LIC of Iowa Life Paid Up at 95	395	151	●	●	●	◑	1.58	3.76	3.47
Kansas City LIC Exec. L 95 Guaranteed Cost	370	154	◑	●	●	◑	−0.04	3.48	3.64
Old Line LIC of Amer. Bus. Whole Life	417	141	●	●	◑	○	4.97	4.10	3.33
Life & Casualty Ins. Co. of Tenn. Pfd. Exec. Whole Life	422	152	◑	●	○	◑	3.22	3.83	3.24
Lincoln National LIC Whole Life [B]	371	161	◑	◑	●	◑	−0.51	3.35	3.72
Amer. States LIC Whole Life	376	160	◑	◑	◑	◑	−0.37	3.27	3.42
Home Beneficial LIC Life Paid Up at 95	375	161	◑	◑	◑	◑	0.08	3.35	3.63
Federal Kemper Life Assurance Soc. OL—4	383	173	●	●	◑	○	0.11	2.95	3.33
All Amer. Life & Casualty Co. Bus. Whole Life	432	162	●	◑	○	○	4.04	3.60	3.08
U.S. LIC in the City of N.Y. Bus. Whole Life	432	162	●	◑	○	○	4.04	3.60	3.08

[A] Available only to "preferred risks."
[B] Available only to nonsmokers.
[C] Available only in Massachusetts.
[D] Available only in New York.
[E] Available only to Lutherans.
[F] Available only to people in certain jobs.
[G] Available only to members of a fraternal organization.

Ratings of Cash Value Policies (Nonpar/$25,000/35 Years) continued

Company and policy	Annual premium	Cost Indexes 20-yr.	Cost Indexes 9-yr.	Cost Indexes 19-yr.	Cost Indexes 29-yr.	Net payment Index	Yields 9-yr.	Yields 19-yr.	Yields 29-yr.
Allstate LIC Exec. Plan [B]	$380	$163	○	●	●	◑	−0.46%	3.26%	3.49%
Time Ins. Co. Whole Life	380	164	○	●	●	◑	−1.21	3.10	3.32
J.C. Penney LIC Value Select-Whole Life	366	165	○	●	●	●	−0.94	3.06	3.54
Lincoln National LIC Whole Life	380	170	○	●	●	●	−1.14	3.03	3.50
Southwestern LIC Executive 85	439	172	●	●	◑	○	1.97	3.16	2.76
Dominion LAC Whole Life	375	173	○	●	●	◑	−1.49	2.86	3.44
Manufacturers LIC Permanent Economic Protection	387	173	○	●	●	◑	−0.73	2.94	3.33
National Life & Acc. Ins. Co. Exec. Whole Life [A]	441	174	●	◑	○	○	2.29	3.09	2.71
Fidelity Union LIC Presidents Pfd. Life	398	171	◑	●	●	●	−0.33	2.98	3.09
Monumental LIC LP at 95 Exec.	423	174	○	●	●	○	0.53	3.10	2.97
Security-Connecticut LIC Bus. Whole Life	411	159	○	●	●	○	0.06	3.53	3.12
Occidental LIC of Calif. Guaranteed Whole Life	439	167	○	◑	●	○	−0.32	3.32	2.87
Colonial LIC of Amer. Whole Life [B]	444	168	○	●	●	○	0.01	3.32	2.84
Travelers Ins. Co. Ordinary Life	424	173	○	○	○	○	0.07	2.99	2.77
IDS LIC Whole Life	385	175	○	●	●	●	−1.39	2.85	3.28
Allstate LIC Exec. Plan	391	175	○	●	●	●	−1.22	2.88	3.23
Colonial LIC of Amer. Endowment at 98 [B]	378	176	○	●	●	●	−1.68	2.76	3.35
Commonwealth LIC Life Paid Up at 95	384	179	○	●	●	●	−2.00	2.54	3.16
INA LIC Whole Life	383	181	○	○	●	●	−2.06	2.57	3.23
National Life & Acc. Ins. Co. Exec. Life Plus [A]	388	181	○	○	●	●	−1.94	2.50	3.11
Aetna LIC Whole Life	392	175	○	○	○	●	−1.27	2.86	3.19
Southwestern LIC Special Exec. 95	397	175	○	○	○	●	−1.55	2.79	3.05
Franklin LIC Pfd. 95	393	177	◑	○	○	●	−1.52	2.81	3.16
Midland National LIC Whole Life	349	179	◑	○	○	◑	−5.08	2.16	3.43

Policy										
Amer. National Ins. Co. Life Paid Up at 90 [B]	397	179	○		○	◐	−0.86	2.68	3.06
Colonial LIC of Amer. Life Paid Up at 92	396	182	◐		○	●	−1.34	2.63	3.11
Durham LIC Life Paid Up at 90	435	183	○		○	○	0.65	2.84	2.77
Paul Revere LIC Exec. Life to 95	397	184	◐		○	◐	−1.57	2.59	3.08
Jefferson Standard LIC Life Paid Up at 90	437	184	◐		○	◐	0.58	2.81	2.75
United Investors LIC Whole Life	400	189	○		○	○	−0.66	2.42	2.94
Time Ins. Co. Exec. Special	431	191	●		◐	●	2.35	2.58	2.59
Monarch LIC Ordinary Life-NP	410	176	○		○	○	−0.25	2.98	3.05
Sun LIC of America L96	400	178	◐		○	◐	−3.33	2.68	2.93
Northwestern National LIC Whole Life Non Par	412	182	○		◐	○	−1.45	2.74	2.97
Provident Life & Acc. Ins. Co. Whole Life	451	182	●		○	●	2.05	2.99	2.57
Home Beneficial LIC Whole Life	434	183	○		○	◐	−0.48	2.84	2.78
Safeco LIC Pfd. Life/Exec. Life	406	184	◐		○	◐	−2.08	2.49	2.86
Connecticut General LIC OL Plus	392	185	●		○	◐	−3.05	2.44	2.65
IDS LIC Select Whole Life	451	185	◐		◐	●	2.45	2.89	2.59
Travelers Ins. Co. Presidential Whole Life—4	387	186	◐		○	◐	−2.44	2.30	3.02
Durham LIC Life Paid Up at 95	398	188	◐		○	◐	−3.25	2.40	2.99
Southland LIC Exec. Pfd. Whole Life	448	180	○		○	◐	0.22	2.89	2.59
Commonwealth LIC Whole Life	451	183	○		○	◐	−0.43	2.80	2.52
Colonial LIC of Amer. Whole Life	460	184	◐		○	◐	−0.89	2.88	2.53
Colonial LIC of Amer. Economiser [B]	464	188	◐		○	◐	−1.09	2.78	2.46
Colonial LIC of Amer. Endowment at 98	394	192	○		◐	◐	−2.78	2.20	2.96
Hartford LIC Whole Life	395	193	○		◐	◐	−2.87	2.16	2.93
Colonial LIC of Amer. Cash Flo [B]	401	200	○		○	◐	−3.27	1.95	2.79

[A] Available only to "preferred risks."
[B] Available only to nonsmokers.
[C] Available only to people in certain jobs.
[D] Available only in New York.
[E] Available only to Lutherans.
[F] Available only in Massachusetts.
[G] Available only to members of a fraternal organization.

Ratings of Cash Value Policies (Nonpar/$25,000/35 Years) continued

Company and policy	Annual premium	Cost Indexes				Net payment index	Yields		
		20-yr.	9-yr.	19-yr.	29-yr.		9-yr.	19-yr.	29-yr.
United Benefit LIC Ordinary Life	$401	$200	◐	◐	○	◑	-3.34%	1.84%	2.70%
Nationwide LIC W.L.P.U. at 95	417	192	◐	◐	○	○	-2.39	2.26	2.70
Jefferson Standard LIC Life Paid Up at 95	413	193	◐	◐	○	○	-1.68	2.33	2.86
Amer. National Ins. Co. Life Paid Up at 95	415	196	◐	◐	◐	○	-1.97	2.12	2.66
Monarch LIC Accelerator 95	454	196	◐	◑	◑	◑	0.80	2.54	2.38
North Amer. Co. for Life & Health Ins. Life Paid Up at 95	462	196	◐	●	●	●	1.21	2.60	2.31
Liberty LIC Liberty Protection 95 (LPU at 95)	464	196	◐	●	●	●	1.20	2.60	2.31
Aetna LIC Life Paid Up at 95	455	209	◐	●	●	◑	0.99	2.12	2.27
J.C. Penney LIC Exec. Select Life Paid Up at 90	466	198	○	○	○	○	0.24	2.40	2.24
Amer. Health & Life Ins. Co. Freedom Whole Life—Level	443	201	◐	●	●	●	-1.67	2.26	2.44
Great-West LAC Life at 90	423	204	◐	◑	◑	●	-2.26	1.98	2.64
United Benefit LIC Life Paid Up at 90	449	208	○	◑	◑	●	-0.73	2.04	2.23
First Colony LIC Whole Life	435	189	●	●	●	○	-5.36	2.50	2.55
Connecticut General LIC Ordinary Life	433	204	●	●	●	●	-3.65	2.07	2.41
Monumental LIC LP at 90 Executive	457	207	◐	●	●	◑	-1.91	2.15	2.31
Security Life & Acc. Co. Whole Life 10	436	220	◑	●	●	○	-2.08	1.51	2.22
National LAC of Canada Exec. Ordinary Life	414	213	◐	●	●	○	-4.29	1.52	2.52
Imperial LAC of Canada Whole Life	416	214	◐	●	●	◑	-4.18	1.49	2.49
Liberty LIC Liberty Exec. Pfd. (WL)	456	216	○	●	●	●	-1.91	1.87	2.19
INA LIC Exec. Whole Life	477	235	○	◐	◑	●	-0.13	1.41	1.82
Bankers Life & Casualty Co. Exec. Ordinary Life	463	222	◐	●	●	●	-1.33	1.72	2.07
Bankers Life & Casualty Co. Life Paid Up at 95	485	244	◐	●	●	◐	-0.56	1.16	1.66

Type: Nonparticipating   Amount: $25,000   Age: 45

Listed in order of increasing cost, based primarily on 19-year cost index (see p. 267). All of the rates are for men's policies; rates for women at the same age are generally lower. Where company and policy listings are the same, difference is indicated by footnote. In addition to standard abbreviations, the following are used: LIC (Life Insurance Co.) and LAC (Life Assurance Co.). All data are based on 1979 rates and include waiver of premium in event of disability.

Best ● ◑ ○ ● Worst

Company and policy	Annual premium	Cost Indexes 20-yr.	9-yr.	19-yr.	29-yr.	Net payment index	Yields 9-yr.	19-yr.	29-yr.
Amer. States LIC Whole Life	$564	$275	●	●	●	◑	1.03%	3.66%	3.67%
Lincoln National LIC Whole Life [B]	563	282	●	●	●	◑	1.22	3.69	3.89
Kansas City LIC Exec. L 95 Guaranteed Cost	577	287	◑	●	●	◑	0.50	3.30	3.44
Life & Casualty Ins. Co. of Tenn. Pfd. Exec. Whole Life	621	284	●	●	●	○	3.08	3.63	3.15
Old Line LIC of Amer. Bus. Whole Life	625	284	●	●	●	○	3.01	3.43	3.01
Security-Connecticut LIC Bus. Whole Life	612	289	◑	◑	●	○	0.54	3.45	3.14
Continental Assurance Co. Maximiser II	583	295	◑	◑	◑	◑	0.30	3.31	3.52
Continental Assurance Co. Economiser	550	298	○	◑	●	◑	-1.67	3.18	3.90
Home Beneficial LIC Life Paid Up at 95	584	298	◑	◑	◑	◑	0.57	3.25	3.50
J.C. Penney LIC Value Select—Whole Life	575	302	◑	◑	◑	◑	-0.35	2.91	3.33
Lincoln National LIC Whole Life	584	302	◑	◑	◑	◑	0.20	3.14	3.48
Dominion LAC Whole Life	580	304	◑	◑	◑	◑	-0.30	3.09	3.52
Colonial LIC of Amer. Endowment at 98 [B]	578	307	◑	◑	◑	◑	-0.23	3.01	3.46

[A] Available only to "preferred risks."
[B] Available only to nonsmokers.
[C] Available only in Massachusetts.
[D] Available only in New York.
[E] Available only to Lutherans.
[F] Available only to people in certain jobs.
[G] Available only to members of a fraternal organization.

Ratings of Cash Value Policies (Nonpar/$25,000/45 Years) *continued*

Company and policy	Annual premium	Cost Indexes 20-yr.	Cost Indexes 9-yr.	Cost Indexes 19-yr.	Cost Indexes 29-yr.	Net payment index	Yields 9-yr.	Yields 19-yr.	Yields 29-yr.
Manufacturers LIC Permanent Economic Protection	$598	$312	●	◐	◐	◐	−0.03%	2.91%	3.22%
All Amer. Life & Casualty Co. Bus. Whole Life	641	302	●	◐	○	○	2.27	3.21	2.84
U.S. LIC In the City of N.Y. Bus. Whole Life	641	302	●	◐	○	○	2.27	3.21	2.84
Allstate LIC Exec. Plan Ⓐ	600	305	○	◐	◐	◐	−0.38	3.04	3.34
Time Ins. Co. Whole Life	598	310	○	◐	◐	◐	−0.96	2.72	2.98
Connecticut General LIC OL Plus	587	304	○	◐	◐	◐	−0.66	3.02	3.00
Equitable LIC of Iowa Life Paid Up at 95	618	309	◐	◐	◐	○	1.00	3.01	2.97
Provident Life & Acc. Ins. Co. Whole Life Paid Up—90	625	312	◐	◐	◐	○	0.75	2.95	2.93
Colonial LIC of Amer. Whole Life Ⓑ	652	308	○	◐	◐	◐	0.27	3.04	2.68
INA LIC Whole Life	593	319	○	○	○	○	−0.97	2.71	3.21
Time Ins. Co. Exec. Special	636	326	●	◐	◐	◐	2.26	2.47	2.50
Amer. National Ins. Co. Life Paid Up at 90 Ⓑ	610	319	●	◐	◐	◐	−0.21	2.55	2.78
National Life & Acc. Ins. Co. Exec. Whole Life Ⓐ	656	321	●	◐	○	○	1.40	2.60	2.39
Midland National LIC Whole Life	578	333	◐	○	○	○	−4.00	1.95	3.02
Allstate LIC Exec. Plan Ⓑ	614	319	○	○	○	○	−1.04	2.69	3.08
Fidelity Union LIC Presidents Pfd. Life	619	320	○	○	○	◐	−0.58	2.51	2.70
Southwestern LIC Executive 85	660	320	○	○	○	◐	1.11	2.62	2.40
Monumental LIC LP at 95 Exec.	644	322	○	○	○	○	−0.08	2.72	2.78
Commonwealth LIC Life Paid Up at 95	604	325	○	○	○	○	−1.41	2.34	2.86
National Life & Acc. Ins. Co. Exec. Life Plus Ⓐ	608	325	○	○	○	○	−1.18	2.34	2.82
Northwestern National LIC Whole Life Non Par	628	325	○	○	○	○	−0.90	2.59	2.82
Federal Kemper Life Assurance Soc. OL—4	610	326	○	○	○	○	−0.32	2.54	2.99
Aetna LIC Whole Life	618	327	○	○	○	○	−1.21	2.50	2.85

Policy	No.	No.				Rating	Value	Rate 1	Rate 2
Travelers Ins. Co. Ordinary Life	647	327				○	−0.49	2.39	2.35
Safeco LIC Pfd. Life/Exec. Life	619	328				○	−1.25	2.31	2.66
Franklin LIC Pfd. 95	620	329				○	−1.36	2.47	2.83
Southwestern LIC Special Exec. 95	621	329				○	−1.36	2.26	2.63
Travelers Ins. Co. Presidential Whole Life—4	604	331				○	−1.77	2.16	2.78
IDS LIC Whole Life	615	332				◐	−1.44	2.37	2.86
Monarch LIC Ordinary Life—NP	638	332				○	−0.37	2.47	2.63
Colonial LIC of Amer. Endowment at 98	607	336				○	−1.61	2.28	2.92
Sun LIC of America L96	617	319		◐		○	−2.31	2.49	2.72
Connecticut General LIC Ordinary Life	638	335		◐		○	−1.96	2.35	2.55
Durham LIC Life Paid Up at 90	662	335		◐	◐	◐	0.61	2.48	2.45
Jefferson Standard LIC Life Paid Up at 90	662	335		◐	◐	◐	0.61	2.47	2.44
Allstate LIC Exec. Plan	631	336		◐	◐	◐	−1.80	2.30	2.79
North Amer. Co. for Life & Health Ins. Life Paid Up at 95	672	339			◐	◐	1.04	2.42	2.23
Home Beneficial LIC Whole Life	661	336			◐	◐	−0.65	2.42	2.44
Commonwealth LIC Whole Life	673	336				◐	−0.96	2.25	2.12
Southland LIC Exec. Pfd. Whole Life	676	338				◐	−0.52	2.21	2.08
Occidental LIC of Calif. Guaranteed Whole Life	665	324				◐	−1.06	2.67	2.46
Colonial LIC of Amer. Whole Life	681	337				◐	−0.89	2.43	2.23
Jefferson Standard LIC Life Paid Up at 95	639	345			◐	○	−1.15	2.14	2.59
United Investors LIC Whole Life	630	347			◐	○	−0.97	2.06	2.60
Durham LIC Life Paid Up at 95	624	341	◐		◐	○	−2.43	2.15	2.71
Hartford LIC Whole Life	613	342	◐		◐	○	−1.89	2.13	2.79
Imperial LAC of Canada Whole Life	620	345	◐		◐	○	−2.22	2.06	2.74
United Benefit LIC Ordinary Life	620	346	◐		◐	○	−2.45	1.80	2.51

A Available only in New York.
B Available only to nonsmokers.
C Available only in Massachusetts.
D Available only to "preferred risks."
E Available only to Lutherans.
F Available only to people in certain jobs.
G Available only to members of a fraternal organization.

Ratings of Cash Value Policies (Nonpar/$25,000/45 Years) continued

Company and policy	Annual premium	Cost Indexes				Net payment Index	Yields		
		20-yr.	9-yr.	19-yr.	29-yr.		9-yr.	19-yr.	29-yr.
Colonial LIC of Amer. Cash Flo [B]	$618	$347	◑	◑	○	○	-2.13%	2.00%	2.71%
IDS LIC Select Whole Life	682	347	◑	◑	◑	◑	1.30	2.24	2.13
Amer. National Ins. Co. Life Paid Up at 95	638	348	○	◑	◑	◑	-1.45	1.87	2.26
Provident Life & Acc. Ins. Co. Whole Life	685	348	◑	◑	◑	◑	0.61	2.22	2.07
Paul Revere LIC Exec. Life to 95	630	349	◑	◑	◑	○	-1.63	1.99	2.57
Aetna LIC Life Paid Up at 95	682	364	◑	◑	◑	◑	0.53	1.84	2.02
Colonial LIC of Amer. Life Paid Up at 92	634	352	○	◑	◑	○	-1.66	1.95	2.45
J.C. Penney LIC Exec. Select Life Paid Up at 90	688	353	◑	◑	◑	◑	-0.55	1.91	1.89
Nationwide LIC W.L.P.U. at 95	650	354	◑	◑	◑	◑	-2.39	1.70	2.19
Great-West LAC Life at 90	649	355	◑	◑	◑	◑	-1.56	1.90	2.44
Liberty LIC Liberty Protection 95 (LPU at 95)	699	361	○	◑	◑	◑	-0.02	1.96	1.89
National LAC of Canada Exec. Ordinary Life	642	367	◑	◑	◑	○	-3.22	1.52	2.35
INA LIC Exec., Whole Life	693	379	○	◑	◑	◑	0.31	1.53	1.84
Colonial LIC of Amer. Economiser [B]	689	346	◑	◑	◑	◑	-1.23	2.25	2.10
Amer. Health & Life Ins. Co. Freedom Whole Life—Level	669	361	◑	◑	◑	◑	-1.43	1.85	2.12
Monarch LIC Accelerator 95	700	368	○	◑	◑	●	0.03	1.81	1.80
Monumental LIC LP at 90 Exec.	693	370	◑	◑	◑	◑	-2.12	1.70	1.92
United Benefit LIC Life Paid Up at 90	684	372	◑	◑	◑	◑	-1.63	1.46	1.76
Liberty LIC Liberty Exec. Pfd. (WL)	687	375	◑	◑	◑	◑	-1.76	1.57	1.92
Security Life & Acc. Co. Whole Life 10	673	382	◑	◑	◑	◑	-2.24	1.29	1.94
First Colony LIC Whole Life	675	356	●	●	●	●	-4.58	1.91	2.09
Bankers Life & Casualty Co. Exec. Ordinary Life	709	396	◑	◑	●	●	-2.20	1.14	1.59
Bankers Life & Casualty Co. Life Paid Up at 95	726	413	◑	◑	●	●	-1.02	0.85	1.34

Type: Participating   Amount: $25,000   Age: 25

Listed in order of increasing cost, based primarily on 19-year cost index (see p. 267). All of the rates are for men's policies; rates for women at the same age are generally lower. Where company and policy listings are the same, difference is indicated by footnote. In addition to standard abbreviations, the following are used: LIC (Life Insurance Co.) and LAC (Life Assurance Co.). All data are based on 1979 rates and include waiver of premium in event of disability.

Best ● ◐ ○ ◑ ● Worst

Company and policy	Annual premium*	Cost Indexes 20-yr.	9-yr.	19-yr.	29-yr.	Net payment index	Yields 9-yr.	19-yr.	29-yr.
Teachers Ins. & Annuity Assoc. of Amer. Ordinary Life [F]	$302	$10	●	●	●	●	1.90%	7.28%	7.88%
State Mutual LAC of Amer. Non-Smoker Whole Life [B]	331	13	●	●	●	●	6.15	7.42	7.39
Massachusetts SBLI Straight Life [C]	236	27	●	●	●	●	8.54	7.97	7.85
New York SBLI Straight Life [D]	280	48	●	●	●	●	5.65	6.34	6.51
New England Mutual LIC Ordinary Life [A]	296	48	●	●	●	●	3.64	6.26	6.45
Massachusetts Mutual LIC Convertible Life	302	55	●	●	●	●	3.40	5.98	6.08
Standard Ins. Co. Whole Life [B]	306	55	●	●	●	●	3.44	5.98	6.34
New England Mutual LIC Ordinary Life	305	57	●	●	●	●	2.69	5.81	6.12
Northwestern Mutual LIC Whole Life	364	60	●	●	●	●	3.19	5.65	6.17
Home LIC Whole Life NSR [B]	277	31	◐	●	●	●	1.84	7.05	6.97
Phoenix Mutual LIC Ordinary Life, NSB [B]	384	35	●	●	●	◐	3.77	6.20	6.30
Home LIC Whole Life	289	43	◐	●	●	●	0.48	6.35	6.47

*Premium changes after number of years in parentheses.

[A] Available only to "preferred risks."
[B] Available only to nonsmokers.
[C] Available only in Massachusetts.
[D] Available only in New York.
[E] Available only to Lutherans.
[F] Available only to people in certain jobs.
[G] Available only to members of a fraternal organization.

Ratings of Cash Value Policies (Par/$25,000/25 Years) continued

Company and policy	Annual premium*	Cost Indexes 20-yr.	9-yr.	19-yr.	29-yr.	Net payment index	Yields 9-yr.	19-yr.	29-yr.
Central LAC Special Whole Life	$340	$52	◐	●	●	◐	5.91%	5.98%	5.88%
Phoenix Mutual LIC Ordinary Life	388	39	●	●	●	○	3.50	6.06	6.20
Union Mutual LIC Whole Life [B]	391	49	◐	●	●	◐	2.68	5.68	5.95
Guardian LIC of Amer. Pension Trust Whole Life [A]	376	51	○	●	●	○	2.56	5.66	6.06
Guardian LIC of Amer. Modified 3 Whole Life [A]	385 (3)	53	○	●	●	○	2.64	5.65	6.00
Guardian LIC of Amer. Whole Life [A]	376	55	◐	●	●	○	2.51	5.52	5.88
Guardian LIC of Amer. Pension Trust Whole Life	382	57	○	●	◐	○	2.14	5.44	5.90
Union Mutual LIC Whole Life	399	58	◐	●	●	○	2.13	5.38	5.73
Guardian LIC of Amer. Modified 3 Whole Life [A]	391 (3)	59	◐	●	●	○	2.15	5.40	5.83
Mutual LIC of New York Whole Life [A]	417	49	○	●	●	○	0.84	5.63	5.82
Continental Assurance Co. Whole Life	335	56	◐	●	○	○	1.80	5.61	4.69
Mutual LIC of New York Whole Life	427	59	◐	●	●	○	0.19	5.29	5.58
USAA LIC Modified-One Whole Life [F]	282 (1)	65	●	●	◐	●	3.96	5.56	5.85
Manufacturers LIC Permanent Economic Protection	306	64	○	●	●	●	-0.21	5.45	6.19
Standard Ins. Co. Whole Life	316	66	○	◐	◐	●	2.41	5.42	5.95
Connecticut Mutual LIC Econolife (Whole Life)	281	74	●	◐	○	●	3.69	5.12	5.34
Guardian LIC of Amer. Whole Life	382	61	○	◐	●	○	2.09	5.29	5.72
Union Mutual LIC Exec. Life (Non-NY) [B]	400	68	○	◐	●	◐	2.62	5.08	5.63
Indianapolis LIC Ordinary Life [B]	345	69	○	◐	◐	●	2.22	5.15	5.40
New York LIC Modified 2 Whole Life	374 (2)	69	○	◐	●	●	-0.53	5.12	5.83
Columbus Mutual LIC Life—100	288	71	○	◐	◐	◐	-0.85	5.12	5.62
Farm Bureau (Iowa) Exec. Pfd. Par	349	72	◐	◐	◐	○	2.05	5.01	5.40
USAA LIC Ordinary Life [F]	345	68	◐	◐	◐	○	1.63	5.15	5.52
Indianapolis LIC Exec. Protector [B]	386	68	◐	◐	◐	○	3.11	5.16	5.34

Company		Age	Rating						Net cost index	Interest-adjusted	
John Hancock Mutual LIC Pfd. 25 [A]	397 (3)	70							1.31	4.98	5.52
State Mutual LAC of Amer. Non-Smoker Exec. Protector Endowment [B]	391	71							2.34	4.96	5.53
Minnesota Mutual LIC Econo-Life	310	72							−0.64	5.01	5.63
Bankers Life Co. Special Whole Life	303	73							1.00	5.04	5.22
Penn Mutual LIC Whole Life [B]	383	73							2.04	4.96	5.27
Equitable Life Assurance Soc. of the U.S. Adjustable Whole Life	384	73							1.60	4.93	5.37
Connecticut Mutual LIC Whole Life	308	75							2.49	4.96	5.36
Security Benefit LIC Exec. Whole Life	310	76							−3.03	4.80	5.49
Union Mutual LIC Exec. Life (Non-NY)	408	76							2.09	4.79	5.42
New York LIC Whole Life	374	65							2.23	5.10	5.54
Lutheran Mutual LIC Whole Life	403	72							2.23	4.89	5.00
Southern Farm Bureau LIC Ordinary Life	387	73							0.86	4.91	5.26
Prudential Ins. Co. of Amer. Modified Life 3	400 (3)	73							1.20	4.91	5.40
Indianapolis LIC Five Year Modified Life	386 (5)	75							−2.43	4.92	5.27
National LIC Life [B]	412	75							2.03	4.76	5.07
Woodmen of the World Life Ins. Soc. Whole Life Minimum $10,000 [C]	318	77							0.50	4.76	5.55
Indianapolis LIC Ordinary Life	356	80							1.36	4.69	5.07
Farm Bureau (Iowa) Whole Life Par	386	80							1.67	4.68	5.26
Acacia Mutual LIC Whole Life [B]	298	82							0.67	4.57	5.03
Aid Association for Lutherans Estate Life [E]	320	86							1.73	4.38	5.34
State Mutual LAC of Amer. Whole Life	392	77							1.24	4.76	5.39
Provident Mutual LIC Protector [A]	386 (2)	79							2.79	4.76	5.23
Indianapolis LIC Exec. Protector	397	79							2.27	4.74	5.04
Prudential Ins. Co. of Amer. Estate 20—Whole Life	377	83							1.62	4.53	5.16

* Premium changes after number of years in parentheses.

[A] Available only to "preferred risks."
[B] Available only to nonsmokers.
[C] Available only in Massachusetts.
[D] Available only in New York.
[E] Available only to Lutherans.
[F] Available only to people in certain jobs.
[G] Available only to members of a fraternal organization.

Ratings of Cash Value Policies (Par/$25,000/25 Years) continued

Company and policy	Annual premium*	Cost indexes 20-yr.	9-yr.	19-yr.	29-yr.	Net payment index	Yields 9-yr.	19-yr.	29-yr.
Mutual Benefit LIC Ordinary Life	$425	$ 84	○	○	○	○	2.32%	4.56%	5.02%
Provident Mutual LIC Protector	393 (2)	86	◐	○	○	○	2.19	4.45	5.01
Provident Mutual LIC Whole Life A	426	86	◐	○	○	○	1.79	4.49	5.04
Lincoln National LIC Whole Life B	394	79	◐	○	○	○	0.74	4.67	4.76
Dominion LAC Whole Life	359	80	○	○	○	○	−0.19	4.65	5.19
State Mutual LAC of Amer. Exec. Protector Endowment at 90 A	401	83	○	○	○	○	1.57	4.52	5.18
Penn Mutual LIC Whole Life	394	84	○	○	○	○	1.24	4.53	4.97
Sun LAC of Canada Sun Permanent Life	318	86	◐	○	○	◐	−1.86	4.37	4.70
Midland Mutual LIC Modified Life	391 (3)	87	◐	○	○	◐	−3.40	4.29	5.08
Penn Mutual LIC Value Builder 90 B	398	88	◐	○	○	◐	2.19	4.40	4.88
Aid Association for Lutherans Whole Life E	382	89	○	○	◐	○	−0.23	4.28	5.22
Sun LAC of Canada Whole Life	435	89	○	○	○	○	0.61	4.33	4.64
North American LAC Whole Life	323	92	○	○	○	○	−0.97	4.15	4.77
Acacia Mutual LIC Whole Life	310	94	○	○	○	○	−0.45	4.00	4.64
Manhattan LIC Challenger B	414	81	○	○	○	◐	0.85	4.64	4.92
Mutual Benefit LIC Life Paid Up at 95	397	82	◐	○	○	◐	1.40	4.60	5.04
National LIC Life	424	86	○	○	○	○	1.26	4.36	4.79
State Farm LIC Whole Life	370	90	◐	○	○	○	−1.75	4.23	4.96
Midland Mutual LIC Paid Up Life at 95	416	90	◐	○	○	◐	−1.86	4.19	4.74
Provident Mutual LIC Whole Life	434	93	○	○	○	◐	1.30	4.22	4.84
Confederation LIC Life to 96	331	95	●	○	○	○	−4.23	3.90	5.09
Fidelity Union LIC Professional Exec. Life	312	97	◐	◐	○	○	−0.92	3.92	4.14
Life & Casualty Ins. Co. of Tenn. Whole Life	375	97	○	◐	○	●	−1.78	3.90	4.53

Plan									
Beneficial LIC Professional Estate Plan	◐	○	○	◐	439	97	1.20	4.11	4.66
Lincoln National LIC Whole Life	○	◐	○	◐	399	84	0.38	4.48	4.63
Mutual Trust LIC Ordinary Life	◐	○	◐	◐	408	88	−0.66	4.34	4.68
Columbus Mutual LIC Pfd. Life	◐	○	○	◐	405	91	−0.18	4.22	4.98
Bankers Life & Casualty Co. Life Paid Up at 98	○	○	○	◐	433	92	1.21	4.31	4.45
Union Central LIC Ordinary Life Pfd. Class	◐	◐	○	◐	421	94	−1.23	4.11	4.72
Canada LAC Exec. Whole Life	○	○	○	○	373	96	−1.76	4.02	4.51
Union Central LIC Ordinary Life	◐	◐	○	◐	421	96	−1.35	4.02	4.64
Penn Mutual LIC Value Builder 90	◐	◐	○	○	409	99	1.45	4.01	4.60
Kansas City LIC Exec. Endowment 90	○	◐	○	○	368	101	1.18	3.91	4.33
Pacific Mutual LIC Adjustable Life	◐	○	◐	○	427	93	−0.60	4.17	4.27
Northwestern National LIC Whole Life Par	●	●	◐	●	380	96	−2.51	4.01	4.57
Minnesota Mutual LIC Adjustable Life	◐	◐	◐	○	337	99	−1.77	3.77	4.89
Metropolitan LIC Whole Life	◐	●	◐	○	342	100	−3.10	3.74	4.83
Nationwide LIC W.L.P.U. at 95	◐	●	◐	◐	403	102	1.61	3.87	4.22
Ohio National LIC Exec. Protector Whole Life	●	●	◐	◐	296	107	−2.41	3.36	4.12
Bankers LIC of Nebraska Whole Life	●	●	○	○	374	94	−8.13	3.47	4.80
Mutual Trust LIC Life Paid Up at 90	○	◐	○	◐	424	100	0.52	3.91	4.42
Ohio National LIC Whole Life	○	◐	○	◐	406	101	0.38	3.93	4.30
John Hancock Mutual LIC 3 Year Modified Life	◐	◐	◐	◐	398 (3)	103	−1.28	3.76	4.72
Great-West LAC Estatemaster "25"	○	◐	◐	◐	399	111	0.01	3.51	4.26
Canada LAC Estate Protector	◐	◐	◐	◐	384	113	−0.68	3.38	4.03
Life & Casualty Ins. Co. of Tenn. Exec. Whole Life	◐	◐	◐	◐	421	117	−0.62	3.16	4.02
Amer. Family LIC Ordinary Life	◐	○	◐	◐	439	100	−1.11	3.94	4.31

* Premium changes after number of years in parentheses.

A Available only to "preferred risks."
B Available only to nonsmokers.
C Available only in Massachusetts.
D Available only in New York.
E Available only to Lutherans.
F Available only to people in certain jobs.
G Available only to members of a fraternal organization.

Ratings of Cash Value Policies (Par/$25,000/25 Years) continued

Company and policy	Annual premium*	Cost Indexes 20-yr.	Cost Indexes 9-yr.	Cost Indexes 19-yr.	Cost Indexes 29-yr.	Net payment Index	Yields 9-yr.	Yields 19-yr.	Yields 29-yr.
Equitable LIC of Iowa Whole Life	$410	$102	◐	◐	◐	◐	−0.55%	3.81%	4.50%
John Hancock Mutual LIC Life Paid Up at 85	394	104	●	◐	○	◐	−1.75	3.74	4.68
Confederation LIC Whole Life	398	104	◐	◐	◐	◐	−0.52	3.72	4.46
Monarch LIC Select Risk Endowment at 95 Ⓐ	416	109	○	◐	◐	●	1.63	3.77	4.17
Connecticut General LIC Life Full Paid at 90 (Par)	397	112	○	◐	◐	◐	0.52	3.60	3.91
Canada LAC Executive 95	414	114	◐	◐	◐	◐	0.06	3.44	4.04
Midland National LIC Exec. Pfd. Par	454	114	◐	◐	◐	◐	−0.44	3.48	4.24
Jefferson Standard LIC Life Paid Up at 90	433	116	○	◐	◐	◐	1.06	3.48	3.97
Occidental LIC of Calif. Pfd. Whole Life	413	98	◐	◐	◐	●	−2.47	3.94	4.21
Manhattan LIC Challenger	436	102	◐	◐	◐	◐	−0.48	3.96	4.45
Monarch LIC Ordinary Life—Par	416	112	◐	●	●	◐	−1.32	3.51	3.98
Bankers LIC of Nebraska Equity Builder	433	112	○	●	●	○	1.04	3.16	4.29
Security Benefit LIC Ultra—Ordinary Life	379	122	●	●	●	○	−2.53	2.86	4.26
Imperial LAC of Canada Whole Life	346	129	●	●	●	○	−6.07	2.44	4.08
Franklin LIC Executive Select—I	427	120	●	●	●	◐	−2.57	3.21	4.08
Amer. National Ins. Co. Whole Life—Participating	426	129	●	●	●	◐	−2.57	2.82	3.90
Amer. Republic Ins. Co. Whole Life	363	144	●	●	●	●	−4.06	2.09	3.44
Colonial LIC of Amer. Whole Life Par	443	135	●	●	●	●	−1.60	2.86	3.43
All Amer. Life & Casualty Co. Life Paid Up at 85	452	136	●	●	●	●	−0.99	2.84	3.61
Aetna LIC Whole Life	453	141	●	●	●	●	−6.40	2.68	3.78
Imperial LAC of Canada Exec. Protector	475	148	●	●	●	●	−1.24	2.49	3.50
Security Life & Acc. Co. Whole Life	438	153	●	●	●	●	−5.54	2.12	3.60
Fidelity Life Assoc. Ordinary Life	468	181	●	●	●	●	−4.89	1.22	2.32

Type: Participating   Amount: $25,000   Age: 35

Listed in order of increasing cost, based primarily on 19-year cost index (see p. 267). All of the rates are for men's policies; rates for women at the same age are generally lower. Where company and policy listings are the same, difference is indicated by footnote. In addition to standard abbreviations, the following are used: LIC (Life Insurance Co.) and LAC (Life Assurance Co.). All data are based on 1979 rates and include waiver of premium in event of disability.

Best ● ◕ ◑ ◔ ○ Worst

Company and policy	Annual premium*	Cost Indexes 20-yr.	Cost Indexes 9-yr.	Cost Indexes 19-yr.	Cost Indexes 29-yr.	Net payment index	Yields 9-yr.	Yields 19-yr.	Yields 29-yr.
Teachers Ins. & Annuity Assoc. of Amer. Ordinary Life Ⓕ	$430	$11	●	●	●	●	4.32%	7.88%	8.21%
Massachusetts SBLI Straight Life Ⓒ	350	49	●	●	●	●	6.95	7.51	7.55
Standard Ins. Co. Whole Life Ⓑ	435	90	●	●	●	●	3.23	5.73	6.12
New York SBLI Straight Life Ⓓ	415	92	◑	●	●	●	4.21	5.67	6.01
Home LIC Whole Life NSR Ⓑ	426	60	●	●	●	●	1.20	6.52	6.70
Phoenix Mutual LIC Ordinary Life, NSB Ⓑ	525	66	●	●	●	◑	3.68	5.97	6.06
Central LAC Special Whole Life	486	82	◑	◑	●	◑	4.97	5.82	5.83
New England Mutual LIC Ordinary Life Ⓐ	418	85	●	●	●	●	2.40	5.83	6.14
Northwestern Mutual LIC Whole Life	512	93	◑	●	●	◑	2.63	5.54	6.10
Union Mutual LIC Whole Life Ⓑ	519	79	○	●	●	●	2.92	5.57	5.78
Home LIC Whole Life	446	80	○	●	●	●	−0.06	5.84	6.18
Guardian LIC of Amer. Pension Trust Whole Life Ⓐ	511	83	◑	●	●	○	2.14	5.52	5.89

* Premium changes after number of years in parentheses.

Ⓐ Available only in New York.
Ⓑ Available only to nonsmokers.
Ⓒ Available only in Massachusetts.

Ⓓ Available only to "preferred risks."
Ⓔ Available only to Lutherans.
Ⓕ Available only to people in certain jobs.

Ⓖ Available only to members of a fraternal organization.

Ratings of Cash Value Policies (Par/$25,000/35 Years) continued

Company and policy	Annual premium*	Cost Indexes 20-yr.	Cost Indexes 9-yr.	Cost Indexes 19-yr.	Cost Indexes 29-yr.	Net payment index	Yields 9-yr.	Yields 19-yr.	Yields 29-yr.
Phoenix Mutual LIC Ordinary Life	$543	$ 85	◐	●	●	○	2.74%	5.46%	5.68%
Guardian LIC of Amer. Modified 3 Whole Life A	522 (3)	88	◐	●	●	○	2.08	5.46	5.82
Guardian LIC of Amer. Whole Life A	511	89	◐	●	●	○	2.08	5.38	5.74
Union Mutual LIC Exec. Life (Non-NY) B	544	92	◐	●	●	◐	2.94	5.24	5.73
Massachusetts Mutual LIC Convertible Life	420	95	○	●	●	○	2.41	5.56	5.73
Mutual LIC of New York Whole Life A	561	103	○	●	●	○	0.93	5.33	5.67
Continental Assurance Co. Whole Life	456	89	◐	●	○	○	2.30	5.50	4.70
USAA LIC Modified-One Whole Life F	409 (1)	98	●	○	●	●	3.66	5.41	5.70
Manufacturers LIC Permanent Economic Protection	438	101	○	○	●	●	0.60	5.29	5.94
Standard Ins. Co. Whole Life	450	105	◐	○	●	●	2.19	5.20	5.73
USAA LIC Ordinary Life F	485	101	◐	○	◐	◐	1.81	5.12	5.50
State Mutual LAC of Amer. Non-Smoker Whole Life B	524	103	○	◐	◐	◐	2.29	5.08	5.57
Columbus Mutual LIC Life—100	410	106	●	◐	○	◐	0.18	5.05	5.53
Connecticut Mutual LIC Econolife (Whole Life)	399	112	○	◐	◐	○	3.32	5.08	5.36
Guardian LIC of Amer. Pension Trust Whole Life	524	97	○	◐	●	◐	1.47	5.15	5.62
Union Mutual LIC Whole Life	537	97	◐	◐	●	◐	1.98	5.08	5.40
Penn Mutual LIC Whole Life B	514	99	◐	◐	●	◐	2.11	5.17	5.44
Guardian LIC of Amer. Modified 3 Whole Life B	536 (3)	101	○	◐	●	◐	1.34	5.07	5.54
New England Mutual LIC Ordinary Life	439	105	○	◐	◐	◐	1.13	5.13	5.62
New York LIC Modified 2 Whole Life	524 (2)	108	○	◐	◐	◐	−0.50	4.91	5.64
Union Mutual LIC Exec. Life (Non-NY)	562	110	◐	◐	◐	◐	2.09	4.77	5.37
Indianapolis LIC Ordinary Life B	487	113	◐	◐	◐	○	1.84	4.88	5.19
Connecticut Mutual LIC Whole Life	432	115	◐	◐	◐	○	2.32	4.89	5.30

Policy										
Guardian LIC of Amer. Whole Life	524	102	○			○		1.41	5.01	5.47
New York LIC Whole Life	524	104	○			○		1.52	4.91	5.36
Equitable Life Assurance Soc. of the U.S. Adjustable Whole Life	526	110	○			○		1.66	4.85	5.27
Indianapolis LIC Exec. Protector Ⓑ	538	111	◐	●		◐		2.45	4.87	5.10
Bankers Life Co. Special Whole Life	434	112	○	○		○		0.88	4.83	5.06
Lutheran Mutual LIC Whole Life	556	111	○	○		○		1.66	4.75	4.84
Mutual LIC of New York Whole Life	583	110	◐	○		◑		−0.09	4.78	5.25
State Mutual LAC of Amer. Non-Smoker Exec. Protector Endowment Ⓑ	547	114	●	●		●		2.44	4.74	5.28
Provident Mutual LIC Protector Ⓐ	525 (2)	115	●	●		●		2.69	4.80	5.27
Confederation LIC Life to 96	442	118	○	●		●		−1.15	4.67	5.46
National LIC Life Ⓑ	553	111	○	●		○		1.90	4.73	5.11
John Hancock Mutual LIC Pfd. 25 Ⓐ	553 (3)	117	○	◐		○		0.99	4.64	5.24
Penn Mutual LIC Value Builder 90 Ⓑ	532	118	◐	◐		○		2.51	4.68	5.07
Security Benefit LIC Exec. Whole Life	433	123	○	○		○		−1.14	4.61	5.24
Indianapolis LIC Five Year Modified Life	552 (5)	123	○	◐		◐		−1.86	4.59	5.01
Aid Association for Lutherans Estate Life Ⓔ	448	127	○	●		○		1.31	4.30	5.29
Woodmen of the World Life Ins. Soc. Whole Life Minimum $10,000 Ⓖ	462	128	○	●		○		0.21	4.30	5.13
Mutual Benefit LIC Ordinary Life	574	131	◐	○		◐		2.04	4.36	4.83
Aid Association for Lutherans Whole Life Ⓔ	523	132	○	○		◐		−0.34	4.16	5.15
Provident Mutual LIC Protector	544 (2)	134	○	○		○		1.67	4.25	4.87
Lincoln National LIC Whole Life Ⓑ	539	122	○	○		○		0.83	4.53	4.64
Prudential Ins. Co. of Amer. Modified Life 3	553 (3)	124	○	○		○		0.87	4.38	5.00
Minnesota Mutual LIC Econo-Life	443	126	○	○		○		−0.72	4.43	5.15
Farm Bureau (Iowa) Exec. Pfd. Par	503	126	○	○		○		1.04	4.45	4.94

* Premium changes after number of years in parentheses.

Ⓐ Available only in New York.
Ⓑ Available only to nonsmokers.
Ⓒ Available only in Massachusetts.

Ⓓ Available only to "preferred risks."
Ⓔ Available only to Lutherans.
Ⓕ Available only to people in certain jobs.

Ⓖ Available only to members of a fraternal organization.

Ratings of Cash Value Policies (Par/$25,000/35 Years) *continued*

Company and policy	Annual premium*	Cost Indexes 20-yr.	9-yr.	19-yr.	29-yr.	Net payment index	Yields 9-yr.	19-yr.	29-yr.
Dominion LAC Whole Life	$503	$126	○	○	○	○	0.05%	4.44%	4.98%
Penn Mutual LIC Whole Life	541	126	○	○	○	○	0.76	4.42	4.88
Southern Farm Bureau LIC Ordinary Life	542	126	○	○	○	○	0.36	4.44	4.93
North American LAC Whole Life	451	127	○	○	○	○	0.01	4.39	4.91
Mutual Benefit LIC Life Paid Up at 95	535	127	○	○	○	○	0.96	4.44	4.92
State Mutual LAC of Amer. Whole Life	542	127	○	○	○	○	1.19	4.43	5.03
Indianapolis LIC Exec. Protector	554	127	○	○	○	○	1.63	4.44	4.78
Indianapolis LIC Ordinary Life	502	128	○	○	○	○	1.00	4.41	4.84
Provident Mutual LIC Whole Life Ⓑ	561	128	○	○	○	○	1.68	4.41	5.00
Acacia Mutual LIC Whole Life Ⓑ	436	129	○	○	○	○	0.11	4.27	4.62
Sun LAC of Canada Sun Permanent Life	447	131	○	○	○	○	-0.22	4.31	4.60
Prudential Ins. Co. of Amer. Estate 20—Whole Life	520	132	○	○	○	○	0.63	4.15	4.90
Farm Bureau (Iowa) Whole Life Par	536	134	○	○	○	○	1.05	4.27	4.91
State Mutual LAC of Amer. Exec. Protector Endowment at 90 Ⓐ	563	136	○	○	○	○	1.48	4.17	4.82
Confederation LIC Whole Life	519	138	○	○	○	○	0.55	4.12	4.63
Equitable LIC of Iowa Whole Life	544	138	○	○	○	○	0.07	4.08	4.63
Manhattan LIC Challenger Ⓑ	552	118	○	○	◐	◐	0.97	4.58	4.87
Lincoln National LIC Whole Life	549	132	○	○	●	◐	0.34	4.26	4.44
National LIC Life	575	133	○	○	○	○	0.85	4.17	4.69
Columbus Mutual LIC Pfd. Life	545	137	◐	◐	◐	○	-0.40	4.05	4.86
State Farm LIC Whole Life	517	138	◐	○	○	○	-1.43	4.01	4.75
Union Central LIC Ordinary Life Pfd. Class	569	139	◐	○	○	○	-0.64	4.09	4.53
Midland Mutual LIC Modified Life	539 (3)	142	●	○	○	○	-2.78	3.84	4.57
Sun LAC of Canada Whole Life	589	143	○	○	◐	○	0.48	4.02	4.38

Policy			Rating				Premium change		
Penn Mutual LIC Value Builder 90	559	145	◐	◐	○		1.20	3.98	4.55
Mutual Trust LIC Ordinary Life	558	132	◐	○	○		−0.63	4.21	4.58
Provident Mutual LIC Whole Life	579	147	○	◐	○		0.81	3.92	4.63
Acacia Mutual LIC Whole Life	453	146	○	◐	○		−0.89	3.74	4.24
Fidelity Union LIC Professional Executive Life	452	149	◐	◐	○		−0.71	3.70	4.03
Metropolitan LIC Whole Life	495	150	○	◐	○		−2.80	3.67	5.46
Beneficial LIC Professional Estate Plan	594	150	○	◐	◐		0.97	3.87	4.46
Beneficial LIC Heritage 100	594	150	○	◐	○		0.97	3.87	4.46
Ohio National LIC Exec. Protector Whole Life	435	156	◐	◐	◐		−1.21	3.53	4.18
Minnesota Mutual LIC Adjustable Life	503	157	○	◐	◐		−2.53	3.50	4.69
Great-West LAC Estatemaster "25"	555	161	○	◐	◐		0.28	3.52	4.22
Bankers LIC of Nebraska Whole Life	514	136	●	◐	○		−5.13	3.59	4.76
Canada LAC Exec. Whole Life	514	145	◐	◐	◐		−0.98	3.92	4.41
Northwestern National LIC Whole Life Par	533	145	◐	◐	◐		−1.96	3.91	4.42
Union Central LIC Ordinary Life	569	145	◐	◐	◐		−0.81	3.94	4.38
Ohio National LIC Whole Life	556	148	◐	◐	◐		0.59	3.89	4.25
Midland Mutual LIC Paid Up Life at 95	561	148	◐	◐	◐		−1.84	3.73	4.28
Mutual Trust LIC Life Paid Up at 90	581	148	○	◐	◐		0.22	3.83	4.33
Bankers Life & Casualty Co. Life Paid Up at 98	603	149	○	◐	◐		0.47	3.90	4.24
Bankers LIC of Nebraska Equity Builder	579	151	○	◐	◐		1.05	3.38	4.30
Life & Casualty Ins. Co. of Tenn. Whole Life	525	153	◐	◐	◐		−1.31	3.65	4.26
Kansas City LIC Exec. Endowment 90	517	154	○	◐	◐		0.76	3.66	4.01
Nationwide LIC W.L.P.U. at 95	562	155	○	◐	◐		1.24	3.64	4.00
John Hancock Mutual LIC 3 Year Modified Life	555 (3)	156	◐	○	◐		−1.18	3.57	4.49

* Premium changes after number of years in parentheses.

Ⓐ Available only to "preferred risks."
Ⓑ Available only to nonsmokers.
Ⓒ Available only in Massachusetts.
Ⓓ Available only in New York.
Ⓔ Available only to Lutherans.
Ⓕ Available only to people in certain jobs.
Ⓖ Available only to members of a fraternal organization.

Ratings of Cash Value Policies (Par/$25,000/35 Years) continued

Company and policy	Annual premium*	Cost indexes 20-yr.	9-yr.	19-yr.	29-yr.	Net payment index	Yields 9-yr.	19-yr.	29-yr.
Security Benefit LIC Ultra—Ordinary Life	$510	168	◐	◐	◐	○	-1.11%	3.21%	4.32%
Pacific Mutual LIC Adjustable Life	582	150	◐	◐	◐	◐	-0.60	3.82	3.99
Amer. Family LIC Ordinary Life	598	159	◐	◐	◐	◐	-0.64	3.61	3.99
John Hancock Mutual LIC Life Paid Up at 85	549	163	◐	◐	◐	◐	-1.83	3.45	4.39
Monarch LIC Select Risk Endowment at 95 Ⓐ	568	166	○	◐	●	○	1.16	3.51	3.64
Canada LAC Estate Protector	538	168	◐	◐	●	◐	-0.87	3.32	3.95
Connecticut General LIC Life Full Paid at 90 (Par)	547	169	○	◐	●	◐	0.38	3.40	3.74
Canada LAC Exec. 95	569	171	○	◐	●	◐	0.01	3.31	3.90
Midland National LIC Exec. Pfd. Par	607	171	○	◐	●	◐	-0.80	3.24	3.99
Jefferson Standard LIC Life Paid Up at 90	586	172	○	◐	●	◐	0.87	3.33	3.74
Occidental LIC of Calif. Pfd. Whole Life	559	160	◐	◐	◐	◐	-2.17	3.54	3.79
Manhattan LIC Challenger	594	161	◐	◐	●	○	-0.93	3.59	4.14
Imperial LAC of Canada Whole Life	478	178	◐	●	●	○	-3.62	2.84	4.12
Life & Casualty Ins. Co. of Tenn. Exec. Whole Life	573	176	◐	●	●	○	-0.71	3.08	3.86
Franklin LIC Exec. Select—I	582	173	●	●	●	◐	-2.13	3.22	4.04
Monarch LIC Ordinary Life—Par	568	174	◐	●	●	◐	-1.21	3.19	3.64
Colonial LIC of Amer. Whole Life Par	592	188	●	●	●	◐	-1.42	2.90	3.40
Amer. National Ins. Co. Whole Life—Participating	578	188	●	●	●	◐	-2.65	2.73	3.62
Amer. Republic Ins. Co. Whole Life	519	203	●	●	●	●	-3.07	2.19	3.36
Aetna LIC Whole Life	606	198	●	●	●	●	-5.04	2.70	3.73
All Amer. Life & Casualty Co. Life Paid Up at 85	622	199	●	●	●	●	-1.46	2.68	3.54
Imperial LAC of Canada Executive Protector	637	215	●	●	●	●	-1.47	2.34	3.37
Security Life & Acc. Co. Whole Life	598	217	●	●	●	●	-4.64	2.11	3.53
Fidelity Life Assoc. Ordinary Life	618	256	●	●	●	●	-4.25	1.19	2.22

Type: Participating   Amount: $25,000   Age: 45

Listed in order of increasing cost, based primarily on 19-year cost index (see p. 267). All of the rates are for men's policies; rates for women at the same age are generally lower. Where company and policy listings are the same, difference is indicated by footnote. In addition to standard abbreviations, the following are used: LIC (Life Insurance Co.) and LAC (Life Assurance Co.). All data are based on 1979 rates and include waiver of premium in event of disability.

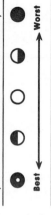

Best ● ◐ ○ ◑ ● Worst

Company and policy	Annual premium*	Cost Indexes				Net payment index	Yields		
		20-yr.	9-yr.	19-yr.	29-yr.		9-yr.	19-yr.	29-yr.
Teachers Ins. & Annuity Assoc. of Amer. Ordinary Life [F]	$648	$ 64	●	●	●	●	6.94%	8.86%	8.93%
Massachusetts SBLI Straight Life [C]	549	131	●	●	●	●	7.52	7.68	7.76
New England Mutual LIC Ordinary Life [A]	617	173	●	●	●	●	3.49	6.17	6.46
Standard Ins. Co. Whole Life [B]	666	187	●	●	●	●	3.51	5.88	6.19
USAA LIC Modified-One Whole Life [F]	638 (1)	189	●	●	●	●	4.94	5.82	5.93
Northwestern Mutual LIC Whole Life	767	189	●	●	●	●	3.13	5.72	6.14
Phoenix Mutual LIC Ordinary Life, NSB [B]	718	140	●	●	●	●	5.26	6.48	6.43
Home LIC Whole Life NSR [B]	691	146	◐	●	●	●	2.39	6.62	6.78
Union Mutual LIC Whole Life [B]	758	172	●	●	●	●	3.07	5.53	5.80
Central LAC Special Whole Life	745	178	●	●	●	◑	5.00	5.90	5.92
Union Mutual LIC Exec. Life (Non-NY) [B]	790	182	●	●	●	●	3.15	5.27	5.75
Home LIC Whole Life	722	177	○	●	●	●	1.01	5.84	6.15

Premium changes after number of years in parentheses.

[A] Available only in New York.
[B] Available only to nonsmokers.
[C] Available only in Massachusetts.
[D] Available only to "preferred risks."
[E] Available only to Lutherans.
[F] Available only to people in certain jobs.
[G] Available only to members of a fraternal organization.

Ratings of Cash Value Policies (Par/$25,000/45 Years) *continued*

Company and policy	Annual premium*	Cost indexes 20-yr.	9-yr.	19-yr.	29-yr.	Net payment index	Yields 9-yr.	19-yr.	29-yr.
Guardian LIC of Amer. Pension Trust Whole Life Ⓐ	$730	$189	◐	●	●	◐	2.27%	5.38%	5.72%
Phoenix Mutual LIC Ordinary Life	768	190	○	●	●	○	3.26	5.36	5.53
Guardian LIC of Amer. Whole Life Ⓐ	734	192	◐	●	●	◐	2.31	5.33	5.64
Guardian LIC of Amer. Modified 3 Whole Life Ⓐ	748 (3)	193	●	●	●	●	2.22	5.36	5.69
Massachusetts Mutual LIC Convertible Life	634	194	●	●	●	●	3.54	5.74	5.86
USAA LIC Ordinary Life Ⓕ	720	194	●	●	●	●	2.68	5.37	5.68
Union Mutual LIC Whole Life	785	200	●	●	●	●	2.07	4.95	5.34
New York SBLI Straight Life Ⓓ	656	201	◐	●	●	◐	4.18	5.50	5.84
National LIC Life Ⓑ	770	190	●	●	●	○	2.97	5.28	5.41
Penn Mutual LIC Whole Life Ⓑ	744	195	○	●	●	○	2.49	5.34	5.47
Mutual LIC of New York Whole Life Ⓐ	806	181	●	●	●	●	1.20	5.40	5.69
State Mutual LAC of Amer. Non-Smoker Whole Life Ⓑ	772	205	●	●	●	●	2.71	5.13	5.57
Provident Mutual LIC Protector Ⓐ	772 (2)	213	●	●	●	●	3.44	5.09	5.47
Manufacturers LIC Permanent Economic Protection	658	211	●	●	●	●	1.53	5.28	5.81
Standard Ins. Co. Whole Life	691	211	●	●	●	○	2.38	5.24	5.69
Union Mutual LIC Exec. Life (Non-NY)	820	212	●	●	●	●	2.14	4.68	5.28
Columbus Mutual LIC Life-100	628	213	●	●	●	●	1.25	5.02	5.45
New England Mutual LIC Ordinary Life	661	218	●	●	●	●	1.45	5.03	5.55
Aid Association for Lutherans Estate Life Ⓔ	677	223	●	●	●	●	1.48	4.65	5.40
Connecticut Mutual LIC Whole Life	653	224	●	●	●	○	2.76	4.96	5.34
Connecticut Mutual LIC Econolife (Whole Life)	623	230	●	●	●	○	3.33	4.93	5.22
Lutheran Mutual LIC Whole Life	809	214	◑	●	●	○	2.00	4.81	4.90
Confederation LIC Life to 96	642	215	○	◐	◐	◐	0.70	5.11	5.64

Policy			Rating	Rating	Rating	Rating			
Penn Mutual LIC Value Builder 90 [B]	770	217	◐	◐		○	2.88	4.87	5.10
New York LIC Modified 2 Whole Life	777	220	○	◐	◐	◐	0.07	4.88	5.43
State Mutual LAC of Amer. Non-Smoker Exec. Protector Endowment [B]	830	222	◐	◐	◐	○	2.92	4.64	5.09
Bankers Life Co. Special Whole Life	664	223	◐	◐	○	◑	1.50	4.73	5.00
Provident Mutual LIC Whole Life [A]	798	230	◐	◐	◐	○	2.23	4.60	5.12
Aid Association for Lutherans Whole Life [E]	764	233	○	◐	◐	◐	0.42	4.39	5.18
Continental Assurance Co. Whole Life	685	207	◐	◐	●	○	2.35	5.06	4.41
Manhattan LIC Challenger [B]	777	208	◐	◐	◐	◐	1.71	4.81	5.01
New York LIC Whole Life	777	214	○	◐	◐	○	1.38	4.79	5.16
Guardian LIC of Amer. Pension Trust Whole Life	756	215	○	◐	◐	○	1.28	4.83	5.29
Guardian LIC of Amer. Whole Life	759	218	○	◐	◐	○	1.32	4.78	5.21
Guardian LIC of Amer. Modified 3 Whole Life	774 (3)	219	○	◐	◐	○	1.15	4.79	5.25
Equitable Life Assurance Soc. of the U.S. Adjustable Whole Life [A]	775	226	○	◐	◐	○	1.56	4.66	5.03
John Hancock Mutual LIC Pfd. 25 [B]	808 (3)	226	○	◐	◐	○	1.43	4.58	5.17
Lincoln National LIC Whole Life	783	227	◐	◐	◐	○	1.87	4.65	4.73
Confederation LIC Whole Life	712	232	◐	◐	◐	○	1.84	4.60	4.89
Indianapolis LIC Exec. Protector [B]	793	233	◐	◐	○	○	2.50	4.58	4.88
Farm Bureau (Iowa) Exec. Pfd. Par	728	234	◐	◐	◐	○	1.66	4.61	4.94
Mutual LIC of New York Whole Life	848	223	◑	◐	◐	○	−0.29	4.57	5.04
Mutual Benefit LIC Life Paid Up at 95	772	234	○	◐	○	○	1.24	4.50	4.88
Indianapolis LIC Ordinary Life [B]	725	240	◐	◐	◐	○	1.77	4.47	4.95
Prudential Ins. Co. of Amer. Modified Life 3	818 (3)	240	○	○	○	○	0.62	4.17	4.77
Prudential Ins. Co. of Amer. Estate 20—Whole Life	769	241	○	○	○	○	0.70	4.11	4.74
Mutual Benefit LIC Ordinary Life	831	246	◐	○	○	○	2.20	4.30	4.67

* Premium changes after number of years in parentheses.

[A] Available only to "preferred risks."
[B] Available only to nonsmokers.
[C] Available only in Massachusetts.
[D] Available only in New York.
[E] Available only to Lutherans.
[F] Available only to people in certain jobs.
[G] Available only to members of a fraternal organization.

Ratings of Cash Value Policies (Par/$25,000/45 Years) continued

Company and policy	Annual premium*	Cost Indexes 20-yr.	Cost Indexes 9-yr.	Cost Indexes 19-yr.	Cost Indexes 29-yr.	Net payment index	Yields 9-yr.	Yields 19-yr.	Yields 29-yr.
Provident Mutual LIC Protector	$810 (2)	$250	◐	○	○	○	1.90%	4.24%	4.80%
Security Benefit LIC Exec. Whole Life	675	258	○	○	○	◑	-0.87	4.12	4.80
Indianapolis LIC Five Year Modified Life	841 (5)	262	○	○	○	◑	-1.74	4.04	4.68
National LIC Life	882	242	○	○	○	○	1.07	4.22	4.57
North American LAC Whole Life	682	244	○	○	○	○	0.61	4.40	4.83
Farm Bureau (Iowa) Whole Life Par	784	244	○	○	○	○	1.48	4.35	4.85
Penn Mutual LIC Whole Life	793	244	○	○	○	○	0.61	4.29	4.64
Minnesota Mutual LIC Econo-Life	672	248	○	○	○	○	-0.48	4.24	4.93
Lincoln National LIC Whole Life	805	250	○	○	○	○	1.05	4.19	4.37
Dominion LAC Whole Life	744	251	○	○	○	○	0.23	4.20	4.71
State Mutual LAC of Amer. Whole Life	803	252	○	○	○	○	1.16	4.15	4.79
Ohio National LIC Whole Life	810	253	○	○	○	○	0.51	4.08	4.38
Union Central LIC Ordinary Life Pfd. Class	825	253	○	○	○	○	0.12	4.14	4.45
Columbus Mutual LIC Pfd. Life	788	254	○	○	●	○	-0.47	3.88	4.71
Woodmen of the World Life Ins. Soc. Whole Life Minimum $10,000 [C]	710	258	○	○	○	○	0.03	3.86	4.66
Indianapolis LIC Exec. Protector	818	258	○	○	○	○	1.59	4.06	4.48
Indianapolis LIC Ordinary Life	750	265	○	○	○	○	0.76	3.92	4.52
Provident Mutual LIC Whole Life	835	267	○	○	○	○	0.85	3.84	4.52
Equitable LIC of Iowa Whole Life	798	271	○	○	○	○	0.07	3.73	4.32
Southern Farm Bureau LIC Ordinary Life	814	256	○	○	○	○	-0.07	4.05	4.64
Sun LAC of Canada Sun Permanent Life	678	257	◐	○	○	○	0.67	4.15	4.42
Metropolitan LIC Whole Life	751	261	◐	○	○	○	-1.72	6.38	7.95
Penn Mutual LIC Value Builder 90	819	265	○	○	○	●	1.10	3.88	4.32
State Mutual LAC of Amer. Exec. Protector Endowment at 90 [A]	857	265	○	○	○	◑	1.63	3.85	4.47

Policy								
Ohio National LIC Exec. Protector Whole Life	671	268	○	○	○	0.01	3.94	4.41
State Farm LIC Whole Life	773	268	○	◐	○	−1.36	3.67	4.44
Acacia Mutual LIC Whole Life B	713	269	○	○	○	−0.16	3.71	4.08
Beneficial LIC Professional Estate Plan	842	269	◐	○	◐	1.07	3.82	4.38
Beneficial LIC Heritage 100	842	269	◐	○	○	1.07	3.82	4.38
Fidelity Union LIC Professional Executive Life	684	270	○	○	◐	−0.25	3.68	4.00
Sun LAC of Canada Whole Life	857	271	○	○	○	0.51	3.80	4.15
Mutual Trust LIC Ordinary Life	816	252	◐	○	◐	−0.51	4.04	4.42
Union Central LIC Ordinary Life	825	267	◐	○	○	−0.18	3.87	4.19
Canada LAC Exec. Whole Life	758	273	○	◐	◐	−0.58	3.76	4.22
Bankers LIC of Nebraska Equity Builder	831	266	◐	○	◐	1.36	3.51	4.37
Security Benefit LIC Ultra—Ordinary Life	734	284	◐	○	○	0.14	3.51	4.35
Life & Casualty Ins. Co. of Tenn. Exec. Whole Life	836	302	●	◐	○	0.16	3.20	3.80
Bankers LIC of Nebraska Whole Life	764	263	●	◐	◐	−3.93	3.50	4.57
Mutual Trust LIC Life Paid Up at 90	852	273	●	○	◐	0.08	3.63	4.14
Minnesota Mutual LIC Adjustable Life	786	278	◐	◐	○	−2.30	3.57	4.53
Midland Mutual LIC Modified Life	799 (3)	279	◐	◐	○	−2.54	3.40	4.08
Northwestern National LIC Whole Life Par	781	280	◐	◐	◐	−1.48	3.57	4.08
Midland Mutual LIC Paid Up Life at 95	814	281	◐	◐	○	−1.56	3.38	3.88
John Hancock Mutual LIC 3 Year Modified Life	814 (3)	283	◐	◐	◐	−0.92	3.45	4.32
Life & Casualty Ins. Co. of Tenn. Whole Life	787	284	◐	◐	○	−0.53	3.55	4.08
Nationwide LIC W.L.P.U. at 95	825	284	◐	◐	◐	1.35	3.40	3.74
Kansas City LIC Exec. Endowment 90	770	290	◐	○	○	0.35	3.29	3.59
Acacia Mutual LIC Whole Life	735	291	◐	○	◐	−1.03	3.23	3.70

* Premium changes after number of years in parentheses.

A Available only to "preferred risks."
B Available only to nonsmokers.
C Available only in Massachusetts.
D Available only in New York.
E Available only to Lutherans.
F Available only to people in certain jobs.
G Available only to members of a fraternal organization.

Ratings of Cash Value Policies (Par/$25,000/45 Years) *continued*

Company and policy	Annual premium*	Cost Indexes 20-yr.	9-yr.	19-yr.	29-yr.	Net payment index	Yields 9-yr.	19-yr.	29-yr.
Great-West LAC Estatemaster "25"	$823	$293	○	◑	◑	◑	0.36%	3.38%	4.00%
Imperial LAC of Canada Whole Life	702	301	◑	◑	◑	○	-2.07	3.10	4.12
Bankers Life & Casualty Co. Life Paid Up at 98	905	284	◑	◑	◑	◑	-0.52	3.50	4.05
Amer. Family LIC Ordinary Life	865	286	◑	◑	◑	◑	-0.39	3.49	2.52
Pacific Mutual LIC Adjustable Life	854	287	◑	◑	◑	◑	-0.63	3.43	3.65
John Hancock Mutual LIC Life Paid Up at 85	805	290	●	◑	◑	◑	-1.51	3.31	4.22
Monarch LIC Select Risk Endowment at 95 △	824	301	○	◑	○	◑	1.17	3.22	3.31
Canada LAC Estate Protector	808	306	◑	◑	◑	◑	-0.98	3.10	3.74
Canada LAC Exec. 95	835	310	◑	◑	◑	◑	-0.05	3.05	3.62
Jefferson Standard LIC Life Paid Up at 90	849	311	○	◑	◑	◑	0.69	3.03	3.40
Franklin LIC Exec. Select—I	849	293	●	◑	◑	◑	-1.62	3.31	4.02
Aetna LIC Whole Life	866	312	●	◑	◑	◑	-3.87	2.96	3.93
Midland National LIC Exec. Pfd. Par	870	312	●	◑	◑	◑	-1.42	2.80	3.61
Connecticut General LIC Life Full Paid at 90 (Par)	814	313	◑	◑	◑	◑	0.21	2.99	3.39
Occidental LIC of Calif. Pfd. Whole Life	804	293	●	◑	●	◑	-1.85	3.28	3.50
Manhattan LIC Challenger	872	303	●	●	●	◑	-1.45	3.11	3.73
Monarch LIC Ordinary Life—Par	824	329	●	●	●	◑	-1.70	2.65	3.16
Amer. National Ins. Co. Whole Life—Participating	835	330	●	●	●	◑	-2.40	2.39	3.24
Colonial LIC of Amer. Whole Life Par	867	336	●	●	●	◑	-1.29	2.56	3.13
Amer. Republic Ins. Co. Whole Life	795	367	●	●	●	◑	-3.54	1.63	2.96
All Amer. Life & Casualty Co. Life Paid Up at 85	921	347	●	●	●	●	-2.13	2.34	3.30
Imperial LAC of Canada Exec. Protector	918	371	●	●	●	●	-2.18	1.96	3.05
Security Life & Acc. Co. Whole Life	872	386	●	●	●	●	-4.96	1.54	2.97
Fidelity Life Assoc. Ordinary Life	878	426	●	●	●	●	-4.26	0.83	1.90

Type: Nonparticipating   Amount: $100,000   Age: 25

Listed in order of increasing cost, based primarily on 19-year cost index (see p. 267). All of the rates are for men's policies; rates for women at the same age are generally lower. Where company and policy listings are the same, difference is indicated by footnote. In addition to standard abbreviations, the following are used: LIC (Life Insurance Co.) and LAC (Life Assurance Co.). All data are based on 1979 rates and include waiver of premium in event of disability.

Best ⟶ Worst

Company and policy	Annual premium	Cost Indexes 20-yr	9-yr	19-yr	29-yr	Net payment index	Yields 9-yr	19-yr	29-yr
Time Ins. Co. The Competitor	$ 826	$210	◑	●	●	●	2.10%	5.34%	4.86%
Continental Assurance Co. Economiser	658	217	◑	●	●	●	−1.01	5.50	5.92
Equitable LIC of Iowa Life Paid Up at 95	956	226	●	●	●	◑	3.67	5.12	4.39
Provident Life & Acc. Ins. Co. Whole Life Paid Up—90	948	228	●	●	●	●	4.25	5.14	4.42
Continental Assurance Co. Maximiser II	825	237	◑	●	●	●	1.71	5.02	4.89
Federal Kemper Life Assurance Soc. Thrift-Life	849	251	◑	●	●	●	0.67	4.80	4.64
Kansas City LIC Exec. L 95 Guaranteed Cost	871	258	◑	◑	●	◑	1.26	4.67	4.49
Connecticut General LIC OL Plus	877	295	◑	◑	◑	○	−0.64	4.15	3.91
Travelers Ins. Co. Ordinary Life—NS [A]	1043	288	●	◑	●	◑	2.60	4.45	3.72
All Amer. Life & Casualty Co. Bus. Whole Life	1154	304	●	●	○	◑	6.52	4.39	3.50
U.S. LIC in the City of N.Y. Bus. Whole Life	1154	304	●	●	○	◑	6.52	4.39	3.50
Allstate LIC Exec. Plan [B]	926	309	◑	◑	◑	●	−0.07	3.99	4.01
Paul Revere LIC Super—Standard Whole Life	877	324	○	◑	●	◑	−1.35	3.71	4.18

* Premium changes after number of years in parentheses.

[A] Available only in New York.
[B] Available only to nonsmokers.
[C] Available only in Massachusetts.
[D] Available only to Lutherans.
[E] Available only to people in certain jobs.
[F] Available only to members of a fraternal organization.

Ratings of Cash Value Policies (Nonpar/$100,000/25 Years) *continued*

Company and policy	Annual premium	Cost indexes 20-yr.	Cost indexes 9-yr.	Cost indexes 19-yr.	Cost indexes 29-yr.	Net payment index	Yields 9-yr.	Yields 19-yr.	Yields 29-yr.
Federal Kemper Life Assurance Soc. OL—4	$923	$325	◐	◐	●	◐	1.71%	3.82%	3.94%
Home Beneficial LIC Life Paid Up at 95	939	335	◐	●	●	◐	-0.33	3.67	3.94
United Investors LIC Whole Life	939	340	◐	●	●	◐	1.90	3.62	3.81
Occidental LIC of Calif. Life—100	924	308	○	●	●	◐	-2.05	4.01	4.02
Fidelity Union LIC Presidents Pfd. Life	977	312	◐	●	●	○	0.83	3.96	3.78
Allstate LIC Exec. Plan	949	332	○	●	●	●	-0.72	3.69	3.81
Amer. States LIC Whole Life	950	334	○	●	●	●	-0.51	3.67	3.77
Northwestern National LIC Pfd. Whole Life Non Par	905	338	○	●	●	●	-1.49	3.56	4.04
Hartford LIC Whole Life	897	341	○	●	●	●	-1.60	3.47	4.01
Aetna LIC Whole Life Pfd. Risk A	957	341	○	●	●	●	-0.97	3.57	3.73
Southwestern LIC Commercial Whole Life	941	342	○	●	●	●	-1.32	3.51	3.72
Lincoln National LIC Whole Life A	933	346	○	●	●	●	-1.63	3.46	3.97
Amer. Health & Life Ins. Co. Enterprise Whole Life—Level	995	347	◐	●	●	○	0.11	3.58	3.64
Travelers Ins. Co. Ordinary Life	1081	327	◐	●	◐	○	1.44	3.88	3.34
Durham LIC Life Paid Up at 95	935	337	●	●	●	○	-3.03	3.56	3.84
Old Line LIC of Amer. Bus. Whole Life	1172	317	●	●	●	●	6.08	4.15	3.38
Security-Connecticut LIC Bus. Whole Life	1076	321	○	●	●	◐	0.01	4.00	3.35
Colonial LIC of Amer. Economiser B	1168	321	●	●	●	●	4.65	4.12	3.37
Provident Life & Acc. Ins. Co. Whole Life	1175	331	●	●	●	●	4.51	4.08	3.17
National Life & Acc. Ins. Co. Executive Whole Life A	1170	341	●	●	◐	○	4.03	3.91	3.20
Sun LIC of America L96	980	345	○	○	○	○	-4.01	3.49	3.57
Life & Casualty Ins. Co. of Tenn. Pfd. Exec. Whole Life	1173	346	●	●	●	◐	3.53	3.87	3.26
Colonial LIC of Amer. Economiser	1193	346	●	●	●	●	4.13	3.87	3.21
Southwestern LIC Executive 85	1169	348	●	●	◐	◐	3.48	3.79	3.18

Policy			Ratings							
Amer. National Ins. Co. Exec. Pfd. 99	1169	340	◗	◗	◗	◗	◗	1.71	3.86	3.24
Connecticut General LIC Ordinary Life	1001	341	◗	○	◗	○	○	−2.15	3.63	3.55
Southland LIC Exec. Pfd. Whole Life	1172	345	◗	◗	◗	◗	◐	1.46	3.77	3.20
First Colony LIC Whole Life	1049	329	●	◗	◗	○	○	−5.75	3.76	3.42
Commonwealth LIC Whole Life	1175	351	○	◗	◗	◗	◗	0.87	3.73	3.17
Travelers Ins.,Co. Presidential Whole Life—4NS [B]	908	352	◗	◗	◗	◗	◗	−1.75	3.43	3.93
Lincoln National LIC Whole Life [B]	944	357	○	◗	○	◗	◗	−1.94	3.31	3.87
Security Life & Acc. Co. Whole Life 100	1016	358	◗	◗	○	◗	◗	2.10	3.50	3.64
Liberty LIC Liberty Exec. Pfd. (WL)	1079	360	◗	○	○	○	○	0.55	3.57	3.38
First Colony LIC Life Paid Up at 96	925	369	○	○	○	◗	◗	−2.43	3.08	3.75
Jefferson Standard LIC Whole Life [B]	943	373	◗	○	○	◗	◗	−2.24	3.09	3.71
Lincoln National LIC Whole Life	961	374	◗	○	○	◗	◗	−2.41	3.09	3.73
Manufacturers LIC Estate Protector	933	377	◗	○	○	◗	◗	−2.66	2.97	3.68
National LAC of Canada Exec. Ordinary Life	933	379	◗	○	○	◗	◗	−2.98	2.94	3.66
J.C. Penney LIC Value Select—Whole Life	938	383	◗	○	○	◗	◗	−2.92	2.88	3.56
Amer. National Ins. Co. Exec. Pfd. 98	953	383	◗	○	○	◗	◗	−2.67	2.91	3.56
Dominion LAC Whole Life	942	386	◗	○	○	◗	◗	−2.92	2.85	3.60
Commonwealth LIC Life Paid Up at 95	956	390	◗	○	○	◗	◐	−3.01	2.77	3.49
National Life & Acc. Ins. Co. Exec. Life Plus [A]	962	390	◗	○	○	◗	◐	−2.97	2.77	3.47
Travelers Ins.,Co. Presidential Whole Life—4	946	391	◗	○	○	◗	◐	−3.20	2.74	3.48
Imperial LAC of Canada Whole Life	948	392	◗	○	○	◗	◐	−3.09	2.77	3.55
Aetna LIC Whole Life	980	364	○	○	○	○	◐	−1.60	3.27	3.53
Liberty LIC Liberty Protection 95 (LPU at 95)	1209	365	◗	◗	●	◗	◗	3.83	3.73	2.96
Colonial LIC of Amer. Cash Flo [B]	954	398	◗	○	◗	○	◐	−3.25	2.69	3.49

[A] Available only to "preferred risks."
[B] Available only to nonsmokers.
[C] Available only in Massachusetts.
[D] Available only in New York.
[E] Available only to Lutherans.
[F] Available only to people in certain jobs.
[G] Available only to members of a fraternal organization.

Ratings of Cash Value Policies (Nonpar/$100,000/25 Years) *continued*

Company and policy	Annual premium	Cost indexes 20-yr.	Cost indexes 9-yr.	Cost indexes 19-yr.	Cost indexes 29-yr.	Net payment index	Yields 9-yr.	Yields 19-yr.	Yields 29-yr.
Durham LIC Life Paid Up at 90	$1110	$358	◐	○	◐	◐	◐	1.65%	3.63%	3.34%
Jefferson Standard LIC Life Paid Up at 90	1113	361	◐	○	◐	◐	◐	1.58	3.60	3.31
Franklin LIC Pfd. 95	985	370	◐	○	○	○	○	−1.91	3.21	3.49
Monumental LIC LP at 95 Exec.	1120	374	◐	○	◐	◐	○	1.52	3.47	3.23
Safeco LIC Pfd. Life/Exec. Life	1022	375	◐	○	○	○	○	−2.11	3.17	3.39
IDS LIC Whole Life	981	382	○	○	○	○	○	−2.27	3.03	3.45
Paul Revere LIC Pfd. Life to 95	992	390	○	○	○	○	○	−1.91	2.98	3.48
Paul Revere LIC Exec. Life to 95	1002	400	○	○	○	○	○	−2.18	2.86	3.40
Manufacturers LIC Permanent Economic Protection	1007	402	○	○	○	○	○	−1.99	2.84	3.37
Home Beneficial LIC Whole Life	1129	380	○	○	○	◐	○	−0.14	3.38	3.19
Monarch LIC Ordinary Life—NP	1075	392	○	○	○	○	○	−1.03	3.10	3.22
J.C. Penney LIC Exec. Select Life Paid Up at 90	1224	392	●	○	◐	◐	●	2.31	3.36	2.88
Northwestern National LIC Whole Life Non Par	1068	394	◐	○	○	○	○	−2.00	3.06	3.22
Midland National LIC Whole Life	833	404	◐	◐	◐	◐	◉	−8.53	1.92	3.59
Jefferson Standard LIC Whole Life	983	413	◐	○	◐	◐	○	−3.34	2.56	3.37
Colonial LIC of Amer. Cash Flo	979	423	◐	○	◐	◐	○	−3.94	2.36	3.28
INA LIC Whole Life	983	427	◐	○	◐	◐	○	−4.05	2.31	3.25
United Benefit LIC Ordinary Life	983	428	◐	○	◐	◐	○	−4.22	2.26	3.16
Great-West LAC Estatemaster "400"	1038	419	◐	○	◐	◐	◐	−2.16	2.65	3.23
United Benefit LIC Life Paid Up at 90	1157	437	○	○	◐	◐	◐	0.38	2.68	2.77
Colonial LIC of Amer. Life Paid Up at 92	1045	440	◐	○	◐	○	○	−2.95	2.38	3.07
IDS LIC Select Whole Life	1247	432	●	○	●	●	●	2.87	3.05	2.70
Monarch LIC Accelerator 95	1201	441	○	○	◐	◐	◐	1.02	2.81	2.65
Monumental LIC LP at 90 Exec.	1190	443	○	○	◐	◐	◐	−1.56	2.73	2.76

Company and policy	Annual premium	Cost Indexes 20-yr.	9-yr.	19-yr.	29-yr.	Net payment Index 9-yr.	19-yr.	29-yr.	Yields 9-yr.	19-yr.	29-yr.
Time Ins. Co. Exec. Special	1185	465	◐	●	●	●	●	●	2.43	2.53	2.60
Nationwide LIC W.L.P.U. at 95	1124	468	●	●	●	◐	●	●	−4.44	2.09	2.69
North Amer. Co. for Life & Health Ins. Life Paid Up at 95	1302	484	○	●	●	●	●	●	1.29	2.60	2.29
Aetna LIC Life Paid Up at 95	1243	506	○	●	●	●	●	●	1.22	2.17	2.34
INA LIC Executive Whole Life	1344	624	◐	●	●	●	●	●	−0.67	1.05	1.65
Bankers Life & Casualty Co. Exec. Ordinary Life	1274	554	●	●	●	●	●	●	−1.74	1.65	2.08
Bankers Life & Casualty Co. Life Paid Up at 95	1375	654	●	●	●	●	●	●	−1.41	0.79	1.48

Type: Nonparticipating   Amount: $100,000   Age: 35

Listed in order of increasing cost, based primarily on 19-year cost index (see p. 267). All of the rates are for men's policies; rates for women at the same age are generally lower. Where company and policy listings are the same, difference is indicated by footnote. In addition to standard abbreviations, the following are used: LIC (Life Insurance Co.) and LAC (Life Assurance Co.). All data are based on 1979 rates and include waiver of premium in event of disability.

Best ⟶ Worst

Company and policy	Annual premium	Cost Indexes 20-yr.	9-yr.	19-yr.	29-yr.	Net payment Index 9-yr.	19-yr.	29-yr.	Yields 9-yr.	19-yr.	29-yr.
Time Ins. Co. The Competitor	$1281	$415	●	●	●	◐	●	●	1.86%	4.68%	4.45%
Travelers Ins. Co. Ordinary Life—NS [B]	1448	445	●	●	●	◑	◑	◑	2.83	4.40	3.78
Provident Life & Acc. Ins. Co. Whole Life Paid Up—90	1425	460	●	●	●	◐	●	●	3.27	4.47	4.02
Continental Assurance Co. Economiser	1162	465	○	●	●	●	●	●	−1.06	4.31	4.94

[A] Available only to "preferred risks."
[B] Available only to nonsmokers.
[C] Available only in Massachusetts.
[D] Available only in New York.
[E] Available only to Lutherans.
[F] Available only to people in certain jobs.
[G] Available only to members of a fraternal organization.

Ratings of Cash Value Policies (Nonpar/$100,000/35 Years) continued

Company and policy	Annual premium	Cost Indexes 20-yr.	9-yr.	19-yr.	29-yr.	Net payment Index	Yields 9-yr.	19-yr.	29-yr.
Continental Assurance Co. Maximiser II	$1315	$468	◐	●	●	●	◐	1.38%	4.34%	4.36%
Kansas City LIC Exec. L 95 Guaranteed Cost	1333	469	◐	●	●	●	◐	1.28	4.18	4.15
Federal Kemper Life Assurance Soc. Thrift—Life	1334	494	◐	●	●	●	◐	0.53	4.09	4.18
Travelers Ins. Co. Presidential Whole Life—4NS [B]	1301	496	◐	●	●	●	◐	0.69	3.91	4.16
Security-Connecticut LIC Bus. Whole Life	1456	451	◐	●	●	●	◐	1.92	4.49	3.82
Connecticut General LIC OL Plus	1321	494	◐	●	●	◐	◐	0.06	4.04	3.87
Equitable LIC of Iowa Life Paid Up at 95	1468	494	●	●	●	◐	◐	2.26	4.14	3.76
Colonial LIC of Amer. Economiser [B]	1566	463	●	●	●	○	○	5.00	4.43	3.60
Paul Revere LIC Super—Standard Whole Life	1325	521	◐	●	◐	◐	◐	0.19	3.81	4.12
Aetna LIC Whole Life Pfd. Risk [A]	1392	525	◐	◐	◐	◐	◐	0.54	3.81	3.87
Lincoln National LIC Whole Life [A]	1378	538	○	◐	◐	◐	◐	0.09	3.68	3.98
Southwestern LIC Commercial Whole Life	1395	553	○	◐	◐	◐	◐	-0.25	3.42	3.65
Northwestern National LIC Pfd. Whole Life Non Par	1383	559	○	◐	◐	◐	◐	-0.27	3.46	3.86
Lincoln National LIC Whole Life [B]	1402	562	○	◐	◐	◐	◐	-0.34	3.47	3.83
Allstate LIC Exec. Plan [A]	1429	562	○	◐	◐	◐	◐	-0.09	3.49	3.67
Colonial LIC of Amer. Economiser	1631	528	●	◐	◐	○	○	4.03	3.95	3.26
Old Line LIC of Amer. Bus. Whole Life	1638	531	●	◐	◐	○	○	4.41	3.85	3.18
All Amer. Life & Casualty Co. Bus. Whole Life	1615	535	●	◐	◐	○	○	4.65	3.94	3.34
U.S. LIC in the City of N.Y. Bus. Whole Life	1615	535	◐	◐	◐	○	○	4.65	3.94	3.34
Fidelity Union LIC Presidents Pfd. Life	1466	554	◐	◐	◐	○	○	0.61	3.50	3.47
Occidental LIC of Calif. Life-100	1423	556	◐	◐	◐	○	◐	-1.19	3.50	3.68
Life & Casualty Ins. Co. of Tenn. Pfd. Exec. Whole Life	1642	562	●	◐	○	○	○	2.89	3.69	3.16
Connecticut General LIC Ordinary Life	1478	559	◐	◐	○	○	○	-0.76	3.56	3.47
Federal Kemper Life Assurance Soc. OL—4	1412	572	◐	○	○	◐	◐	0.96	3.42	3.68

Policy									
United Investors LIC Whole Life	○	○	1422	581	◐	◐	1.12	3.36	3.62
Colonial LIC of Amer. Cash Flo [B]	○	○	1380	574	◐	○	−0.63	3.33	3.77
Jefferson Standard LIC Whole Life [B]	○	○	1408	578	◐	○	−0.52	3.33	3.74
Home Beneficial LIC Life Paid Up at 95	○	○	1433	581	◐	○	−0.02	3.34	3.64
J.C. Penney LIC Value Select—Whole Life	○	○	1393	588	◐	○	−0.95	3.09	3.59
Hartford LIC Whole Life	○	○	1396	590	◐	○	−0.92	3.19	3.67
Amer. National Ins. Co. Exec. Pfd. 98	○	○	1422	593	◐	○	−0.91	3.06	3.52
Safeco LIC Pfd. Life/Exec. Life	○	○	1458	570	◐	○	−0.55	3.30	3.45
Aetna LIC Whole Life	○	○	1439	572	◐	○	−0.28	3.39	3.59
Franklin LIC Pfd. 95	○	○	1443	578	◐	○	−0.54	3.35	3.56
Amer. States LIC Whole Life	○	○	1448	583	◐	○	−0.62	3.19	3.39
Allstate LIC Exec. Plan [B]	○	◐	1451	584	◐	○	−0.49	3.29	3.54
Security Life & Acc. Co. Whole Life 100	○	◐	1531	595	○	○	1.37	3.31	3.51
Lincoln National LIC Whole Life	○	●	1438	598	◐	○	−0.97	3.15	3.61
Amer. Health & Life Ins. Co. Enterprise Whole Life—Level	○	●	1477	590	◐	○	0.00	3.31	3.45
National Life & Acc. Ins. Co. Exec. Whole Life [A]	○	◐	1665	598	◐	○	2.70	3.33	2.90
Provident Life & Acc. Ins. Co. Whole Life	○	◐	1677	603	◐	○	2.85	3.42	2.89
IDS LIC Whole Life	○	◐	1445	604	○	○	−0.97	3.10	3.48
Dominion LAC Whole Life	○	◐	1415	609	◐	○	−1.25	3.01	3.57
Manufacturers LIC Estate Protector	○	◐	1420	614	◐	○	−1.34	2.97	3.55
Commonwealth LIC Life Paid Up at 95	○	◐	1443	622	◐	○	−1.60	2.79	3.35
Southland LIC Exec. Pfd. Whole Life	○	◐	1652	578	◐	○	1.20	3.42	2.98
Amer. National Ins. Co. Exec. Pfd. 99	○	◐	1661	579	◐	○	1.21	3.43	2.97
Travelers Ins. Co. Ordinary Life	○	◐	1591	588	◐	○	0.57	3.28	2.99
Monumental LIC LP at 95 Executive	○	○	1593	596	○	○	0.98	3.37	3.18

[A] Available only to "preferred risks."
[B] Available only to nonsmokers.
[C] Available only in Massachusetts.
[D] Available only in New York.
[E] Available only to Lutherans.
[F] Available only to people in certain jobs.
[G] Available only to members of a fraternal organization.

Ratings of Cash Value Policies (Nonpar/$100,000/35 Years) continued

Company and policy	Annual premium	Cost Indexes 20-yr.	9-yr.	19-yr.	29-yr.	Net payment index	Yields 9-yr.	19-yr.	29-yr.
Northwestern National LIC Whole Life Non Par	$1524	$602	◐	○	○	○	−0.58%	3.21%	3.32%
Southwestern LIC Executive 85	1681	610	●	◐	◐	◐	2.05	3.24	2.84
Sun LIC of America L96	1492	599	●	◐	○	○	−2.69	3.04	3.21
Commonwealth LIC Whole Life	1683	611	○	○	○	○	0.26	3.18	2.82
First Colony LIC Whole Life	1589	607	●	◐	○	◐	−4.14	3.14	3.02
Midland National LIC Whole Life	1305	627	●	◐	◐	●	−4.73	2.39	3.61
National Life & Acc. Ins. Co. Exec. Life Plus Ⓐ	1457	627	◐	◐	◐	◐	−1.50	2.76	3.32
INA LIC Whole Life	1438	632	◐	○	○	○	−1.66	2.81	3.43
Great-West LAC Estatemaster "100"	1505	632	○	◐	◐	○	−0.46	2.93	3.30
First Colony LIC Life Paid Up at 96	1439	633	◐	◐	◐	○	−1.67	2.80	3.42
Travelers Ins. Co. Presidential Whole Life—4	1443	638	◐	◐	◐	◐	−1.88	2.62	3.26
Colonial LIC of Amer. Cash Flo	1445	639	●	◐	◐	◐	−1.78	2.75	3.36
Time Ins. Co. Exec. Special	1625	662	●	◐	◐	◐	2.80	2.84	2.80
Allstate LIC Exec. Plan	1497	630	◐	◐	○	○	−1.26	2.90	3.27
J.C. Penney LIC Exec. Select Life Paid Up at 90	1713	641	●	◐	◐	◐	1.32	2.98	2.67
Paul Revere LIC Pfd. Life to 95	1492	642	◐	◐	◐	○	−1.18	2.82	3.26
Jefferson Standard LIC Whole Life	1478	648	◐	◐	◐	○	−1.73	2.72	3.32
Manufacturers LIC Permanent Economic Protection	1511	656	◐	◐	◐	○	−1.30	2.70	3.18
Imperial LAC of Canada Whole Life	1467	661	◐	◐	◐	◐	−2.16	2.56	3.26
Jefferson Standard LIC Life Paid Up at 90	1640	632	○	○	○	○	1.10	3.11	2.98
Durham LIC Life Paid Up at 90	1644	636	●	●	○	○	1.04	3.08	2.96
Durham LIC Life Paid Up at 95	1479	638	◐	●	◐	●	−2.56	2.79	3.28
North Amer. Co. for Life & Health Ins. Life Paid Up at 95	1720	657	◐	◐	◐	○	1.98	3.03	2.64
Monarch LIC Ordinary Life—NP	1595	659	◐	◐	◐	○	−0.64	2.82	2.97

Policy			Ratings									
Liberty LIC Liberty Protection 95 (LPU at 95)	1745	670	◑	○	◑	●	◑	◑	◑	4.78	2.93	2.57
National LAC of Canada Exec. Ordinary Life	1477	673	○	●	◑	○	◑	○	○	−2.53	2.45	3.19
Paul Revere LIC Exec. Life to 95	1526	676	○	●	◑	◑	◑	◑	◑	−1.74	2.54	3.07
IDS LIC Select Whole Life	1758	695	◑	◑	◑	◑	◑	◑	◑	2.12	2.76	2.53
Home Beneficial LIC Whole Life	1658	654	●	◑	◑	◑	◑	◑	◑	−0.36	2.94	2.88
Liberty LIC Liberty Exec. Pfd. (WL)	1638	675	○	◑	◑	◑	◑	◑	◑	−0.24	2.75	2.83
Monumental LIC LP at 90 Exec.	1681	682	◑	●	◑	◑	◑	◑	◑	−0.84	2.73	2.74
United Benefit LIC Ordinary Life	1492	687	◑	●	○	◑	◑	◑	●	−2.68	2.22	2.99
United Benefit LIC Life Paid Up at 90	1685	719	◑	●	○	◑	◑	◑	●	−0.14	2.37	2.49
Colonial LIC of Amer. Life Paid Up at 92	1584	729	○	●	◑	◑	◑	◑	●	−2.46	2.11	2.77
Aetna LIC Life Paid Up at 95	1730	745	◑	◑	◑	◑	●	●	●	1.28	2.31	2.42
Nationwide LIC W.L.P.U. at 95	1637	735	◑	◑	◑	●	◑	◑	●	−2.98	2.00	2.54
Monarch LIC Accelerator 95	1769	741	◑	◑	●	●	●	●	●	0.48	2.41	2.32
INA LIC Executive Whole Life	1832	867	●	●	●	●	●	●	●	−0.06	1.48	1.90
Bankers Life & Casualty Co. Executive Ordinary Life	1820	855	●	●	●	●	●	●	●	−1.83	1.51	1.95
Bankers Life & Casualty Co. Life Paid Up at 95	1909	945	●	●	●	●	●	●	●	−1.03	0.96	1.54

Type: Nonparticipating   Amount: $100,000   Age: 45

Listed in order of increasing cost, based primarily on 19-year cost index (see p. 267). All of the rates are for men's policies; rates for women at the same age are generally lower. Where company and policy listings are the same, difference is indicated by footnote. In addition to standard abbreviations, the following are used: LIC (Life Insurance Co.) and LAC (Life Assurance Co.). All data are based on 1979 rates and include waiver of premium in event of disability.

Best ● ◐ ○ ◑ ○ Worst

A Available only to "preferred risks."
B Available only to nonsmokers.
C Available only in Massachusetts.
D Available only in New York.
E Available only to Lutherans.
F Available only to people in certain jobs.
G Available only to members of a fraternal organization.

Ratings of Cash Value Policies (Nonpar/$100,000/45 Years) continued

Company and policy	Annual premium	Cost indexes 20-yr.	9-yr.	19-yr.	29-yr.	Net payment index	Yields 9-yr.	19-yr.	29-yr.
Time Ins. Co. The Competitor	$2104	$950	◐	●	●	◐	1.75%	4.17%	4.08%
Lincoln National LIC Whole Life Ⓐ	2106	981	◐	●	●	◐	2.25	4.26	4.33
Paul Revere LIC Super—Standard Whole Life	2068	985	◐	●	●	●	2.06	4.24	4.40
Connecticut General LIC OL Plus	2092	963	●	●	●	◐	1.73	4.31	4.04
Colonial LIC of Amer. Economiser Ⓑ	2367	993	◐	◐	●	○	4.50	4.08	3.46
Security-Connecticut LIC Business Whole Life	2283	994	◐	◐	●	◐	1.67	4.07	3.62
Kansas City LIC Exec. L 95 Guaranteed Cost	2164	1002	◐	◐	◐	◐	1.44	3.83	3.85
Travelers Ins. Co. Ordinary Life—NS Ⓑ	2290	1009	◐	◐	◐	◐	2.04	3.74	3.38
Travelers Ins. Co. Presidential Whole Life—4NS Ⓑ	2119	1024	◐	◐	◐	◐	1.04	3.68	3.92
Lincoln National LIC Whole Life Ⓑ	2162	1037	◐	◐	◐	◐	1.51	3.87	4.04
Federal Kemper Life Assurance Soc. Thrift—Life	2173	1044	◐	◐	◐	◐	0.89	3.80	3.96
Aetna LIC Whole Life Preferred Risk Ⓐ	2206	1044	◐	◐	◐	◐	1.15	3.78	3.82
Amer. States LIC Whole Life	2203	1046	◐	◐	◐	◐	0.83	3.58	3.64
Colonial LIC of Amer. Cash Flo Ⓑ	2142	1059	◐	◐	◐	◐	1.06	3.73	4.02
Jefferson Standard LIC Whole Life Ⓑ	2203	1067	◐	◐	◐	◐	1.06	3.65	3.86
Continental Assurance Co. Maximiser II	2219	1068	◐	◐	◐	◐	0.84	3.63	3.79
Amer. National Ins. Co. Exec. Pfd. 98	2206	1073	◐	◐	◐	◐	0.67	3.41	3.65
Fidelity Union LIC Presidents Pfd. Life	2298	1099	◐	◐	◐	◐	0.68	3.22	3.25
Great-West LAC Estatemaster "100"	2270	1106	○	◐	◐	◐	1.23	3.43	3.57
Continental Assurance Co. Economiser	2080	1071	○	◐	◐	◐	-0.97	3.59	4.23
Connecticut General LIC Ordinary Life	2286	1076	○	◐	◐	◐	0.28	3.57	3.48
Provident Life & Accident Ins. Co. Whole Life Paid Up—90	2327	1076	◐	◐	◐	○	1.95	3.61	3.44

Company	Code	Code							
All Amer. Life & Casualty Co. Bus. Whole Life	2431	1076	○	●	◐	○	3.00	3.61	3.16
U.S. LIC in the City of N.Y. Bus. Whole Life	2431	1076	●	●	◐	○	3.00	3.61	3.16
Life & Casualty Ins. Co. of Tenn. Pfd. Exec. Whole Life	2440	1089	●	●	◐	○	2.83	3.54	3.10
Northwestern National LIC Pfd. Whole Life Nonpar	2221	1100	○	◐	◐	○	0.56	3.43	3.73
Old Line LIC of Amer. Business Whole Life	2468	1104	◐	◐	◐	○	2.62	3.27	2.90
Occidental LIC of Calif. Life—100	2268	1106	○	◐	◐	◐	-0.27	3.37	3.52
Safeco LIC Pfd. Life/Exec. Life	2274	1107	○	◐	◐	◐	0.28	3.16	3.30
Dominion LAC Whole Life	2213	1111	○	◐	◐	◐	0.14	3.36	3.73
Hartford LIC Whole Life	2195	1112	○	◐	◐	◐	0.37	3.37	3.73
J.C. Penney LIC Value Select—Whole Life	2209	1113	○	◐	◐	◐	-0.05	3.11	3.50
Home Beneficial LIC Life Paid Up at 95	2257	1114	○	◐	◐	◐	0.71	3.36	3.61
Lincoln National LIC Whole Life	2245	1120	○	◐	◐	◐	0.46	3.32	3.63
Southwestern LIC Commercial Whole Life	2254	1127	○	◐	○	○	-0.26	3.01	3.31
Amer. National Ins. Co. Exec. Pfd. 99	2432	1065	●	◐	◐	◐	1.93	3.51	3.05
Colonial LIC of Amer. Economiser	2482	1108	●	◐	○	◐	3.24	3.42	2.97
Equitable LIC of Iowa Life Paid Up at 95	2355	1117	◐	◐	◐	◐	1.58	3.35	3.24
United Investors LIC Whole Life	2281	1150	◐	◐	◐	◐	0.97	3.13	3.42
Allstate LIC Exec. Plan Ⓐ	2331	1151	○	○	◐	◐	-0.37	3.08	3.39
Aetna LIC Whole Life	2316	1154	○	○	◐	◐	-0.20	3.07	3.29
Federal Kemper Life Assurance Soc. OL—4	2288	1156	○	○	◐	◐	0.63	3.09	3.42
Franklin LIC Pfd. 95	2322	1162	○	○	◐	◐	-0.35	3.04	3.28
INA LIC Whole Life	2269	1171	○	○	◐	◐	-0.55	2.97	3.43
Colonial LIC of Amer. Cash Flo	2257	1174	○	○	◐	◐	-0.40	2.96	3.44
Manufacturers LIC Estate Protector	2275	1174	○	○	○	◐	-0.62	2.93	3.41

Ⓐ Available only to "preferred risks."
Ⓑ Available only to nonsmokers.
Ⓒ Available only in Massachusetts.
Ⓓ Available only in New York.
Ⓔ Available only to Lutherans.
Ⓕ Available only to people in certain jobs.
Ⓖ Available only to members of a fraternal organization.

Ratings of Cash Value Policies (Nonpar/$100,000/45 Years) *continued*

Company and policy	Annual premium	Cost Indexes 20-yr.	9-yr.	19-yr.	29-yr.	Net payment index	Yields 9-yr.	19-yr.	29-yr.
Commonwealth LIC Life Paid Up at 95	$2296	$1178	○	○	○	◐	−0.82%	2.69%	3.14%
National Life & Acc. Ins. Co. Exec. Life Plus Ⓐ	2312	1178	○	○	○	◐	−0.56	2.71	3.11
Imperial LAC of Canada Whole Life	2285	1184	○	○	○	◐	−0.74	2.88	3.37
IDS LIC Whole Life	2314	1185	○	○	○	◐	−0.56	2.87	3.25
Time Ins. Co. Exec. Special	2444	1202	●	○	○	○	2.63	2.69	2.68
Midland National LIC Whole Life	2193	1212	◐	○	◐	●	−3.37	2.32	3.32
Security Life & Acc. Co. Whole Life 100	2441	1151	○	○	○	○	1.13	3.14	2.98
Monumental LIC LP at 95 Exec.	2454	1167	○	○	○	○	0.49	3.06	3.05
Northwestern National LIC Whole Life Non Par	2385	1173	○	○	○	○	−0.25	2.97	3.12
Amer. Health & Life Ins. Co. Enterprise Whole Life-Level	2336	1181	○	○	○	○	0.19	2.94	3.19
Jefferson Standard LIC Whole Life	2328	1192	◐	○	○	○	−0.47	2.85	3.26
Travelers Ins. Co. Presidential Whole Life—4	2303	1207	◐	○	○	◐	−1.24	2.48	3.03
Manufacturers LIC Permanent Economic Protection	2356	1214	◐	○	○	○	−0.41	2.74	3.12
First Colony LIC Life Paid Up at 96	2315	1215	◐	○	○	○	−1.10	2.69	3.22
Paul Revere LIC Ptd. Life to 95	2344	1221	◐	○	○	○	−0.40	2.68	3.11
National Life & Acc. Ins. Co. Exec. Whole Life Ⓐ	2501	1163	●	○	◐	◐	1.98	2.93	2.66
Sun LIC of America L96	2359	1165	●	○	○	○	−1.85	2.77	2.96
North Amer. Co. for Life & Health Ins. Life Paid Up at 95	2520	1189	◐	○	●	◐	2.06	2.99	2.68
Travelers Ins. Co. Ordinary Life	2473	1191	○	○	●	◐	0.01	2.68	2.59
Southwestern LIC Exec. 85	2566	1203	◐	○	●	○	1.20	2.69	2.48
Allstate LIC Exec. Plan Ⓑ	2389	1208	○	○	○	○	−1.03	2.73	3.13
Provident Life & Acc. Ins. Co. Whole Life	2567	1220	◐	○	○	◐	1.67	2.81	2.53
United Benefit LIC Ordinary Life	2340	1243	○	○	○	○	−1.65	2.26	2.87

Policy									
Southland LIC Exec. Pfd. Whole Life	2538	1186	○		◐	◐	0.46	2.76	2.51
Jefferson Standard LIC Life Paid Up at 90	2526	1220	○	◐	◐	◐	1.17	2.79	2.70
J.C. Penney LIC Exec. Select Life Paid Up at 90	2570	1229	○	◐	◐	◐	0.60	2.56	2.40
Durham LIC Life Paid Up at 90	2543	1234	○	◐	◐	◐	0.99	2.71	2.65
Commonwealth LIC Whole Life	2573	1222	◐	◐	◐	◐	−0.44	2.56	2.37
First Colony LIC Whole Life	2506	1229	●	◐	◐	◐	−3.26	2.63	2.65
Durham LIC Life Paid Up at 95	2388	1257	○	○	○	○	−1.97	2.43	2.95
National LAC of Canada Exec. Ordinary Life	2370	1270	○	○	○	○	−1.77	2.33	2.97
Allstate LIC Exec. Plan	2457	1275	○	○	○	○	−1.80	2.33	2.84
Liberty LIC Liberty Protection 95 (LPU at 95)	2683	1330	○	◐	○	◐	0.42	2.23	2.12
Paul Revere LIC Exec. Life to 95	2461	1338	◐	○	○	○	−1.72	1.98	2.59
IDS LIC Select Whole Life	2684	1345	○	◐	○	◐	1.10	2.16	2.09
Aetna LIC Life Paid Up at 95	2630	1360	○	◐	○	◐	0.83	2.03	2.18
Home Beneficial LIC Whole Life	2555	1253	◐	●	◐	◐	−0.42	2.58	2.58
Monarch LIC Ordinary Life—NP	2506	1285	○	◐	◐	◐	−0.62	2.38	2.58
Monumental LIC LP at 90 Exec.	2582	1289	◐	◐	◐	◐	−0.89	2.38	2.46
Liberty LIC Liberty Exec. Pfd. (WL)	2562	1312	◐	●	◐	◐	−0.55	2.25	2.45
United Benefit LIC Life Paid Up at 90	2596	1347	◐	●	●	◐	−0.92	1.87	2.08
INA LIC Exec. Whole Life	2677	1424	○	○	●	◐	0.57	1.71	1.99
Nationwide LIC W.L.P.U. at 95	2572	1383	●	●	●	◐	−2.78	1.54	2.09
Colonial LIC of Amer. Life Paid Up at 92	2535	1409	◐	◐	●	●	−2.39	1.60	2.21
Monarch LIC Accelerator 95	2756	1428	●	●	●	●	−0.18	1.74	1.76
Bankers Life & Casualty Co. Exec. Ordinary Life	2804	1554	●	●	●	●	−2.53	1.01	1.51
Bankers Life & Casualty Co. Life Paid Up at 95	2872	1621	●	●	●	●	−1.34	0.71	1.26

A Available only to "preferred risks."
B Available only to nonsmokers.
C Available only in Massachusetts.
D Available only in New York.
E Available only to Lutherans.
F Available only to people in certain jobs.
G Available only to members of a fraternal organization.

Type: Participating   Amount: $100,000   Age: 25

Listed in order of increasing cost, based primarily on 19-year cost index (see p. 267). All of the rates are for men's policies; rates for women at the same age are generally lower. Where company and policy listings are the same, difference is indicated by footnote. In addition to standard abbreviations, the following are used: LIC (Life Insurance Co.) and LAC (Life Assurance Co.). All data are based on 1979 rates and include waiver of premium in event of disability.

Best ● ◐ ○ ◐ → Worst

Company and policy	Annual premium*	20-yr.	Cost Indexes 9-yr.	19-yr.	29-yr.	Net payment index	Yields 9-yr.	19-yr.	29-yr.
Teachers Ins. & Annuity Assoc. of Amer. Ordinary Life [E]	$1207	$−14	●	●	●	●	1.11%	6.91%	7.64%
New England Mutual LIC Ordinary Life [A]	1140	148	●	●	●	●	2.95	5.95	6.24
Massachusetts Mutual LIC Convertible Life	1147	160	●	●	●	●	3.09	5.86	6.02
New England Mutual LIC Ordinary Life	1175	183	●	●	●	●	2.09	5.50	5.92
Standard Ins. Co. Whole Life [B]	1187	184	●	●	●	●	2.61	5.54	6.05
Northwestern Mutual LIC Whole Life	1411	196	●	●	●	●	2.58	5.36	5.98
Home LIC Whole Life NSR [B]	1081	98	◐	●	●	◐	0.56	6.44	6.55
Union Mutual LIC Whole Life [B]	1502	136	●	●	●	◐	2.55	5.63	5.93
Central LAC Special Whole Life	1315	162	●	●	●	◐	5.34	5.72	5.72
Connecticut Mutual LIC Econolife (Whole Life) [A]	1018	191	◐	●	●	●	4.64	5.60	5.70
Mutual LIC of New York Mony—One [A]	999	193	◐	●	●	●	−1.12	5.50	5.97
Central LAC Maximum Life	1054	196	●	●	●	○	0.49	5.42	5.93
Phoenix Mutual LIC Ordinary Life, NSB [B]	1499	103	●	●	●	○	3.15	5.91	6.11
Phoenix Mutual LIC Ordinary Life	1514	118	●	●	●	○	2.89	5.77	6.01
Home LIC Whole Life	1131	148	○	●	●	●	−0.73	5.78	6.09

Policy									
Guardian LIC of Amer. Modified 3 Whole Life [A]	1496 (3)	169	●	●	●	○	2.10	5.42	5.87
Knights of Columbus Directors Plan (L95) [G]	1310	170	●	●	◐	◐	1.93	5.50	6.05
Union Mutual LIC Exec. Life (Non-NY) [B]	1520	190	●	●	●	○	2.92	5.26	5.78
Connecticut Mutual LIC Whole Life [A]	1129	200	●	●	●	◐	3.22	5.36	5.66
Guardian LIC of Amer. Pension Trust Whole Life [A]	1457	158	●	◐	◐	○	2.15	5.46	5.94
Union Mutual LIC Whole Life	1535	169	●	●	◐	○	2.00	5.33	5.71
Guardian LIC of Amer. Whole Life [A]	1457	176	●	●	◐	○	2.09	5.31	5.76
Guardian LIC of Amer. Pension Trust Whole Life	1481	182	●	●	◐	○	1.72	5.24	5.78
New York LIC Whole Life	1421	186	●	●	◐	○	2.33	5.18	5.62
General Amer. LIC Limited Payment Life [A]	1541	135	●	●	◐	◐	1.39	5.60	5.87
General Amer. LIC Limited Payment Life	1568	162	●	●	○	◐	0.93	5.38	5.71
Mutual LIC of New York Whole Life [A]	1616	146	●	●	○	◐	0.50	5.50	5.75
Mutual LIC of New York Whole Life	1656	186	●	◐	◐	◐	-0.14	5.17	5.51
Continental Assurance Co. Whole Life	1311	194	●	◐	◐	○	0.94	5.23	4.45
Farm Bureau (Iowa) Special Whole Life	1030	212	◐	◐	●	●	2.21	5.22	5.60
Standard Ins. Co. Whole Life	1229	226	◐	◐	●	●	1.59	5.01	5.68
New York LIC Modified 2 Whole Life	1421 (2)	200	◐	◐	○	●	-0.46	5.20	5.91
State Mutual LAC of Amer. Non-Smoker Whole Life [B]	1478	209	◐	◐	◐	◐	1.72	5.05	5.65
Bankers Life Co. Century 100	1045	216	◐	◐	◐	●	0.32	5.10	5.41
Manufacturers LIC Estate Protector	1088	217	◐	◐	○	●	-1.63	5.10	6.09
Acacia Mutual LIC Whole Life	1086	221	◐	◐	●	●	1.44	5.00	5.35
Manufacturers LIC Permanent Economic Protection	1187	221	◐	●	○	●	-1.07	5.04	5.92
Connecticut Mutual LIC Econolife (Whole Life)	1062	235	◐	●	●	○	3.44	4.99	5.28

Premium changes after number of years in parentheses.

[A] Available only to "preferred risks."
[B] Available only to nonsmokers.
[C] Available only in Massachusetts.
[D] Available only in New York.
[E] Available only to Lutherans.
[F] Available only to people in certain jobs.
[G] Available only to members of a fraternal organization.

Ratings of Cash Value Policies (Par/$100,000/25 Years) continued

Company and policy	Annual premium*	Cost Indexes 20-yr.	Cost Indexes 9-yr.	Cost Indexes 19-yr.	Cost Indexes 29-yr.	Net payment index	Yields 9-yr.	Yields 19-yr.	Yields 29-yr.
Connecticut Mutual LIC Whole Life	$1170	$241	●	◑	◑	◑	2.26%	4.86%	5.31%
USAA LIC Modified-One Whole Life [F]	1129(1)	257	●	◑	◑	◑	2.16	4.72	5.28
Guardian LIC of Amer. Modified 3 Whole Life	1520(3)	193	◑	◑	●	○	1.63	5.19	5.70
Guardian LIC of Amer. Whole Life	1481	200	◑	◑	●	○	1.67	5.09	5.60
Equitable Life Assurance Soc. of the U.S. Adjustable Whole Life	1445	201	◑	◑	●	○	1.98	5.15	5.55
John Hancock Mutual LIC Pfd. 25 [A]	1528(3)	220	◑	◑	●	○	1.10	4.92	5.50
Union Mutual LIC Exec. Life (Non-NY)	1551	221	◑	◑	●	○	2.42	4.99	5.58
Columbus Mutual LIC Life—100	1098	228	○	◑	◑	◔	−1.29	4.93	5.51
Southern Farm Bureau LIC Whole Life	1269	247	◑	◑	◑	◑	0.85	4.77	5.36
Canada LAC The Century	1146	248	●	◑	○	◑	1.73	4.80	5.14
Pacific Mutual LIC Special Whole Life	1127	249	◑	◑	◑	◑	1.11	4.73	5.33
State Farm LIC Estate Protector (L95)	1130	202	○	◑	◑	◑	−0.48	5.23	5.56
Penn Mutual LIC Whole Life [B]	1455	216	◑	◑	◑	◑	2.15	5.03	5.35
Dominion LAC Whole Life	1339	225	○	◑	◑	◔	0.28	4.94	5.42
Mutual LIC of New York Mony—One	1039	233	◑	◑	◑	●	−2.23	4.95	5.60
Mutual Benefit LIC Life Paid Up at 95	1492	233	◑	◑	◑	○	1.86	4.87	5.25
State Mutual LAC of Amer. Non-Smoker Exec. Protector Endowment [B]	1519	240	◔	◑	○	○	1.95	4.76	5.40
Indianapolis LIC Exec. Protector [B]	1514	242	◑	◑	○	◑	2.36	4.80	5.10
Bankers Life Co. Special Whole Life	1167	244	◑	◑	○	◑	0.40	4.77	5.06
Security Benefit LIC Exec. Whole Life	1179	246	◑	◑	○	◔	−3.33	4.69	5.44
Indianapolis LIC Ordinary Life [B]	1351	247	◑	◑	○	◑	1.40	4.75	5.13
Minnesota Mutual LIC Econo-Life	1181	229	◑	◑	◑	◑	−0.90	4.92	5.59
Prudential Ins. Co. of Amer. Modified Life 3 [A]	1546 (3)	234	○	◑	◑	○	0.94	4.81	5.35

Policy							
Occidental LIC of Calif. Par 90 F	1224	240		●		2.77	4.85	4.43
USAA LIC Ordinary Life F	1350	240		○		0.85	4.78	5.28
Confederation LIC Life to 96 B	1188	242		◐		−2.79	4.69	5.67
Lincoln National LIC Whole Life A	1485	227		○		1.10	4.89	4.94
Lincoln National LIC Whole Life B	1499	241		○		0.84	4.76	4.85
Provident Mutual LIC Protector Plus A	1364 (2)	259		●		2.88	4.64	5.20
Acacia Mutual LIC Whole Life	1135	270		◐		0.29	4.42	4.95
Prudential Ins. Co. of Amer. Modified Life 3	1566 (3)	254		○		0.59	4.63	5.22
North American LAC Whole Life	1183	257		○		−0.14	4.60	5.11
Farm Bureau (Iowa) Exec. Pfd. Par	1367	260		◐		1.25	4.63	5.15
Beneficial LIC Heritage 100	1077	261		○		−1.21	4.59	5.18
Penn Mutual LIC Whole Life	1500	261		◐		1.32	4.61	5.05
Metropolitan LIC Whole Life A	1230	262		◐		−1.70	4.48	5.38
State Mutual LAC of Amer. Whole Life	1522	262		○		0.81	4.55	5.26
John Hancock Mutual LIC Whole Life 100	1474	266		◐		0.89	4.48	5.21
Equitable LIC of Iowa Life Paid Up at 95	1545	266		○		1.17	4.51	4.98
Woodmen of the World Life Ins. Soc. Whole Life Minimum $10,000 G	1236	272		○		−0.24	4.42	5.34
Mutual Benefit LIC Ordinary Life	1639	275		○		2.21	4.51	5.00
Prudential Ins. Co. of Amer. Estate 20—Whole Life A	1450	276		◐		1.37	4.44	5.12
Lutheran Mutual LIC Whole Life	1583	258		○		1.59	4.56	4.79
Ohio National LIC Pfd. Exec. Whole Life	1082	269		○		−0.82	4.50	4.87
Indianapolis LIC Five Year Modified Life	1513 (5)	271		○		−3.89	4.38	4.94
Penn Mutual LIC Value Builder 90 B	1517	277		◑		2.30	4.48	4.96

*Premium changes after number of years in parentheses.

A Available only to "preferred risks."
B Available only to nonsmokers.
C Available only in Massachusetts.
D Available only in New York.
E Available only to Lutherans.
F Available only to people in certain jobs.
G Available only to members of a fraternal organization.

Ratings of Cash Value Policies (Par/$100,000/25 Years) continued

Company and policy	Annual premium*	Cost Indexes				Net payment Index	Yields		
		20-yr.	9-yr.	19-yr.	29-yr.		9-yr.	19-yr.	29-yr.
Ohio National LIC Pfd. Whole Life	$1471	$258	◐	○	◕	◕	1.63%	4.64%	4.76%
National LIC Life [B]	1613	264	○	○	◕	◐	1.45	4.50	4.91
Canada LAC Exec. Whole Life	1383	274	◑	○	◐	◕	−0.99	4.47	4.86
Life & Casualty Ins. Co. of Tenn. Whole Life	1389	278	◐	○	◐	◕	−0.93	4.38	4.89
Manhattan LIC Challenger [B]	1597	262	◐	○	◐	◐	0.69	4.59	4.91
Jefferson Standard LIC Life Paid Up at 95 [B]	1593	258	◐	○	◐	◐	0.01	4.56	4.81
Lincoln National LIC Whole Life	1520	262	◐	○	◐	◐	0.47	4.57	4.71
Provident Mutual LIC Protector Plus	1394 (2)	289	●	○	◐	◐	2.21	4.30	4.96
Great-West LAC Estatemaster "100"	1206	292	◐	○	◐	◐	−2.18	4.18	5.27
Aid Association for Lutherans Estate Life [E]	1253	316	○	○	◐	○	0.85	3.98	5.08
Confederation LIC Whole Life [B]	1455	279	◐	○	○	○	0.62	4.36	4.95
Indianapolis LIC Exec. Protector	1557	285	○	○	○	○	1.60	4.39	4.81
State Mutual LAC of Amer. Exec. Protector Endowment at 90 [A]	1558	288	○	○	○	○	1.17	4.33	5.06
Farm Bureau (Iowa) Whole Life Par	1513	290	○	○	○	○	0.97	4.34	5.04
Fidelity Union LIC Professional Exec. Life	1159	298	○	○	◐	◐	−0.51	4.17	4.33
Minnesota Mutual LIC Adjustable Life	1259	308	◐	○	◐	◐	−1.38	4.01	5.09
Kansas City LIC Exec. Endowment 90	1378	308	◐	○	◐	○	1.62	4.18	4.54
Imperial LAC of Canada Whole Life	1189	322	◐	○	◐	◐	−3.45	3.81	5.06
Bankers LIC of Nebraska Whole Life Special	1415	284	●	○	◐	◐	−3.72	3.81	4.99
Indianapolis LIC Ordinary Life	1394	290	○	○	◐	◐	0.56	4.30	4.82
Prudential Ins. Co. of Amer. Estate 20 — Whole Life	1470	296	○	○	◐	◐	1.03	4.26	4.99
Union Central LIC 100,000 Minimum Life	1037	302	◐	○	◐	◐	−4.04	4.01	4.95
Metropolitan LIC Whole Life	1272	304	◐	○	○	○	−2.60	4.03	5.06

Policy	No.							Premium change	Cost index (10 yr)	Cost index (20 yr)
Penn Mutual LIC Value Builder 90	1562			◐	◐	◐	◐	1.53	4.09	4.68
Aid Association for Lutherans Whole Life Ⓔ	322			◐	○	○	○	-0.98	3.91	4.98
Canada LAC Exec. 95	1501			○	◐	○	○	0.73	3.84	4.34
Southern Farm Bureau LIC Ordinary Life	1545			◐	◐	◐	○	-0.40	4.28	4.83
Columbus Mutual LIC Pfd. Life	1549			◐	◐	○	◐	-0.45	4.12	4.93
Beneficial LIC Professional Estate Plan	1567			○	◐	◐	○	1.37	4.23	4.76
Sun LAC of Canada Sun Permanent Life	1677			◐	◐	◐	◐	-2.79	3.95	4.43
Midland Mutual LIC Modified Life	1243			●	◐	◐	◐	-4.38	3.83	4.78
Provident Mutual LIC Whole Life Plus Ⓐ	1537 (3)			○	◐	◐	◐	1.16	4.08	4.80
Mutual Trust LIC Life Paid Up at 85	1596			○	◐	◐	◐	1.46	3.94	4.33
Canada LAC Estate Protector	1579			◐	◐	◐	○	0.04	3.81	4.36
Life & Casualty Ins. Co. of Tenn. Exec. Whole Life	1427			◐	◐	○	○	0.11	3.59	4.36
Mutual Trust LIC Ordinary Life	1573			◐	◐	◐	◐	-0.84	4.29	4.67
Jefferson Standard LIC Life Paid Up at 95	1572			●	◐	◐	◐	-0.64	4.23	4.57
National Life of Vermont Life	1633			◐	◐	○	○	0.70	4.11	4.63
State Farm LIC Whole Life	1659			●	◐	◐	◐	-2.25	4.01	4.82
Amer. Family LIC Ordinary Life	1433			○	◐	◐	◐	-1.03	4.02	4.39
Sun LAC of Canada Whole Life	1681			●	◐	◐	◐	-0.07	4.00	4.42
Midland Mutual LIC Paid Up Life at 95	1708			●	◐	◐	○	-2.69	3.79	4.48
Northwestern National LIC Whole Life Par	1641			●	◐	◐	◐	-2.98	3.80	4.44
Mutual Trust LIC Life Paid Up at 90	1476			◐	◐	◐	◐	0.36	3.87	4.42
John Hancock Mutual LIC 3 Year Modified Life	1636			○	◐	◐	◐	-1.48	3.71	4.71
Provident Mutual LIC Whole Life Plus	1533 (3)			◐	◐	◐	◐	0.65	3.82	4.62
Pacific Mutual LIC Adjustable Life	1626			◐	●	◐	◐	-1.02	3.99	4.17

*Premium changes after number of years in parentheses.

Ⓐ Available only to "preferred risks."
Ⓑ Available only to nonsmokers.
Ⓒ Available only in Massachusetts.
Ⓓ Available only in New York.
Ⓔ Available only to Lutherans.
Ⓕ Available only to people in certain jobs.
Ⓖ Available only to members of a fraternal organization.

Ratings of Cash Value Policies (Par/$100,000/25 Years) *continued*

Company and policy	Annual premium*	Cost Indexes 20-yr.	Cost Indexes 9-yr.	Cost Indexes 19-yr.	Cost Indexes 29-yr.	Net payment index	Yields 9-yr.	Yields 19-yr.	Yields 29-yr.
Union Central LIC Ordinary Life Preferred Class	$1637	$330	●	◐	◐	◐	−1.66%	3.92%	4.61%
Bankers Life & Casualty Co. Life Paid Up at 98	1699	335	◐	◐	●	◐	0.62	4.03	4.27
Union Central LIC Ordinary Life	1637	340	●	◐	●	◐	−1.79	3.83	4.53
Manhattan LIC Challenger	1682	347	◐	◐	●	●	−0.63	3.92	4.44
Nationwide LIC W.L.P.U. at 95	1588	381	○	●	●	◐	0.84	3.50	3.98
Franklin LIC Exec. Select—II	1652	374	◐	●	●	●	−1.81	3.57	4.33
Connecticut General LIC Life Full Paid at 90 (Par)	1529	388	◐	●	●	◐	0.36	3.56	3.90
Monarch LIC Select Risk Endowment at 95 Ⓐ	1618	391	○	●	●	●	1.24	3.61	4.08
U.S. LIC in the City of N.Y. Life Paid Up at 85	1654	407	◐	●	●	◐	0.22	3.39	3.97
Bankers LIC of Nebraska Equity Builder	1694	413	●	●	●	○	0.52	2.92	4.15
Security Benefit LIC Ultra—Ordinary Life	1455	429	●	●	●	◐	−2.73	2.79	4.23
Monarch LIC Ordinary Life—Par	1618	404	●	●	●	◐	−1.74	3.33	3.88
Midland National LIC Exec. Pfd. Par	1784	423	●	●	●	◐	−1.02	3.20	4.06
Amer. National Ins. Co. Whole Life—Participating	1669	480	●	●	●	●	−3.11	2.58	3.76
Amer. Republic Ins. Co. Whole Life	1428	550	●	●	●	●	−4.89	1.72	3.20
Union Central LIC Plan 50 Pfd. Class Ⓐ	1716	364	●	●	●	●	−0.69	3.81	4.25
Union Central LIC Plan 50	1716	374	●	●	●	●	−0.79	3.74	4.18
All Amer. Life & Casualty Co. Life Paid Up at 85	1725	464	●	●	●	●	−0.83	2.96	3.72
Colonial LIC of Amer. Whole Life Par	1727	494	●	●	●	●	−1.98	2.71	3.35
Aetna LIC Whole Life	1766	517	●	●	●	●	−6.75	2.54	3.71
Imperial LAC of Canada Exec. Protector	1841	532	●	●	●	●	−1.37	2.45	3.49
Security Life & Acc. Co. Whole Life	1690	551	●	●	●	●	−5.70	2.08	3.60
Fidelity Life Assoc. Ordinary Life	1810	663	●	●	●	●	−5.04	1.18	2.32

Type: Participating   Amount: $100,000   Age: 35

Listed in order of increasing cost, based primarily on 19-year cost index (see p. 267). All of the rates are for men's policies; rates for women at the same age are generally lower. Where company and policy listings are the same, difference is indicated by footnote. In addition to standard abbreviations, the following are used: LIC (Life Insurance Co.) and LAC (Life Assurance Co.). All data are based on 1979 rates and include waiver of premium in event of disability.

Best ← → Worst

Company and policy	Annual premium	Cost indexes 20-yr.	Cost indexes 9-yr.	Cost indexes 19-yr.	Cost indexes 29-yr.	Net payment index	Yields 9-yr.	Yields 19-yr.	Yields 29-yr.
Teachers Ins. & Annuity Assoc. of Amer. Ordinary Life [F]	$1718	$-12	●	●	●	●	3.84%	7.67%	8.07%
New England Mutual LIC Ordinary Life [A]	1628	295	●	●	●	●	2.05	5.65	6.02
Central LAC Maximum Life	1567	303	●	●	●	●	1.50	5.65	6.06
Northwestern Mutual LIC Whole Life	2004	327	●	●	●	●	2.26	5.37	5.99
Home LIC Whole Life NSR [B]	1678	215	◐	●	●	●	0.47	6.17	6.45
Phoenix Mutual LIC Ordinary Life, NSB [B]	2062	229	●	●	●	◐	3.26	5.78	5.94
Union Mutual LIC Whole Life [B]	2018	256	●	●	◐	◐	2.81	5.55	5.78
Union Mutual LIC Exec. Life (Non-NY) [B]	2073	264	●	●	◐	◐	3.34	5.50	5.95
Knights of Columbus Directors Plan (L95) [G]	1827	296	●	●	●	◐	2.82	5.53	5.99
Bankers Life Co. Pfd. Century 100 [A]	1559	309	●	●	●	●	1.31	5.48	5.71
Connecticut Mutual LIC Econolife (Whole Life) [A]	1461	313	●	●	●	●	4.46	5.71	5.85
Standard Ins. Co. Whole Life [B]	1702	323	●	●	●	◐	2.67	5.46	5.95

*Premium changes after number of years in parentheses.

[A] Available only to "preferred risks."
[B] Available only to nonsmokers.
[C] Available only in Massachusetts.
[D] Available only in New York.
[E] Available only to Lutherans.
[F] Available only to people in certain jobs.
[G] Available only to members of a fraternal organization.

Ratings of Cash Value Policies (Par/$100,000/35 Years) *continued*

Company and policy	Annual premium	Cost Indexes 20-yr.	9-yr.	19-yr.	29-yr.	Net payment index	Yields 9-yr.	19-yr.	29-yr.
Central LAC Special Whole Life	$1900	$284	●	●	◐	○	4.62%	5.67%	5.73%
Phoenix Mutual LIC Ordinary Life	2136	303	●	●	●	○	2.34	5.28	5.57
Massachusetts Mutual LIC Convertible Life	1620	318	●	●	●	◐	2.29	5.51	5.71
Penn Mutual LIC Whole Life [B]	1979	321	●	●	●	●	2.23	5.25	5.52
Confederation LIC Life to 96 [B]	1622	326	○	●	●	○	0.04	5.35	5.99
Union Mutual LIC Exec. Life (Non-NY)	2140	331	●	●	●	○	2.54	5.05	5.61
Connecticut Mutual LIC Whole Life [A]	1600	332	●	●	●	○	3.27	5.41	5.70
Guardian LIC of Amer. Pension Trust Whole Life [A]	1997	288	◐	●	●	○	1.89	5.39	5.82
Guardian LIC of Amer. Modified 3 Whole Life [A]	2044	306	◐	●	●	○	1.75	5.32	5.74
Guardian LIC of Amer. Whole Life [A]	1997	310	◐	●	●	○	1.81	5.25	5.66
General Amer. LIC Limited Payment Life [A]	2155	286	○	●	●	○	0.98	5.31	5.65
Home LIC Whole Life	1757	294	◐	●	◐	○	−0.75	5.51	5.95
Union Mutual LIC Whole Life	2089	328	●	●	●	○	1.92	5.06	5.40
Mutual LIC of New York Whole Life [A]	2193	363	○	●	◐	○	0.74	5.25	5.63
Continental Assurance Co. Whole Life	1791	321	◐	◐	◐	○	1.80	5.28	4.56
Mutual LIC of New York Mony—One [A]	1506	347	●	●	◐	●	−0.28	5.29	5.91
Manufacturers LIC Estate Protector	1604	365	●	○	◐	●	−0.11	5.12	5.93
Standard Ins. Co. Whole Life	1762	383	●	●	◐	◐	1.71	4.94	5.56
Provident Mutual LIC Protector Plus [A]	1923 (2)	384	●	●	◐	◐	3.23	4.96	5.39
USAA LIC Modified-One Whole Life [F]	1635 (1)	392	●	●	●	◐	2.47	4.84	5.31
Connecticut Mutual LIC Whole Life	1667	399	●	●	●	◐	2.21	4.85	5.29
Bankers Life Co. Century 100	1559	364	◐	●	●	◐	0.65	5.01	5.30
State Mutual LAC of Amer. Non-Smoker Whole Life [B]	2052	366	◐	●	◐	●	1.99	4.95	5.49

Policy								
Columbus Mutual LIC Life—100	1586	367	◑	◑	◑	−0.08	4.95	5.47
New England Mutual LIC Ordinary Life	1710	377	◑	◑	◑	0.76	4.96	5.51
Connecticut Mutual LIC Econolife (Whole Life)	1535	387	●	○	◑	3.14	5.02	5.34
North American LAC Whole Life	1682	389	◑	◑	◑	0.76	4.83	5.25
Penn Mutual LIC Value Builder 90 [B]	2053	396	●	◑	○	2.59	4.76	5.17
Canada LAC The Century	1648	399	●	◑	◑	1.90	4.86	5.14
Pacific Mutual LIC Special Whole Life	1673	401	◑	◑	◑	0.97	4.77	5.31
Southern Farm Bureau LIC Whole Life	1835	406	◑	◑	◑	0.82	4.75	5.30
Guardian LIC of Amer. Pension Trust Whole Life	2051	342	○	•	○	1.21	5.02	5.55
New York LIC Whole Life	2019	343	◑	◑	○	1.62	4.99	5.44
Equitable Life Assurance Soc. of the U.S. Adjustable Whole Life	2014	350	◑	◑	○	1.97	5.03	5.42
Guardian LIC of Amer. Modified 3 Whole Life	2098 (3)	360	◑	◑	○	1.02	4.94	5.46
Manufacturers LIC Permanent Economic Protection	1714	369	○	◑	◑	0.07	5.03	5.77
USAA LIC Ordinary Life [F]	1909	374	◑	◑	○	1.31	4.86	5.33
State Farm LIC Estate Protector (L95)	1648	387	○	◑	◑	−0.17	4.77	5.14
Mutual Benefit LIC Life Paid Up at 95	2032	397	◑	◑	◑	1.48	4.74	5.17
Acacia Mutual LIC Whole Life [B]	1629	399	◑	◑	◑	0.76	4.65	4.92
Bankers Life Co. Special Whole Life	1693	403	◑	◑	◑	0.51	4.67	4.96
New York LIC Modified 2 Whole Life	2019 (2)	359	◑	◑	◑	−0.43	4.99	5.72
Guardian LIC of Amer. Whole Life	2051	364	○	◑	○	1.14	4.89	5.39
Lincoln National LIC Whole Life [A]	2036	371	◑	◑	○	1.46	4.90	4.94
Confederation LIC Whole Life [B]	1928	404	◑	○	○	1.56	4.70	5.08
Lincoln National LIC Whole Life [B]	2063	398	◑	◑	○	1.12	4.71	4.80
Occidental LIC of Calif. Par 90	1770	399	◑	◑	○	1.69	4.74	4.63

* Premium changes after number of years in parentheses.

[A] Available only to "preferred risks."
[B] Available only to nonsmokers.
[C] Available only in Massachusetts.
[D] Available only in New York.
[E] Available only to Lutherans.
[F] Available only to people in certain jobs.
[G] Available only to members of a fraternal organization.

Ratings of Cash Value Policies (Par/$100,000/35 Years) *continued*

Company and policy	Annual premium	Cost indexes 20-yr.	Cost 9-yr.	Cost 19-yr.	Cost 29-yr.	Net payment index	Yields 9-yr.	Yields 19-yr.	Yields 29-yr.
General Amer. LIC Limited Payment Life	$2216	$347	◐	◐	●	●	0.27%	4.93%	5.37%
Mutual LIC of New York Whole Life	2282	391	◐	●	●	●	−0.30	4.70	5.22
Provident Mutual LIC Protector Plus	1998 (2)	459	●	○	○	●	2.12	4.37	4.96
Prudential Ins. Co. of Amer. Modified Life 3 [A]	2125 (3)	410	◐	◐	◐	○	1.11	4.55	5.14
State Mutual LAC of Amer. Non-Smoker Exec. Protector Endowment [B]	2143	413	◐	○	●	○	2.16	4.62	5.21
Farm Bureau (Iowa) Special Whole Life	1573	419	◐	○	●	●	1.13	4.69	5.14
Great-West LAC Estatemaster "100"	1738	424	○	○	●	●	−0.24	4.58	5.44
John Hancock Mutual LIC Preferred 25 [A]	2153 (3)	407	○	○	○	○	0.88	4.61	5.24
Dominion LAC Whole Life	1917	411	○	○	○	○	0.41	4.66	5.16
Indianapolis LIC Exec. Protector [B]	2123	415	●	○	○	●	1.96	4.64	4.95
Indianapolis LIC Ordinary Life [B]	1916	421	●	○	○	○	1.34	4.62	5.02
Metropolitan LIC Whole Life [A]	1815	430	◐	○	●	◐	−1.46	4.42	5.30
Mutual LIC of New York Mony—One	1595	436	◐	○	●	●	−1.78	4.51	5.34
Beneficial LIC Heritage 100	1594	438	○	○	○	○	1.12	3.98	4.56
Prudential Ins. Co. of Amer. Estate 20—Whole Life [A]	1993	439	◐	○	○	○	0.86	4.32	5.04
Provident Mutual LIC Whole Life Plus [A]	2129	452	◐	○	○	○	1.68	4.39	4.99
Mutual Benefit LIC Ordinary Life	2237	463	◐	○	○	○	1.94	4.34	4.84
National LIC Life [B]	2176	406	○	○	○	◐	1.51	4.56	5.00
Lutheran Mutual LIC Whole Life	2195	414	○	○	○	○	1.20	4.54	4.70
Penn Mutual LIC Whole Life	2087	429	○	○	○	○	0.86	4.50	4.96
Security Benefit LIC Exec. Whole Life	1673	430	●	○	○	●	−1.31	4.56	5.22
Union Central LIC 100,000 Minimum Life	1576	433	●	○	○	●	−1.54	4.52	5.13
Equitable LIC of Iowa Life Paid Up at 95	2115	443	○	○	○	○	0.86	4.39	4.85

Policy									
Ohio National LIC Pfd. Exec. Whole Life	1641	457	○	◐	○	◐	−0.20	4.37	4.79
Prudential Ins. Co. of Amer. Modified Life 3	2175 (3)	460	○	○	○	○	0.47	4.21	4.89
State Mutual LAC of Amer. Whole Life	2124	461	○	○	○	○	0.94	4.31	4.96
Indianapolis LIC Five Year Modified Life	2177 (5)	462	○	◐	○	◐	−2.76	4.24	4.79
Manhattan LIC Challenger [B]	2146	414	◑	◐	○	◐	0.88	4.57	4.88
Ohio National LIC Pfd. Whole Life	2071	435	○	◐	○	◑	1.52	4.49	4.66
Lincoln National LIC Whole Life	2104	439	○	◐	○	○	0.62	4.44	4.59
Minnesota Mutual LIC Econo-Life	1712	444	◐	◐	○	○	−0.86	4.40	5.15
Jefferson Standard LIC Life Paid Up at 95 [B]	2138	428	◑	◐	○	◐	0.43	4.48	4.66
Aid Association for Lutherans Estate Life [E]	1764	479	◐	◐	◐	◐	0.73	4.03	5.12
Woodmen of the World Life Ins. Soc. Whole Life Minimum $10,000 [G]	1812	473	○	◐	◐	○	−0.25	4.09	5.00
Farm Bureau (Iowa) Exec. Pfd. Par	1983	475	◐	◐	◑	◑	0.53	4.21	4.79
Imperial LAC of Canada Whole Life	1718	518	◐	◐	○	○	−1.82	3.83	4.86
Acacia Mutual LIC Whole Life	1698	468	◐	◐	○	○	−0.27	4.11	4.53
Indianapolis LIC Exec. Protector	2186	478	◐	◐	◑	◑	1.20	4.22	4.63
Indianapolis LIC Ordinary Life	1979	484	◐	◐	◑	●	0.49	4.16	4.68
Aid Association for Lutherans Whole Life [E]	2065	500	◐	◐	◑	◑	−0.84	3.92	4.99
State Mutual LAC of Amer. Exec. Protector Endowment at 90 [A]	2208	500	◐	◐	◑	◑	1.24	4.06	4.75
Life & Casualty Ins. Co. of Tenn. Whole Life	1991	503	◐	◐	◑	◑	−0.74	4.00	4.54
Fidelity Union LIC Professional Exec. Life	1718	504	○	◐	◑	◑	−0.42	3.89	4.20
Farm Bureau (Iowa) Whole Life Par	2113	504	◐	◑	◑	◑	0.60	4.05	4.76
Kansas City LIC Exec. Endowment 90	1974	521	●	◑	◑	◑	1.09	3.87	4.19
Bankers LIC of Nebraska Whole Life Special	1964	427	◑	○	○	○	−2.85	4.01	5.06
Canada LAC Exec. Whole Life	1945	469	◑	◐	○	◑	−0.43	4.26	4.68

* Premium changes after number of years in parentheses.

[A] Available only to "preferred risks."
[B] Available only to nonsmokers.
[C] Available only in Massachusetts.
[D] Available only in New York.
[E] Available only to Lutherans.
[F] Available only to people in certain jobs.
[G] Available only to members of a fraternal organization.

Ratings of Cash Value Policies (Par/$100,000/35 Years) continued

Company and policy	Annual premium	Cost Indexes 20-yr.	9-yr.	19-yr.	29-yr.	Net payment index	Yields 9-yr.	19-yr.	29-yr.
John Hancock Mutual LIC Whole Life 100	$2082	$480	◐	◐	○	◐	0.55%	4.14%	4.91%
Prudential Ins. Co. of Amer. Estate 20-Whole Life	2043	489	◐	◐	○	◐	0.24	3.99	4.79
Columbus Mutual LIC Pfd. Life	2128	491	◐	◐	○	◐	-0.57	3.99	4.84
Sun LAC of Canada Sun Permanent Life	1756	495	○	○	◐	○	-0.81	4.04	4.43
Penn Mutual LIC Value Builder 90	2161	504	○	◐	◐	○	1.29	4.06	4.63
Southern Farm Bureau LIC Ordinary Life	2166	505	○	◐	◐	○	-0.47	4.01	4.63
State Farm LIC Whole Life	2022	507	◐	◐	◐	○	-1.74	3.88	4.68
Metropolitan LIC Whole Life	1893	508	●	◐	○	○	-2.56	3.84	4.87
Mutual Trust LIC Life Paid Up at 85	2185	513	○	◐	◐	◐	1.36	3.95	4.30
Beneficial LIC Professional Estate Plan	2294	520	○	◐	◐	◐	1.12	3.98	4.56
Beneficial LIC Heritage 100	2294	520	○	◐	◐	◐	1.12	3.98	4.56
Provident Mutual LIC Whole Life Plus	2204	527	○	◐	◐	◐	0.79	3.90	4.63
Canada LAC Estate Protector	2042	562	◐	◐	◐	◐	-0.36	3.64	4.21
Mutual Trust LIC Ordinary Life	2172	470	◐	◐	◐	◐	-0.73	4.20	4.59
National LIC Life	2265	495	◐	◐	◐	◐	0.47	4.01	4.59
Jefferson Standard LIC Life Paid Up at 95	2208	498	◐	◐	◐	◐	-0.40	4.03	4.33
Union Central LIC Ordinary Life Pfd. Class	2231	512	◐	◐	◐	◐	-0.93	3.97	4.46
Union Central LIC Plan 50 Pfd. Class Ⓐ	2298	518	◐	◐	◐	◐	0.25	3.99	4.26
Mutual Trust LIC Life Paid Up at 90	2263	532	●	◐	◐	◐	0.13	3.82	4.34
Northwestern National LIC Whole Life Par	2086	533	◐	◐	○	○	-2.25	3.78	4.34
Union Central LIC Ordinary Life	2231	535	◐	◐	◐	◐	-1.09	3.82	4.32
Union Central LIC Plan 50	2298	541	◐	◐	◐	◐	0.10	3.86	4.13
Sun LAC of Canada Whole Life	2326	541	●	◐	○	○	0.05	3.80	4.24
Midland Mutual LIC Modified Life	2131 (3)	542	◐	◐	◐	○	-3.40	3.55	4.38
Amer. Family LIC Ordinary Life	2317	561	○	◐	◐	◐	-0.56	3.69	4.07

Company					No.	Premium		Δ (year 1)	Δ (year 2)	Δ (year 3)
Midland Mutual LIC Paid Up Life at 95	○			●	2221	565	○	−2.37	3.47	4.12
John Hancock Mutual LIC 3 Year Modified Life	◐	○	○	◐	2160 (3)	566	◐	−1.29	3.55	4.50
Bankers Life & Casualty Co. Life Paid Up at 98	◐	○	○	◐	2381	566	◐	0.08	3.72	4.12
Canada LAC Exec. 95	◐	○	○	●	2166	572	◐	0.51	3.62	4.15
Minnesota Mutual LIC Adjustable Life	○	○	●	◐	1920	539	○	−2.26	3.68	3.78
Pacific Mutual LIC Adjustable Life	◐	○	●	○	2282	554	◐	−0.87	3.71	3.93
Life & Casualty Ins. Co. of Tenn. Exec. Whole Life	○	○	●	●	2181	593	○	−0.20	3.41	4.12
Security Benefit LIC Ultra—Ordinary Life	○	○	●	●	1979	611	○	−1.23	3.19	4.32
Bankers LIC of Nebraska Equity Builder	◐	○	●	●	2280	569	◐	0.72	3.23	4.21
U.S. LIC in the City of N.Y. Life Paid Up at 85	◐	●	●	●	2231	584	◐	0.53	3.55	4.07
Nationwide LIC W.L.P.U.,at 95	◐	●	●	●	2224	593	◐	0.75	3.40	3.84
Franklin LIC Exec. Select—II	◐	◐	●	●	2272	594	◐	−1.70	3.44	4.22
Connecticut General LIC Life Full Paid at 90 (Par)	◐	●	●	●	2128	614	◐	0.28	3.38	3.75
Manhattan LIC Challenger	◐	○	●	●	2316	584	◐	−1.02	3.58	4.16
Monarch LIC Select Risk Endowment at 95 A	●	◐	●	●	2228	618	●	0.91	3.41	3.59
Monarch LIC Ordinary Life—Par	●	◐	●	●	2228	652	●	−1.48	3.08	3.58
Midland National LIC Exec. Ptd. Par	◐	●	●	●	2398	654	●	−1.20	3.05	3.88
Amer. National Ins. Co. Whole Life—Participating	◐	●	●	●	2277	713	●	−3.01	2.58	3.53
Amer. Republic Ins. Co. Whole Life	◐	●	●	●	2052	788	●	−3.62	1.93	3.20
All Amer. Life & Casualty Co. Life Paid Up at 85	●	●	●	●	2375	685	●	−1.01	2.97	3.77
Colonial LIC of Amer. Whole Life Par	●	●	●	●	2323	709	●	−1.67	2.80	3.35
Aetna LIC Whole Life	●	●	●	●	2377	749	●	−5.27	2.62	3.69
Imperial LAC of Canada Exec. Protector	●	●	●	●	2487	801	●	−1.54	2.33	3.39
Security Life & Acc. Co. Whole Life	●	●	●	●	2333	808	●	−4.73	2.10	3.54
Fidelity Life Assoc. Ordinary Life	●	●	●	●	2413	964	●	−4.33	1.19	2.24

* Premium changes after number of years in parentheses.

A Available only to "preferred risks."
B Available only to nonsmokers.
C Available only in Massachusetts.
D Available only in New York.
E Available only to Lutherans.
F Available only to people in certain jobs.
G Available only to members of a fraternal organization.

Type: Participating Amount: $100,000 Age: 45

Listed in order of increasing cost, based primarily on 19-year cost index (see p. 267). All of the rates are for men's policies; rates for women at the same age are generally lower. Where company and policy listings are the same, difference is indicated by footnote. In addition to standard abbreviations, the following are used: LIC (Life Insurance Co.) and LAC (Life Assurance Co.). All data are based on 1979 rates and include waiver of premium in event of disability.

Best ● ◐ ○ ◑ ● Worst

Company and policy	Annual premium*	Cost indexes 20-yr	9-yr	19-yr	29-yr	Net payment index	Yields 9-yr	19-yr	29-yr
Teachers Ins. & Annuity Assoc. of Amer. Ordinary Life [F]	$2591	$200	●	●	●	●	6.66%	8.74%	8.84%
Phoenix Mutual LIC Ordinary Life, NSB [B]	2836	523	●	●	●	●	4.94	6.34	6.33
New England Mutual LIC Ordinary Life [A]	2421	648	●	●	●	●	3.21	6.05	6.38
Central LAC Maximum Life	2465	650	●	●	●	●	2.90	6.12	6.42
Central LAC Special Whole Life	2936	667	●	●	●	●	4.78	5.80	5.86
Bankers Life Co. Preferred Century 100 [A]	2434	680	●	●	●	●	2.48	5.72	5.92
Connecticut Mutual LIC Whole Life [A]	2408	691	●	●	●	●	4.34	5.89	6.08
Standard Ins. Co. Whole Life [B]	2628	710	●	●	●	●	3.13	5.70	6.07
Northwestern Mutual LIC Whole Life	3023	712	●	●	●	●	2.89	5.62	6.07
Home LIC Whole Life NSR [B]	2739	558	◐	●	●	●	1.90	6.38	6.60
Union Mutual LIC Exec. Life (Non-NY) [B]	3029	595	●	●	●	◐	3.75	5.66	6.07
Union Mutual LIC Whole Life [B]	2971	628	●	●	●	◐	3.01	5.53	5.82
Confederation LIC Life to 96 [B]	2389	682	◐	●	●	●	2.00	5.86	6.25
Connecticut Mutual LIC Econolife (Whole Life) [A]	2271	699	●	●	●	●	5.25	6.03	6.09
Union Mutual LIC Exec. Life (Non-NY) [A]	3139	704	●	●	●	◐	2.80	5.10	5.62
Mutual LIC of New York Money—One [A]	2409	707	◐	●	●	●	1.03	5.73	6.24

Knights of Columbus Directors Plan (L95) [G]	2784	711	3.30	5.49	5.90
Massachusetts Mutual LIC Convertible Life	2475	717	3.44	5.72	5.86
USAA LIC Modified-One Whole Life [F]	2552 (1)	756	4.06	5.38	5.61
Home LIC Whole Life	2862	681	0.55	5.61	5.99
Penn Mutual LIC Whole Life [B]	2901	706	2.57	5.42	5.55
Phoenix Mutual LIC Ordinary Life	3037	724	2.97	5.23	5.45
USAA LIC Ordinary Life [F]	2850	745	2.30	5.19	5.55
Confederation LIC Whole Life [B]	2671	753	2.95	5.26	5.43
Guardian LIC of Amer. Pension Trust Whole Life [A]	2876	712	2.06	5.30	5.67
Guardian LIC of Amer. Whole Life [A]	2889	724	2.10	5.25	5.60
National LIC Life [B]	3044	724	2.68	5.16	5.33
Guardian LIC of Amer. Modified 3 Whole Life [A]	2947 (3)	727	1.99	5.27	5.64
Union Mutual LIC Whole Life	3081	738	2.01	4.95	5.36
Lincoln National LIC Whole Life [A]	2975	755	2.71	5.17	5.16
General Amer. LIC Limited Payment Life [A]	3118	662	1.36	5.34	5.68
Mutual LIC of New York Whole Life [A]	3173	673	1.05	5.35	5.67
Provident Mutual LIC Protector Plus [A]	2916 (2)	776	3.85	5.25	5.60
Bankers Life Co. Century 100	2434	787	1.62	5.06	5.33
Columbus Mutual LIC Life—100	2458	797	1.12	4.97	5.43
Manufacturers LIC Estate Protector	2480	801	0.98	5.20	5.84
Manufacturers LIC Permanent Economic Protection	2596	808	1.16	5.11	5.69
Connecticut Mutual LIC Whole Life	2553	836	2.67	4.95	5.35
State Mutual LAC of Amer. Non-Smoker Whole Life [B]	3043	774	2.50	5.04	5.52

* Premium changes after number of years in parentheses.

[A] Available only to "preferred risks."
[B] Available only to nonsmokers.
[C] Available only in Massachusetts.
[D] Available only in New York.
[E] Available only to Lutherans.
[F] Available only to people in certain jobs.
[G] Available only to members of a fraternal organization.

Ratings of Cash Value Policies (Par/$100,000/45 Years) continued

Company and policy	Annual premium*	Cost Indexes 20-yr.	9-yr.	19-yr.	29-yr.	Net payment Index	Yields 9-yr.	19-yr.	29-yr.
Penn Mutual LIC Value Builder 90 [B]	$3005	$791	●	◑	◑	○	2.96%	4.95%	5.18%
Standard Ins. Co. Whole Life	2726	808	◑	◑	◑	◑	2.02	5.08	5.58
New England Mutual LIC Ordinary Life	2599	826	◑	◑	◑	◑	1.20	4.92	5.49
Canada LAC The Century	2537	847	●	◑	○	◑	2.39	4.92	5.12
Connecticut Mutual LIC Econolife (Whole Life)	2432	860	●	○	○	◑	3.22	4.91	5.23
Manhattan LIC Challenger [B]	3047	771	◑	◑	●	◑	1.65	4.82	5.04
Metropolitan LIC Whole Life [A]	2777	789	◑	◑	●	◑	-0.13	4.85	5.56
Mutual Benefit LIC Life Paid Up at 95	2955	805	○	○	◑	○	1.84	4.88	5.19
Equitable Life Assurance Soc. of the U.S. Adjustable Whole Life	3011	812	○	◑	◑	○	1.78	4.82	5.17
Prudential Ins. Co. of Amer. Modified Life 3 [A]	3132 (3)	816	○	◑	◑	○	1.37	4.62	5.14
Prudential Ins. Co. of Amer. Estate 20—Whole Life [A]	2933	821	○	◑	◑	◑	1.43	4.54	5.10
North American LAC Whole Life	2583	833	○	◑	◑	◑	1.44	4.88	5.22
Great-West LAC Estatemaster "100"	2628	842	○	◑	○	◑	0.93	4.88	5.51
Bankers Life Co. Special Whole Life	2611	847	◑	◑	○	◑	1.26	4.63	4.94
Pacific Mutual LIC Special Whole Life	2654	850	◑	◑	○	◑	1.32	4.80	5.23
Provident Mutual LIC Whole Life Plus [A]	3068	851	○	◑	●	○	2.43	4.66	5.17
New York LIC Whole Life	3034	779	◑	◑	●	○	1.45	4.87	5.24
New York LIC Modified 2 Whole Life	3034 (2)	806	◑	◑	●	◑	0.17	4.96	5.52
Lincoln National LIC Whole Life [B]	3034	814	○	◑	●	○	2.15	4.85	4.90
Guardian LIC of Amer. Pension Trust Whole Life	2979	815	○	◑	●	○	1.08	4.75	5.24
Lutheran Mutual LIC Whole Life	3206	823	○	◑	●	○	1.68	4.66	4.80
Guardian LIC of Amer. Whole Life	2992	827	○	◑	◑	○	1.12	4.70	5.17
Guardian LIC of Amer. Modified 3 Whole Life	3050 (3)	830	○	◑	◑	○	0.96	4.71	5.21
Union Central LIC 100,000 Minimum Life	2528	835	○	◑	◑	●	0.22	4.98	5.38

Company			Rating	Rating	Rating	Rating			
State Mutual LAC of Amer. Non-Smoker Exec. Protector Endowment [B]	3275	844	◑	◑	◑	◑	2.74	4.58	5.06
Continental Assurance Co. Whole Life	2700	788	○	◑	◑	○	2.07	4.95	4.34
General Amer. LIC Limited Payment Life	3267	811	◑	◑	●	◑	0.08	4.62	5.12
Occidental LIC of Calif. Par 90	2788	828	○	◑	○	○	1.21	4.72	4.89
Ohio National LIC Preferred Whole Life	3087	841	◑	◑	○	○	1.39	4.63	4.80
Mutual LIC of New York Whole Life	3342	842	◑	◑	◑	○	-0.41	4.53	5.03
John Hancock Mutual LIC Pfd. 25 [A]	3173 (3)	845	◑	◑	◑	◑	1.38	4.58	5.19
Aid Association for Lutherans Estate Life [E]	2680	860	○	○	◑	◑	1.13	4.47	5.28
Farm Bureau (Iowa) Special Whole Life	2542	864	◑	◑	○	◑	1.83	4.79	5.10
Southern Farm Bureau LIC Whole Life	2840	861	○	○	○	◑	1.10	4.71	5.21
Beneficial LIC Heritage 100	2522	876	◑	○	○	◑	1.19	3.92	4.48
Mutual LIC of New York Mony—One	2578	876	◑	◑	○	◑	-0.92	4.65	5.36
Ohio National LIC Pfd. Exec. Whole Life	2581	901	◑	○	○	◑	0.90	4.60	4.96
Indianapolis LIC Exec. Protector [B]	3141	902	◑	○	○	○	2.16	4.42	4.78
Provident Mutual LIC Protector Plus	3066 (2)	926	○	○	○	○	2.25	4.36	4.90
Indianapolis LIC Ordinary Life [B]	2869	931	◑	◑	○	○	1.40	4.30	4.83
Aid Association for Lutherans Whole Life [E]	3029	900	○	○	◑	○	0.12	4.23	5.07
Farm Bureau (Iowa) Exec. Pfd. Par	2881	905	○	○	○	○	1.29	4.43	4.82
Dominion LAC Whole Life	2881	910	○	◑	○	○	0.52	4.39	4.88
Mutual Benefit LIC Ordinary Life	3263	925	◑	○	○	○	2.15	4.30	4.69
Farm Bureau (Iowa) Whole Life Par	3107	944	◑	◑	○	○	1.15	4.20	4.75
Jefferson Standard LIC Life Paid Up at 95 [B]	3089	857	◑	◑	○	○	1.04	4.55	4.63
Lincoln National LIC Whole Life	3123	903	◑	◑	○	○	1.31	4.38	4.53
State Farm LIC Estate Protector (L95)	2542	907	○	◑	○	○	0.31	4.29	4.56

Premium changes after number of years in parentheses.

[A] Available only to "preferred risks."
[B] Available only to nonsmokers.
[C] Available only in Massachusetts.
[D] Available only in New York.
[E] Available only to Lutherans.
[F] Available only to people in certain jobs.
[G] Available only to members of a fraternal organization.

Ratings of Cash Value Policies (Par/$100,000/45 Years) continued

Company and policy	Annual premium*	Cost Indexes				Net payment index	Yields		
		20-yr.	9-yr.	19-yr.	29-yr.		9-yr.	19-yr.	29-yr.
Prudential Ins. Co. of Amer. Modified Life 3	$3238 (3)	$ 922	○	○	○	○	0.35%	4.06%	4.70%
Minnesota Mutual LIC Econo-Life	2628	933	○	○	○	○	-0.57	4.24	4.94
Acacia Mutual LIC Whole Life B	2720	942	◐	○	◐	○	0.51	4.11	4.40
Penn Mutual LIC Whole Life	3096	901	◐	○	○	○	0.71	4.37	4.72
Prudential Ins. Co. of Amer. Estate 20—Whole Life	3039	927	○	○	○	◐	0.46	4.00	4.68
Union Central LIC Plan 50 Preferred Class A	3289	934	○	○	◐	◐	1.54	4.21	4.37
State Mutual LAC of Amer. Whole Life	3166	963	○	◐	◐	◐	0.98	4.08	4.75
John Hancock Mutual LIC Whole Life 100	3090	947	○	◐	◐	◐	1.00	4.06	4.80
Equitable LIC of Iowa Life Paid Up at 95	3136	957	○	◐	◐	◐	0.88	4.10	4.60
Columbus Mutual LIC Ptd. Life	3097	959	○	◐	◐	○	-0.58	3.86	4.71
Metropolitan LIC Whole Life	2957	970	◐	◐	◐	◐	-1.95	3.84	4.77
Security Benefit LIC Exec. Whole Life	2640	973	◐	◐	◐	◐	-0.96	4.11	4.81
Fidelity Union LIC Professional Exec. Life	2644	988	○	◐	◐	◐	-0.01	3.85	4.15
Mutual Trust LIC Life Paid Up at 85	3237	994	◐	◐	◐	◐	1.78	3.86	4.15
Sun LAC of Canada Sun Permanent Life	2680	997	○	○	○	○	0.29	3.96	4.30
State Mutual LAC of Amer. Exec. Protector Endowment at 90 A	3383	1014	○	○	○	◐	1.47	3.79	4.44
Bankers LIC of Nebraska Whole Life Special	2947	887	●	●	●	○	-2.03	4.08	4.97
Canada LAC Exec. Whole Life	2922	983	○	○	◐	◐	-0.15	4.04	4.45
Penn Mutual LIC Value Builder 90	3200	986	○	◐	◐	◐	1.21	3.96	4.40
Union Central LIC Plan 50	3289	986	○	◐	◐	◐	1.26	3.97	4.14
Woodmen of the World Life Ins. Soc. Whole Life Minimum $10,000 C	2802	994	◐	○	○	○	-0.27	3.73	4.58
Beneficial LIC Professional Estate Plan	3288	994	○	◐	◐	◐	1.19	3.92	4.48
Beneficial LIC Heritage 100	3288	994	○	◐	◐	◐	1.19	3.92	4.48

			Ratings					Premium change*		
Provident Mutual LIC Whole Life Plus	3218	1001	○	◐	◐	◐	◐	1.07	3.89	4.56
Imperial LAC of Canada Whole Life	2612	1009	◐	◐	◐	◐	○	−0.75	3.87	4.73
Indianapolis LIC Exec. Protector	3241	1016	○	◐	◐	◐	◐	1.36	3.92	4.38
Indianapolis LIC Five Year Modified Life	3333 (5)	1020	◐	◐	◐	◐	○	−2.39	3.79	4.53
State Farm LIC Whole Life	3048	1024	◐	◐	◐	◐	○	−1.56	3.59	4.40
Life & Casualty Ins. Co. of Tenn. Whole Life	3037	1027	◐	◐	◐	◐	○	−0.09	3.83	4.31
Acacia Mutual LIC Whole Life	2809	1031	○	◐	◐	◐	○	−0.41	3.61	4.02
Indianapolis LIC Ordinary Life	2969	1031	◐	◐	◐	◐	◐	0.44	3.76	4.44
Kansas City LIC Exec. Endowment 90	2983	1062	○	◐	◐	◐	◐	0.61	3.46	3.74
Security Benefit LIC Ultra—Ordinary Life	2877	1076	◐	◐	◐	◐	○	0.09	3.50	4.37
Life & Casualty Ins. Co. of Tenn. Exec. Whole Life	3232	1100	●	◐	◐	◐	◐	0.58	3.47	4.03
National Life of Vermont Life	3252	932	●	◐	◐	◐	◐	0.81	4.11	4.51
Mutual Trust LIC Ordinary Life	3205	947	●	◐	◐	◐	◐	−0.55	4.05	4.45
Union Central LIC Ordinary Life Preferred Class	3256	967	○	◐	◐	◐	◐	−0.06	4.07	4.41
Jefferson Standard LIC Life Paid Up at 95	3214	982	○	◐	◐	◐	◐	−0.09	3.93	4.14
Union Central LIC Ordinary Life	3256	1022	●	◐	◐	◐	◐	−0.36	3.80	4.15
Minnesota Mutual LIC Adjustable Life	3053	1024	●	◐	◐	◐	◐	−2.09	3.73	4.67
Southern Farm Bureau LIC Ordinary Life	3256	1024	○	◐	◐	◐	◐	−0.64	3.75	4.42
Bankers LIC of Nebraska Equity Builder	3289	1030	○	◐	◐	◐	◐	1.12	3.40	4.31
Mutual Trust LIC Life Paid Up at 90	3346	1032	○	◐	◐	◐	◐	0.05	3.64	4.17
U.S. LIC in the City of N.Y. Life Paid Up at 85	3255	1034	○	◐	◐	◐	◐	0.75	3.67	4.20
Sun LAC of Canada Whole Life	3398	1053	○	◐	◐	◐	◐	0.19	3.65	4.05
John Hancock Mutual LIC 3 Year Modified Life	3195 (3)	1071	●	◐	◐	◐	◐	−0.98	3.45	4.34
Midland Mutual LIC Modified Life	3172 (3)	1089	●	◐	◐	◐	○	−2.95	3.22	3.95
Nationwide LIC W.L.P.U. at 95	3275	1110	○	◐	◐	◐	◐	0.99	3.22	3.62

Premium changes after number of years in parentheses.

A Available only to "preferred risks."
B Available only to nonsmokers.
C Available only in Massachusetts.
D Available only in New York.
E Available only to Lutherans.
F Available only to people in certain jobs.
G Available only to members of a fraternal organization.

Ratings of Cash Value Policies (Par/$100,000/45 Years) continued

Company and policy	Annual premium*	Cost indexes 20-yr.	9-yr.	19-yr.	29-yr.	Net payment index	Yields 9-yr.	19-yr.	29-yr.
Canada LAC Estate Protector	$3120	$1113	◐	○	○	○	−0.58%	3.35%	3.92%
Amer. Family LIC Ordinary Life	3384	1070	◐	◐	○	◐	−0.30	3.56	2.60
Franklin LIC Exec. Select—II	3336	1075	●	◐	○	◐	−1.31	3.50	4.18
Northwestern National LIC Whole Life Par	3079	1076	●	●	○	●	−1.67	3.50	4.04
Midland Mutual LIC Paid Up Life at 95	3233	1098	●	●	○	●	−1.93	3.21	3.77
Pacific Mutual LIC Adjustable Life	3372	1101	◐	◐	○	◐	−0.81	3.36	3.62
Bankers Life & Casualty Co. Life Paid Up at 98	3590	1106	●	●	○	◐	−0.77	3.39	3.97
Canada LAC Exec. 95	3229	1128	◐	●	●	●	0.34	3.30	3.84
Monarch LIC Select Risk Endowment at 95 [A]	3252	1160	◐	●	●	●	1.02	3.16	3.28
All Amer. Life & Casualty Co. Life Paid Up at 85	3464	1169	●	●	●	●	−0.95	3.03	3.86
Connecticut General LIC Life Full Paid at 90 (Par)	3194	1190	●	●	●	●	0.17	3.00	3.41
Aetna LIC Whole Life	3417	1201	●	●	○	○	−4.03	2.91	3.94
Manhattan LIC Challenger	3427	1151	●	●	●	●	−1.49	3.13	3.76
Midland National LIC Exec. Pfd. Par	3451	1218	●	●	●	●	−1.70	2.68	3.53
Monarch LIC Ordinary Life—Par	3252	1270	●	●	●	●	−1.88	2.59	3.13
Amer. National Ins. Co. Whole Life—Participating	3304	1283	●	●	●	●	−2.64	2.29	3.18
Colonial LIC of Amer. Whole Life Par	3422	1300	●	●	●	●	−1.46	2.50	3.10
Amer. Republic Ins. Co. Whole Life	3156	1441	●	●	●	●	−3.90	1.47	2.85
Imperial LAC of Canada Exec. Protector	3613	1423	●	●	●	●	−2.21	1.98	3.08
Security Life & Acc. Co. Whole Life	3429	1483	●	●	●	●	−5.01	1.56	3.00
Fidelity Life Assoc. Ordinary Life	3452	1643	●	●	●	●	−4.30	0.84	1.93

* Premium changes after number of years in parentheses.

A Available only to "preferred risks."
B Available only to nonsmokers.
C Available only in Massachusetts.
D Available only in New York.
E Available only to Lutherans.
F Available only to people in certain jobs.
G Available only to members of a fraternal organization.

Alphabetical Summary of Cash Value Policies

If you've been offered a particular cash value policy, and you want to get a rough idea of its relative merit, you can use this alphabetical summary of all companies whose policies are rated in Chapter 17. It's important to remember that you are shopping for the best possible policy, and not necessarily the best company. Some companies offer policies that may be excellent buys at certain ages and at certain face amounts but not as good buys at other ages or face amounts. As an example, note that the various policies issued by Colonial Life Insurance Company of America ranged (in nineteen-year net cost) from best to worst, touching every rung of the ladder in between.

A few companies, though, did consistently well or poorly in Consumers Union's cost survey of cash value policies. Two companies ranked near the bottom of CU's Ratings at all ages and face amounts: American Republic Insurance Company and Fidelity Life Association. Six companies were consistently near the top. They were (in alphabetical order): Central Life Assurance Company, Home Life Insurance

Company, Massachusetts Mutual Life Insurance Company, Northwestern Mutual Life Insurance Company, Phoenix Mutual Life Insurance Company, and Teachers Insurance and Annuity Association of America.

Prices can change from year to year. The symbols in this table, based on 1979 rates, show roughly how each policy ranked compared with other similar policies, as measured by the nineteen-year interest-adjusted net cost index. This gives a good basic idea of a policy's comparative cost, in CU's view. A more complete idea of comparative cost can be obtained by looking at the detailed information about a policy in the tables in Chapter 17.

Summary Table of Cash Value Policies

Listed alphabetically by company. Judgments are based on 19-year cost index (see p. 267), using rates for men. Types indicated are Participating (P) and Nonparticipating (N). Where company and policy listings are the same, difference is indicated by footnote. In addition to standard abbreviations, the following are used: LIC (Life Insurance Co.) and LAC (Life Assurance Co.). All data are based on 1979 rates and include waiver of premium in event of disability.

Best ⊙ ◐ ○ → ◑ ● Worst

Company and policy	Type	Age 25 $25M	Age 25 $100M	Age 35 $25M	Age 35 $100M	Age 45 $25M	Age 45 $100M
Acacia Mutual LIC Whole Life	P	○	○	◑	◑	◑	○
Acacia Mutual LIC Whole Life [B]	P	○	◐	◐	◑	○	○
Aetna LIC Whole Life	P	●	●	●	●	●	●
Aetna LIC Whole Life	N	○	○	◑	○	○	○
Aetna LIC Whole Life Preferred Risk [A]	N	◑	◑	●	●	◑	●
Aetna LIC Life Paid Up at 95	N	●	●	●	●	○	○
Aid Association for Lutherans Whole Life [E]	P	○	○	○	○	◐	◐
Aid Association for Lutherans Estate Life [E]	P	○	○	○	○	○	○
All Amer. Life & Casualty Co. Business Whole Life	N	◑	◑	●	●	●	◑
All Amer. Life & Casualty Co. Life Paid Up at 85	P	●	⊙	●	●	◐	◑
Allstate LIC Executive Plan	N	◑	◑	○	○	○	○
Allstate LIC Executive Plan [A]	N					○	◑
Allstate LIC Executive Plan [B]	N	◐	◑	◐	◐	◑	◑
Amer. Family LIC Ordinary Life	P	◑	◑	◑	◑	○	○

[A] Available only to "preferred risks."
[B] Available only to nonsmokers.
[C] Available only in Massachusetts.
[D] Available only in New York.
[E] Available only to Lutherans.
[F] Available only to people in certain jobs.
[G] Available only to members of a fraternal organization.

Summary Table of Cash Value Policies *continued*

Company and policy	Type	Age 25		Age 35		Age 45	
		$25M	$100M	$25M	$100M	$25M	$100M
Amer. Health & Life Ins. Co. Enterprise Whole Life—Level	N		◐		○		○
Amer. Health & Life Ins. Co. Freedom Whole Life—Level	N	◐		◐		◐	
Amer. National Ins. Co. Life Paid Up at 95	N	◐	●	◐	●	●	●
Amer. National Ins. Co. Whole Life—Participating	P	●		●	●	●	●
Amer. National Ins. Co. Life Paid Up at 90 [B]	N	○		○		○	
Amer. National Ins. Co. Executive Preferred 98	N		○			◐	◐
Amer. National Ins. Co. Executive Preferred 99	N		◐		○	◐	●
Amer. Republic Ins. Co. Whole Life	P	●	◐	●	●	●	●
Amer. States LIC Whole Life	N	◐	◐	◐	◐	◐	◐
Bankers Life & Casualty Co. Life Paid Up at 95	N	●	◐	●	◐	●	●
Bankers Life & Casualty Co. Life Paid Up at 98	P	○	◐	◐	●	●	●
Bankers Life & Casualty Co. Executive Ordinary Life	N	◐	◐	●	●	●	●
Bankers Life Co. Special Whole Life	P	◐	◐	◐	●	◐	●
Bankers Life Co. Century 100	P	◐	◐	◐	◐	◐	◐
Bankers Life Co. Preferred Century 100 [A]	P			⊙	⊙	⊙	●
Bankers LIC of Nebraska Whole Life	P	◐		◐			◐
Bankers LIC of Nebraska Whole Life Special	P		◐		●	◐	◐
Bankers LIC of Nebraska Equity Builder	P	●	◐		●	◐	●
Beneficial LIC Heritage 100	P	○	○	○	◐	○	◐
Beneficial LIC Professional Estate Plan	P	◐	○	○	◐	○	◐
Canada LAC Estate Protector	P	◐	○	◐	◐	◐	◐
Canada LAC Executive Whole Life	P	○		◐	◐	○	●
Canada LAC The Century	P	◐		◐	◐	◐	●
Canada LAC Executive 95	P	◐	◐	◐	◐	◐	●

Product		1	2	3	4	5	6
Central LAC Special Whole Life	P	●	●	●	●	●	●
Central LAC Maximum Life	P	●	●	●	●	●	●
Colonial LIC of Amer. Whole Life	N	◑	○	○			
Colonial LIC of Amer. Whole Life [B]	N	○	◑	◑			○
Colonial LIC of Amer. Economiser	N	◑	◑	◑	●	◑	◑
Colonial LIC of Amer. Economiser [B]	N		○	◑	●	◑	◕
Colonial LIC of Amer. Cash Flo	N			○	○	○	◑
Colonial LIC of Amer. Cash Flo [B]	N	◑	◑	◑	◑	◑	○
Colonial LIC of Amer. Life Paid Up at 92	N	●	◑	○	◑	●	◑
Colonial LIC of Amer. Whole Life Par	P	●	●	●	●	●	●
Colonial LIC of Amer. Endowment at 98	N	○	◑	○	◑		
Colonial LIC of Amer. Endowment at 98 [B]	N		○				
Columbus Mutual LIC Life—100	P	◑	◑	◑	◑	◑	◑
Columbus Mutual LIC Preferred Life	P	○	○	○	○	○	○
Commonwealth LIC Whole Life	N	○	○	○	○	○	○
Commonwealth LIC Life Paid Up at 95	N	◑	◑		○	○	○
Confederation LIC Whole Life	P	◑	●				●
Confederation LIC Whole Life [B]	P	○	◑				
Confederation LIC Life to 96	P	◑	○		●		●
Confederation LIC Life to 96 [B]	P	○	◑				
Connecticut General LIC Ordinary Life	N	◑	◑	◑	◑	◑	◑
Connecticut General LIC OL Plus	N	◑	●	○	○	○	●
Connecticut General LIC Life Full Paid at 90 (Par)	P	◑	●	●	●	●	●
Connecticut Mutual LIC Whole Life	P	◑	◑	◑	◑	◑	◑
Connecticut Mutual LIC Whole Life [A]	P	◑	◑	●	◑	●	◑
Connecticut Mutual LIC Econolife (Whole Life)	P	◑	◑	◑	◑	●	◑

[A] Available only to "preferred risks."
[B] Available only to nonsmokers.
[C] Available only in Massachusetts.
[D] Available only in New York.
[E] Available only to Lutherans.
[F] Available only to people in certain jobs.
[G] Available only to members of a fraternal organization.

Summary Table of Cash Value Policies *continued*

Company and policy	Type	Age 25 $25M	Age 25 $100M	Age 35 $25M	Age 35 $100M	Age 45 $25M	Age 45 $100M
Connecticut Mutual LIC Econolife (Whole Life) Ⓐ	P		●		●	◐	●
Continental Assurance Co. Whole Life	P	●	●	●	●	◐	◐
Continental Assurance Co. Economiser	N	●	●	●	●	◑	◑
Continental Assurance Co. Maximiser II	N	◐	●	◑	●	◑	◑
Dominion LAC Whole Life	P	○	◑	○	○	◐	○
Dominion LAC Whole Life	N	○	○	◑	○	◑	◐
Durham LIC Life Paid Up at 95	N	○	◐	○	○	○	◐
Durham LIC Life Paid Up at 90	N	○	◐	○		◐	○
Equitable Life Assurance Soc. of the U.S. Adjustable Whole Life	P	◐	◐	◐		◐	◐
Equitable LIC of Iowa Whole Life	P	◑	○	○	○	○	○
Equitable LIC of Iowa Life Paid Up at 95	P		●		○	◐	◑
Equitable LIC of Iowa Life Paid Up at 95	N	●	●	●	●	●	○
Farm Bureau (Iowa) Special Whole Life	P		◐		◑	◑	◑
Farm Bureau (Iowa) Whole Life Par	P	○	◑	○	◑	◑	◑
Farm Bureau (Iowa) Executive Preferred Par	P	◐	◑	○	◑	○	○
Federal Kemper Life Assurance Soc. OL—4	N	◐	◐	◐	◑	◐	◑
Federal Kemper Life Assurance Soc. Thrift—Life	N	●	◑	●	◑	●	◑
Fidelity Life Association Ordinary Life	P	●	●	●	●	●	◐
Fidelity Union LIC Presidents Preferred Life	N	◑	◑	◑	◑	◑	◑
Fidelity Union LIC Professional Executive Life	P	○	◑	◑	◑	◑	○
First Colony LIC Whole Life	N	○	○	○	○	◐	○
First Colony LIC Life Paid-Up at 96	N			◐		◐	○
Franklin LIC Executive Select—I	P	●	●	●	●	◐	
Franklin LIC Executive Select—II	P	○	●	○	●	○	◑

Policy	
Franklin LIC Preferred 95	N
General Amer. LIC Limited Payment Life	P
General Amer. LIC Limited Payment Life Ⓐ	P
Great-West LAC Estatemaster "100"	P
Great-West LAC Estatemaster "100"	N
Great-West LAC Estatemaster "25"	P
Great-West LAC Life at 90	N
Guardian LIC of Amer. Whole Life	P
Guardian LIC of Amer. Whole Life Ⓐ	P
Guardian LIC of Amer. Modified 3 Whole Life	P
Guardian LIC of Amer. Modified 3 Whole Life Ⓐ	P
Guardian LIC of Amer. Pension Trust Whole Life	P
Guardian LIC of Amer. Pension Trust Whole Life Ⓐ	P
Hartford LIC Whole Life	N
Home Beneficial LIC Whole Life	N
Home Beneficial LIC Life Paid Up at 95	N
Home LIC Whole Life	P
Home LIC Whole Life NSR Ⓑ	P
IDS LIC Whole Life	N
IDS LIC Select Whole Life	N
Imperial LAC of Canada Whole Life	P
Imperial LAC of Canada Whole Life	N
Imperial LAC of Canada Executive Protector	P
INA LIC Whole Life	N
INA LIC Executive Whole Life	N

Ⓐ Available only to "preferred risks."
Ⓑ Available only to nonsmokers.
Ⓒ Available only in Massachusetts.
Ⓓ Available only in New York.
Ⓔ Available only to Lutherans.
Ⓕ Available only to people in certain jobs.
Ⓖ Available only to members of a fraternal organization.

Summary Table of Cash Value Policies *continued*

Company and policy	Type	Age 25 $25M	Age 25 $100M	Age 35 $25M	Age 35 $100M	Age 45 $25M	Age 45 $100M
Indianapolis LIC Ordinary Life	P	◐	◐	○	◐	◐	◐
Indianapolis LIC Ordinary Life B	P	◐	◐	◐	○	○	○
Indianapolis LIC Executive Protector	P	○	○	○	○	○	○
Indianapolis LIC Executive Protector B	P	◐	◐	◐	○	◐	◐
Indianapolis LIC Five Year Modified Life	P	◐	○	○	○	○	◐
J.C. Penney LIC Value Select—Whole Life	N	○		○	○		○
J.C. Penney LIC Executive Select Life Paid Up at 90	N	○		◐	○		◐
Jefferson Standard LIC Whole Life	N						○
Jefferson Standard LIC Whole Life B	N	○	○	○	○	○	○
Jefferson Standard LIC Life Paid Up at 95	N	◐	◐	◐	◐	◐	◐
Jefferson Standard LIC Life Paid Up at 95	N	○	○				
Jefferson Standard LIC Life Paid Up at 95 B	P			◐	○	◐	○
Jefferson Standard LIC Life Paid Up at 90	P	◐	○			◐	◐
Jefferson Standard LIC Life Paid Up at 90	N	◐	○	○	◐	◐	◐
John Hancock Mutual LIC Life Paid Up at 85	P	◐	○	◐	○	◐	◐
John Hancock Mutual LIC Whole Life 100	P	◐	◐	○	○	◐	◐
John Hancock Mutual LIC Preferred 25 A	P	◐	◐	○	○	◐	◐
John Hancock Mutual LIC 3 Year Modified Life	P	◐	◉	◉	◉	◉	◉
Kansas City LIC Executive L 95 Guaranteed Cost	N	○	◐	◐	◐	◉	◉
Kansas City LIC Executive Endowment 90	P			○	○	◐	◐
Knights of Columbus Directors Plan (L95) C	P	◐	◉	●	●	●	●
Liberty LIC Liberty Executive Preferred (WL)	N	○	○	◐	◐	◐	◐
Liberty LIC Liberty Protection 95 (LPU at 95)	N			◐	◐	◐	◐
Life & Casualty Ins. Co. of Tenn. Whole Life	P	○		◐	◐	◐	◐

Policy	
Life & Casualty Ins. Co. of Tenn. Executive Whole Life	P
Life & Casualty Ins. Co. of Tenn. Preferred Executive Whole Life	N
Lincoln National LIC Whole Life	P
Lincoln National LIC Whole Life	N
Lincoln National LIC Whole Life A	P
Lincoln National LIC Whole Life A	N
Lincoln National LIC Whole Life B	P
Lincoln National LIC Whole Life B	N
Lutheran Mutual LIC Whole Life	P
Manhattan LIC Challenger	P
Manhattan LIC Challenger B	P
Manufacturers LIC Estate Protector	P
Manufacturers LIC Estate Protector	N
Manufacturers LIC Permanent Economic Protection	P
Manufacturers LIC Permanent Economic Protection	N
Massachusetts Mutual LIC Convertible Life	P
Massachusetts SBLI Straight Life C	P
Metropolitan LIC Whole Life	P
Metropolitan LIC Whole Life A	P
Midland Mutual LIC Modified Life	P
Midland Mutual LIC Paid Up Life at 95	P
Midland National LIC Whole Life	N
Midland National LIC Executive Preferred Par	P
Minnesota Mutual LIC Econo-Life	P

A Available only to "preferred risks."
B Available only to nonsmokers.
C Available only in Massachusetts.
D Available only in New York.
E Available only to Lutherans.
F Available only to people in certain jobs.
G Available only to members of a fraternal organization.

Summary Table of Cash Value Policies *continued*

Company and policy	Type	Age 25 $25M	Age 25 $100M	Age 35 $25M	Age 35 $100M	Age 45 $25M	Age 45 $100M
Minnesota Mutual LIC Adjustable Life	P	○	○	◐	◐	○	○
Monarch LIC Ordinary Life—Par	P	◐	●	●	●	●	●
Monarch LIC Select Risk Endowment at 95 [A]	P	◐	●	●	●	◐	●
Monarch LIC Ordinary Life—NP	N	◐	○	○	○	○	○
Monarch LIC Accelerator 95	N	○	○	○	○	○	○
Monumental LIC LP at 95 Executive	N	◐	◐	◐	◐	◐	◐
Monumental LIC LP at 90 Executive	N	◐	◐	◐	◐	◐	◐
Mutual Benefit LIC Life Paid Up at 95	P	○	○	○	○	○	○
Mutual Benefit LIC Ordinary Life	P	○	○	○	○	○	○
Mutual LIC of New York Whole Life	P	◉	◉	◐	◐	◐	◐
Mutual LIC of New York Whole Life [A]	P	◉	◉	◉	◉	◉	●
Mutual LIC of New York Mony—One	P		◐	○	○	○	○
Mutual LIC of New York Mony—One [A]	P		●	○	○	●	○
Mutual Trust LIC Life Paid Up at 85	P	○	◐	○	○	○	◐
Mutual Trust LIC Ordinary Life	P	○	◐	◐	◐	◐	◐
Mutual Trust LIC Life Paid Up at 90	P	◐	◐	◐	◐	○	○
National Life & Accident Ins. Co. Executive Whole Life [A]	N	◐	◐	○	○	○	◐
National Life & Accident Ins. Co. Executive Life Plus [A]	N	○	○	○	○	○	○
National LAC of Canada Executive Ordinary Life	N	◐	○	◐	◐	○	○
National LIC Life	P	○	○	○	○	○	◐
National LIC Life [B]	P	◐	○	○	○	◉	◉
Nationwide LIC W.L.P.U. at 95	P	◐	●	●	●	◐	◐
Nationwide LIC W.L.P.U. at 95	N	◐	●	●	●	◐	◐

Policy	Rating
New England Mutual LIC Ordinary Life	P
New England Mutual LIC Ordinary Life [A]	P
New York LIC Whole Life	P
New York LIC Modified 2 Whole Life	P
New York SBLI Straight Life [C]	P
North Amer. Co. for Life & Health Ins. Life Paid Up at 95	N
North Amer. LAC Whole Life	P
Northwestern Mutual LIC Whole Life	P
Northwestern National LIC Whole Life Par	P
Northwestern National LIC Preferred Whole Life Nonpar	N
Northwestern National LIC Whole Life Nonpar	N
Occidental LIC of California Life—100	N
Occidental LIC of California Guaranteed Whole Life	N
Occidental LIC of California Preferred Whole Life	P
Occidental LIC of California Par 90	P
Ohio National LIC Whole Life	P
Ohio National LIC Preferred Whole Life	P
Ohio National LIC Executive Protector Whole Life	P
Ohio National LIC Preferred Executive Whole Life	P
Old Line LIC of Amer. Business Whole Life	N
Pacific Mutual LIC Special Whole Life	P
Pacific Mutual LIC Adjustable Life	P
Paul Revere LIC Super—Standard Whole Life	N
Paul Revere LIC Executive Life to 95	N
Paul Revere LIC Preferred Life to 95	N

[A] Available only to "preferred risks."
[B] Available only to nonsmokers.
[C] Available only in Massachusetts.
[D] Available only in New York.
[E] Available only to Lutherans.
[F] Available only to people in certain jobs.
[G] Available only to members of a fraternal organization.

Summary Table of Cash Value Policies continued

Company and policy	Type	Age 25 $25M	Age 25 $100M	Age 35 $25M	Age 35 $100M	Age 45 $25M	Age 45 $100M
Penn Mutual LIC Whole Life	P	○	○	●	○	○	●
Penn Mutual LIC Whole Life [B]	P	◐	◐	●	◉	◉	●
Penn Mutual LIC Value Builder 90	P	○	◐	○	◐	○	◐
Penn Mutual LIC Value Builder 90 [B]	P	○	◐	◐	◐	◐	◐
Phoenix Mutual LIC Ordinary Life	P	◉	◉	◉	◉	◉	◉
Phoenix Mutual LIC Ordinary Life, NSB [B]	P	◉	◉	◉	◉	◉	◉
Provident Life & Accident Ins. Co. Whole Life	N	◐	◐	○	○	◐	◐
Provident Life & Accident Ins. Co. Whole Life Paid Up—90	N	◉	◉	◉	◉	◐	◐
Provident Mutual LIC Whole Life	P	○				◐	
Provident Mutual LIC Whole Life [A]	P	○				○	
Provident Mutual LIC Whole Life Plus	P		◐	◐			◐
Provident Mutual LIC Whole Life Plus [A]	P		◐	○		○	◐
Provident Mutual LIC Protector	P	○		○			
Provident Mutual LIC Protector [A]	P	○		○		◐	
Provident Mutual LIC Protector Plus	P		◐		◐		○
Provident Mutual LIC Protector Plus [A]	P		◐		◐		◐
Prudential Ins. Co. of Amer. Estate 20—Whole Life	P	○	◐	○	◐	○	◐
Prudential Ins. Co. of Amer. Estate 20—Whole Life [A]	P		◐	○	◐	○	◐
Prudential Ins. Co. of Amer. Modified Life 3	P	◐	○	○	○	○	○
Prudential Ins. Co. of Amer. Modified Life 3 [A]	P	◐	◐	○	◐	◐	◐
Safeco LIC Preferred Life/Executive Life	N	◐	◐	○	○	○	○
Security Benefit LIC Executive Whole Life	P	◐	●	○	○	◐	◐
Security Benefit LIC Ultra—Ordinary Life	P	●	●	●	●	◉	◉
Security-Connecticut LIC Business Whole Life	N	○	○	◐	◉	●	●

Product	P/N
Security Life & Accident Co. Whole Life	P
Security Life & Accident Co. Whole Life 100	N
Security Life & Accident Co. Whole Life 100	N
Southern Farm Bureau LIC Whole Life	P
Southern Farm Bureau LIC Ordinary Life	P
Southland LIC Executive Preferred Whole Life	N
Southwestern LIC Commercial Whole Life	N
Southwestern LIC Special Executive 95	N
Southwestern LIC Executive 85	N
Standard Ins. Co. Whole Life	P
Standard Ins. Co. Whole Life Ⓑ	P
State Farm LIC Whole Life	P
State Farm LIC Estate Protector (L95)	P
State Mutual LAC of Amer. Whole Life	P
State Mutual LAC of Amer. Non-Smoker Whole Life Ⓑ	P
State Mutual LAC of Amer. Executive Protector Endowment at 90 Ⓐ	P
State Mutual LAC of Amer. Non-Smoker Exec. Protector Endowment at 90 Ⓐ Ⓑ	P
Sun LAC of Canada Whole Life	P
Sun LAC of Canada Sun Permanent Life	P
Sun LIC of America L96	N
Teachers Ins. & Annuity Assoc. of Amer. Ordinary Life Ⓕ	P
Time Ins. Co. Whole Life	N
Time Ins. Co. The Competitor	N
Time Ins. Co. Executive Special	N

Ⓐ Available only to "preferred risks."
Ⓑ Available only to nonsmokers.
Ⓒ Available only in Massachusetts.
Ⓓ Available only in New York.
Ⓔ Available only to Lutherans.
Ⓕ Available only to people in certain jobs.
Ⓖ Available only to members of a fraternal organization.

Summary Table of Cash Value Policies *continued*

Company and policy	Type	Age 25 $25M	Age 25 $100M	Age 35 $25M	Age 35 $100M	Age 45 $25M	Age 45 $100M
Travelers Ins. Co. Ordinary Life	N	◑		◑	○		○
Travelers Ins. Co. Ordinary Life—NS [A]	N		●				●
Travelers Ins. Co. Ordinary Life—NS [B]	N				●	●	●
Travelers Ins. Co. Presidential Whole Life—4NS [B]	N		○		● ◑		◑ ●
Travelers Ins. Co. Presidential Whole Life—4	N	○	○	○ ◑	◑ ◑	○	◑ ◑
Union Central LIC Ordinary Life	P	○	◑	◑ ◑	◑ ◑	○	◑ ◑
Union Central LIC Ordinary Life Preferred Class	P	○	◑		◑	○	◑
Union Central LIC Plan 50	P		●		◑		○ ◑
Union Central LIC Plan 50 Preferred Class [A]	P		●				
Union Central LIC 100,000 Minimum Life	P		○		○		○
Union Mutual LIC Whole Life	P	●	●	◑ ◑	● ●	●	● ●
Union Mutual LIC Whole Life [B]	P	●	●	● ●	● ●	●	● ●
Union Mutual LIC Executive Life (Non-NY)	P	◑	◑	● ●	● ●	◑	◑ ●
Union Mutual LIC Executive Life (Non-NY) [B]	P	◑	●	● ◑	● ●	●	● ◑
United Benefit LIC Ordinary Life	N	◑	◑	◑ ○	◑ ○	◑	○ ◑
United Benefit LIC Life Paid Up at 90	N	◑	◑	◑	◑	◑	◑ ◑
United Investors LIC Whole Life	N	○	◑	○	○	◑	◑ ◑
U.S. LIC in the City of N.Y. Business Whole Life	N	◑	●	◑	●	◑	◑ ●
U.S. LIC in the City of N.Y. Life Paid Up at 85	P		●		●		○ ◑
USAA LIC Ordinary Life [F]	P	◑	◑	◑	◑	●	● ◑
USAA LIC Modified-One Whole Life [F]	P	◑	◑	◑	◑	●	● ◑
Woodmen of the World Life Ins. Soc. Whole Life Minimum $10,000 [G]	P	○			○	○	○

[A] Available only to "preferred risks."
[B] Available only to nonsmokers.
[C] Available only in Massachusetts.
[D] Available only in New York.
[E] Available only to Lutherans.
[F] Available only to people in certain jobs.
[G] Available only to members of a fraternal organization.

A Note to Beneficiaries

If you are the beneficiary of a life insurance policy, you should take special note of certain information in this book that is of particular importance to you.

During the lifetime of the insured, you would be well advised to discuss with him or her the exact location of the policies and the identity of any agents. This can help to prevent confusion if and when you should need to file a claim. Include a notation about such information along with your important papers.

Filing a claim is a chore that usually must be done during a time of grief and emotional turmoil. But ordinarily it should not otherwise be a difficult process. The claim procedure is briefly discussed on page 164, under the heading *Payment when insured dies.*

Two problems you may face shortly after the insured's death are probate costs and estate taxes. Probate costs, and ways to minimize them, are briefly discussed in Chapter 3. Estate taxes, and ways to minimize them, are touched on in Chapter 3 and discussed in Appendix IV.

In most cases, you as the beneficiary will have a choice of what to do with your insurance money—take it in a lump sum, take it in a series of fixed installments, take it as an annuity, or leave the principal with the company and take only the interest. These settlement options, as they're known, are discussed in detail in Chapter 4 and in Chapter 11.

Term Versus Whole Life: Investment Values

Although investment strategy is only a secondary consideration in buying life insurance, it can still be an important one. As we have stated (see Chapter 5), Consumers Union's studies indicate that the success of a buy-term-and-invest-the-difference strategy depends substantially on the aftertax rate of return that the term insurance policyholder is able to get on the money saved initially as a result of the lower premiums for the term policy. If the long-run aftertax return were only 4 percent or less, you would be better off (in terms of long-run investment strategy) with a low-cost whole life policy. If the return were 5 percent, there would be roughly a standoff between the lowest-cost participating whole life and term policies (see Table A–1 on pages 350–351), while the edge would go to term insurance with nonparticipating policies. If the return were 6 percent after taxes, you would generally be better off buying term and investing the difference.

These conclusions are consistent with our belief that term insurance is preferable for most life insurance buyers. The

Table A-1
CU's Format for Measuring Term Versus Whole Life

All figures in the table below are rounded to the nearest dollar. Numbers in parentheses are negative. Data are based on CU's 1973 cost survey. A 5 percent return rate is assumed.

Age	Term Premium	Term Dividend	Term Face Amount	Whole Life Premium	Whole Life Dividend	Yearly Savings of Term Policyholder	Accumulated Savings of Term Policyholder	Cash Value of Whole Life Policy*
35	$136	$ 0	$25,000	$561	$ 0	$ 425	$ 447	
36	136	8	25,000	561	36	398	887	
37	136	12	25,000	561	43	394	1,345	
38	136	15	25,000	561	51	390	1,821	
39	136	19	25,000	561	61	383	2,314	
40	159	26	23,000	561	76	352	2,800	
41	159	28	23,000	561	94	335	3,292	
42	159	32	23,000	561	115	319	3,792	
43	159	36	23,000	561	138	299	4,296	
44	159	40	23,000	561	163	279	4,804	$ 4,250
45	197	44	21,000	561	187	221	5,277	
46	197	46	21,000	561	212	198	5,749	

47	197	49	21,000	561	236	177	6,222	
48	197	51	21,000	561	258	158	6,698	
49	197	54	21,000	561	278	141	7,182	
50	241	57	18,000	561	293	84	7,630	
51	241	54	18,000	561	304	70	8,085	
52	241	58	18,000	561	313	64	8,557	
53	241	61	18,000	561	322	59	9,047	
54	241	64	18,000	561	331	53	9,555	9,354
55	313	68	16,000	561	341	(24)	10,006	
56	313	69	16,000	561	350	(33)	10,473	
57	313	74	16,000	561	359	(37)	10,958	
58	313	80	16,000	561	368	(40)	11,464	
59	313	87	16,000	561	377	(42)	11,993	
60	382	94	13,000	546	386	(127)	12,459	
61	382	90	13,000	546	394	(141)	12,935	
62	382	99	13,000	546	404	(141)	13,433	
63	382	108	13,000	546	413	(141)	13,958	
64	382	118	13,000	546	422	(140)	14,509	14,502

*Includes the terminal dividend—a dividend paid by some companies upon termination of the policy.

rate of return figures cited above assume that the insured will buy a whole life policy at age thirty-five and, at age sixty-five, will surrender the policy for its cash value. If the policy-holder were to die with the policy still in force, term insurance would almost invariably prove to be a better buy than whole life.

Moreover, CU has stressed in the past and still believes that the primary purpose of life insurance is to provide financial security for a family, not to be an investment. Term insurance allows most buyers to purchase a greater amount of protection than they could with whole life. In many cases, the purchase of term insurance may allow a family to be adequately protected, whereas with a cash value policy the family would not be. The conditions under which CU believes the purchase of whole life is reasonable, as well as other aspects of the term-versus-cash-value controversy, are discussed in Chapter 5.

Table A–1 shows the format we used in 1973 to reach our conclusions about the investment merits of the two major forms of insurance. (Our 1979 survey provided further evidence to support these conclusions.) In this comparison of two participating policies, our actuaries reduced the face amount of the term policy every five years to keep the total estate (life insurance plus separate savings resulting from the buy-term-and-invest-the–difference strategy) constant at roughly $25,000. The face amount of the whole life policy was kept constant at $25,000. Dividends, in this illustration, were assumed to be applied toward the next year's premium. The term policy was a 1973 five-year renewable and convertible term policy, with a face amount of $25,000, issued by the National Life Insurance Company (Montpelier, Vermont); it was the most economical participating policy for a thirty-five-year-old man generally available in CU's 1973 cost survey. The whole life policy, which was chosen in the same manner, was a 1973 policy issued by Home Life Insurance Company (New York, New York). The aftertax interest rate assumed for the purposes of this illustration was 5 percent.

If one analyzes the policies in the illustration using a different assumption about the rate of interest, the results shift markedly. If a 4 percent rate of return were assumed, the whole life policy would be superior in investment terms by $3,599. At 5 percent, as Table A–1 shows, the two policies would be almost identical from an investment standpoint over thirty years. If a 6 percent aftertax return were assumed, the term policy would be superior by a margin of $4,762.

A comparison of the tenth-ranked participating term policy against the tenth-ranked participating whole life policy from CU's 1973 survey yielded roughly similar results. At 4 percent interest, the whole life policy was superior by $5,300; at 5 percent, the whole life policy was better by $1,683; at 6 percent, the term was better by $2,708.

A comparison of the top-ranked generally available nonparticipating policies from CU's 1973 survey produced the following results: At 4 percent interest, the whole life was $1,299 better; at 5 percent, the term was better by $1,804; at 6 percent, the term was better by $5,828.

Comparing the tenth-ranked nonparticipating policies, our consulting actuaries found that at 4 percent the whole life was better by $363; at 6 percent, the term was better by $9,191. At 5 percent (by interpolation), the term would have been better by approximately $4,400.

Addresses of Insurance Departments

State insurance departments can help in answering questions about life insurance and in resolving consumer problems concerning life insurance—though, as noted in Chapter 13, the degree of effectiveness varies greatly, depending on who the insurance commissioner is and how well staffed and well funded the department is. In resolving problems, the department in the state where a company is domiciled, as well as the department in the buyer's state, can sometimes be of assistance. The addresses of the insurance departments in the fifty states, the District of Columbia, and Puerto Rico follow. (Address your letters to Commissioner of Insurance, unless otherwise indicated.)

Alabama
Department of Insurance, 453 Administrative Building, 64 North Union Street, Montgomery, Alabama 36130

Alaska
Director of Insurance, Division of Insurance, Department

of Commerce, Pouch D, Juneau, Alaska 99811

Arizona
Director of Insurance, Department of Insurance, 1601 West Jefferson Street, Phoenix, Arizona 85007

Arkansas
Insurance Department, 400 University Tower Building, Little Rock, Arkansas 72204

California
Department of Insurance, 600 South Commonwealth Avenue, Suite 1401, Los Angeles, California 90005

Colorado
Insurance Division, 201 East Colfax Avenue, State Office Building, Room 106, Denver, Colorado 80203

Connecticut
Insurance Department, P.O. Box 816, Hartford, Connecticut 06115

Delaware
Insurance Department, 21 The Green, Dover, Delaware 19901

District of Columbia
Superintendent of Insurance, Department of Insurance, 614 H Street, N.W., Room 512, Washington, D.C. 20001

Florida
Office of State Treasurer and Insurance Commissioner,

State Capitol Building, Tallahassee, Florida 32301

Georgia
Insurance Department, Room 238, State Capitol, Atlanta, Georgia 30334

Hawaii
Insurance Division, Department of Regulatory Agencies, P.O. Box 3614, Honolulu, Hawaii 96811

Idaho
Director of Insurance, Department of Insurance, 700 West State Street, Boise, Idaho 83720

Illinois
Director of Insurance, Department of Insurance, 320 West Washington Street, Springfield, Illinois 62767

Indiana
Department of Insurance, 509 State Office Building, Indianapolis, Indiana 46204

Iowa
Insurance Department, Lucas State Office Building, Des Moines, Iowa 50319

Kansas
Insurance Department, State Office Building, Topeka, Kansas 66612

Kentucky
Department of Insurance, 151 Elkhorn Court, Frankfort, Kentucky 40601

Louisiana
Commissioner of Insurance, P.O. Box 44214, Baton Rouge, Louisiana 70804

Maine
Superintendent, Bureau of Insurance, State House Station #34, Augusta, Maine 04333

Maryland
Insurance Division, One South Calvert Street, Baltimore, Maryland 21210

Massachusetts
Division of Insurance, 100 Cambridge Street, Boston, Massachusetts 02202

Michigan
Insurance Bureau, Department of Commerce, P.O. Box 30220, Lansing, Michigan 48909

Minnesota
Division of Insurance, Metro Square Building, St. Paul, Minnesota 55101

Mississippi
Insurance Department, 1804 Walter Sillers Office Building, P.O. Box 79, Jackson, Mississippi 39205

Missouri
Division of Insurance, P.O. Box 690, Jefferson City, Missouri 65102

Montana
Commissioner of Insurance and State Auditor, P.O. Box

4009, Mitchell Building, Helena, Montana 59601

Nebraska
Department of Insurance, 301 Centennial Mall South, Lincoln, Nebraska 68509

Nevada
Division of Insurance, 201 South Fall Street, Carson City, Nevada 89710

New Hampshire
Insurance Department, 169 Manchester Street (Box 2005), Concord, New Hampshire 03301

New Jersey
Insurance Department, 201 East State Street (P.O. Box 1510), Trenton, New Jersey 08625

New Mexico
Department of Insurance, PERA Building, P.O. Box 1269, Santa Fe, New Mexico 87501

New York
Superintendent of Insurance, New York State Insurance Department, Two World Trade Center, New York, New York 10047

North Carolina
Department of Insurance, P.O. Box 26387, Raleigh, North Carolina 27611

North Dakota
Insurance Department, State Capitol Building, Bismarck, North Dakota 58505

Ohio
Department of Insurance, 2100 Stella Court, Columbus, Ohio 43215

Oklahoma
State Insurance Department, 408 Will Rogers Office Building, Oklahoma City, Oklahoma 73105

Oregon
Insurance Division, 158 Twelfth Street, N.E., Salem, Oregon 97310

Pennsylvania
Commissioner of Insurance, Pennsylvania Insurance Department, 13th Floor, Strawberry Square, Harrisburg, Pennsylvania 17120

Puerto Rico
Commissioner of Insurance, Department of the Treasury, San Juan, Puerto Rico 00904

Rhode Island
Department of Business Regulation, Insurance Division, 100 North Main Street, Providence, Rhode Island 02903

South Carolina
Chief Insurance Commissioner, South Carolina Department of Insurance, P.O. Box 4067, Columbia, South Carolina 29240

South Dakota
Director of Insurance, Division of Insurance, Insurance Building, Pierre, South Dakota 57501

Tennessee
Department of Insurance, 114 State Office Building, Nashville, Tennessee 37219

Texas
State Board of Insurance, 1110 San Jacinto, Austin, Texas 78786

Utah
Insurance Department, 326 South 5th East, Salt Lake City, Utah 84102

Vermont
Department of Banking and Insurance, Insurance Division, 120 State Street, Montpelier, Vermont 05602

Virginia
Bureau of Insurance, State Corporation Commission, P. O. Box 1157, Richmond, Virginia 23209

Washington
Insurance Commissioner's Office, Insurance Building, Olympia, Washington 98504

West Virginia
Insurance Department, 2100 Washington Street East, Charleston, West Virginia 25305

Wisconsin
Office of the Commissioner of Insurance, 123 West Washington Avenue, Madison, Wisconsin 53702

Wyoming
Insurance Department, 2424 Pioneer Avenue, Cheyenne, Wyoming 82002

Estate Taxes

As we state in Chapter 3, your estate is the sum of the wealth you leave to your heirs. Under some circumstances, your estate is subject to federal estate tax and, in some states, to a state levy as well. If you have substantial assets, Consumers Union strongly urges you to consult a knowledgeable lawyer or expert financial adviser to aid you in your estate planning. Such planning would be directed at, among other things, minimizing estate taxes and distributing your estate to your intended heirs as you would wish.

If the value of your estate—including life insurance—is less than $161,563 (or, starting in 1981, $175,625), it is ordinarily exempt from federal estate tax. The reason is that under the Tax Reform Act of 1976 you get a tax credit that may be subtracted directly from any federal estate tax you would otherwise owe. The tax credit, $42,500 in 1980, rises to $47,000 in 1981 and subsequent years. The effect of a $42,500 tax credit on the federal estate tax (as shown in Table A-2 on page 363) is to enable you to bequeath, tax free, an estate of less than $161,563 in 1980. As of 1981, the

$47,000 tax credit works out to a tax exemption for an estate of less than $175,625.

However, applying the tax credit is not quite as simple and straightforward as you might wish. It is a "unified" tax credit that applies not only to estate taxes but to gift tax as well. If you use part (or all) of the tax credit to defray gift tax you'd otherwise owe, only part (or none) of the tax credit would be left to reduce your estate taxes.

Here's how the unified tax credit works: Each year, you may give gifts of up to $3,000 each to as many individuals as you want without having to pay a tax on such gifts. If you give someone an amount in excess of $3,000 in a year, you owe gift tax on the excess. From 1976 until December 1979, you could choose whether to pay gift tax separately or to use the unified tax credit to defray gift tax. Then, the Internal Revenue Service issued a ruling making the latter use mandatory. In effect, under the new ruling, you can't pay any gift tax until you use up the unified tax credit. Thus, if some of your unified tax credit is used to defray gift tax, less of the unified tax credit would be available to your estate when it comes time to determine estate taxes.

Even if your estate is larger than $161,563, or $175,625 after 1980, you still may not have any estate tax liability. The 1976 law permits a substantial marital deduction, if part of your estate is left to your spouse. You can leave to your spouse, tax free, up to $250,000 or half the value of your estate, whichever is greater. The marital deduction cannot, however, exceed the dollar value of the portion of the estate actually left to your spouse.

Here are some examples. If you leave a $250,000 estate with all of it going to your spouse, your estate is not taxable. On a $400,000 estate left entirely to your spouse, $250,000 would be tax free, and the remaining $150,000 would be potentially taxable. The tax on $150,000, however, would be

Table A–2
Computing Federal Estate Tax

Step 1. If all or part of the estate is to be left to a spouse, deduct up to $250,000 or half the value of the estate, whichever is greater (but not more than the actual dollar sum to be left to a spouse).
Step 2. Using the value of the estate after any marital deduction (Step 1), find the tentative estate tax in the listing below. (For reasons of space, figures for the tentative estate tax for an estate of $1 million to $5 million—after deduction—are omitted in the table below.)

Size of Estate After Deduction	Tentative Estate Tax
Less than $10,000	18% of total
$10,000 to $19,999	$1,800 + 20% of amount over $10,000
$20,000 to $39,999	$3,800 + 22% of amount over $20,000
$40,000 to $59,999	$8,200 + 24% of amount over $40,000
$60,000 to $79,999	$13,000 + 26% of amount over $60,000
$80,000 to $99,999	$18,200 + 28% of amount over $80,000
$100,000 to $149,999	$23,800 + 30% of amount over $100,000
$150,000 to $249,999	$38,800 + 32% of amount over $150,000
$250,000 to $499,999	$70,800 + 34% of amount over $250,000
$500,000 to $749,999	$155,800 + 37% of amount over $500,000
$750,000 to $999,999	$248,300 + 39% of amount over $750,000
$1 million to $5 million	Not shown here; consult IRS, lawyer, or tax adviser
$5 million and above	$2,550,800 + 70% of amount over $5 million

Step 3. From the tentative estate tax (Step 2), subtract the unified tax credit ($42,500 in 1980 and $47,000 in 1981 and thereafter), unless some of it has been used previously to defray gift tax. If it has, subtract any portion of the credit that is still due you. The resulting figure is an approximation of estate tax liability under federal law. An exact calculation will require the help of a tax adviser, who should take cognizance of any recent changes in laws and regulations.

shielded by the unified tax credit. On a $600,000 estate left entirely to your spouse, $300,000 would be tax free and $300,000 potentially taxable. As calculated with the help of Table A-2, the tax would be $87,800—minus the unified tax credit. But if you have a $600,000 estate and leave only $100,000 to your spouse, the remaining $500,000 would be potentially taxable. Here the tax would be $155,800—minus the unified tax credit.

Because of the combined effects of the unified tax credit and the marital deduction, you could, as of 1980, leave as much as $411,563 to your spouse, tax free. As of 1981, that figure rises to $425,625. Appealing as that may be, CU cautions against your assuming, without authoritative counseling, that you should leave your full estate to your spouse. That question should be decided in the context of total estate planning, conducted in cooperation with a trusted adviser.

Keep in mind, too, that you and your spouse might die at exactly the same time, or within a few weeks or months of each other. In that case, the marital deduction might not effectively shield your assets from taxation, and future heirs might find a diminished estate. This is another reason why advance estate planning is desirable.

Estate tax liability is determined according to a progressive tax rate schedule, shown in Table A-2. The figures were current as of early 1980. When you actually undertake your estate planning, it would be wise to check with your lawyer or tax adviser to ascertain the laws and rates in effect then.

The proceeds of life insurance are a potentially taxable part of your estate. One way to minimize estate taxes is to transfer the ownership of a life insurance policy in order to exclude the life insurance proceeds from your taxable gross estate. The policy can be legally owned by the beneficiary or by a trustee, but this arrangement requires the irrevocable transfer of policy ownership.

Under certain conditions, you may continue to pay the premiums on the life insurance without jeopardizing the estate tax shelter. If you should die during the three years after the transfer, the life insurance proceeds would still be taxable. It takes a lawyer with a thorough knowledge of state inheritance tax laws and federal estate tax laws to provide adequate advice on the pros and cons of transferring insurance ownership for tax purposes.

If you transfer policy ownership, you give up direct control of a substantial portion of your estate. There may be undesirable consequences if you irrevocably transfer policy ownership rights, including the right to change the beneficiary. Such a transfer should not be undertaken before you have fully explored the matter with an attorney.

Glossary

Words and phrases printed in *italics* are defined elsewhere in this glossary of life insurance terms. (For explanations of some types of life insurance policies not included in the Glossary, readers should refer to Chapter 9.)

Accidental death benefit. A *rider,* which may be purchased at an additional *premium,* providing for payment of double (or triple) the *face amount* of a policy, should the policyholder's death result from an accident. Also known as double (or triple) indemnity.

Annuity. A contract that provides periodic payments, either for a certain number of years or for a lifetime. When an annuity is purchased by a policyholder under a *nonforfeiture option* of a life insurance policy, the *cash value* of the policy pays for the annuity. When an annuity is purchased by a *beneficiary* under a *settlement option* of a life insurance policy, the *death benefit* from the policy pays for the annuity. Annuities can also be purchased independently of a life insurance policy and are often used to provide regular income during retirement.

Attained age conversion. Transaction in which a *term insurance* policyholder converts the policy to a *cash value insurance* policy by paying a *premium* on the new policy based on his or her age at the time the change is made. See also *conversion clause, convertible term insurance, original age conversion.*

Beneficiary. The person (or entity) named in a policy to receive the *death benefit* in the event of the policyholder's death. There may be one or more beneficiaries, and there may be primary and secondary beneficiaries.

Breakpoints. Specific *face amounts* in the price structure of life insurance policies—often $10,000, $25,000, or $100,000, for example—at which point the *premium* per thousand dollars of *coverage* is less than what it was at a lower face amount. The total annual premium for $100,000 of insurance, for example, may be only a shade higher—or in some cases, even lower—than for $95,000.

Cash value. The money that accumulates in a *cash value insurance* policy (and in some long-term *term insurance* policies) during the time the policy is in force. This money may be borrowed against by the policyholder. It goes to the policyholder on *surrender* of the policy or if the policyholder lives to the *maturity date* of the policy.

Cash value insurance. A type of policy that provides both an insurance protection component and a savings component (the *cash value*). The policy usually has a *level premium.*

Claim. A notice filed with an insurance company that payment is due under the provisions of an insurance policy.

Conversion clause. A provision of most *term insurance* policies guaranteeing the policyholder the right to convert the insurance *coverage* to a *cash value insurance* policy without evidence of insurability. The clause usually specifies the age by which conversion of the policy must take place. See also *attained age conversion, convertible term insurance, original age conversion.*

Coverage. The amount of insurance protection a policyholder has in force. See also *face amount.*

Convertible term insurance. *Term insurance* that guarantees the policyholder the right to transfer the insurance *coverage* to *cash value insurance* without evidence of insurability. See also *attained age conversion, conversion clause, original age conversion.*

Death benefit. Amount payable to the *beneficiary* of a life insurance policy upon the death of the policyholder. See also *face amount.*

Debit insurance. A relatively costly form of insurance (including life insurance and other types of insurance) in which *premiums,* due weekly or monthly, are collected in person by a company representative. Also called home service insurance, industrial insurance, or monthly debit ordinary insurance.

Decreasing term. A form of *term insurance* with a *level premium* and a *death benefit* that gradually decreases from year to year, in accordance with a schedule specified at the time of purchase.

Dividend options. The ways in which the *dividends* of a *participating policy* can be taken.

Dividends. Payments made to a policyholder at regular intervals under certain forms of insurance, known as *participating (or par) policies.* The amount of the payments is based in part on the difference between the *premium* charged and the company's actual expenses, investment, and mortality experience. Dividends are not taxed when they are paid. The Internal Revenue Service considers them to be refunds of previous overpayments on premiums. See also *dividend options.*

Endowment. The payment to a policyholder of the *cash value* accumulated in a policy on its *maturity date.*

Endowment policy. A *cash value insurance* policy in which *endowment* occurs earlier than at age one hundred.

Estate liquidity. The availability of assets with which to pay estate taxes and other expenses that occur in connection with a death. See also *liquidity.*

Extended term insurance. A *nonforfeiture option* allowing continued life insurance *coverage* at the original *face amount* for a specified period of years, paid for with the *cash value* accumulated in a policy.

Face amount. The sum payable to a *beneficiary* in the event a policyholder's death occurs while a policy is in force. It does not include such items as *dividends* or sums payable because of *riders* added to the policy. See also *coverage, death benefit.*

Forgone interest. Interest not earned because a person's money was committed to a use other than investment (or to a relatively low-yielding investment).

Group life insurance. Plans often available at a place of employment. The plans usually consist of group term insurance. (Members of an organization sometimes are also able to purchase group insurance.)

Guaranteed insurability. A *rider* often available with *cash value* policies, giving the policyholder the right to purchase additional *cash value insurance* at specified times in the future. The additional insurance is available at standard rates despite changes in the policyholder's health or occupation.

Illustration. Table listing an insurance company's current *dividend* figures, often shown to prospective purchasers of a *participating policy.* These figures are neither estimates nor guarantees of the dividends a policyholder will receive over the years. The dividends actually paid may be larger or smaller than those illustrated.

Interest-adjusted method. A way of calculating the relative cost of similar life insurance policies over a given period of time that takes into account not only the amount of *premium* and *dividend* payments but also their timing. The timing is important because of the interest policyholders can earn on money that is in their possession. The method makes certain hypothetical assumptions about the time a policy will be in force; dividends to be paid, if any; and probable interest rates. See also *interest-adjusted net cost index, interest-adjusted net payment index.*

Interest-adjusted net cost index. A dollar figure derived by the *interest-adjusted method,* used to compare the costs of similar policies. The index is an indicator of the cost of a policy, assuming the policy is *surrendered* after a given number of years. See also *interest-adjusted net payment index.*

Interest-adjusted net payment index. A dollar figure derived by the *interest-adjusted method,* used to compare the costs of similar policies. The index is an indicator of the cost of a policy, assuming the policyholder dies while it is in force. See also *interest-adjusted net cost index.*

Level premium. A *premium* that is fixed for the entire time the policy is in force.

Liquidity. The ready availability of cash. An asset is liquid only if it can be readily converted to cash. See also *estate liquidity.*

Maturity date. The time at which the insurance *coverage* of a *cash value insurance* policy ends and the policyholder, if still alive, is normally given the amount of money that has accumulated in the *cash value* component of the policy—which at that point equals the full *face amount* of the policy.

Nonforfeiture options. Often called *surrender* options. Choices available to a policyholder who surrenders the policy before the *maturity date.* Most policies offer three options: a cash payment (which can be taken as a lump sum under the *settlement options*); a reduced amount of *paid-up whole life insurance;* or *extended term insurance.*

Nonpar policy. See *nonparticipating policy.*

Nonparticipating policy. A policy that does not pay *dividends* to the policyholder. Also known as a nonpar policy.

371

Ordinary life. Life insurance as conventionally sold to individuals (whether in the form of *cash value* or *term insurance*); distinguished from *debit insurance* and *group life insurance*. Also often used by life insurance companies as synonymous with *whole life*.

Original age conversion. Transaction in which a *term insurance* policyholder converts the policy to a *cash value insurance* policy by paying a *premium* for the new policy based on his or her age at the time of the original purchase of the term policy. In addition, the buyer usually pays the difference between the total term premiums paid and the total of what the cash value premiums would have been up to the conversion date, plus interest. See also *attained age conversion, conversion clause, convertible term insurance.*

Paid-up life insurance. Life insurance on which no further *premiums* need be paid. When a *cash value insurance* policy is paid up, the *cash value* may continue to accumulate and *dividends* may continue to be paid to the policyholder. Paid-up insurance may be purchased directly. Or it may be taken as a *nonforfeiture option;* in the latter case, the *face amount* of the paid-up policy will be smaller than the face amount of the original policy.

Par policy. See *participating policy.*

Participating policy. A policy that pays *dividends* to the policyholder. Also known as a par policy.

Policy loan. A loan made by a life insurance company to the owner of a *cash value insurance* policy. The *cash value* provides collateral for the loan, which is made from company funds.

Premium. Money paid by a policyholder—annually, semiannually, quarterly, monthly, or even weekly—for insurance *coverage.* Premiums are usually lowest if paid annually. See also *level premium.*

Premium rate. The *premium* per thousand dollars of life insurance *coverage.* Also used loosely as a synonym for premium.

Renewable term insurance. *Term insurance coverage*—usually for a period of one or five years—which guarantees the policyholder, without evidence of insurability, the right to continue the coverage for successive, equal periods—each time at an increased *premium rate*—up to a specified age. See also *convertible term insurance.*

Rider. An option providing an additional benefit that may be added to an insurance policy, at an increase in *premium.* See also *accidental death benefit, guaranteed insurability, waiver of premium.*

Settlement options. The ways in which life insurance money may be paid to the *beneficiary* after the death of the insured or to the policyholder upon *surrender* or *endowment* of a *cash value insurance* policy. See also *annuity.*

Straight life. A *cash value insurance* policy with a *level premium* payable to age one hundred, *endowment* at age one hundred, and a level *death benefit.*

Surrender. To terminate or cancel a policy before the *maturity date.* In the case of a *cash value insurance* policy, the policyholder may exercise one of the *nonforfeiture options* at the time of surrender.

Terminal dividend. A *dividend* paid by some life insurance companies at the time a policy is *surrendered.*

Terminate. See *surrender.*

Term insurance. A type of policy that provides insurance protection for a specific number of years (the term). With *renewable term insurance, coverage* can be continued for one or more subsequent terms by paying increased annual *premiums.* One-year and five-year term policies ordinarily have no *cash value.* Some longer-term term policies have substantial cash value. See also *decreasing term.*

Waiver of premium. A provision, available as a *rider* with most policies (but standard in some policies), releasing the policyholder, in the event he or she becomes totally disabled, from the obligation to pay the *premium* for the duration of the disability. Eligibility to take advantage of this rider usually ends at a specified age.

Whole life. A *cash value insurance* policy designed to cover the policyholder for a lifetime. Includes *straight life* and *paid-up life insurance* (with *endowment* at age one hundred).

Index

Accidental death benefit, 140–141
Adjustable life, 122–125
Aetna Life Insurance Company, 133, 149, 266
Agents:
   and life insurance sales, 21, 22, 72–73
   service, 86, 120, 189
American Council of Life Insurance, 102n
American Life Convention, 102n
American National Insurance Company, 158
American Republic Insurance Company, 333
Annual Percentage Rate, 117, 157–158, 195
Annuity, 68, 138, 166–167

Armed Forces Reserve, 49
Attained age conversion, 74, 159–160
Automatic payment plan, 157, 158
Average indexed yearly earnings, 24–29, 39–40

Bankers Life Company (of Iowa), 122–124
Belth, Joseph M., 93, 109, 157, 194, 195
Beneficiaries, 164, 347–348
Beneficiary clause, 151
Best's Insurance Reports, 152
   ratings, 109, 201
Best's Review, 96
Breakpoints, 116–117
Burial insurance, 128
Business Men's Assurance

Company of America, 204

Campus life insurance, 125
Capitol Life Insurance Company, 204
Carter, President, 193
Cash value, 99–100
  and loans against, 63, 83, 85, 172–174
  and rate of return, 82, 195
Cash value insurance, 61, 62–63, 66–71, 103
  adjustable life, 122–125
  campus life insurance, 125
  contingent life, 134
  cost indexes of (table), 112–113
  cost-of-living insurance, 126
  dividend options of, 89, 154–155, 174–175
  economatic policies, 129–132
  endowment policies, 66–67, 70, 154
  as forced savings, 80–83
  and guaranteed insurability rider, 145–146
  and level premium, 67, 73–74
  limited payment life, 134–135
  and minimum deposit plan, 135–137
  and nonforfeiture options, 67–69
policies, Ratings of, 263–332
policies, summary of, 333–346
settlement options of, 68, 164–168
shopping for, 109, 111, 113
table of values, 168–172
as tax shelter, 82–84
variable life insurance, 138–139
versus term insurance, 72–86
yield on, 203–204, 264–266
See also Cash value, Investment strategy and life insurance
Central Life Assurance Company, 194, 195, 266, 333
Charity, insurance to benefit, 16
Children, insurance for, 16, 17, 20–22, 125
  and Social Security benefits, 31–32
College students, insurance for, 22, 54–56, 114, 125
Colonial Life Insurance Company of America, 333
Connecticut Mutual Life Insurance Company, 158
Connecticut Savings Bank Life Insurance, 205
Consumers Union life insurance survey, 201–205
  Ratings of policies, proce-

dure for, 206–207, 263–268

Continental Association of Funeral and Memorial Societies, 49

Continental Assurance Company, 149, 253

Contingent life, 134

Conversion, 64, 65–66, 74–75, 143, 158–162, 185

Cost comparisons, 98–107

Cost disclosure, need for, 92, 193–197

Cost-of-living insurance, 126 and adjustable life, 124

Coverage, average amount of, 74

Credit life insurance, 126–127

Credit report, 119

Debit insurance, 127–128

Debt repayment, planning for, 51

Declining term insurance, 64–66

Decreasing term insurance, 64–66

Deferred annuity, 137–138

Deposit term insurance, 128–129

Disability:
and Social Security benefits, 35, 37
insurance, 144
and waiver of premium, 141–144

Dividends, 87–96
options, 88–89, 137, 153–155, 174–175
and questionable practices, 92–94, 196–197
for cash value policies, 174–175
for term policies, 153–155

Dorfman, John, 6

Double indemnity, 140–141

Economatic policies, 129–132
versus participating whole life (table), 131

Education fund, planning for, 54–56

Emergency fund, planning for, 51

Endowment policies, 66–67, 70, 154

Equitable Life Assurance Society of the U.S., 94, 138, 149, 155*n*, 158, 160, 174

Equitable Life Insurance Company, 204

Equivalent level dividend, 95, 194

Estate taxes, 50–51, 361–365
computing federal estate tax (table), 363

Extended term insurance, as nonforfeiture option, 69

Face amount of policies, 62, 63, 64, 66

Fair Credit Reporting Act, 119

Family income fund, planning for, 51–54
Family income plan, 132
Family maintenance plan, 132–133
Family plan, 15, 22
Farmers New World Life Insurance Company, 205
Federal Kemper Life Assurance Company, 149, 156
Federal Trade Commission report on life insurance, 72, 77, 192–193
Fidelity and Guaranty Life Insurance Company, 204
Fidelity Life Association, 194, 195, 267, 333
Fidelity Union Life Insurance Company (Dallas, Texas), 125
First Colony Life Insurance Company, 253
Flesch Readability Scale, 147–149
Flexible premium nonpar, 133
Front-end load, 178, 187, 203
Funeral costs, planning for, 16, 21, 48–49

General Accounting Office report on life insurance, 191–192
Grace period, 134, 152–153
Graded-death-benefit life insurance, 118

Great Southern Life Insurance Company, 204
Group insurance, 45, 114–115
Guaranteed insurability rider, 125, 145–146
Guardian Life Insurance Company of America, 253

Health problems and life insurance, 117–118
Historical cost indexes, 95–96, 121
Home Life Insurance Company, 333, 352
Homemaker, insurance for, 18–20, 66
Home service insurance, 127

INA Life Insurance Company, 149
Incontestability clause, 162–163, 179
Indexes, cost-comparison, 98, 100, 103–105, 110
Indianapolis Life Insurance Company, 149, 155n
Industrial insurance, 127
Inflation and life insurance planning, 43–44
accounting for inflation (table), 57
Institute of Life Insurance, 102n
Insurance companies, financial stability of, 109

Insurance Forum, The, 109, 157

Integon Life Insurance Company, 94

Interest-adjusted index, 106–107 (table), 109, 193

Interest-adjusted net cost index, 103–107, 109–111, 112–113, 207, 266–267
    calculating, for a policy (table), 181–184
    using cash value insurance cost indexes (table), 112–113
    using term insurance cost indexes (table), 110

Interest-adjusted net payment index, 103–107, 111, 188, 267
    using cash value insurance cost indexes (table), 112–113

Internal Revenue Service, 89, 362

Investment strategy and life insurance, 78–80, 349–353

Joint life, 134

Joint Special Committee on Life Insurance Costs, 102

Kansas City Life Insurance Company, 196

Level nonrenewable term insurance, 64

Level premium, 67, 73–74

Level renewable term insurance, 63–64

Life and Casualty Insurance Company of Tennessee, 196

Life Insurance Association of America, 102n

Life Insurance Company of Georgia, 205

Life Insurance Fact Book, 157

Life Insurance Marketing and Research Association, 54, 56

Limited payment life, 134–135

Linton-yield method, 264–265

Loans against cash value, 63, 83, 85, 172–174

Massachusetts Insurance Department, 148–149

Massachusetts Mutual Life Insurance Company, 334

Massachusetts Savings Bank Life Insurance, 149, 155n, 174

McCarran-Ferguson Act of 1944, 190, 192

Medical costs and planning life insurance, 48

Metropolitan Life Insurance Company, 132, 149, 150,

152–155, 158–159, 160–162, 163–164, 169, 170–171 (table), 172–173
Midland National Life Insurance Company, 149, 174
Minimum deposit plan, 135–137
Minnesota Mutual Life Insurance Company, 122–124
Modified Whole Life, 67
Monthly debit ordinary insurance, 127
Mortgage payments, planning for, 45, 52
Mortgage term insurance, 64–66

National Association of Insurance Commissioners, 90, 102, 149, 193–194
National Guard, 49
National Life Insurance Company (Montpelier, Vermont), 201*n,* 352
Nationwide Life Insurance Company, 149, 155*n,* 156, 174, 253
Net cost, 99
    See also Interest-adjusted index, Interest-adjusted net cost index
Net payment, 99
    See also Interest-adjusted index, Interest-adjusted net payment index
Net rates, 175

New England Mutual Life Insurance Company, 149, 155*n,* 252
Nonforfeiture options, 67–69
Nonparticipating policies, 87–88, 89–92
Northwestern Mutual Life Insurance Company, 132, 149, 155*n,* 163–164, 334

Occidental Life Insurance Company of California, 66*n,* 145*n*
Ohio State Life Insurance Company, 204
Old Line Life Insurance Company of America, 253
Options:
    dividend, 88–89, 137, 153–155, 174–175
    nonforfeiture, 67–69
    settlement, 68, 164–168
    See also Riders
Ordinary life insurance
    See Whole life insurance
Original age conversion, 74–75, 159–161
Ownership, 162

Paid-up additional insurance, 154, 175
Paid-up policy, 67, 68
Participating policies, 87–96
Payroll deduction plans, 81
Penn Mutual Life Insurance

Company, 253
Pensions and planning life insurance, 45
Philadelphia Life Insurance Company, 204
Phoenix Mutual Life Insurance Company, 334
Policies:
and definitions, 152
and determining costs of present policy, 180
payment when insured dies, 164
premium payments on, 152–153, 156–158
rates of, lower for women, 111
Ratings, basis for, 204, 207, 267–268
readability of, 120, 147–149
reinstatement of, 152–153
renewal of term, 155–156
shopping for, 108–121
specifications of, 150–152
switching, 177–189
See also Cash value, Cash value insurance, Conversion, Dividends, Options, Riders, Term insurance
Preferred risk policies, 111
Premiums, 61–62, 63, 64, 65, 66, 67, 70, 87–88, 98
advantage of annual payment, 117
automatic premium loan, 174

cash value versus term, 73–74, 85
and reinstatement, 152–153
Probate costs, planning for, 49–50
Probe (industry newsletter), 120
Prudential Insurance Company of America, 132, 149, 153, 154, 155*n,* 161
Puritan Life Insurance Company, 205

Rate of return, 77, 82–83, 84, 195
Real estate and life insurance planning, 45
Reducing term insurance, 64–66
Rejection by insurance companies, 119
Renewable and convertible term insurance, 63–64, 75
one-year term, 116, 126, 175
Renewable term insurance, 61–62, 63–64, 86, 155–156
Renewal premiums, table of, 156–157
Replacement, 177–189
Reserve Officers Training Corps, 49
Retirement fund, planning for, 56, 75–76, 79–80

Riders:
  accidental death benefit,
    140–141
  guaranteed insurability,
    125, 145–146
  waiver of premium, 141–
    145
Risk, insurance, 117–119
  and health, 117–118
  and lifestyle, 119
  and occupation, 119
  substandard, 117, 119

Savings, forced, 80–83
Savings Bank Life Insurance,
    113–114, 128
Securities and Exchange
    Commission, 138
Securities and life insurance
    planning, 45
Security-Connecticut Life In-
    surance Company, 253
Security Life and Accident
    Company, 94
Settlement options, 68, 164–
    168
  fixed payment settlement
    option (table), 167
  lifetime annuity settlement
    option (table), 166
Shopping for a policy, 108–
    121, 169, 176, 206, 266
Single person, insurance for,
    15–16
Single-premium life insur-
    ance, 67
Social Security, 23–40

average indexed yearly
    earnings, 24–29, 39–40
benefits record (table), 34
death benefits, 37–38
disability benefits, 35, 37,
    38 (table), 144
earnings, 24
eligibility standards for, 24,
    29, 30 (table), 31 (table),
    32, 35 (table), 37–38
retirement benefits, 32–35,
    36 (table)
survivors benefits, 29–32,
    33 (table)
work credit, 29, 30 (table)
Social Security Administra-
    tion, 23n, 40
Society of Actuaries, 265
Split life, 137
State insurance departments:
  addresses, 354–360
  complaints to, 186
  licensing of insurance com-
    panies, 120–121
  regulating insurance mar-
    ketplace, 190–193
State Mutual Life Insurance
    Company, 150
Straight life, 66, 67
Suicide clause, 163–164, 179
Sun Life Insurance Company
    of America, 253
Switching policies, 177–189

Tax Reform Act of 1976, 361
Taxes:
  and adjustable life, 124

and cash value policies, 82–84

computing federal estate tax (table), 363

estate, 50–51, 361–365

gift, 362

and limited payment life, 135

marital deduction, 362–364

and minimum deposit plan, 136–137

unified tax credit, 362–364

Teachers Insurance and Annuity Association of America, 94–95, 150, 153, 174, 252, 266, 334

Term insurance, 61–62, 63–66, 103

adjustable life, 122–125

cost indexes of (table), 110

decreasing term, 64–66

deposit term, 128–129

dividend options, 88–89, 153–155

level nonrenewable, 64

level renewable, 63–64

policies, Ratings of, 206–251

policies, summary of, 252–262

shopping for, 109, 111, 113

split life, 137

versus cash value, 72–86

See also Conversion, Investment strategy and life insurance

Thrift plans, 81

Time Insurance Company, 91

Travelers Insurance Company, 133

Underwriting, 118–119

Unified tax credit, 362–364

Union Mutual Life Insurance Company, 253

United Benefit Life Insurance Company, 158

United Investors Life Insurance Company, 253

USAA Life Insurance Company, 253

U.S. Government EE bonds, 81

Variable life insurance, 138–139

Veterans Administration death benefits, 49

Veterans' insurance, 115–116

Waiver of premium, 141–145

Wall Street Journal, The, 191

Western and Southern Life Insurance Company, 204

Whole life insurance, 66–67

See also Cash value insurance, Investment strategy and life insurance

Wisconsin Insurance Department, 110, 112

Worksheet, Life Insurance Planning, 41–42, 44–60